Communications
in Computer and Information Science

2448

Series Editors

Gang Li, *School of Information Technology, Deakin University, Burwood, VIC, Australia*
Joaquim Filipe , *Polytechnic Institute of Setúbal, Setúbal, Portugal*
Zhiwei Xu, *Chinese Academy of Sciences, Beijing, China*

Rationale

The CCIS series is devoted to the publication of proceedings of computer science conferences. Its aim is to efficiently disseminate original research results in informatics in printed and electronic form. While the focus is on publication of peer-reviewed full papers presenting mature work, inclusion of reviewed short papers reporting on work in progress is welcome, too. Besides globally relevant meetings with internationally representative program committees guaranteeing a strict peer-reviewing and paper selection process, conferences run by societies or of high regional or national relevance are also considered for publication.

Topics

The topical scope of CCIS spans the entire spectrum of informatics ranging from foundational topics in the theory of computing to information and communications science and technology and a broad variety of interdisciplinary application fields.

Information for Volume Editors and Authors

Publication in CCIS is free of charge. No royalties are paid, however, we offer registered conference participants temporary free access to the online version of the conference proceedings on SpringerLink (http://link.springer.com) by means of an http referrer from the conference website and/or a number of complimentary printed copies, as specified in the official acceptance email of the event.

CCIS proceedings can be published in time for distribution at conferences or as post-proceedings, and delivered in the form of printed books and/or electronically as USBs and/or e-content licenses for accessing proceedings at SpringerLink. Furthermore, CCIS proceedings are included in the CCIS electronic book series hosted in the SpringerLink digital library at http://link.springer.com/bookseries/7899. Conferences publishing in CCIS are allowed to use Online Conference Service (OCS) for managing the whole proceedings lifecycle (from submission and reviewing to preparing for publication) free of charge.

Publication process

The language of publication is exclusively English. Authors publishing in CCIS have to sign the Springer CCIS copyright transfer form, however, they are free to use their material published in CCIS for substantially changed, more elaborate subsequent publications elsewhere. For the preparation of the camera-ready papers/files, authors have to strictly adhere to the Springer CCIS Authors' Instructions and are strongly encouraged to use the CCIS LaTeX style files or templates.

Abstracting/Indexing

CCIS is abstracted/indexed in DBLP, Google Scholar, EI-Compendex, Mathematical Reviews, SCImago, Scopus. CCIS volumes are also submitted for the inclusion in ISI Proceedings.

How to start

To start the evaluation of your proposal for inclusion in the CCIS series, please send an e-mail to ccis@springer.com.

Kun Zhang · Xianhua Song ·
Mohammad S. Obaidat · Anas Bilal · Jun Hu ·
Zeguang Lu
Editors

Computer Science and Educational Informatization

6th International Conference, CSEI 2024
Haikou, China, November 1–3, 2024
Revised Selected Papers, Part II

 Springer

Editors
Kun Zhang (iD)
Hainan Normal University
Haikou, China

Xianhua Song (iD)
Harbin University of Science and Technology
Harbin, China

Mohammad S. Obaidat (iD)
University of Jordan
Amman, Jordan

Anas Bilal (iD)
Hainan Normal University
Haikou, China

Jun Hu (iD)
Harbin University of Science and Technology
Harbin, China

Zeguang Lu (iD)
National Academy of Guo Ding Institute
of Data Science
Beijing, China

ISSN 1865-0929   ISSN 1865-0937 (electronic)
Communications in Computer and Information Science
ISBN 978-981-96-3737-9   ISBN 978-981-96-3738-6 (eBook)
https://doi.org/10.1007/978-981-96-3738-6

Preface

The 6th International Conference on Computer Science and Educational Informatization (CSEI 2024) was held in Haikou, China, on November 1–2, 2024, hosted by Hainan Normal University, CCF Computer Applications Technical Committee, and co-organized by CCF Haikou Member Activity Center, Hainan University, Hainan Tropical Ocean University, Hainan College of Economics and Business, the First-level discipline Master's Program in Cyberspace Security of the School of Information Science and Technology at Hainan Normal University, and the Master's Program in Computer Technology of the School of Information Science and Technology at Hainan Normal University. The goal of this conference was to provide a forum for computer scientists, engineers, and educators.

This conference attracted 171 paper submissions. After the hard work of the Program Committee, 51 papers of CSEI 2024 were accepted to be presented in the conference, with an acceptance rate of 29.82%. There were at least 3 reviewers for each article, and each reviewer reviewed no more than 4 articles. The major topics of this conference were Computer Science, Education Informatization, and Engineering Education. The accepted papers cover a wide range of areas related to educational information science and technology, educational informatization and big data for education, innovative applications for the deeper integration of education practice and information technology, and university engineering education.

We would like to thank all the Program Committee members for their hard work in completing the review tasks. Their collective efforts made it possible to attain quality reviews for all the submissions within a few weeks. Their diverse expertise in each research area helped us to create an exciting program for the conference. Their comments and advice helped the authors to improve the quality of their papers and gain deeper insights.

We thank the team at Springer, whose professional assistance was invaluable in the production of the proceedings. A big thanks also to the authors and participants for their tremendous support in making the conference a success.

Besides the technical program, this year CSEI offered different experiences to the participants. We hope you enjoyed the conference.

January 2025

Xianhua Song
Yu Zhou
Anas Bilal

Organization

Honorary Chair

Rajkumar Buyya — University of Melbourne, Australia

General Chairs

Mohammad S. Obaidat — University of Jordan, Jordan
Kun Zhang — Hainan Normal University, China
Bin Wen — Hainan Normal University, China

Program Chairs

Xianhua Song — Harbin University of Science and Technology, China
Yu Zhou — Hainan Normal University, China
Anas Bilal — Hainan Normal University, China

Program Co-chairs

Xiaowen Liu — Hainan Normal University, China
Haixia Long — Hainan Normal University, China
Zhengjie Deng — Hainan Normal University, China
Ali Haider Khan — Lahore Garrison University, Pakistan
Mostafa Ghobaei-Arani — Islamic Azad University, Iran
Sibghat Ullah Bazai — Balochistan University of Information Technology, Engineering, and Management Sciences, Pakistan

Organising Chairs

Qingchen Zhang — Hainan University, China
Haifeng Wang — Hainan Tropical Ocean University, China
Heping Gou — Qiongtai Normal University, China

Yuxi Liu	Harbin Normal University, China
Hongzhi Wang	Harbin Institute of Technology, China
Mir Muhammad Nizamani	Hainan University, China
Amin Qourbani	Amirkabir University of Technology, Iran

Publication Chairs

Jun Hu	Harbin University of Science and Technology, China
Emad Mahrous Awwad	King Saud University, Saudi Arabia
Uzair Aslam Bhatti	Hainan University, China

Registration/Financial Chair

| Fa Yue | National Academy of Guo Ding Institute of Data Science, China |

Academic Committee Chairman

| Hongzhi Wang | Harbin Institute of Technology, China |

Academic Committee Vice Presidents

Jianhou Gan	Yunnan Normal University, China
Dong Liu	Henan Normal University, China
Guanglu Sun	Harbin University of Science and Technology, China

Academic Committee Secretary General

| Zeguang Lu | National Academy of Guo Ding Institute of Data Science, China |

Academic Committee Executive Members

Xiaoju Dong	Shanghai Jiao Tong University, China
Qilong Han	Harbin Engineering University, China
Lan Huang	Jilin University, China
Ying Jiang	Kunming University of Science and Technology, China
Junna Zhang	Henan Normal University, China
Junxiang Zhou	Yunnan Normal University, China

Program Committee Members (In Alphabetical Order)

Jinliang An	Henan Institute of Science and Technology, China
Hongtao Bai	Jilin University, China
Chunguang Bi	Jilin Agriculture University, China
Xiaochun Cao	Sun Yat-sen University, China
Yuefeng Cen	Zhejiang University of Science And Technology, China
Wanxiang Che	Harbin Institute of Technology, China
Juntao Chen	Hainan College of Economics and Business, China
Lei Chen	Sanya Aviation and Tourism College, China
Yarui Chen	Tianjin University of Science and Technology, China
Haoran Chen	Zhengzhou University of Light Industry, China
Fei Dai	Southwest Forestry University, China
Shoujian Duan	Baoshan University, China
Congyu Duan	Shenzhen University, China
Yuxuan Feng	Jilin Agricultural University, China
Ping Feng	Changchun University, China
Jianhou Gan	Yunnan Normal University, China
Qiuei Han	Changchun University, China
Jia Hao	Yunnan Normal University, China
Yaqiong He	Zhengzhou University of Light Industry, China
Xinhong Hei	Xi'an University of Technology, China
Wenjuan Jia	Dalian University of Finance and Economics, China
Ying Jiang	Kunming University of Science and Technology, China
Jiaqiong Jiang	Hunan University, China
Zhejun Kuang	Changchun University, China

Guohou Li	Henan Institute of Science and Technology, China
Yuanhui Li	Sanya Aviation and Tourism College, China
Shanshan Li	Sanya Aviation and Tourism College, China
Hua Li	Changchun University of Science and Technology, China
Yanting Li	Zhengzhou University of Light Industry, China
Zedong Li	Dalian Nationalities University, China
Zijie Li	Yunnan Normal University, China
Chengrong Lin	Hainan University, China
Zongli Lin	University of Virginia, USA
Kaibiao Lin	Xiamen University of Technology, China
Chunhong Liu	Henan Normal University, China
Dong Liu	Henan Normal University, China
Xia Liu	Sanya Aviation and Tourism College, China
Kang Liu	Sanya Aviation and Tourism College, China
Ying Liu	Tianjin University of Science and Technology, China
Wanquan Liu	Sun Yat-sen University, China
Sanya Liu	Central China Normal University, China
ChinaDong Liu	Henan Normal University, China
Shijian Luo	Zhejiang University, China
Juan Luo	Hunan University, China
Wei Meng	Guangdong University of Technology, China
Yashuang Mu	Henan University of Technology, China
Cong Qu	Hainan University, China
Jiannji Ren	Henan Polytechnic University, China
Jinmei Shi	Hainan Vocational University of Science and Technology, China
Xiaobo Shi	Henan Normal University, China
Yancui Shi	Tianjin University of Science and Technology, China
Wenjun Shi	Zhengzhou University of Light Industry, China
Jing Su	Tianjin University of Science and Technology, China
Peng Sun	University of Electronic Science and Technology of China, China
Weizhi Sun	Sanya Aviation and Tourism College, China
Guanglu Sun	Harbin University of Science and Technology, China
Lin Tang	Yunnan Normal University, China
Mingjing Tang	Yunnan Normal University, China
Hongwei Tao	Zhengzhou University of Light Industry, China
Yiyuan Wang	Northeast Normal University, USA

Junchao Wang	North Dakota State College of Science, China
Xiaoyu Wang	Jilin Normal University, China
Cong Wang	Tianjin University of Science and Technology, China
Yuan Wang	Tianjin University of Science and Technology, China
Jun Wang	Yunnan Normal University, China
Min Wang	Yunnan Normal University, China
Haiyan Wang	Changchun University, China
Xiao Wang	Zhengzhou University of Light Industry, China
Cunru Wang	Dalian Nationalities University, China
Xinkai Wang	Ningbo Technology University, China
Yongheng Wang	Hunan University, China
Zumin Wang	Dalian University, China
Wei Wei	Xi'an University of Technology, China
Changji Wen	Jilin Agriculture University, China
Bin Wen	Yunnan Normal University, China
Yang Weng	Sichuan University, China
Huaiguang Wu	Zhengzhou University of Light Industry, China
Di Wu	Yunnan Normal University, China
Yonghui Wu	Fudan University, China
Bin Xi	Xiamen University, China
Yuelong Xia	Yunnan Normal University, China
Xiaoxu Xiao	Shaanxi Normal University, China
Meihua Xiao	East China Jiaotong University, China
Min Xie	Yunnan Normal University, China
Jian Xu	Qujing Normal University, China
Mingliang Xue	Dalian Nationalities University, China
Yajun Yang	Tianjin University, China
Fan Yang	Xiamen University, China
Kehua Yang	Hunan University, China
Chen Yao	Zhejiang University, China
Zhenyan Ye	Sanya Aviation and Tourism College, China
Shouyi Yin	Tsinghua University, China
Xiaohui Yu	Shandong University, China
Yue Yu	Beijing Institute of Technology, China
Lingyun Yuan	Yunnan Normal University, China
Ye Yuan	Northeastern University, China
Congpin Zhang	Henan Normal University, China
Junna Zhang	Henan Normal University, China
Chuanlei Zhang	Tianjin University of Science and Technology, China

Contents – Part II

**Innovative Application for the Deeper Integration of Education
Practice and Information Technology**

Contents – Part I

Educational Informatization and Big Data for Education

Research on the Construction and Application of Smart Campuses in Applied Colleges

Juan Li[1]([✉]), Wanxiong Zhao[1], Beilei Shi[2], and Qian Xie[2]

[1] Wuchang Institute of Technology, Wuhan, China
Lijuan770107@126.com
[2] Naval University of Engineering, Wuhan, China

Abstract. The smart campus represents a significant educational reform aimed at leveraging the latest information technologies to increase educational quality and facilitate innovation and reform in teaching methodologies. On the basis of thorough research into the current state of information technology adoption and the need for smart campus development for applied colleges, a blueprint for constructing smart campuses has been proposed that encompasses upgrading network infrastructure, establishing a big data-assisted decision-making platform, constructing a unified application integration platform, and enhancing information security measures and safety management protocols. The implementation process of this project ensures smooth progress by strengthening organizational management and clarifying and implementing management tasks at each stage, thus providing robust support for smart campus construction. The smart teaching solutions and practical cases supported by the smart campus platform demonstrate the superior effect of technology-empowered education. The development of smart campuses is an inevitable choice for the informatization of applied higher education institutions, representing a powerful initiative to increase the level of information management, service efficiency, and, ultimately, the competitiveness and influence of these institutions.

Keywords: Smart Campus · Educational Informationization · Smart Teaching

1 Introduction

With the development of the times, the construction of educational informatization has transformed from digitization to intelligence. Smart campuses constitute a future trend and an inevitable path for the development of educational informatization[1–3]. The construction of smart campuses, which involves the informatization and intelligent empowerment of teaching environments, teaching processes, educational management, and campus services, will promote education toward a higher level and goal. As an in-depth development and upgrade of digital campuses and a more advanced form of educational informatization, smart campuses organically connect physical spaces with information spaces, enabling convenient access to resources and services regardless of time and place [4, 5].

© The Author(s), under exclusive license to Springer Nature Singapore Pte Ltd. 2025
K. Zhang et al. (Eds.): CSEI 2024, CCIS 2448, pp. 3–13, 2025.
https://doi.org/10.1007/978-981-96-3738-6_1

With the goal of cultivating skilled craftsmen and highly skilled application-oriented talent, applied colleges have a certain foundation for information construction, but the level of smart campus construction is still relatively low, making them unable to meet the needs of modern education for digitization and intelligence. Focusing on the needs of smart campus construction in applied colleges, corresponding design and implementation plans for smart campuses are proposed. By deeply integrating information system technology and applications, it aims to promote intelligent classroom teaching, research, management, and services. This will establish a comprehensive smart campus and enhance the overall quality and competitiveness of applied colleges.

2 Requirement Analysis

Education informatization in applied colleges is crucial for cultivating highly skilled and applied talent. With the continuous promotion of national education informatization reform and the continuous advancement of information technology, the informatization of applied colleges has undergone stages such as multimedia teaching, basic campus network construction, individual MIS system application, and comprehensive smart campus construction coverage.

However, the majority of the existing infrastructure in applied colleges has been in use for a relatively long time and can no longer meet the needs of future development. Fundamental support platforms for smart campuses, such as unified identity authentication platforms, unified user portal platforms, and unified data center platforms, have not been established. Many application systems, including smart teaching management platforms and smart student affairs management systems, are still in the initial stages of planning and construction.

Using modern information technology and intelligent technology, the construction of smart campuses in applied colleges should intelligently upgrade campus-related businesses such as the campus environment, campus management, campus services, education and teaching, and educational research. Guided by service and driven by application innovation, the construction of smart campuses deeply integrates advanced information technologies such as 5G networks, virtualization, big data, the Internet of Things, and the mobile internet with the teaching, research, and management of applied colleges. With teaching as the center and service improvement as the foundation, it aims to create a convenient educational environment for smart campuses, enabling on-demand teaching services, readily available course resources, flexible scientific and technological research and development, and timely auxiliary decision-making, thereby improving the quality of education [6].

3 Project Design

Adhering to the principles of education-oriented and moral cultivation, the construction of smart campuses in applied colleges promotes the digitization and intelligent transformation and upgrading of various businesses in private higher education, including teaching, management, and services by information technology.

3.1   General Framework of Smart Campuses

The overall design for the construction of smart campuses in applied colleges should adhere to the national standards for the general framework of smart campuses and fully incorporate the characteristics of applied colleges. According to the needs for smart campus construction in applied colleges derived from various surveys and interviews, the core goals of smart campus construction in applied colleges are to upgrade network infrastructure, establish a big data-assisted decision-making platform, construct a unified application integration platform, ensure information security and standardize operation and maintenance management.

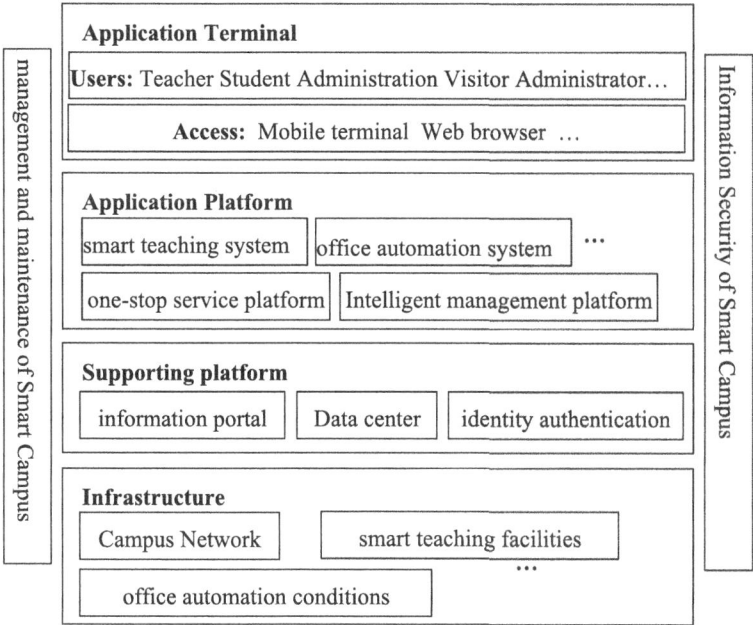

Fig. 1. Overall design for the construction of smart campuses

The framework for the construction of smart campuses in applied colleges is shown in Fig. 1. The infrastructure layer primarily comprises the foundational hardware facilities of the smart campus, encompassing the campus network, smart teaching facilities, office automation conditions and so on. The support layer provides services such as portal access, identity authentication, and data sharing for the application platform layer. The application platform layer consists of various smart management platforms and systems for the smart campus, including a smart teaching system, an office automation system, a one-stop service platform, an intelligent management platform and other business systems. The application terminal layer serves users in roles such as teachers, students, administrative personnel, administrators and external personnel.

3.2 Construction Contents Involving Smart Campuses

Network infrastructure construction is the basic context of smart campuses. The campus network should provide high-speed, convenient, and flexible network access methods to meet the demands of educational informatization. It mainly covers several aspects, including the Gigabit wired network, comprehensive wireless network, and IoT network. Gigabit wired networks can achieve high-speed connections and improve operation and maintenance efficiency, addressing issues such as outdated existing networks, incomplete coverage, and messy wiring. A comprehensive wireless network with high speed covering the entire campus will satisfy the wireless service needs of teachers and students anytime and anywhere while facing challenges in coverage, security, and management. The IoT network, which is applied in smart campuses, provides an integrated, seamless acquisition platform and intelligent campus service platform, transforming campus teaching and management methods to improve educational quality.

The development of a data support platform is a key component of a smart campus. Following scientific, normal and practical data standards. Unified data resource platforms should be built with rich content, complete dimensions, a clear hierarchy, and reliable quality. Moreover, a sophisticated, user-friendly, and visually intuitive data management tool software system also needs to be deployed to achieve full-lifecycle management of data resources. Specifically, tailored to the needs of applied colleges, we can integrate relevant application systems, resolve data exchange and share issues between different systems. Big data technology can be applied to provide teaching references, as well as planning and decision-making support for students, demonstrating excellent adaptability.

The construction of an application platform is an important component of a smart campus, which includes many intelligent business systems. Under an individualized, flexible, and efficient smart teaching environment, smart teaching resources can be taken full advantage of to gain diverse and personalized teaching content and tools that support educational innovation and enhance learning outcomes. Moreover, through smart campus management, applied colleges can comprehensively manage and optimize various aspects, improving the efficiency and quality of educational management. Moreover, smart campus services can provide convenient and efficient campus life services.

3.3 Information Security and Operations Management

The prevention of information security is a comprehensive project encompassing technology, management, and personnel [7]. The construction of smart campus information security in applied colleges can be approached from three perspectives: the establishment of an information security technology system, the formulation of information security regulations, and the improvement of awareness of information security protection. The specific measures are shown in Table 1.

Operation and maintenance management is an important task to ensure the normal operation of various hardware and software systems on smart campuses. The operation and maintenance of a smart campus requires the support of a corresponding professional IT team. Establishing an operation and maintenance organization for smart campuses, strengthening the training of relevant technical personnel, improving the maintenance system of smart campuses, and clarifying job responsibilities can provide safeguards for smart campuses. Moreover, by deploying a unified smart operation and maintenance management system, we can achieve whole-process and comprehensive unified intelligent monitoring and management of various equipment resources in a college, actively detect faults in time, and realize rapid fault location and fault recovery.

Table 1. Specific measures for information security

Domain	Method	Measures
Technology	Establish the information security technology system	Network access authenticating, deploying professional web protection equipment, website protection platform, arranging online behavior audit system, unified information security operation and maintenance management, timely classified protection evaluating and so on
Management	Formulate the information security regulations	Information security management measures, data center workflow and management systems, information security agreements for faculty and staff, information security emergency plans and disposal management measures, etc
Personnel	Improve awareness of information security protection	Specialized training for leading cadres to increase their attention and responsibility, training, lectures, and other means for teachers and students to promote information security awareness, specialized technical training for security professionals and train a professional and competent campus information security team

4 Project Implementation

In applied colleges, the construction of a smart campus is a complex and crucial task. It not only involves technological innovation and application but also requires rigorous project management to ensure the smooth progress of the project. Therefore, applying project management theory to the construction of smart campuses is the key to ensuring the successful implementation of the project. Following project management theory to oversee the implementation process of smart campus construction projects, we can ensure smooth project progression, increase project success rates, and provide robust support for the development of applied colleges.

4.1 Team Organization

Because the smart campus project at Applied College has large-scale construction, numerous stakeholders involved, and high technological content, a matrix-style organizational structure for management is adopted to ensure the successful completion of the project, which encompasses both the project management organization of the college and performance, as illustrated in Fig. 2. Both parties include a project leadership team, an expert committee, a project director, and project managers. During the specific implementation process, the college's project management organization still needs positions such as a business review team, a project implementation team, a discipline inspection and supervision team, a bidding and procurement team, and a user experience team. Moreover, the implementation side's project management organization needs a business analysis team, a design and development team, a project implementation team, a quality supervision team, and an after-sales service team.

For the project leader, it is crucial to be familiar with the project's organizational structure, scope, and management processes, as well as the roles and responsibilities of each project member. Each project member, on the other hand, must have a clear understanding of the project's objectives, scope of construction, team members, and individual work tasks. Both the implementation team members and college staff must be familiar with their respective work tasks and job responsibilities to ensure smooth vertical and horizontal communication.

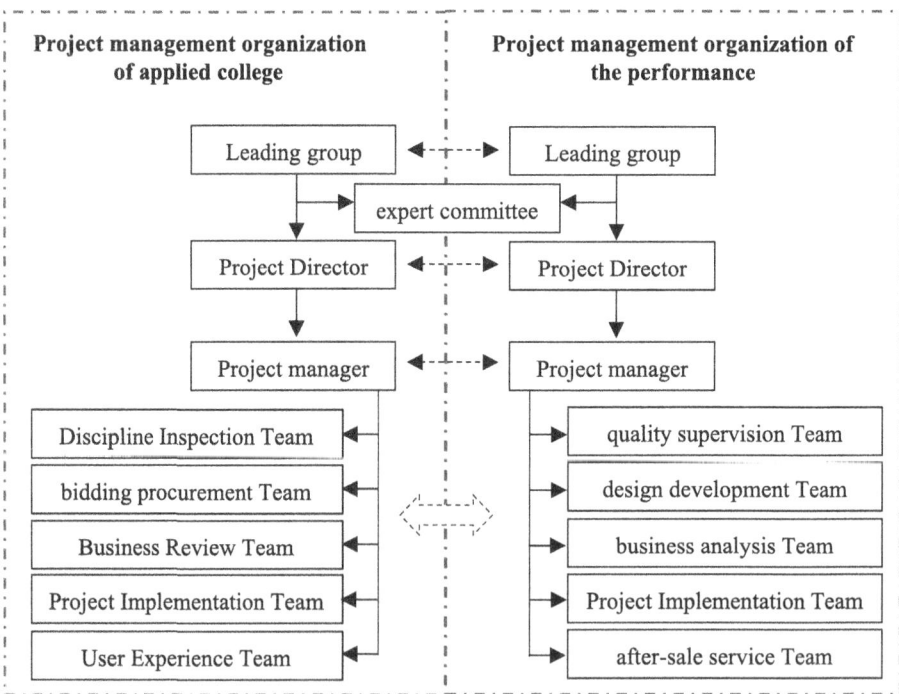

Fig. 2. Team organization for the construction of smart campuses

4.2   Project Management

During project implementation, management can be conducted through three phases: initiation, execution, and closure.

At the initiation phase, the smart campus project teams and their members must clearly define their respective responsibilities and strictly adhere to relevant norms, thereby guaranteeing the project's progress and quality. During this process, documents such as the project task statement, charter, member assignments, implementation plan, and schedule should be compiled to ensure the smooth accomplishment of the project.

Comprehensive management of the project is undertaken throughout the entire implementation process to ensure that it proceeds smoothly as planned. The execution phase specifically breaks down into several stages, including requirements analysis, scheme formulation, software development, deployment, and pilot runs, with the detailed tasks outlined in Table 2.

Table 2.   Detailed tasks in each execution phase

Phase	Main tasks	Key documents
Requirement	After determining the project scope, conduct detailed requirement research on each sub project of the smart campus	Project Scope Statement, Project Requirements Survey Form
Scheme	Develop detailed implementation plans for each subproject, clearly defining the key links and responsible persons., prepare detailed requirements specifications for the customized software	Project Implementation Details, Software Customization Development Requirements Specification, System Installation Manual
Development	According design of customized software complete its development, conduct system testing following testing plan making corrections to ultimately achieve the desired results	Software Design Documentation, Software Customization Development Program, System Test Report"
Deployment	Follow the relevant operational procedures to complete the deployment and implementation of the project. Conduct a series of tests on the system to ensure its normal operation	Quality Inspection Checklist, System Implementation Report
Pilot run	Observe the operation of the system and promptly resolve related issues. Additionally, the implementing engineer will also provide training to the college's system maintenance personnel	Training Record Form, System Operation Manual

5   Application and Effects

The core of a smart campus lies in leveraging advanced information technology to facilitate the optimal allocation of educational resources and the intelligent management of educational processes. The smart teaching supported by the smart campus platform has fundamentally transformed traditional teaching methods and management models [8–10]. The central idea of smart teaching is to develop students' wisdom through knowledge impartation, using the teaching of knowledge as a means to cultivate students' thinking abilities and achieve the integration of knowledge and wisdom. As a typical application of smart campuses, smart teaching has become an essential component of the digital transformation of higher education, with its importance becoming increasingly prominent.

5.1   Smart Teaching Solutions

The smart teaching solution supported by the smart campus is illustrated in Fig. 3. With the backing of the smart network platform, students engage in online autonomous learning through the online cloud classroom, whereas offline face-to-face classes are organized in smart classrooms. After-class reinforcement and expansion are accomplished primarily through platform support, enabling students to engage in broader learning and exploration on the basis of their individual needs.

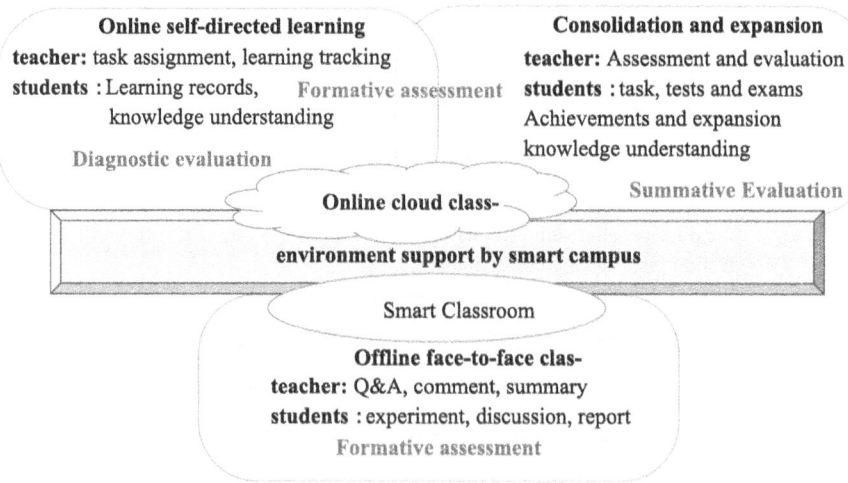

Fig. 3. Solution framework of smart teaching

The smart network platform provides infrastructure and resources for smart teaching, enabling the establishment of online cloud classrooms for online teaching. Smart classrooms are connected to the smart classroom teaching platform through network technology, forming an intelligent teaching space for offline teaching. The smart teaching platform can also record the entire teaching process dynamically and leverage big data in education. It will provide teachers with insights for individualized and precise teaching, making teaching activities more tailored to students' needs, facilitating their understanding and mastery of knowledge, and effectively enhancing students' autonomous learning and self-development capabilities, transforming knowledge into students' intellectual wisdom.

The preclass stage involves online autonomous learning, during which teachers track students' learning progress and provide necessary instructional guidance and feedback. On the basis of students' online learning performance, teachers devise strategies for implementing face-to-face classes, which can be organized as seminars, presentations, Q&A sessions, etc. The cultivation of higher-order learning abilities such as inquiry-based learning and collaborative learning is emphasized to help students develop their own learning systems and foster habits of active knowledge seeking. After-class reinforcement also takes place online, where students review and consolidate their learning. The smart teaching network platform also provides necessary support for teaching evaluation, leveraging its advantages to integrate diagnostic, formative, and summative evaluations.

5.2 Implementation Case

"Data Structures", the core course of computer science at a certain Applied College, is selected as a case study to investigate the application of smart teaching. This college has completed the first phase of its "Smart Campus" construction project, which includes the upgrading of network infrastructure and smart classrooms, as well as the deployment of a smart teaching platform. This has facilitated the construction of the "Data Structures" course website. On this basis, blending learning has been developed to achieve smart teaching.

Guided by the goals of knowledge acquisition, skill development, and wisdom generation, an implementation plan for smart teaching is designed. The course resources are developed on the course website. The teaching content system is integrated and reconstructed on the basis of a project-driven approach and the integration of theory and practice. Then, teaching plans and implementation schemes are formulated, and teaching activities are designed. The teaching implementation primarily encompasses autonomous learning in online classrooms, flipped classrooms in smart classrooms, and programming practices on online platforms. During implementation, teachers closely monitor the big data generated by the teaching platform and provide timely feedback on these data to ensure that smart teaching proceeds as planned, effectively improving teaching efficiency and precisely aligning with teaching objectives.

Course assessment spans the entire teaching process. Process-based evaluation relies primarily on learning data from the teaching platform, whereas practical ability is evaluated on the basis of the completion of practical projects. A summary assessment is conducted in the form of a closed-book final exam. Teaching evaluations are conducted on the basis of the actual implementation of the teaching plan, summarizing the effectiveness of the teaching with insights from big data and student exam scores. Furthermore, through discussions between teachers and students, team seminars, and exchanges with peers both inside and outside the college, the effectiveness of smart teaching, teacher–student satisfaction, and goal achievement can be investigated and analyzed. On the basis of these findings, we refine and optimize the goals and application models of smart teaching, summarize experience, distill achievements, and promote their application in other courses and majors.

5.3 Effect Evaluation

The effectiveness of smart teaching supported by a smart campus needs to be verified through teaching practices. The "Data Structures" course adopted traditional teaching methods before 2020, underwent pilot teaching from 2021--2022, and was fully implemented from 2023--2024. An annual questionnaire survey was conducted for all course sessions, and the survey results are presented in Table 3.

Table 3. Survey results of the teaching case

Classes	A	B1	B2	C
Average score	72.62	74.63	80.18	84.26
satisfaction degree	70.86%	76.24%	89.45%	94.12%
Knowledge Understanding				
Good	12.23%	16.15%	32.72%	38.65%
Normal	28.63%	34.81%	40.72%	45.23%
Pass	36.25%	32.47%%	16.86%	12.28%
Poor	22.89%	16.57%	9.70%	5.84%
Acceptance of smart teaching	---------	82.16%	92.53%	96.28%

note: A means the traditional teaching class for 2019 and 2020; B means the teaching class for 2021 and 2022, with B1 being the traditional teaching class and B2 being the pilot class for smart teaching; C means a smart teaching class for 2023 and 2024. Good - Implementing typical algorithms based on mastering basic knowledge Normal - Understand typical algorithms based on mastering basic knowledge Pass -Only mastering basic knowledge Poor- Only understand basic concepts

As shown in the table, the level of satisfaction with smart teaching is high, and students have the best grasp of knowledge. Compared with those in previous years, traditional classes in the 2021 and 2022 classes presented improved knowledge mastery, primarily due to the sharing of course website resources within the smart campus environment.

The smart teaching of the "Data Structures" course features advanced concepts and novel methods, leading to high student engagement and excellent teaching outcomes. Students evaluate classes as lively, highly interactive, and significantly enhancing their self-learning and innovative abilities. The teaching practices and research achievements have been repeatedly exchanged and showcased at various levels within schools, departments, and similar colleges, garnering praise from peer teachers. Smart teaching supported by a smart campus can guide applied colleges' teaching from a focus on knowledge to a focus on wisdom, helping students transform knowledge into wisdom and enhancing both knowledge and ability.

6   Conclusion

A smart campus is a significant educational reform that leverages the latest informa-tion technologies to enhance educational quality and promote innovation and reform in teaching methodologies. The construction of smart campuses is an inevitable choice for the informatization of private higher education institutions, serving as a potent measure to increase the level of information management, service efficiency, and, ultimately, the competitiveness and influence of these institutions. On the basis of a clear understand-ing of the construction needs of smart campuses in applied colleges, this paper proposes corresponding construction plans and project implementation management schemes. The use of smart teaching as a case study illustrates the specific applications of smart campuses and demonstrates their superiority through effect analysis.

The construction of smart campuses in applied colleges not only facilitates teachers' work and promotes the intelligent and scientific development of education and teach-ing but also creates a modern and technological learning environment for students. It enhances students' learning motivation and initiative, improves their overall quality, and provides effective assistance in building high-quality, application-oriented, and excellent applied colleges.

Acknowledgment.   This research was supported by grants from the Educational Research Project of Hubei Higher Education Association (2023XD105), the Teaching Reform Research Key Project of Wuchang Institute of Technology (2023JY01), and the Science and Technology Innovation Team Project of Hubei Province Excellent Young and Middle Aged in Colleges and Universities (T2021042).

References

1. Fortes, S., Santoyo-Ramon, J.A., Palacios, D., et al.: The campus as a smart city: university of Malaga environmental, learning, and research approaches. Sensors (6), 1–23 (2019)
2. Chagnon-Lessard, N., Gosselin, L., Barnabe, S., et al.: Smart campuses: extensive review of the last decade of research and current challenges. IEEE Access **9**, 124200–124234 (2021)
3. Dong, Z.Y., Zhang, Y., Yip, C., et al.: Smart campus: definition, framework, technologies, and services. IET Smart Cities **2**(1), 43–54 (2020)
4. Zhang, Y., Yip, C., Lu, E., et al.: A systematic review on technologies and applications in smart campus: a human-centered case study. IEEE Access **10**, 16134–16149 (2022)
5. Sneesl, R., Jusoh, Y.Y., Jabar. M.A., et al.: Revising technology adoption factors for IoT-based smart campuses: a systematic review. Sustainability **14**(8), 4840 (2022)
6. Mustafa, M.F., Mohd-isa, M.R., Abdul-Rauf, U.F., et al.: Student perception study on smart campus: a case study on higher education institution. Malaysian J. Comput. Science **7**, 1–20 (2021)
7. Robert, K., Macrobiotic, F.T.: Managing Complex IT Security Processes with Value Based Measures. Ali Mili (2011)
8. He, F.N., Gao, X.Y., et al.: Construction of functional model of smart teaching space based on teaching motivation optimizaton. Teach. Admin. **09**, 1–6 (2024)
9. Luo, S.H., Zhang, X.: Different understandings and new interpretation of smart instruction. Chin. J. Dist. Educ. **11**, 6–14 (2022)
10. Xing, X.S., Guan, J.: Wisdom teaching in the new era: classroom practice, problem thinking and development strategies. e-Education Res. **43**(05), 109–114 (2022)

Research on the Digital Ability of Tourism Major Students in Higher Vocational Colleges

Han Wu[✉]

Sanya Aviation and Tourism College, Sanya Hainan 572000, China
516095898@qq.com

Abstract. The rise and development of digital tourism has prompted various tourism enterprises to have new requirements for the digital ability of talent engaged in the tourism industry in the future. The digital ability of tourism talent determines whether it can survive and develop in fierce industry competition in the future. On the basis of a previous literature review and analysis, the author found that the digital ability of tourism talent plays a crucial role in their future career development. However, for various reasons, research in academia on the cultivation of the digital ability of vocational tourism talent is currently limited, and even less research has been conducted on Hainan Province. To further advance the reform and research of digital ability training for vocational tourism talent in Hainan against the background of digital tourism, this paper takes 394 students majoring in tourism at Sanya Aviation and Tourism College as the objects of study, designs a questionnaire to investigate the level of students' digital ability, analyzes the existing problems of their digital ability, and suggests solutions to the relevant problems.

Keywords: Digital ability · Tourism major students · Problems and suggestions

1 Introduction

With the advancement and development of digital technology, the tourism industry is also undergoing digital transformation. Students who work in the tourism industry in the future need to master digital skills to adapt to the application of emerging technologies such as smart tourism, online booking, and big data analysis. To improve students' digital ability, teachers should first clarify students' digital ability. By analyzing students' digital ability, teachers can better understand students' strengths and weaknesses in digital technology so that they can adjust their teaching methods and course content and improve their teaching quality. Students' digital skills are developed, which helps stimulate their innovative thinking, enable them to use digital tools and platforms for innovative practices, and enable them to be more competitive in the future job market and better adapt to digital jobs in the tourism industry. For colleges and universities engaged in training tourism professionals, cultivating students' digital ability can promote the digital transformation of tourism-related professional education and help build a talent training system suitable for the digital age. In June 2020, the Ministry of Education

K. Zhang et al. (Eds.): CSEI 2024, CCIS 2448, pp. 14–26, 2025.
https://doi.org/10.1007/978-981-96-3738-6_2

revised the previously issued Code for the Construction of Digital Campus in Vocational Colleges, which made clear requirements for the training of information-based talent in vocational colleges. With the rapid development of information technology, digital technology is widely used, and a good grasp of digital ability is crucial to the future employment and development of students. In this national standard, the requirements for students' numerical ability are described in detail. The formulation of this national standard will help improve the level of digital ability of vocational students and provide better support for their future employment and development. Moreover, it can promote the rapid development of digital education. As one of the most popular tropical coastal tourist destinations in China, Hainan's tourism industry is one of its pillar industries, contributing significantly to GDP. Since 2018, with the continuous development of the construction of the Hainan Free Trade Zone port, the development of tourism has also provided clear guidance. In the future, Hainan will be built into a demonstration province of all-regional tourism and an international tourism consumption center. The future of Hainan tourism is bright. On the basis of the above background, this paper takes 394 students majoring in tourism at Sanya Aviation and Tourism College as the research object, designs a questionnaire to investigate the level of students' digital ability, analyzes the existing problems of students' digital ability, and process solutions to the relevant problems.

2   A Survey of the Digital Ability of Students Majoring in Tourism at a Higher Vocational College

2.1   Research Methods

A Questionnaire survey.

2.2   Research Questions

The digital ability level of tourism major students in higher vocational colleges;

Difference in digital ability level across genders, grades and majors in higher vocational colleges.

2.3   Research Objectives and Tools

In this paper, 394 students with tourism-related majors at Sanya Aviation and Tourism College are taken as the objects of study, and the digital ability of tourism-related majors is investigated via a questionnaire. The designed questionnaire was sent to the students in the form of a questionnaire star. The whole questionnaire is designed by reading many relevant studies, referring to the items in the framework of digital competence cultivation of European citizens, interviewing managers and practitioners of relevant tourism-related industries, and analyzing all aspects involved in the digital competence training of tourism-related talent and the main components of digital competence. In this questionnaire, students' digital ability is divided into three aspects: information skills, media marketing ability, and innovation ability. This questionnaire uses a five-level Likert scale. For the questions in the scale, corresponding scores are set for the students' answers. A score of 1 indicates none, not understood or very inconsistent, and a score of 5 indicates very much, very understanding and very consistent. Each subject's digital ability level is obtained by calculating the average of the items given. All the data in the questionnaire were imported into SPSS 22.0 for data analysis, and the current level of students' digital ability level across different genders, grades and majors was determined. The questions related to each dimension of the questionnaire are listed in Table 1. According to the results of the data analysis for the questionnaires, the level of digital competence of students majoring in the tourism of vocational college students is clarified.

Table 1. Questions on each dimension

Dimension	Question
Information skill	1. I am proficient in daily office software, such as Word, Excel and so on
	2. Familiar with online booking system, various travel apps and electronic maps related to digital tourism
	3. I can master travel-related information through the internet, and I can obtain tourism information through internet technology
	4. Through tourism industry data, I can analyze tourists' consumption behaviors and interests, better serve them, and carry out accurate marketing
	5. I can use software to analyze tourism data and solve practical problems
Media marketing ability	6. I have good logical ability and clear thinking in writing digital tourism documents
	7. I can promote the destination through microblog, wechat, travel website or video account
	8. I can provide consultation, product marketing and other services to tourists through the internet
	9. I can use network big data to forecast tourism information and carry out media marketing
	10. With the help of various media platforms, I can promote tourism enterprises at a lower cost and attract more potential consumers
Innovation ability	11. I can put forward innovative views on digital tourism, and I am good at thinking about the problems encountered in the development of digital tourism with new thinking, new methods and new angles

(*continued*)

Table 1. (*continued*)

Dimension	Question
	12. Good memory ability for digital-intelligence travel related knowledge
	13. The log-smart tourism market has a keen observation ability, and can provide tourists with diversified and high-quality travel experience
	14. I can flexibly deal with problems in digital tourism events, and have sufficient awareness of risk prevention
	15. Log-intelligent tourism has strong independent learning ability, and can quickly acquire and constantly update digital-intelligent tourism knowledge

2.4 Analysis of the Research Results

In this research, questionnaires were issued in the form of questionnaire stars. A total of 400 questionnaires were issued and 394 valid questionnaires were collected. All questionnaires were analyzed via SPSS 22.0.

Testing of Reliability and Validity. In general, the reliability coefficient should be between 0 and 1. Table 2 shows that the Cronbach's alpha coefficient of the questionnaire is 0.992. This means that the reliability of the scale is very good. In Table 3 below, the KMO value is 0.968, and the Sig. Value of the Bartlett sphericity test is 0.000, which is less than 0.05, indicating that the questionnaire has good validity.

Table 2. Reliability statistics

Cronbach'Alpha	N of Items
.992	15

Table 3. KMO and Bartlett test

Kaiser–Meyer–Olkin Measure of Sampling Adequacy		.968
Bartlett's Test of Sphericity	About chi-square	12473.917
	Df	105
	Sig	.000

The Level of Students' Digital Ability Majored in Tourism in Higher Vocational Colleges. *Overall level of digital ability.* Descriptive statistical analysis was conducted on the questions in the questionnaire via SPSS 22.0. According to Table 4, the overall mean value of the 15 questions is 56.0102. The average value for each question is 3.73. On the basis of a total mean of 5 points, 3.73 points is in the middle, so the total number of students majoring in tourism can reach the medium level.

Table 4. Descriptive statistics

	N	Minimum	Maximum	Mean	Standard deviation
Total Value	394	15.00	75.00	56.0102	14.66955
Valid N (listwise)	394				

The Level of Digital Ability in Different Dimensions. In Table 5, a descriptive statistical analysis of the students' information skill levels reveals that the students' information technology ability is moderate, with an average value of 3.74. Students are generally familiar with daily office applications and some travel apps, electronic maps and digital travel online booking systems. The ability of students to use the internet to master travel information is greater than other abilities in this dimension, but the overall level is still average. According to the research results of students, the ability to analyze tourism data, create portraits for tourists, and analyze their preferences for targeted online marketing is also average.

Table 5. Descriptive statistics

	N	Minimum	Maximum	Mean	Standard deviation
Information technology level	394	5.00	25.00	18.7030	4.94094
Valid N (listwise)	394				

In Table 6, a descriptive statistical analysis of the students' marketing ability level reveals that their media marketing ability level is also moderate, with an average value between 3.69 and 3.77. The overall level of students' media marketing ability is moderate. Students can promote their travel destinations through Weibo, WeChat, travel websites, or video accounts. They can also provide consultation, product marketing, and other services to tourists through the internet. They can also use media platforms to promote tourism enterprises at a lower cost and attract potential consumers. With the rapid advancement of mobile internet technology, smartphones have been a part of people's daily lives. In addition to obtaining simple information from the internet and relaxing themselves online, the use of new media to solve work problems has become a current trend. Students have this awareness, and most people have media marketing skills; however, their level still needs to be improved.

Table 6. Descriptive statistics

	N	Minimum	Maximum	Mean	Standard deviation
Media marketing capability level	394	5.00	25.00	18.6497	4.97722
Valid N (listwise)	394				

In Table 7, the overall level of students' innovation ability is average, with an average value between 3.71 and 3.75. Currently, students are willing to accept new ideas and things, and they do not like to learn boring theoretical knowledge. They are more willing to engage in practical operations and apply their imaginative innovative ideas to reality. According to the table data, although students have strong innovation abilities, they still need professional training and practice to apply these abilities to future positions.

Table 7. Descriptive statistics

	N	Minimum	Maximum	Mean	Standard deviation
Innovation capability level	394	5.00	25.00	18.6574	4.96162
Valid N (listwise)	394				

Differences in the Digital Ability of Students Majoring in Different Genders, Grades and Majors. An independent sample T test was conducted to determine whether there are significant differences in digital ability for students majoring in tourism.

Independent Sample T Test for Students of Different Genders. According to Table 8, after an overall analysis of students' information technology ability, media marketing ability, and innovation ability level is conducted the differences between these three abilities among students of different genders are further analyzed. For ease of presentation, students' information technology skills, media marketing skills, and innovation skills are represented as B1, B2, and B3, respectively. After SPSS 22.0 analysis, the F value corresponding to B1, which is the student's information technology ability, is 4.402, and the sig value is 0.038, which is less than 0.05, suggesting that the homogeneity of variance is not valid. Therefore, the T test result is $T = 2.358$, $P = 0.018 < 0.05$. According to the analysis above, there are significant differences in the information technology ability levels of students of different genders. Combining the mean values, the average information technology ability of men is significantly greater than that of women. The F value corresponding to B2, which is the media marketing ability, is 4.222, and the sig value is 0.042, which is 0.05, suggesting that homogeneity of variance does not hold. Therefore, the T test result is $T = 2.518$, $P = 0.013$, which is less than 0.05, indicating that there is a significant difference in media marketing ability between male students and female students. The average media marketing ability of male students is significantly greater than that of female students. The F value corresponding to innovation ability in B3 is 4.158, and the sig value is 0.043, which is less than 0.05, meaning that homogeneity of variance does not hold. Therefore, the T test result is T = 2.943, P = 0.003, which is less than 0.05, indicating that there is a significant difference in innovation ability levels between students of different genders. Combining the mean values, it can be concluded that the average innovation ability of male students is significantly greater than that of female students.

Table 8. Independent- samples T test

	Levene's test forequality of variances		T test for whether the mean is equal					95% Confidence Interval	
	F	Sig.	T	df	Sig. (2-tailed)	Mean difference	Standard error	Lower Bound	Upper Bound
B1	4.402	.038	2.311	391	.022	.24019	.10395	.03578	.44457
			2.358	293.788	.018	.24019	.10193	.03961	.44075
B2	4.222	.042	2.461	391	.015	.25742	.10464	.05171	.46313
			2.518	296.339	.013	.25742	.10227	.05618	.45864
B3	4.158	.043	2.886	391	.004	.30004	.10402	.09556	.50452
			2.943	293.717	.003	.30004	.10196	.09936	.50072

Independent Sample T Test for Students of Different Majors.   According to Table 9, the F values corresponding to B1, B2, and B3 are 1.114, 1.396, and 3.438, respectively and the sig values are 0.291, 0.237, and 0.066, respectively, all of which are > 0.05. This means that the variances are consistent, and there is no significant difference in the levels of information technology ability, marketing ability, and innovation ability among students from different majors.

Table 9. Independent- samples T test

	Levene's test forequality of variances		T test for whether the mean is equal					95% Confidence Interval	
	F	Sig.	T	df	Sig. (2-tailed)	Mean difference	Standard error	Lower Bound	Upper Bound
B1	1.114	.291	1.318	393	.188	.13132	.09972	−.06475	.32737
			1.325	390.527	.187	.13132	.09914	−.06364	.32626
B2	1.396	.237	.469	393	.641	.04714	.10064	−.15076	.24501
			.472	390.458	.639	.04714	.10007	−.14965	.24391
B3	3.438	.066	.544	393	.588	.05448	.10034	−.14274	.25175
			.548	391.353	.586	.05448	.09961	−.14134	.25033

Independent Sample T Test for Students in Different Grades. Table 10 shows that the F values corresponding to B1, B2, and B3 are 0.001, 0.071, and 0.087, respectively, and the sig values are 0.986, 0.793, and 0.768, respectively, all of which are > 0.05. This means that the variances are consistent, and there is no significant difference in the levels of information technology ability, marketing ability, and innovation ability among students of different grades.

Table 10. Independent- samples T test

	Levene's test forequality of variances		T test for whether the mean is equal						
	F	Sig.	T	df	Sig. (2-tailed)	Mean difference	Standard error	95% Confidence Interval	
								Lower Bound	Upper Bound
B1	.001	.986	.354	393	.724	.05931	.16688	−.26882	.38742
			.343	45.933	.735	.05931	.17331	−.28957	.40817
B2	.071	.793	−.396	393	.694	−.06637	.16812	−.39686	.26413
			−.383	46.047	.705	−.06637	.17362	−.41582	.28308
B3	.087	.768	.634	393	.528	.10608	.16754	−.22328	.43543
			.595	45.402	.557	.10608	.17868	−.25374	.46587

2.5   Summary and Analysis of Digital Ability Cultivation Issues

According to the questionnaire survey, this research summarizes the cultivation of digital abilities in vocational tourism professionals. The current level of awareness of digital tourism among vocational tourism professionals is relatively low, and their goal of improving their own digital abilities is vague, resulting in passive learning. In classroom teaching, teachers provide simple descriptions of the concept of digital tourism, which leads to insufficient student awareness and limited understanding of the digitalization, intelligence, and practical applications of tourism in the tourism industry. The goal of cultivating digital abilities for tourism majors in schools is relatively abstract and has not been specifically refined. However, curriculum design still focuses on the cultivation of traditional tourism knowledge and skills, lacking a high emphasis on digital skills. In terms of practical teaching, there is insufficient practical and hands-on teaching, and students lack practical operation and use of digital tools. Therefore, students often find it difficult to use digital skills effectively in practice. In terms of teaching faculties, teachers' quality urgently needs to be improved. Some teachers lack and have limited digital abilities, making it difficult to guide students in developing their digital skills. School enterprise cooperation is not close enough; therefore, it is difficult for students to acquire practical work skills and digital skills training. From an international perspective, students' current internships are mostly in China, so they know little about the needs of digital skills and the current status of digital development in international companies such as Fortune 500 companies, resulting in a lack of high-quality employment opportunities. In terms of students' digital ability, their information technology skills, media marketing ability, and innovation ability are moderate, so there is still great room for improvement in their digital ability. Owing to the significant difference in the digital ability level between male students and female students, when cultivating students' digital abilities, attention should also be given to the differences between male students and female students, and personalized teaching should be provided for students of different genders. Vocational college students are different from ordinary undergraduate students in that their cultural knowledge level is lower and their ability to learn theoretical knowledge is weaker. However, these students have strong hands that can receive correct guidance, and they will surely contribute to the tourism industry in Hainan in the future.

3   Countermeasures and Suggestions for Cultivating the Digital Abilities of Tourism Talent

3.1   Clarifying Professional Talent Training Objectives

According to the above survey results, students' cognitive level of digital tourism is not very high. Although digital tourism and smart tourism are now well known, for students majoring in tourism, the talent development goals related to digital tourism in their field of study are not particularly clear. The training objectives are the top-level design of talent cultivation, which determines the setting of training processes, curriculum systems, and training methods and determines the quality standards of talent cultivation. Therefore, higher vocational colleges should consider the background of the great development of digital tourism, deeply analyze the new demand for the digital abilities of tourism talent in the context of the transformation of the tourism industry against the background of digital tourism, and closely contact tourism-related enterprises. According to the actual demand of the tourism market, schools should open new digital tourism-related majors or add digital tourism-related courses to existing professional courses and clearly demonstrate the training objectives of this major or a certain course in digital tourism to students so that students can clearly know what the goals of their major or course are to be achieved, understand the latest developments in the industry, and know what new knowledge, skills, and qualities they need for future employment in their major. In short, schools should start from industry and market demand, combine their educational positioning and characteristics, and have a clear summary and conclusion of the knowledge, abilities, and quality goals for cultivating the digital abilities of tourism-related talent.

3.2   Adjustment of Professional Course Settings

On the basis of the above survey results, students generally believe that the courses related to digital tourism offered by schools are generally in line with the needs of the tourism market and its various enterprises. Currently, the courses offered by various tourism-related majors still focus on the cultivation of traditional tourism knowledge and skills, lacking a high degree of emphasis on digital skills. Because of insufficient practical and hands-on teaching, especially the lack of practical operation and the use of digital tools, it is very difficult for students to use this skill effectively in practice. In response to the above issues, to cultivate the digital abilities of students, a comprehensive and innovative tourism talent digital ability training curriculum system should first be established, digital technology and tourism professional knowledge should be integrated, and the core knowledge and digital technology of the tourism profession, such as big data, cloud computing, artificial intelligence, etc., should be combined. In terms of curriculum design, new courses should be developed, such as tourism big data analysis, tourism e-commerce, and tourism information management, to enable students to obtain a vocational skill level certificate in tourism big data analysis and strengthen their digital skills to enhance their understanding and application ability of digital technology in the tourism industry. In terms of professional courses, the original basic public courses such as Computer Foundation can be adjusted to Computer and Artificial Intelligence to strengthen students' learning of digital knowledge, to reform the existing teaching contents of Tourism Marketing and Tourism E-Commerce, and to increase the content of digital marketing so that students can experience digital tourism consumption scenarios and improve their awareness of internet rules. New courses related to digital tourism, such as courses on new media operations, should be added to cultivate students' digital communication skills, and other courses that can exercise students' innovation and marketing abilities should be opened.

3.3   Construction of Teaching Staff

According to the survey above, students believe that the teaching attitudes of tourism teachers in vocational colleges are correct and that hey will also share the new progress of digital tourism development with students in the classroom. However, the overall level of informatization of teachers is uneven, and their quality urgently needs to be improved. Owing to the limited digital abilities of some teachers, it is difficult to guide students in developing their digital skills. Some teachers have graduated from universities for many years, but their knowledge is outdated. Faced with the rapid growth of digital tourism, these teachers need to have a keen perception of new technologies and the ability to quickly learn and integrate to better guide students' learning and meet the needs of digital development in the future tourism industry. At present, most of the teachers engaged in tourism courses at Sanya Aviation Tourism Vocational College have a master's degree, and a considerable number of teachers have industry qualification certificates. However, most teachers enter the teaching position directly after graduating from universities and lack frontline work experience. Therefore, relevant training is needed to help teachers master knowledge and tools related to digital technology, including data analysis, digital marketing, and virtual reality. This training will increase the ability of teachers to lead students in facing future challenges. In addition to cultivating existing teachers, it is also possible to supplement existing teaching staff by actively recruiting teachers with digital teaching experience and skills. Invite experts from the tourism industry and digital technology field to give lectures or hold workshops so that teachers can have a first-hand understanding of the latest trends and technological developments in the industry. Create an interactive communication platform for the teaching staff, encourage teachers to share their teaching experience, explore digital teaching methods, and regularly hold teaching seminars or lectures. A performance evaluation mechanism for teaching staff should be established, with digital teaching ability as an important assessment indicator. On the basis of the evaluation results, personalized training and guidance can be provided to teachers to motivate them to continuously improve their digital teaching skills. Tourism teachers should be encouraged to engage in interdisciplinary collaboration with teachers from other disciplines to develop digital teaching content and projects jointly. This can integrate professional knowledge from different fields and provide a more comprehensive digital teaching experience.

3.4   Improving Teaching Facilities and the International Perspective

With respect to campus teaching facilities, students believe that they can only generally meet their training requirements. For vocational college students, practical skills are particularly important. According to research, even in Germany, where vocational education is highly developed, the main obstacle to cultivating digital skills lies in hardware facilities. The hardware facilities used for classroom teaching in vocational colleges are seriously inadequate, with insufficient provision of tablets, interactive whiteboards, desktops, and laptops. The campus network connection signal is poor or almost nonexistent. In China, hardware improvement still requires a relatively long period of time and government investment for vocational colleges. However, to enable students to have strong practical abilities, schools need to first update their existing teaching facilities. At present, the school only has a regular computer room to ensure the learning of the course "Computer Fundamentals" for students, and the multimedia equipment in the classroom is limited to the use of teachers, resulting in poor interactivity. Therefore, interactive facilities such as interactive whiteboards and electronic projection boards should be added to allow students to easily showcase their ideas and work while also stimulating their creativity and imagination. These facilities can also provide teachers with more teaching resources and tools to better guide students' learning. By improving such facilities, tourism professionals can better develop and enhance their digital abilities. Second, it is necessary to provide students with professional training equipment and training rooms for practical exercises within the school. At present, schools equipped with catering training rooms, guest room training rooms, bar training rooms, hotel information system training rooms, and etiquette makeup rooms, but professional artificial intelligence equipment and training rooms are still relatively lacking. The existing training room system is outdated, and the purchase of newer information systems used in hotels or scenic spots requires a significant amount of funds, resulting in the inability of students to carry out campus practice effectively. In addition to existing training rooms and equipment, schools need to continuously update practical facilities, such as simulated airports and hotel lobbies, so that students can practice digital skills in real environments. Third, introducing the latest digital teaching tools and software, such as virtual reality technology and online simulation platforms, is a key measure for improving teaching facilities and helping cultivate the digital abilities of tourism professionals. Through virtual reality technology, students can immerse themselves in tourist destinations, deepen their understanding of actual attractions, and enhance their observation and analysis abilities. Online simulation platforms can also provide students with opportunities to practice in real-life scenarios, allowing them to practice in simulated environments and better master digital skills and the ability to respond to various tourism business scenarios. The introduction of these digital teaching tools and software will help cultivate the digital literacy of tourism majors and enhance their competitiveness in the digital age. Fourth, for schools lacking funds, building VR virtual tour guide training rooms or updating the information system versions of training rooms requires a large amount of funding. Therefore, it is necessary to actively open off campus training bases, deeply integrate school enterprise cooperation, establish relevant industry colleges, and use advanced information systems or professional equipment from enterprises to improve students' practical operation ability.

3.5 Evaluation and Supervision Mechanism

The cultivation of digital abilities for vocational tourism talent requires the establishment of a comprehensive, scientific, and dynamic evaluation and supervision mechanism to ensure the effectiveness and adaptability of talent cultivation. First, the goal-oriented evaluation system and evaluation supervision mechanism should be guided by training objectives, clarifying the digital ability standards that digital tourism talent should possess, including data analysis, e-commerce, and smart tourism platform applications. These standards should be closely aligned with industry needs to ensure the practicality and foresight of the evaluation content. Second, diversified evaluation subjects, including industry experts, business partners, and student self-evolution, in addition to school teachers and management personnel, should be introduced to form a multiangle and multidimensional evaluation system that comprehensively reflects the development of students' digital abilities. Third, the combination of process and outcome evaluation should be emphasized, and the evaluation and supervision mechanism should focus on the process management of students' digital ability cultivation, including process indicators such as learning attitudes, participation, and progress. Moreover, attention should also be given to the final learning outcomes, such as the project completion status, skill mastery level, and other outcome indicators. Fourth, dynamic adjustment and feedback should be provided, and the evaluation and supervision mechanism should have the ability to dynamically adjust talent training programs and evaluation standards in a timely manner on the basis of students' learning progress and industry development changes. Moreover, an effective feedback mechanism should be established to enable students to understand their learning status and clarify their direction for improvement. Fifth, evaluation tools for technical support, which utilize information technology such as online learning platforms and simulation training systems, can be used to develop scientific evaluation tools and methods and improve the accuracy and convenience of evaluation. Moreover, through technologies such as big data analysis, an in-depth analysis of the evaluation results is conducted to provide a basis for teaching improvement.

4 Conclusion

Digital ability is extremely important for future talent in the tourism industry. With strong support from national and local policies, tourism talent who master digital ability can stand invincible in the face of fierce competition in the future. As universities cultivate tourism talent for the country and local areas, there is a long way to go to cultivate students' digital ability continuously, but the future will be bright.

References

1. Zhang, Z., Yang, X.: Composition elements and model construction of digital competence for clinical nurses. J. Nurse Train. Mag. (17), 1577–1583 (2023)
2. Wang, H., Liu, D.: The connotation and improvement path of digital ability for international Chinese teachers. J. Res. Ethnic Educ. **33**(06), 148–155 (2022)
3. Yuan, P.: Research on the investigation and cultivation of digital abilities of international students majoring in Chinese language education. J. Chin. Char. Cult. (S1), 73–74+79 (2019)
4. Yi, Y., Xue, F.: Research on enhancing digital literacy of vocational college teachers against the background of "digital economy": empirical analysis based on 335 full time teachers in Zhejiang Province. J. Voc. Tech. Educ. in China **5**, 55–61 (2022)
5. Zhou, Y., Kong, Z.: Investigation and improvement strategies for digital literacy and skills of applied undergraduate students. J. Educ. Observ. **12**(13), 19–22 (2023)
6. Guo, G., Li, Y., Li, M.: Research on analysis framework and promotion strategy of digital competence of teachers in higher vocational colleges. J. Shenzhen Polytech. **23**(04), 32–38 (2024)
7. Li, T., Wei, C.: Digital competence framework and promotion path of accounting talents from the perspective of big data. Commer. Account. **14**, 25–29 (2024)
8. Wang, Y., Xu, F., Yang, L.: Current situation and development trend of digital ability research abroad. Libr. Sci. Res. Work (06), 5–14 (2024)
9. Dou, J.: Research on digital ability of higher vocational college students against the background of education digital transformation -- based on the survey of higher vocational students in X City, Guangdong Province. J. Guilin Normal Coll. **38**(03), 57–63+93 (2024)
10. Gao, C., Q, Y.: From Practical thinking to inclusive conceptual change: an interpretation of the Digital Competence Framework for European Citizens (DigComp2.2). Shanxi Lib. J. (03), 18 (2024)
11. Yan, M.: A study on the construction of digital literacy competence framework for foreign language majors in China. Fore. Lang. Res. **02**, 67–74 (2024)
12. Chen, Y.: Research on the methodology for formulating the digital literacy framework for all: experience and enlightenment of the digital competence framework for EU citizens. Library **01**, 65–72 (2024)
13. Li, X.: SPSS 22.0 Statistical Analysis from Entry to the Master. Electronic Industry Press, Beijing (2015)
14. Huang, K.: Cultivation and exploration of innovation and entrepreneurship ability of smart tourism talents. Soc. Sci. **01**, 56–60 (2021)
15. Zhao, L.: An analysis on the training path of tourism innovative talents against the background of digital economy. China Market **01**, 66–69 (2024)
16. Lu, K., Guo, L.: Thoughts on the reform of college tourism management personnel training mode under the digital economy. J. Western Travel **01**, 94–96 (1960)
17. Qiu, Y.: Explore the path of college tourism talent training against the background of smart tourism. Tourism Overview **14**, 55–57 (2024)
18. Ji, D., Du, K., Zhou, B.: OTSW analysis of tourism translation talent training mode in Jilin Province in digital economy era. Tourism Overview (16), 36–38 (2022)
19. Yang, Y., Huang, Y.: Digital competence and tourism consumption inequality: a conceptual analysis and research perspective. Tourism Tribune **39**(05), 1–3 (2024)
20. Zhang, Y., Ma, W.: Research on the construction mechanism of vocational tourism talent training base in digital economy era. Jiangsu Commer. Forum **07**, 108–111 (2023)

Research on the Construction of a "Seven-Dimensional" Education System in Vocational Colleges Under the Background of Intelligent Education

Mingming Fu[✉]

Heilongjiang Institute of Teacher Development, Harbin 150080, China
fumingming1980@163.com

Abstract. The ongoing integration of artificial intelligence and the field of education has reshaped the form of educational development, driving education toward informatization, digitization, and intellectualization. This integration has also introduced new requirements for the education system to promote high-quality educational development through intelligent technological means. In response, there is a critical need to establish a comprehensive education system in vocational colleges that encompasses three levels: conceptual transformation, practical innovation, and development goals. This system is designed to foster coordinated development across seven dimensions: technology; the integration of science and education; the integration of vocational and general education; industry-education integration; and schools, teachers, and students. By integrating intelligent technological means and resources, implementing intelligent educational and teaching concepts, and pioneering strategic innovations, this system can effectively promote smart education and the intellectual growth of both teachers and students.

Keywords: Intelligent education · Vocational colleges · Seven-dimensional education system · Construction of the education system

1 AI Empowers Vocational Education

1.1 AI Empowers the Transformation of Educational Concepts

Adhering to the Fundamental Task of Cultivating Virtue and Talent. The prosperity of a nation relies on its moral foundation, just as an individual's integrity determines their personal growth. Adhering to the fundamental task of cultivating virtue and talent and upholding the mission of vocational education are crucial for the continuous development and new achievements in China's vocational education. Therefore, it is imperative that vocational education prioritizes moral education as a cornerstone while also fulfilling its mandate to cultivate virtue alongside practical skills. On the one hand, we should actively explore and promote practical innovations in the implementation of "cultivating virtue and talent" within the field of vocational education, nurturing useful

K. Zhang et al. (Eds.): CSEI 2024, CCIS 2448, pp. 27–42, 2025.
https://doi.org/10.1007/978-981-96-3738-6_3

talents who "cultivate both morality and skills." This involves not only training excellent vocational skills but also fostering good professional ethics. While emphasizing skill orientation, we should also focus on nurturing students' character and enhancing their professional qualities; enabling them to grow into individuals with ideals, abilities, and responsibilities; and becoming new-era talents capable of shouldering the great rejuvenation of the nation. On the other hand, with the rapid development of information and intelligent technologies, smart campuses have begun to take shape, presenting both opportunities and challenges for implementing the strategy of cultivating virtue and talent. By fully leveraging technological advancements, we should actively explore implementation pathways for advancing the "cultivating virtue and talent" strategy on the basis of intelligent technologies and smart education platforms.

Adhering to the People-Oriented Concept of Talent Cultivation. In the era of intelligent education, technological advancements have become the primary driving force behind the transformation and modernization of vocational education, serving as the fundamental impetus for change. However, education essentially aims to promote human development and is an activity focused on talent cultivation that enhances both educators and learners. In educational and teaching practices, teachers and students remain the primary subjects. Therefore, vocational education must realign itself with its foundational mission of nurturing individuals and adhering to the people-oriented concept of talent cultivation. On the one hand, the demand for skilled, versatile, and highly qualified talent is growing, while a knowledge-centered educational philosophy can no longer meet the evolving needs of our time. It necessitates adhering to the basic teaching principles of vocational education, fully leveraging the role of traditional skill-based talent cultivation models, inheriting the craftsmanship spirit, tacit knowledge, and mentorship traditions, achieving a balance between manual and intellectual skills, integrating learning with doing, and combining work with study, thereby returning vocational education to its essence of nurturing individuals. However, the sole criterion for assessing the effectiveness of technology in vocational education is whether it effectively promotes the growth of students and the development of teachers. As education continues to advance, it must increasingly address the diverse and personalized needs of students; stimulate their autonomy, initiative, and creativity; facilitate their free and comprehensive development; and enable each student to become the best version of themselves.

Establishing the Concept of Lifelong Education for Personal Development. With the development of information technology, the lifelong education system has become a trend in modern education. Only by making vocational education accessible to all and lifelong can we cultivate more high-quality, highly skilled applied talent to meet the needs of modern social development. Therefore, vocational education must be oriented toward inclusivity and sustainable future development, establishing the concept of lifelong education for personal development. On the one hand, the application of intelligent technology in education and teaching significantly enhances the precision and efficiency of vocational practices, with more flexible and convenient teaching methods. On the basis of the construction of information-based teaching facilities such as smart campuses, learning environments have been created for intelligent platform applications, digital resource sharing, and personalized learning situation analysis, enabling everyone to learn anytime and anywhere, thereby promoting the realization of lifelong education for all and the enhancement of lifelong skills. On the other hand, the application of information technology has accelerated the realization of intelligent office operations, digital teaching, and convenient management. The advantages of technology broaden the development horizons of vocational education, making the vocational education system and models more flexible and diverse and forming an educational and teaching system that promotes the development of lifelong education [1].

1.2 Exploration of AI-Enabled Educational Practices

Collaborative Construction and Sharing of Digital Resources for Education and Teaching. Vocational education leverages information technology tools such as intelligent and network technologies to establish smart learning environments and conduct smart teaching, thereby enhancing the overall development quality and modernization level of vocational education. China's National Smart Education Platform for Vocational Education offers more than 10,000 online quality courses, providing a wide range of high-quality courses on a large scale and continuously leading the development of digital resources for education and teaching worldwide. This platform supports smooth and effective implementation of teachers' "teaching" activities. Through activities such as lesson introductions, knowledge instruction, explanations of difficult points, exercise explanations, experimental demonstrations, and motion demonstrations, particularly for difficult content in classroom teaching or teaching activities that are challenging to conduct owing to limitations in real-world school classroom environments or resources, it provides actionable demonstrations for teachers.

Utilization of Intelligent Teaching Tools. Technological advancements have significantly enhanced teaching formats, evolving from basic PowerPoint presentations to the adoption of sophisticated intelligent teaching tools. Teaching formats have become increasingly convenient and flexible, enabling the automatic analysis of education and teaching-related indicators. Especially with respect to difficulties in classroom teaching, intelligent teaching tools provide teachers with strategies for improving their teaching methods. According to the "Report on the Development of Vocational Education Informatization (2021 Edition)", 74.54% of vocational education teachers regularly use multimedia teaching equipment such as computers, projectors, and electronic whiteboards. In addition to multimedia teaching equipment, over half of vocational education teachers frequently use course resources on online teaching platforms and integrate them into their educational and teaching practices [2].

Renewal of Majors and Curriculum Systems. As digital industries and artificial intelligence continue to expand, vocational education, as the type of education most closely linked to economic and industrial development, must actively explore the renewal and improvement of majors and curriculum systems to enhance the quality and level of vocational education in serving industrial chains, innovation chains, and educational chains [3]. For example, Liaoning Province has promoted the digital upgrading and transformation of 100 traditional majors and added 84 majors in new fields, such as intelligent control. It has also established a provincial-level big data platform for vocational education to promote the digitization of educational management. Furthermore, it has initiated the construction of a data infrastructure covering vocational colleges across the province, created several information technology benchmark schools, and promoted the comprehensive popularization of digital campuses.

2 The Value of Constructing an Educational System for Vocational Colleges

2.1 Knowledge Objectives: Facilitating Deepened Research and Understanding of the Educational System and Enriching Educational and Pedagogical Theories

In the context of intelligent education, the reform and development of vocational education face new challenges and opportunities, necessitating high-level educational scientific research to explore patterns, solve problems, and lead innovations [3]. Establishing a comprehensive educational system for vocational colleges guided by vocational educational and pedagogical theories is conducive to deepening research and understanding of the educational system, as well as enriching educational and pedagogical theories. On the one hand, by constructing such a system, it highlights the direction and path for the conceptual transformation and practical innovation of vocational colleges, providing a more comprehensive and objective understanding of educational and pedagogical theories, thereby enriching and improving them. On the other hand, by constructing the system, it seeks a motivational mechanism for studying educational and pedagogical theories, enriching theories with vocational educational and pedagogical practices, and allowing educational theories to meet the needs of educational practices, as well as the development needs of schools, teachers, and students, thereby enriching and improving theories related to teaching factors.

2.2 Practical Objectives: Facilitating the Practice and Demonstration of Smart Education and Advancing the High-Quality Development of Vocational Education

With the continuous development and orderly advancement of intelligent education, constructing an educational system for vocational colleges helps vocational colleges accurately grasp educational laws and opportunities, implement intelligent assessment and demonstrations of smart education, and promote the high-quality development of vocational education [4]. On the one hand, by constructing such a system, schools can conduct teaching and research, management, and services based on intelligent technology, promote the deep integration of technology with education and teaching, and advance the digital and smart transformation of vocational education, thereby promoting its high-quality development. On the other hand, by constructing the system, the sensitivity to intelligent education is continuously improved, and related experiences and methods are continuously accumulated. The understanding of technology-based education and teaching becomes deeper, and practical actions become more conscious. This enables more scientific and precise decision-making in teaching and the agile and efficient resolution of practical problems in education and teaching, thereby promoting improvements in teaching effectiveness and quality.

2.3 Values: Facilitating the Formation of Thinking and Wisdom in the Intelligent Age and Promoting the Intelligent Growth of Teachers and Students

In the era of intelligent education, technology is incorporated into the framework of educational and pedagogical wisdom, resulting in the reconstruction of teaching wisdom. The construction of an educational system for vocational colleges, the understanding of teaching and learning behaviors from a technological perspective, the gradual development of thinking and wisdom in the intelligent age, and the promotion of the intelligent growth of teachers and students. On the one hand, by constructing such a system, it leverages technological advantages to explore the laws of teachers' professional development and students' growth in depth; focuses on individual diversity and personalized needs; inspires teachers' autonomy, initiative, and creativity; and promotes their comprehensive and individualized development. On the other hand, by constructing the system, it facilitates a shift from traditional teaching to nurturing, focuses on the professionalism and depth of education itself, converts the love and responsibility for education into educational power, and allows education to occur naturally and effortlessly [5].

3 Construction of the Vocational College Education System

3.1 The Basic Framework of the "Seven-Dimensional" Education System

The basic framework of the vocational college education system, from the foundational level to the apex of smart campus construction, encompasses four levels: the smart environment, smart management and smart services, smart teaching and smart research, and smart teachers and students. The smart environment represents the hardware aspect of smart campus construction. It includes intelligent hardware devices, information systems, and information resources, providing green, intelligent, and smart environmental support for vocational education. The level of smart management and smart services involves technology-supported management and services, encompassing campus management and campus services in vocational colleges. This provides scientific, efficient, meticulous, and convenient logistical support for vocational education. Smart teaching and smart research involve the integration of technology into teaching and research. It encompasses smart teaching methods and smart learning, as well as smart research and reflective thinking, offering intellectual support for the implementation of smart education in vocational colleges. Smart teachers and students represent the human development dimension supported by technology and constitute the apex level of smart campus construction. It encompasses the intelligent development of teachers and the intellectual growth of students, providing directional guidance for the advancement of smart education [6] (Fig. 1).

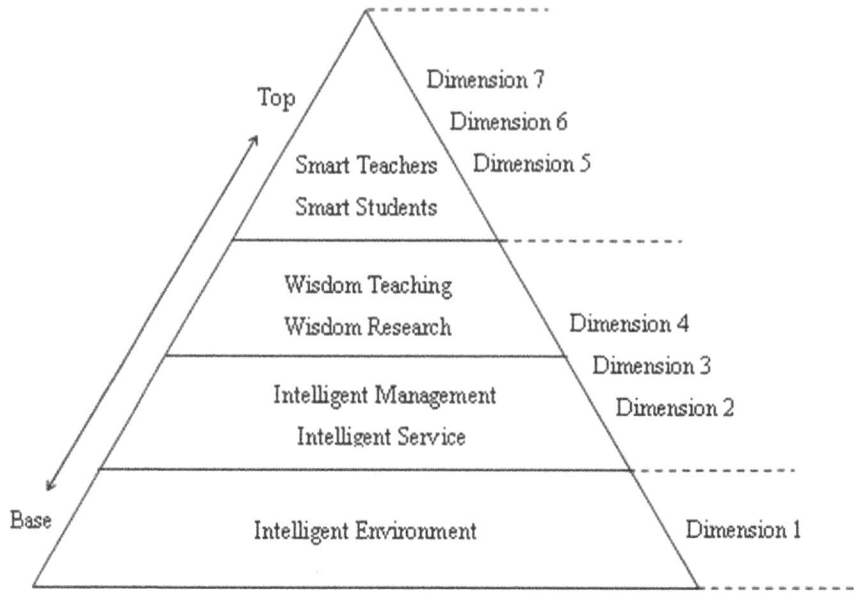

Fig. 1. The basic level framework of the seven-dimensional education system.

3.2 The "Seven-Dimensional" Education System Model

In the era of intelligent education, technological advancements have facilitated the transformation of vocational education concepts, driven practical innovations in vocational education, and accelerated the gradual achievement of vocational education development goals. On the basis of the construction of smart campuses and the integration of the unified theory of acceptance and use of technology (UTAUT) [7], a "seven-dimensional" education system for vocational colleges is established, encompassing three modules and seven dimensions. The three modules are conceptual transformation, practical innovation, and development goals. The first module includes the single dimension of Technology; the second module encompasses three dimensions: the integration of science and education, the integration of vocational and general education, and industry-education integration; and the third module includes the three dimensions of School, Teachers, and Students. The overarching idea is to leverage the smart environment, smart management, and smart services of smart campuses; fully utilize various resources available within these campuses; carry out teaching and research that is deeply integrated with technology, as well as technology-supported management and services; effectively promote the convergence of vocational and general education; advance industry-education and science-education synergies; actively explore strategies to advance smart education in schools; facilitate the smart development of teachers; and accelerate the smart growth of students [8] (Fig. 2).

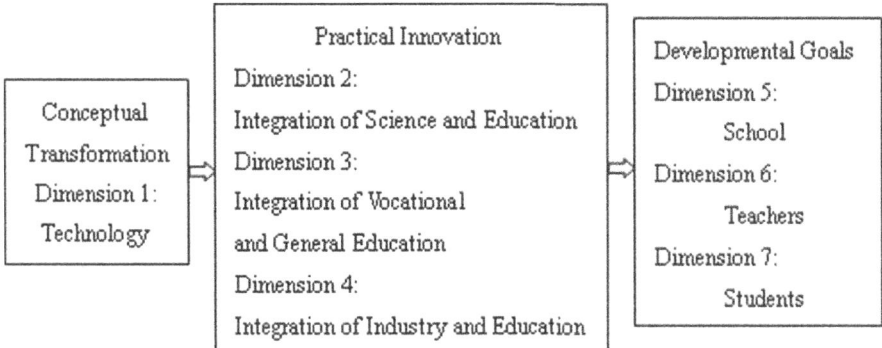

Fig. 2. The basic modules of the "seven-dimensional" education system model.

Module 1: Conceptual Transformation. The transformation of educational concepts supported by technology is currently an important trend in the field of education. This transformation is not merely an upgrade at the technological level but also a reconstruction of the original ideas, beliefs, and value systems (Fig. 3).

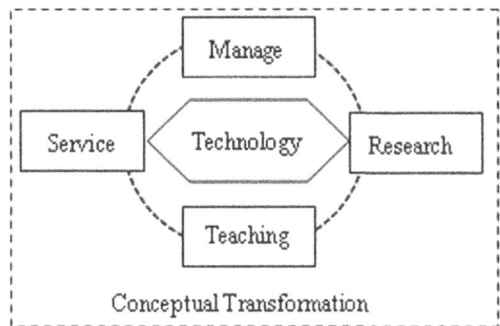

Fig. 3. Conceptual transformation in the "seven-dimensional" education system model.

Technically Supported Teaching Development. The integration of intelligent technology into education and teaching has led to profound changes and innovations in the teaching environment, teaching methods, teaching content, teaching evaluation and teaching management. The intelligent transformation of education and teaching has brought new opportunities and new challenges to education and teaching. One is to change the teaching concept. A shift toward a student-centered teaching paradigm is essential, involving the creation of interactive, intelligent, and open learning spaces; considering the actual needs of teachers and students; meeting different personalized needs; paying attention to students' learning experiences and learning processes; and promoting students' development. Second, teaching management should be improved. The one-way transmission system of knowledge should be improved, the diversification of teacher–student relationships should be promoted, teachers and students should become a learning community, and a final consensus should be reached through equal communication, friendly dialog and timely sharing. Third, intelligent evaluation is carried out. Through the collation and analysis of data, intelligent learning analysis technology is used to carry out personalized learning evaluation, provide personalized learning evaluation for learners, describe the learning process progress, performance and learning results of learners, carry out process evaluation and comprehensive evaluation, and propose learning suggestions [9].

Technically supported research transformation. Given the current situation of comprehensively promoting intelligent education, how to change traditional educational ideas, lead to the comprehensive integration of intelligent technology and curriculum, improve the quality of education, promote educational equity, and improve teachers' intelligent literacy has become an important task for the transformation and development of research. The first is to promote the transformation of research ideas from traditional to intelligent. Rationally, the macro policies and strategies of intelligent education should be considered, the problems encountered in education and teaching with new intelligent thinking should be considered, and guidance for education and teaching practices should be provided. The second is to promote the transformation of the research model from empirical to evidence-based. Relying on traditional experience or building a car behind closed doors can no longer meet the needs of intelligence. We must rely on all forces, rely on intelligent technology to focus on regional and wider development, and turn to open cooperative research. The third is to promote the transformation of research content from single to multiple. Deeply understanding the connotations of the integration of intelligent technology and classroom teaching, strengthening the research and exploration of the integration of information technology and classroom teaching, and strengthening the research and exploration of digital education evaluation are needed.

Technically Supported Management Upgrade. The development of information technology provides new ideas and new kinetic energy for school management, and digital management has become one of the key components of smart campus construction. One is the management of digital conversion. Through the use of information equipment, the development of digital resources and the construction of information platforms, the exploration of information technology applications is carried out to advance toward the goal of modernization of the school governance system. Second, digital upgrades are managed. By strengthening the top-level design, promoting the application of information technology and data integration, the phenomenon of "informatization for informatization" can be avoided, and the correct understanding and practice of the concept of campus digital management construction can be strengthened. The third is management digital innovation. Owing to the characteristics of the current development of intelligent education and the needs of future society, with the comprehensive application of cloud computing, the Internet of Things, big data, artificial intelligence and other technologies, data are used to empower the digital management mode and reshape the digital management form [10].

Technically Supported Service Improvement. Intelligent technology promotes school education from the "mass production" mode to the "private customization" mode. Intelligent services provide precise and personalized services for teachers and students, providing tailored and efficient support for educators and students. The first is intelligent service conversion. Relying on the internet, promoting the opening and coordination of the platform, transferring various services offline to online, and realizing the whole process of online processing. The second is the intelligent upgrading of services. Mobile phone appointments, instant connections, remote interactions, onsite confirmations and other methods are used to provide more efficient and convenient services for teachers and students, which improves their sense of acquisition and satisfaction. The third is intelligent service innovation. By leveraging cognitive computing and cloud-based technologies, we can provide more accurate and intelligent services for teachers and students and promote improvements in the service personalization level.

Module 2: Practical Innovation. Innovation in educational practices supported by technology is transforming teaching and learning methods. This innovation is not merely an upgrade in the application of technology but rather an effective exploration of the deep integration of technology and education [11] (Fig. 4).

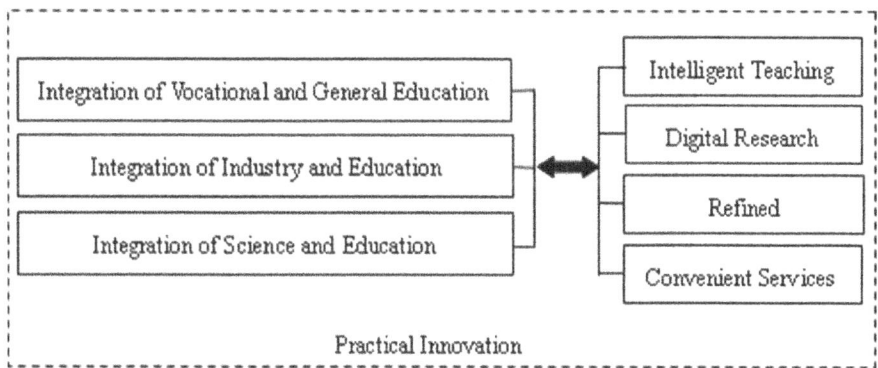

Fig. 4. Practice innovation in the "seven-dimensional" education system model.

Promoting Development through Integration of Vocational and General Education. The modernization of the vocational education system has brought renewed attention to the integration of vocational and general education [12]. This integration refers to the mutual connection between vocational education and general education, aiming to break down internal barriers within the education system and achieve synergistic development of the two types of educational resources. First, top-level national planning sets the direction. In recent years, multiple documents have been issued to clarify the importance of integrating vocational and general education, promoting mutual integration between the two, effectively connecting different levels of vocational education, and coordinating the collaborative innovation of vocational education, higher education, and continuing education. Integration at the higher education level represents a practical innovation in promoting education integration at this level. Third, innovative development at the grassroots level facilitates practical integration. Through approaches such as school-to-school partnerships, class-to-class collaborations, and curriculum integration, the professional advantages of vocational schools are fully leveraged to guide the understanding of their technical skills; foster the idea of serving the country and achieving success through skills; and promote joint school operations, mutual cooperation, and cross-interaction between vocational colleges and high schools. Together, they advance curriculum reforms in each other's systems to promote overall development.

School-Enterprise Cooperation and Industry-Education Integration. School-enterprise cooperation and industry-education integration are the fundamental educational models of vocational education and the most characteristic talent cultivation modes of vocational education, which are formed to meet the demand for talent in economic development [13]. First, policies are issued at the national level to provide support. Support is provided for "industry" and "education" in terms of educational resources and employment information, fully leveraging the advantages and value of industry-education integration and the school-enterprise cooperation talent cultivation model to cultivate talent that meets the needs of social development. Second, diversified school-enterprise cooperation is carried out to form new models. Multiple vocational education groups covering enterprises, schools, industries, and research institutions have been established nationwide, constructing a new model of industry–education integration with cities as nodes, industries as pivots, and enterprises as key points. Third, comprehensive school-enterprise cooperation is conducted to create a new situation. Vocational schools and enterprises have jointly built practical training bases, gradually creating a new situation of joint professional construction, joint talent cultivation, joint process management, resource sharing, and shared responsibility in school-enterprise cooperation [14].

Technology Leadership and Integration of Science and Education. As its core, the integration of science and education involves the intersection of scientific knowledge, technological advancement, and educational practices. Essentially, science and technology are the foundation for national prosperity, and through research in science, technology, and their applications, new momentum is injected into the innovative development of vocational education, promoting the integration and intersection of educational models, teaching methods, and research mechanisms. First, technological innovation is integrated into the development of vocational colleges. By establishing both short-term and long-term goals for technological innovation and development in vocational colleges, institutions can deepen their understanding of science-education integration, scientifically construct a system for the integration of science and education, and closely combine the power of technological innovation with educational work. Second, technological innovation is integrated into the growth process of teachers. In educational and teaching practice, emphasis is placed on enhancing educator research capabilities. By conducting educational and scientific research projects and encouraging teachers to practice in universities, research institutions, and high-tech enterprises, improvements in teachers' research abilities and professional skills can be promoted. Third, technological innovation is integrated into the student cultivation process. By conducting innovative entrepreneurship education and project practice activities, students are guided to participate in scientific research projects, cultivating their innovative spirit and sense of cooperation and promoting the enhancement of their scientific research literacy [15].

Module 3: Development Goals. The development goals supported by technology aim to promote the comprehensive development of smart education in schools, the smart growth of teachers, and the personalized growth of students through measures such as building smart campuses, optimizing the curriculum system, enhancing teachers' technological literacy and professional competence, and fostering students' individualized growth (Fig. 5).

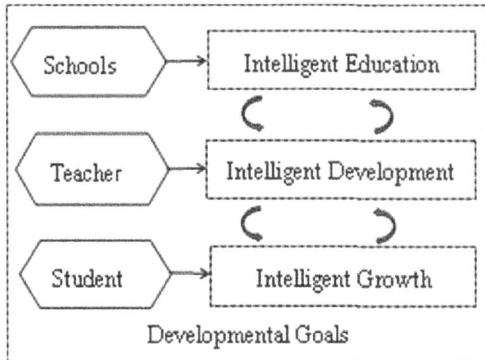

Fig. 5. Development goals in the "seven-dimensional" education system model.

Promoting Smart Education in Schools. A student-centered smart campus should be established, intelligent resources that effectively support smart teaching and learning should be developed, and intelligent teaching, research, and practice that facilitate the joint development of teachers and students should be carried out [16]. Trigger change with the concept of smart education to promote high-quality development in vocational education. First, creating an intelligent environment is fundamental. This involves seamlessly integrating technologies such as artificial intelligence, cloud computing, and virtual reality to advance the construction of an intelligent educational environment. Suitable intelligent educational systems, intelligent management systems, and intelligent evaluation systems, as well as appropriate intelligent assistants and robots, are selected to provide equipment support for intelligent education. Second, intelligent resources should be developed. New technologies such as big data, cloud computing, artificial intelligence, virtual reality, augmented reality, and mixed reality can be fully utilized to develop interactive curriculum resources and educational resources that meet the requirements of the times. Third, intelligent teaching should be conducted. Flexible educational and teaching methods can be adopted, online and offline courses can be integrated to present new forms, diverse courses can be developed, and effective adjustments can be made to solve problems in teaching practice, which is better suited to the development of the artificial intelligence era. Fourth, engage in intelligent research and training. The platform for teacher research and training based on intelligent technology should be upgraded, and the content and paths of teacher research and training should be expanded. By conducting thorough analysis and reflection on educational performance, schools can better support the continuous growth of teachers in the era of intelligent education.

Promoting the Smart Development of Teachers. With the continuous integration of intelligent technology and education, there have been tremendous changes in teacher development concepts and practices, and artificial intelligence has enabled new paths and methods for teacher development. First, in terms of the development of teachers' concepts, teachers should prioritize their professional growth by shifting from mobile learning to ubiquitous learning, learning to learn, actively learning, and lifelong learning. Only by consciously improving themselves can they better facilitate the development and improvement of students. Second, the expansion of teachers' activities is essential. In the era of intelligent education, mere knowledge updating and technical training are no longer sufficient to meet the needs of modern teacher teaching. Through diversified development paths, classroom teaching, teacher research, and teacher training can be integrated to carry out professional innovation and creation on the basis of learning and understanding. Third, in teaching practice, there is a need to carry out classroom teaching supported by intelligent technology, focusing on the integration of industry and education and human–machine collaboration, finding scientific evidence for improving and perfecting teaching, and accurately pointing out the gains and losses in the teaching process. Fourth, teachers' research and innovation are needed. Conducting data-driven research based on big data and artificial intelligence; comprehensively collecting, analyzing, and interpreting data from the educational and teaching process; changing the previous reliance on experience and reflection; and encouraging teachers to conduct reflection and research scientifically and normatively enables them to have a deeper understanding of learning and research [17].

Promoting the Smart Growth of Students. Define and cultivate students' growth with a "people-oriented" value orientation. The ultimate educational goal remains to promote student development; enhance innovative ability, communication skills, and learning ability; and promote personalized and comprehensive development. The first is to expand students' horizons. Cultivate students with cross-cultural understanding and a global perspective, emphasizing communication, collaboration and teamwork awareness. Having a broad knowledge base and sufficient vision to navigate the future is suitable for the development of the intelligent education era. Second, enhancing students' skills is fundamental. Students' innovative abilities, communication skills, and autonomous learning abilities should be cultivated. When encountering any viewpoint and information, they can think independently; effectively share their thoughts, viewpoints, and solutions; and solve problems with innovative and critical thinking. (Note: The repetition of "students' ability innovation" in the original text has been corrected here by focusing on different aspects of ability development.) The third is to personalize students' development. Conducting a detailed analysis of students' characteristics and learning situations, customizing personalized learning plans, providing students with unique information environments and services, and providing convenient self-study platforms and fully functional learning service systems to create favorable conditions for personalized learning and lifelong learning. Fourth, promoting students' comprehensive development means recognizing and respecting the individuality of each learner. Respecting and understanding students; returning growth to students; cultivating their scientific and correct learning attitudes; maximizing their initiative, enthusiasm, and creativity; and allowing students to develop comprehensively and become the best version of themselves.

3.3   Indicators of the Seven-Dimensional Education System Model

On the basis of school education and teaching practices, formulating indicators for the seven-dimensional educational system model can more comprehensively evaluate a school's performance in smart education, teachers' wisdom development, and students' intelligent growth. This study provides scientific guidance and a reference for enhancing the quality of education and teaching (Tables 1, 2 and 3).

Table 1.   Three-level indicators for the schools' smart education.

Indicator Classification	First-level Indicator	Second-level Indicator	Third-level Indicator
School	Smart Education	Intelligent Environment	Planning for Smart Campus Construction
			Campus Network Construction
			Intelligent Teaching Facilities
		Intelligent Resources	Digital Teaching Resource Development
			Resource Co-construction and Sharing
			Smart Library
		Smart Teaching	Intelligent Learning Platform
			Innovation in Smart Teaching Modes
			Intelligent Evaluation
			Personalized Learning
		Smart Research and Training	Training and Assessment
			Exchange and Cooperation
			Evaluation and Feedback
		Management and Service	Intelligent Management Platform
			Intelligent Service Platform

Table 2. Three-level indicators of teachers' intellectual development.

Indicator Classification	First-level Indicator	Second-level Indicator	Third-level Indicator
Teacher	Intellectual Development	Professional Knowledge	Subject Knowledge
			Pedagogical Knowledge
			Technical Knowledge
			Interdisciplinary Knowledge
		Professional Competence	Intelligent Educational Teaching Ability
			Intelligent Educational Practice Ability
			Ability to Promote Student Development
			Autonomous Development Ability
		Technical Tools	Information Technology Application
			Data Application
			Intelligent Resource Integration
			Intelligent Collaboration
		Professional Emotion	Professional Attitude
			Emotional Integrity
			Psychological Quality
		Ethics and Morals	Data Ethics
			Ethical Standards

Table 3. Three-level indicators of students' intellectual growth.

Indicator Classification	First-level Indicator	Second-level Indicator	Third-level Indicator
Student	Intellectual Growth	Learning Ability	Autonomous Learning Ability
			Critical Thinking
			Collaborative Learning Ability

(*continued*)

Table 3. (*continued*)

Indicator Classification	First-level Indicator	Second-level Indicator	Third-level Indicator
		Intellectual Literacy	Awareness of Intelligence
			Intelligent Knowledge and Skills
			Application of Intelligence
			Social Responsibility in the Age of Intelligence
		Innovative Thinking	Practical Operation
			Interdisciplinary Integration
		Digital Life	Healthy Social Interaction
			Self-Management
		Mental Health	Emotions, Attitudes and Values
			Self-Regulation Skills

4   Conclusion

Currently, the integration of intelligent technology and education has brought numerous unprecedented changes, ushering vocational education into a new era. The operation of vocational colleges requires alignment with the evolving technological environment, necessitating continuous refinement and upgrading of their educational systems to adapt to the evolving educational landscape across different eras.

Practical data demonstrate that by establishing a "seven-dimensional" educational system in vocational colleges within the context of intelligent education, not only is the traditional transmission of knowledge emphasized, but greater focus is placed on leveraging intelligent technologies to advance smart education, thereby fostering the comprehensive development of both teachers and students. This system underscores the deep integration of intelligent technology with education, enabling a more precise understanding of the circumstances of both students and teachers. It provides personalized learning and teaching support, which not only cultivates students' innovative thinking and practical abilities but also enhances teachers' professional competence and instructional effectiveness. Furthermore, it serves as a driving force for the continuous improvement and innovation of education and teaching.

For vocational colleges, systematically constructing an educational system that incorporates novel elements such as intelligent technology and innovation capabilities, thoroughly implementing the new concept of integrating intelligent elements into vocational education, actively exploring new practices within the context of intelligent education, and striving to pioneer new innovations in the deep integration of intelligence and education represent a practical and sustainable pathway for the development of vocational colleges.

References

1. Yue, J.: Artificial intelligence deeply empowers the innovation and development of vocational education. Vocation. Tech. Educ. **43**(24), 45 (2022)
2. Zhang, Z.: The connotation characteristics, structural elements and practical strategies of digital. Chin. Vocation. Tech. Educ. **27**, 40–45 (2024)
3. Li, Y.: The persistence and breakthrough of digital transformation of vocational education. Vocation. Tech. Educ. **44**(22), 1 (2023)
4. Wang, J.: Goal, motivation and practice path of digital transformation of vocational education. Adult Educ. **44**(1), 61 (2024)
5. Fu, M.: Path of teachers' professional development in the era of intelligent education. J. Heilongjiang Inst. Teach. Dev. **41**(7), 21 (2022)
6. Zhang, J.: Thinking and practice of constructing a smart education system with Chinese characteristics. China Higher Educ. (Z2), 9 (2022)
7. Venkatesh, V., Morris, M., Davis, G., et al.: User acceptance of information technology: toward a unified view. MIS Q. **27**(3), 425–478 (2003)
8. Meng, F., Wang, S.: Promotion of the Integration of science and education: new vision, new field New Track. Vocation. Tech. Educ. **43**(33), 30–34 (2022)
9. Xu, G.: The Fundamental transformation of talent training model in vocational education in the era of intelligence. Educ. Res. **37**(03), 72–78 (2016)
10. Fu, M., Ran, L.: Digital transformation of school education: cognitive misconceptions, potential challenges and strategies for solutions. China Educ. Technol. **444**(1), 44–50 (2024)
11. Deng, L.: Accelerate the construction of vocational education system. People's Tribune (16), 53–57 (2024)
12. Sun, Q., Chen, Y., Mao, H., et al.: Deepen the reform and construction of the modern vocational education system to comprehensively serve and support Chinese-style modernization. Chin. Vocation. Tech. Educ. (2),10–19 (2023)
13. Hu, J.: The practical issues and corresponding solutions of industry-education integration. Vocation. Educ. Anhui Province (19),100–105 (2024)
14. Liu, F.: Connotation analysis and promotion path of the integration between industry and education in vocational education from the perspective of the new quality productive forces. Vocation. Educ. Res. **10**, 23–29 (2024)
15. An, P., Sun, B., Liu, C.: Era substance, implementation basis and action strategies of science-education integration in vocational education. Vocation. Tech. Educ. **45**(31), 62–67 (2024)
16. Fu, M.: Research on the improvement path of teachers' intelligent education literacy in the era of artificial intelligence. J. Heilongjiang Inst. Teach. Dev. **43**(5), 32–34 (2024)
17. Liu, D.: Innovative thinking on continuing education of professional and technical personnel based on network. Adult Educ. **44**(1), 43 (2024)

Research on the Blended Teaching Mode of Computer Network Courses Under the Background of New Engineering

Yujing Wang[1,2,3], Yuanyuan Wei[1,2], Ying Du[1,2,3]([✉]), Pu Cheng[4], and Xiaoyu Du[1,2,3]

[1] School of Computer and Information Engineering, Henan University,
Kaifeng 475004, Henan, China
duying@henu.edu.cn

[2] Henan Province Engineering Research Center of Spatial Information Processing, Henan
University, Kaifeng 475004, People's Republic of China

[3] Henan Engineering Research Center for Industrial Internet of Things,
Zhengzhou 450046, China

[4] School of Software, Henan University, Kaifeng 475004, Henan, China

Abstract. The construction of New Engineering has higher requirements for computer professionals. Computer network is a core course in computer science. In order to enhance the effectiveness of course teaching and highlight students' ability to solve complex engineering problems, Computer Network course need to change the traditional teaching mode and innovate course teaching methods. This paper proposes a blended teaching mode for Computer Network based on the BOPPPS+TBL model. This mode includes a multidimensional teaching platform, online and offline blended learning, and comprehensive evaluation methods. The statistical results of teaching practice show that blended teaching can stimulate students' interest in learning, promote their deep participation in course teaching, and effectively improve teaching quality.

Keywords: Computer Network · Blended Teaching · BOPPPS · TBL

1 Introduction

The Ministry of Education is actively promoting the comprehensive development of new engineering disciplines, emphasizing the integration of education, technology, and talent, with a requirement for unified planning and coordinated implementation [1]. The computer science discipline plays a fundamental role in the construction of new engineering programs, facilitating and supporting the development of many emerging fields, and has formed a "Computer Plus" model for new engineering discipline innovation and talent cultivation. Computer networks have become one of the most important information infrastructures in today's society.

The Computer Networks course is a fundamental core course designed to strengthen the professional foundation of computer science students. It is a critical part of developing

K. Zhang et al. (Eds.): CSEI 2024, CCIS 2448, pp. 43–50, 2025.
https://doi.org/10.1007/978-981-96-3738-6_4

the ability to solve complex engineering problems. This course is based on the reference model of network architecture principles, with the TCP/IP framework at its core. It focuses on the basic concepts, principles, technologies, methods, and applications of network protocols. The course is highly theoretical and practical, requiring students not only to grasp professional knowledge of network principles but also to develop practical skills for solving complex network engineering problems.

Computer Network course has undergone continuous reform and innovation in terms of teaching content, methods, and models [2–6]. However, the development of new engineering disciplines continuously places higher demands on the construction of the curriculum and its content. The cultivation of versatile and multi-skilled computer network professionals is the starting point of the new engineering talent development philosophy. It is also the ultimate goal. During the teaching process, based on traditional disciplinary knowledge and skills, purposeful interdisciplinary education is carried out within the course content. A comprehensive curriculum system and knowledge structure are established, and a multi-faceted course innovation platform is built to continuously train students' ability to learn and adapt to development. By staying abreast of the frontiers in the field of computer networks, the course aims to enhance students' abilities in applying engineering knowledge, analyzing problems, designing and developing solutions, conducting engineering research, and selecting and using modern tools. Moreover, by aligning with ideological and political theory courses, it creates a synergistic effect that helps students fully understand the relationship between engineering and society, as well as clarifying their responsibilities and obligations.

In this paper, building on existing research with the aim of enhancing the effectiveness of computer network teaching and developing students' ability to solve complex engineering problems. It combines the characteristics of our computer network course and existing achievements. Based on the BOPPPS + TBL model, it constructs a multi-dimensional teaching platform for the course and proposes a blended online and offline teaching solution for computer networks in the context of new engineering disciplines.

2   Design of Blended Teaching

2.1   A Model of BOPPPS + TBL

In recent years, teaching based on the BOPPPS model [7, 8] has enhanced students' learning motivation as well as their abilities for independent thinking and divergent thinking, achieving satisfactory teaching results. The BOPPPS teaching model emphasizes a student-centered approach. To facilitate deep student engagement in learning activities, it divides classroom teaching into six components: Bridge-in, Objective, Pre-assessment, Participatory Learning, Post-assessment, and Summary. This model is based on course construction and promotes student engagement, interaction, and feedback, providing ideas for the reform of blended teaching in computer networks.

Team-Based Learning is a teaching method, based on team learning, characterized by a collective and active learning approach in small groups. Its goal is to enhance communication among students, thereby effectively improving their self-learning abilities, problem-solving skills, and teamwork capabilities. In the Computer Network course, students are divided into several groups to engage in both theoretical learning and experimental expansion of network topics. Through team collaboration and information gathering, students broaden their perspectives, effectively increase their classroom engagement, deepen their understanding of fundamental network knowledge, and enhance their practical skills in network engineering and teamwork.

The teaching design of the computer network course adopts the open BOPPPS teaching model, effectively integrating the TBL teaching method. This approach aligns with students' cognitive patterns and stimulates their learning initiative.

2.2 Multidimensional Course Teaching Platform

The computer network course platform serves both students and teachers. It is not only an organization of course content but also a collection of high-quality teaching resources. It functions as a place for students' learning progress and a venue for teachers' exchange and improvement. Leveraging Rain Classroom for online course development, the computer network course integrates electronic teaching resources, builds the overall framework and structure of the course, and constructs a multidimensional teaching platform.

Currently, in line with the course objectives and teaching content, and keeping up with the times, the platform has established 22 chapter nodes and 232 learning units. It also includes a question bank, past exam papers for graduate school entrance exams, and other resources. The 22 chapter nodes encompass teacher-specific content, ideological and political integration, national examination papers for subject code "408", network experiments, post-class research, classic reference books, and 16 course teachings. The 232 learning units primarily consist of videos, text and images, exams, and assignments, covering both theoretical and practical aspects of the course teaching resources.

The overall teaching process of the network course is divided into two major parts: theoretical teaching and experimental teaching. The theoretical teaching includes seven units: basic network knowledge, physical layer and data communication fundamentals, a data link layer, a network layer, a transport layer, an application layer, wireless networks, and network security. According to the computer network teaching syllabus and the academic year teaching schedule, the teaching content is organized into 3-h blocks, comprising a total of 16 classroom teaching modules.

Each classroom teaching module includes relevant pre-class announcements, micro-course videos, course PPTs, class recordings, class conditions, and post-class tests. Pre-class announcements record the main content, teaching focus, difficulties, requirements, and assignment expectations for the respective module. Carefully selected micro-course videos correspond to the teaching focus of the module, meeting students' pre-class preparation needs. Class recordings provide assistance for students' post-class review.

The experimental teaching part is crucial in computer network course instruction. While the theoretical content is relatively abstract, experimental teaching allows students to concretize abstract theoretical knowledge through practical experience, thereby integrating theory with practice and deepening their understanding and mastery of the theory. The experimental teaching in the computer network course mainly includes the following: making network jumpers, analyzing MAC frame formats, constructing and configuring switched networks, network interconnection and router configuration, IP datagram analysis, and enterprise-level network construction and configuration implementation. Each experiment typically includes experimental guidance, report templates, instructional videos, related documents, experiment reports, and help documents.

The computer network course incorporates research topics aligned with the course schedule, such as understanding network devices, the PPPOE protocol, and Internet checksum algorithms. Students are required to either research and gather relevant information or use computer technology for programming implementation within a specified timeframe. They must then organize their findings into a document following academic paper standards and submit it online. This approach encourages students to explore more up-to-date computer network technologies, fosters self-learning abilities, broadens their knowledge base, and deepens their understanding of computer networks.

2.3 Online and Offline Blended Learning

The Computer Network course adopts a blended online and offline teaching model, divided into three stages: pre-class, in-class, and post-class. Before each class, pre-class announcements and teaching videos are published online through the course platform, allowing students to preview the material, understand the main content and key points of the upcoming lesson, and watch the corresponding micro-course videos.

During classroom teaching, each session is organized based on the BOPPPS model, integrating online and offline teaching. The teacher publishes teaching content online through Rain Classroom, conducts class introductions, and clarifies the teaching objectives and key points for the session. A quiz is administered to assess students' preparation based on the materials. Various methods, including case studies, comparative analysis, inquiry-based approaches, and experiments, are used to vividly explain the course content, incorporating board writing, text, and animation demonstrations. Students enter the classroom via QR code scanning on Rain Classroom, participate in online interactions, and discuss and summarize course content with the teacher offline. The teacher uses online feedback and offline observations of student status to monitor students' understanding of key concepts, adjust the teaching pace, and enhance teaching effectiveness through discussions, Q&A sessions, and student presentations.

After each class, corresponding tests are published online to reinforce and consolidate learning. Students are required to submit their work in a single attempt, focusing on completing the test within the specified time and duration to strengthen their grasp of fundamental knowledge and improve learning efficiency. The teacher summarizes the course through classroom teaching and post-class tests, identifies any shortcomings, and makes timely improvements.

At the end of each semester, a course evaluation questionnaire is published to collect student feedback. A comprehensive evaluation of students' performance across different majors is conducted, involving multi-faceted analysis. This process helps summarize teaching experiences, reflect on teaching practices, and identify areas for improvement.

Throughout the teaching process, students actively participate and think critically. They gain learning outcomes and feedback through online previews and assessments, and expand their knowledge through offline team-based learning (TBL) and teacher interactions. The implementation of blended online and offline teaching based on the BOPPPS + TBL model before, during, and after class effectively enhances students' classroom engagement and the depth and breadth of their learning, achieving positive interactions between teachers and students as well as among students themselves.

2.4   Comprehensive Evaluation Methods for Course

The computer network course based on the blended teaching model employs various forms of comprehensive course evaluation methods. The comprehensive grades of the course assessment include classroom online interaction grades, laboratory grades, homework grades, research reports, and paper grades, which are composed of 60% of the final exam and 40% of the regular assessment.

The regular assessment consists of four components: classroom exercises, research reports, post-class assignments, and experiments.

(1) Classroom exercises account for 5% of the comprehensive score. These exercises are released during the class, submitted online, and automatically graded. They primarily assess students' understanding and mastery of core computer network knowledge.
(2) Research reports account for 5% of the comprehensive score. They are released after the completion of relevant knowledge units and must be submitted online in a standard academic paper format. Evaluation is based on completion progress, adherence to formatting standards, and content completeness. These reports primarily assess students' ability to investigate computer network systems and devices, conduct literature research, and demonstrate self-learning and adaptability skills.
(3) Post-class assignments account for 10% of the comprehensive score. Multiple-choice and fill-in-the-blank questions are submitted online and automatically graded, while subjective questions are submitted as photos or documents. These assignments primarily assess students' ability to analyze complex network engineering problems and their capacity to apply relevant network theories to solve these issues.
(4) Experimental assessments account for 20% of the comprehensive score and are divided into two main aspects: the completion of experimental tasks and the writing of the experiment report. The completion of experimental tasks is evaluated during the experiment and focuses on assessing students' ability to design and implement solutions for complex network engineering problems, as well as their skills in testing, analyzing, and comparing computer network systems. After the experiment is completed, the students must write and submit an experiment report online. This report is evaluated based on students' ability to draft solutions for complex network problems, as well as their skills in analyzing, summarizing, and evaluating experimental data and solutions.

3 Effectiveness of Blended Teaching

From 2020 to 2023, the blended teaching of the computer network course has been conducted for four sessions. Statistical results from post-class surveys indicate that over 92% of the students each session recognize the effectiveness of the blended online and offline teaching approach, as shown in Fig. 1.

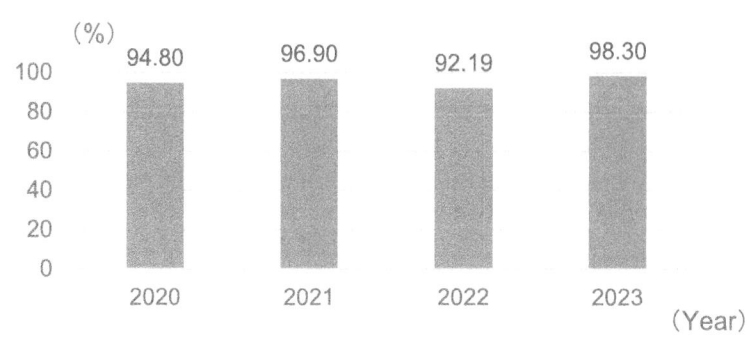

Fig. 1. Students' acceptance of blended learning

Statistics from the past four years show that the overall goal achievement rate of the computer network course using blended teaching exceeds 0.80, as shown in Fig. 2.

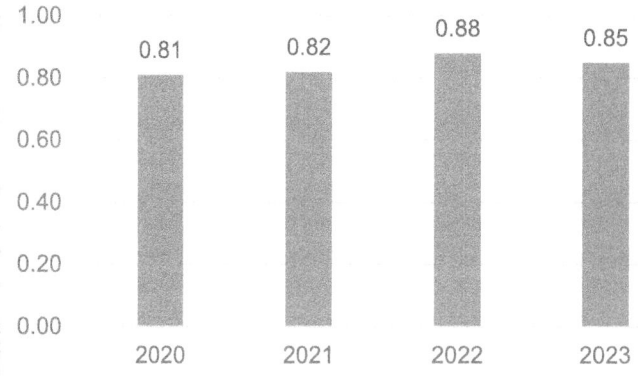

Fig. 2. Overall goal achievement of blended teaching courses over the past 4 years

The achievement rates for the five specific course objectives are all above 0.77, as shown in Fig. 3.

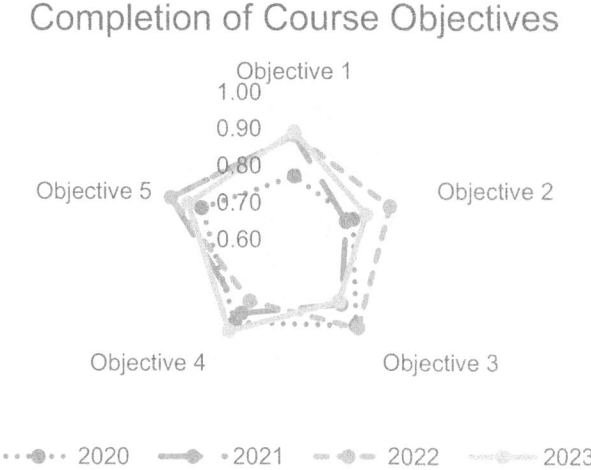

Fig. 3. Complention of the five course objectives in blended teaching over the past 4 years

4 Conclusions

Under the background of new engineering education reform and with a focus on engineering education accreditation, the blended online and offline teaching of the computer network course based on the BOPPPS + TBL model has achieved excellent results. It helps students reinforce fundamental network knowledge, develop practical skills, master key network technologies, and enhance their ability to solve complex engineering problems. Adhering to a results-oriented, student-centered, and continuously improving approach, the teaching of the computer network course should continue to keep pace with the times, continually update and refine, and further enhance the quality of course instruction.

Acknowledgments. This work was supported by the Henan Province Scientific and Technological Research (232102211009), Henan University undergraduate teaching reform research and practice project (HDXJJG2023-013, HDXJJG2023-048), Henan University graduate graduate education innovation and quality improvement project (SYLAL2023011, SYLAL2023018, SYLAL2022018), and Henan University graduate teaching reform research and practice project (YJSJG2022XJ056).

References

1. Ministry of Education of the People's Republic of China. http://www.moe.gov.cn/s78/A08/ton gzhi/201702/t20170223_297158.html. Accessed 15 Sept 2024
2. Shang, F.: Research and practice of outcome-oriented blended online and offline teaching for computer networks. In: 6th China Conference on Computer Practice Education. School of Computer Science and Technology, Chongqing University of Posts and Telecommunications (2022)

3. Z. M. J., et al.: Teaching reform practice of computer network course under the background of new engineering education. Comput. Educ. (03), 154–160 (2024)
4. Liu, D., Y. L., et al.: Reform of computer network course teaching based on OBE concept. Comput. Educ. (3), 159–163 (2023)
5. Zheng, Y.: Exploration of "computer network" course teaching for engineering education accreditation. Ind. Inf. Educ. 1, 40–44 (2023)
6. Cao, H., Chen, Y., et al.: Exploration of blended teaching for computer network principles course based on OBE+BOPPPS. High. Educ. (06), 45–48 (2024)
7. Zhao, Q., Lu, X., exploration of blended teaching based on the BOPPPS model. Comput. Educ. (04), 188–193 (2024)
8. Gao, Z.: Blended teaching design based on the BOPPPS model under the new engineering education background: a case study of the "big data technology" course. Commun. Inf. Technol. (04), 124–129 (2024)

Influence of Peer Evaluation on College Students' Critical Thinking in a Blended Learning Environment

Qingyi Wu and Ying Yang[(✉)]

Yunnan Normal University, Kunming 650500, China
79261313@qq.com

Abstract. As one of the highest-level cognitive abilities, critical thinking has become the focus of education research in the core literacy framework of the 21st century. In a blended learning environment, peer evaluation, as a popular learning activity in teaching, has attracted the attention of many researchers. The purpose of this study was to explore the impact of peer review on college students' critical thinking, design peer review activities, and conduct a follow-up investigation and in-depth analysis of college students participating in peer review through two months of empirical research. Peer evaluation plays a positive role in promoting the development of college students' critical thinking. Communication and feedback among peers can stimulate students' reflective consciousness and improve their ability to analyze and evaluate. Moreover, college students who participate in peer evaluation activities have greater acceptance of and satisfaction with peer evaluation activities, which can promote the learning of college students.

Keyword: Critical Thinking · Higher-Order Cognitive Ability · Peer Evaluation

1 Introduction

With the advent of the educational information age, all countries insist on deepening the reform of education to promote the development of individual core literacy. Core literacy is the essential characteristic and key ability that an individual should possess and can adapt to the needs of lifelong development and social development. Among them, critical thinking in high-level thinking, which is considered the core of the national training of innovative talent, is highly emphasized in the framework of core literacy in many countries and regions in the 21st century. Against the background of core literacy, cultivating talent with higher-order thinking is the direction of future education, and critical thinking is an important part of higher-order thinking ability that attracts educational researchers from all countries. Chinese education scholar Man et al. analyzed the literacy items in 29 frameworks, including the European Union, Russia, the United States, Singapore, Hong Kong, Asia, etc., and finally formed 18 core literacies and divided these 18-core literacies into two categories: domain literacy and general literacy. General literacy includes higher-order cognition, which is subdivided into critical

K. Zhang et al. (Eds.): CSEI 2024, CCIS 2448, pp. 51–62, 2025.
https://doi.org/10.1007/978-981-96-3738-6_5

thinking, creativity and problem-solving, and learning and lifelong learning [1]. Critical thinking has become a necessary requirement for the core quality of talent training in various countries and has also become a necessary ability for innovative talent in the 21st century.

Another reason why critical thinking is so important in educational research is that in today's highly competitive environment, conformity is bound to hinder the development of individuals and society as a whole. The cultivation of thinking is the most important thing in education today, especially in higher education. Critical thinking involves teaching people to think as a starting point to enhance their personal understanding of problems and seek solutions to problems [2].

Judging from the above research results, critical thinking plays a very important role in today's times. However, different scholars have different views on how to understand critical thinking. On the basis of existing research, this study summarizes critical thinking as the ability to analyze, explain, judge, reason, evaluate, and self-regulate current problems to draw conclusions and solve problems [3–7].

Currently, although colleges and universities, as educational institutions that provide talent for the country and society, have realized the significance of cultivating students' critical thinking, they have also taken a series of measures to cultivate college students' critical thinking, such as encouraging curriculum reform, enriching teaching resources, organizing discussions or debates, etc., but they have not achieved the expected achievements. Cultivating college students' critical thinking has become a difficult problem in current research and is also a hot topic discussed by researchers. This study focuses on the peer evaluation perspective in a blended learning environment to explore the impact of peer evaluation learning activities on college students' critical thinking.

2   Research Review

2.1   Research Status of Critical Thinking

Foreign Research Status of Critical Thinking.   Research on critical thinking in foreign countries is relatively early. Early research started with a concise and clear definition of the concept of critical thinking and gradually focused on cultivation methods and the importance of critical thinking. Early researchers proposed that critical thinking is a rational form of reflective thinking and explored methods of cultivating this thinking through thematic teaching. Another study revealed that when critical thinking tests include questions specific to a particular subject, their cultivation effect is more significant than when general subject questions are used [8, 9]. In 2019, the OECD published a document on developing and accessing students' creative and critical thinking skills in higher education, highlighting the implications and understanding that effective teaching in higher education extends beyond the dissemination of knowledge. This also involves the development of higher-order skills such as critical thinking and creativity, as well as other cognitive, social, and emotional skills [10].

Domestic Research Status of Critical Thinking.   To promote the development of learners' critical thinking, most domestic scholars choose a teaching practice path to promote the development of critical thinking. Empirical studies have focused on the ability of technology to promote the development of students' critical thinking. Through the teaching practice of argumentative writing in junior middle school, it has been proven that the application of technology has a positive effect on the development of students' critical thinking and the improvement of their argumentative writing ability. In addition, the design of learning activities based on blended collaborative learning has been proven to effectively promote the development of students' critical thinking. Moreover, trying to use real problems as test situations and using material-based argumentation writing can predict students' critical thinking level through their performance in real problem situations [11–13].

2.2 Research Status of Peer Evaluation

Foreign Research Status of Peer Evaluation. From the results of the literature review, the following conclusions can be drawn from foreign research on the application of peer evaluation activities in education: peer evaluation has a positive effect on learners' learning, can also improve learners' enthusiasm for active learning, and has a significant impact on the development of learners' thinking ability. For example, research has shown that peer evaluation is considered an effective teaching strategy that can actively attract students and improve their learning motivation. By empowering students with autonomy in the evaluation process, peer evaluation encourages the development of autonomy and critical analysis skills, broadens students' understanding of the topic, and enhances their problem-solving and self-assessment abilities [14, 15]. In addition, combining computer-mediated peer evaluation activities, such as exchanging drafts and feedback through email and using interactive software programs for communication, can not only improve students' learning outcomes but also help alleviate the psychological pressure of peer evaluation for some learners. Combining reflection with peer evaluation has also been proven to be a teaching tool suitable for higher education, allowing students to learn knowledge from peer feedback and apply it to subsequent learning and discussion. Moreover, peer anonymous peer evaluation activities supported by technology have also been found to significantly enhance learners' critical thinking skills [16, 17].

Domestic research status of peer evaluation. The use of online peer evaluation as an interactive learning activity has been proven to effectively promote the development of critical thinking among college students. From the perspective of knowledge construction, peer evaluation can also optimize learners' knowledge structure and promote their progress in deep cognition [18, 19]. Moreover, some studies have shown that in MOOC environments, learners' reflective awareness, reflected in the length and quality of comments, is significantly correlated with learning outcomes, indicating the importance of reflection in peer evaluation. In addition, a trustworthy peer evaluation model empowered by artificial intelligence has been proposed to increase trust among learners during the peer evaluation process. These studies collectively demonstrate the multidimensional role of peer evaluation in promoting learning and development [20, 21].

3   Research Model

On the basis of the general process of peer evaluation activities, this study designed a peer evaluation learning activity model, as shown in Fig. 1. The model is divided into five stages: design of peer evaluation activities, initiation of peer evaluation activities, implementation of peer evaluation activities, feedback of peer evaluation activities, and summary reflection.

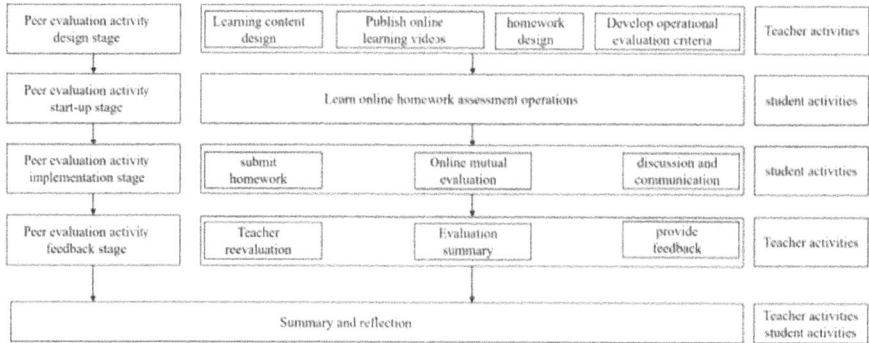

Fig. 1. Design of a peer assessment learning activity model based on critical thinking

3.1   Peer Evaluation Activity Design Stage

The first step in this stage is the design of learning content for teachers. The second step is to provide students with online learning videos as a supplement to classroom learning according to the corresponding learning content. The third step is to carry out homework design according to students' learning content; homework design involves not only testing students' learning effects but also consolidating students' learning results. The fourth step is to establish evaluation criteria for the designed assignments so that students can make objective and fair evaluations according to the evaluation criteria during peer evaluation learning activities.

3.2   Peer Evaluation Activity Start-Up Stage

This study used our school's online teaching platform, where teachers can publish learning resource tasks and assignments for courses and classes and supervise the completion of tasks and assignments by all students from the teacher's end. Students can then learn according to the requirements of the learning tasks published by the teacher. Owing to the research subjects and their proficiency in the basic operation of the platform, the main focus of this study is to provide training and learning on online homework peer evaluation and homework evaluation standards for students.

3.3 Peer Evaluation Activity Implementation Stage

Students use the school's online teaching platform for homework submission, online mutual evaluation and discussion. Each student's work is randomly assigned to the other three students' accounts and reviewed by the other three students, and each student is required to review three copies of the other students' work. Each student's final score is the average of the scores of the other three students.

3.4 Peer Evaluation Activity Feedback Stage

After each peer assessment activity, teachers grade each student's homework again. The purpose of this is to observe whether there is a significant difference between the teacher's rating and the student's rating and to avoid the practice of some students maliciously giving low scores or perfunctory grades. The teacher then summarizes the situation of the students' mutual evaluation and teacher re-evaluation, sorts out and analyzes it, and finally provides feedback to the students.

3.5 Summary and Reflection Stage

The final stage of the peer assessment activity in the fifth stage focuses on teachers' and students' collective reflection. Students conduct self-reflection on the basis of feedback from peers and teachers to improve their learning and performance; teachers improve their own teaching according to students' homework and mutual evaluation.

4 Research Design

4.1 Research Object

This study selected 31 undergraduate students in the "Computer Foundation" of educational technology major at Y University in 2023 as the research objects, including 23 male students and 8 female students. These students have just entered university and have some experience operating online teaching platforms.

4.2 Research Process Design

In this study, a single-group pretest and posttest design was adopted. Pretest questionnaires on critical thinking and peer-peer evaluation were issued before the beginning of the course to understand the current situation of students' critical thinking and peer-peer evaluation. Peer evaluation activities were then designed in the course, and a posttest was conducted after the course to verify the differences between the pretest and posttest. The entire peer evaluation activity is carried out for two months, and the learning platform adopts a learning pass.

4.3 Questionnaire Design

The critical thinking level measurement part of this study mainly refers to the California Critical Thinking Tendency Test Scale (Chinese version) and the California Critical Thinking Skills Test Scale (Chinese version). The measurement of critical thinking level includes a test of critical thinking tendency and a test of critical thinking skills. The specific measurement dimensions are shown in Figs. 2 and 3.

The pretest questionnaire selected questions from different dimensions of the two scales as the pretest of this study. In addition to the critical thinking level test, the posttest questionnaire also included open questions about the students' mastery of the relevant content learned in the course "Computer Foundation" this semester, their satisfaction with and acceptance of peer evaluation activities, and their perception of their own level of critical thinking.

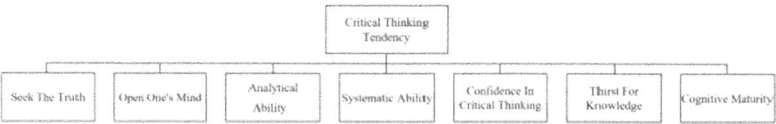

Fig. 2. Evaluation dimension of critical thinking tendency

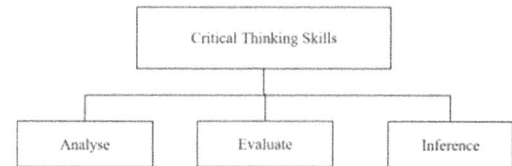

Fig. 3. Evaluation dimensions of critical thinking skills

5 Data Analysis

5.1 Peer Evaluation Has a Significant Effect on the Improvement of College Students' Critical Thinking Level

Through the two-month peer evaluation teaching activities, to test the overall changes in students' critical thinking ability, this study takes students' scores before and after critical thinking ability as variables and conducts a paid-sample t test to understand the significance of changes in students' critical thinking ability. As shown in Table 1, the average total scores of the pretest and posttest data are 33.48399 and 36.3871, respectively, and the posttest data are significantly better than the pretest data. The value of Sig is 0.013, $P < 0.05$, which proves that students' critical thinking levels significantly improve after peer evaluation activities.

A comparison of the average scores of the measurement dimensions of critical thinking before and after the test, as shown in Fig. 4, revealed that, with the exception of the dimensions of open mind and thirst for knowledge, which showed a downward trend, and the dimensions of analytical ability, which remained at the same level as before, the other dimensions showed an upward trend, especially the critical thinking skills of college students, which significantly improved. This may be related to research design, process, student learning, etc.

Table 1. Paired sample t test results.

Measurement of critical thinking	Average	Standard Deviation	T	Freedom Analysis	Sig
Pre-test	33.4839	5.74961	−2.642	30	0.013
Post-test	36.3871	5.24517			

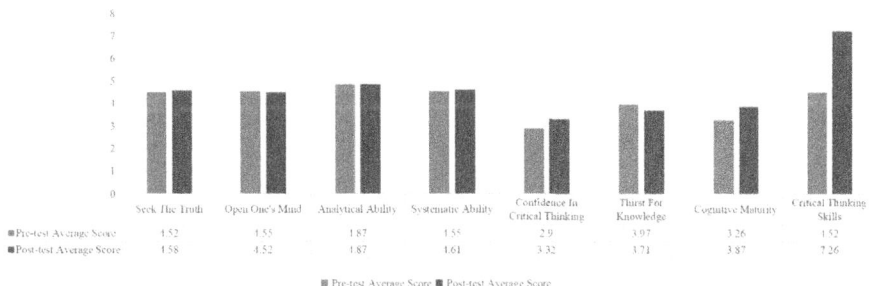

Fig. 4. Comparison chart of the mean scores before and after critical thinking measurement

5.2 College Students Believing that Peer Evaluation Can Promote Their Own Level of Critical Thinking

According to the results of the questionnaire analysis, as shown in Fig. 5 and Table 2, 94% of the students believe that peer evaluation can promote their own learning; 94% of the students believe that the peer review interactive platform is very easy to operate; and 82% of the students are willing to use peer evaluation to grade work. Although most students are willing to participate in peer assessment activities, the results of the survey show that some students are still unwilling to participate in peer assessment. This may be because different students have different standards for evaluation, resulting in different impacts on students' final grades. Overall, 92.3% of the students believed that peer evaluation activities improved their level of critical thinking. In the interview process, this study revealed that college students believe that peer evaluation can improve their critical thinking ability. The main changing aspect of the student's task is that through peer review, they are able to compare themselves with others and see the differences between themselves and others. Most students believe that in the process of peer evaluation, they can gain learning experience from others' work completion and understand their own shortcomings. The study also revealed that students who were given peer ratings and cross-shaped comments before and after the critical thinking assessment had higher scores in the post-critical thinking assessment. For example, students A and C gave high-quality comments while grading, and their scores increased from 22 and 26 points to 46 and 45 points, respectively. During the peer evaluation process, students C and D occasionally wrote comments, which improved their critical thinking skills. However, there was no significant difference in their scores before and after the evaluation.

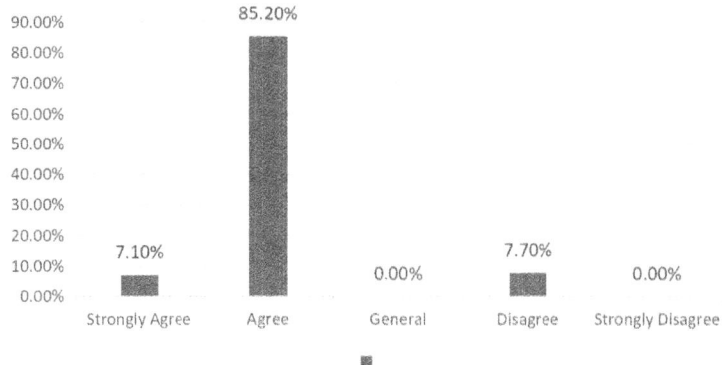

Fig. 5. Peer evaluation can promote the development of critical thinking skills

Table 2. College students' views on peer evaluation

Views	Strongly Agree	Agree	General	Disagree	Strongly Disagree
Peer evaluation can promote learning	6%	88%	0%	3%	3%
Peer evaluation platform is easy to use	13%	81%	0%	3%	3%
Be willing to grade work in a peer-review manner	7%	75%	0%	15%	3%

5.3 Students' Acceptance and Satisfaction of Peer Evaluation Activities Are Higher

During the research process, we randomly selected 7 students, including 4 males and 3 females, for interviews. All the interviewed students provided positive answers to the question of whether they enjoy peer evaluation. However, regarding the question of whether corresponding comments will be given during peer evaluation activities, nearly 29% of the students will choose to ignore writing comments, while approximately 10% of the students will consider whether to write comments on the basis of their own time situation, and 10% of the students will sometimes forget to write comments. Overall, the results of the interviews revealed that, given the blended learning environment online and offline, students have relatively high acceptance of and satisfaction with peer evaluation activities. On the one hand, the reason is that through peer evaluation, students can identify their own shortcomings and view problems from different perspectives on the basis of others' evaluations and assignments. This reflects that students' reflective awareness has been greatly enhanced in the process of peer evaluation. On the other hand, students also believe that using peer evaluation can compensate for the problem of teachers' untimely feedback.

Although students' evaluation of peer evaluation activities is relatively high in general, this study still collects some students' opinions on peer evaluation activities in the interview process. For example, some students said that it would be inconvenient to use mobile phones to perform peer evaluation, such as incomplete page display, but mobile phones are more portable than computers are; thus, this study considers the diversity of evaluation methods in the implementation of peer evaluation. A few students thought that others' evaluation of them was very casual. On the basis of this phenomenon, this study considers adopting the method of complaint reappraisal to solve the situation of disagreement with others' evaluation. Moreover, the interviews revealed that there are differences among students in the process of peer evaluation activities, and these differences are caused mainly by different personal backgrounds, interests, and learning atmospheres.

6 Research Conclusions

Peer evaluation has a significant effect on the development of students' critical thinking. The results show that peer evaluation has a positive influence on the development of students' critical thinking. Peer evaluation is highly important for students' learning.

6.1 Peer Evaluation Has a Positive Impact on the Development of Students' Critical Thinking

The significant differences in critical thinking among students vary with various factors, and there are significant differences when critical thinking is analyzed as a whole. In this study, peer evaluation activities provided students with an open and inclusive learning environment, which is crucial for the development of critical thinking. In the activity, students are encouraged to fully express their opinions, fully respect students, and evaluate and make progress in discussions and evaluations. This atmosphere encourages students to participate more confidently in discussions and dare to question and challenge themselves, thereby promoting the improvement of their critical thinking abilities. In addition, peer evaluation activities emphasize discussion and evaluation based on mutual respect. Students need to carefully analyze and make rational judgments when evaluating their peers' work and provide constructive feedback. This process not only requires students to have the ability to think critically but also encourages them to exercise continuously and improve this ability in practice.

6.2 Peer Evaluation is Highly Important for Student Learning

First, peer evaluation not only has a positive effect on the learning of the evaluated individual but also has a promoting effect on the evaluator's own learning. The forms of peer evaluation used in this study include "scores", "comments", and "scores + comments". When conducting peer evaluation activities, students can help the evaluated person discover strengths and problems in homework in a timely manner by scoring their peers and giving corresponding comments and can also improve their critical thinking level. At the same time, evaluators themselves will also compare and reflect on their own learning outcomes while evaluating, which is also beneficial for learning. In addition, peer evaluation can also allow students to see the completion status of other students, which is not only a process of grading homework but also a process of comparison and learning. Students can directly observe excellent homework and its evaluation, thereby stimulating internal learning motivation and cultivating self-directed learning ability. Finally, owing to the high acceptance and satisfaction of peer evaluation learning activities among college students, this learning method gradually changes their study habits and thinking patterns, further promoting their learning progress.

6.3 Discussion and Prospects

Although the research results show that peer evaluation learning activities have a significant effect on college students' critical thinking, this study also notes that the effect of peer evaluation is not achieved overnight but rather requires a certain amount of time and processing. In the early stage, students may be unfamiliar with the methods and techniques of mutual evaluation, which may lead to poor evaluation quality and even some misunderstandings. However, with the deepening of mutual evaluation activities, students gradually mastered the essentials of mutual evaluation, and the evaluation quality significantly improved. Therefore, when implementing peer evaluation, teachers need to provide students with enough guidance and support to help them better adapt and integrate into this learning process. Moreover, to improve the quality of peer evaluation, on the one hand, teachers can provide training to students, and on the other hand, they can improve the peer evaluation mechanism, such as by giving students the opportunity to appeal and then having teachers conduct a review to meet the needs of different students.

In addition, there are several limitations to this study. First, the sample size was relatively small, which may limit the generalizability of the results. Future studies can expand the sample size to include more schools and majors to improve the representativeness and credibility of the research. Second, this study adopted a questionnaire survey method to collect data. Although it has certain objectivity and operability, it may also be affected by subjective factors.

At the same time, this study also reflects on the research results that have not reached the expected effect and summarizes three reasons. First, the entire experiment lasted only two months, so the experimental period was relatively short. Second, in the process of posttest research, the students finish all the courses at the end of the semester, the learning pressure on all the courses is high, and urgent anxiety may affect the test results. Finally, in the process of questionnaire design, the difficulty of completing the questionnaire may lead to some students' fear of difficulty, which has a partial impact on the research results.

In response to the issues identified in this study, future research should further expand the scope of this area by constructing a theoretical framework for the relationship between peer evaluation and critical thinking, clarifying the interaction mechanism between the two, and optimizing strategies for implementing peer evaluation learning activities to better leverage the educational value of peer evaluation in higher education.

Acknowledgments. This research was financially supported by the 2023 Undergraduate Education and Teaching Reform Project of Yunnan Normal University: Strategic Research on Promoting the Development of College Students' Advanced Thinking through Classroom Interaction in the Smart Classroom Environment.

References

1. Man, S., et al.: Framework and elements of core literacy in the 21st century. J. East China Normal Univ. (Education Science Edition) **34**(03), 29–37+115 (2016)
2. Mohammadi, M., Abbasian, G.R., Siyyari, M.: Adaptation and validation of a critical thinking scale to measure the 3d critical thinking ability of EFL readers. Lang. Testing Asia **12**(1), 24 (2022)
3. Xiajuan, S., Mengdi, W., Rui, F.: Deep learning capability: conceptual framework, core dimensions and measurement system. Res. Audio-Visual Educ. **12**, 1–7 (2023)
4. Qingxu, L.: On the cultivation of college students' critical thinking. Educ. Res. Tsinghua Univ. **04**, 81–85 (2000)
5. Hyytinen, H., Nissinen, K., Kleemola, K., Ursin, J., Toom, A.: How do selfregulation and effort in test-taking contribute to undergraduate students' critical thinking performance? Stud. High. Educ. **49**(1), 192–205 (2024)
6. Facione, P.: Critical thinking: a statement of expert consensus for purposes of educational assessment and instruction/research findings and recommendations. ED315423 (1990)
7. Sheffield Jr, C.B.: Promoting critical thinking in higher education: my experiences as the inaugural Eugene H. Fram chair in applied critical thinking at rochester institute of technology. Topoi **37**(1), 155–163 (2018)
8. Ennis, R.H.: Critical thinking and subject specificity: clarification and needed research. Educ. Res. **18**(3), 4–10 (1989)
9. Renaud, R.D., Murray, H.G.: A comparison of a subject-specific and a general measure of critical thinking. Thinking Skills Creativity **3**(2), 85–93 (2008)
10. Saroyan, A.: Fostering creativity and critical thinking in university teaching and learning: considerations for academics and their professional learning (2022)
11. Jinggang, B., Yuqi, H.Y.D.: A practical exploration of the teaching path of technology promoting students' critical thinking development – a case study of argumentative essay writing in junior middle school. Mod. Educ. Technol. **33**(04), 65–73 (2023)
12. Yuchen, L., Yuchen, L.: An empirical study on the promotion of hybrid collaborative learning to the development of critical thinking. Open Educ. Res. **30**(02), 109–119 (2024)
13. Liming, J., Yujie, L., Fang, L.: Critical thinking assessment based on real problem situations: current situation and challenges. China Dist. Educ. (12), 58– 67+77+83 (2022)
14. Brkić, L., Mekterović, I., Fertalj, M., Mekterović, D.: Peer assessment methodology of open-ended assignments: Insights from a two-year case study within a university course using novel open source system. Comput. Educ. **213**, 105001 (2024)

15. Al Muzahmi, M.S., Bataineh, A., Douzandeh, E., et al.: Eng students' attitude toward peer review. J. English Lang. Teach. Appl. Linguist. **6**(1), 62–68 (2024)
16. Väyrynen, K., Lutovac, S., Kaasila, R.: Reflection on peer reviewing as a pedagogical tool in higher education. Act. Learn. High. Educ. **24**(3), 291–303 (2023)
17. Barahona, C., et al.: Technology-scaffolded peer assessment for developing critical thinking in preservice teacher training: the importance of giving feedback. Educ. Tech. Res. Dev. **71**(2), 667–688 (2023)
18. Tao, Z., Si, Z., Qianqian, G., Qianqian, G.: Promoting learners' critical thinking development in online peer assessment. Electrochem. Educ. Res. **43**(06), 53–60 (2022)
19. Wei, X., Sixuan, Z.: An empirical study of peer evaluation on learners' knowledge construction process: Cognitive network analysis based on time series. Mod. Educ. Technol. **32**(01), 44–53 (2022)
20. Qiong, W., Jiayu, O., Yizhou, F.: The relationship between reflective awareness and learning effectiveness in MOOC peer assessment. Electrochem. Educ. Res. **40**(06), 58–67 (2019)
21. Weiliang, K., Xiaoli, Y., Shuyun, H., Minjie, D.: Construction and verification of trusted peer evaluation model for artificial intelligence empowerment. Mod. Dist. Educ. Res. **35**(03), 93–101+112 (2023)

Data Mining in Smart Education that is Based on the Fuzzy Density Peaks Algorithm

Degang Yang, Jing Chen, and Ji Feng[⊠] [iD]

Chongqing Normal University, Chongqing 400030, China
jifeng@cqnu.edu.cn

Abstract. Education is an essential part of the growth process for students; hence, educational institutions strive to provide high-quality education to students. Nevertheless, accurately assessing students' performance becomes exceedingly challenging because of the diverse sources and structures of educational data. Moreover, considering the differences in students' learning abilities, adopting various teaching strategies is necessary. To unearth hidden knowledge from educational data, clustering algorithms have emerged as effective tools. This paper proposes a fuzzy density peak clustering algorithm based on graph distance and natural neighbors (FDPC-GDNN). The core idea is to enhance the separability of clusters via a fuzzy kernel and minimize the influence of outliers. When student portrait assessment and classification are conducted within educational contexts, the categorization of each student is inherently fuzzy, making it difficult to assign them to a specific category. Therefore, the FDPC-GDNN algorithm has significant advantages. We evaluated the FDPC-GDNN on several real-world and synthetic datasets, and the results demonstrated that this method can effectively cluster data of various shapes and densities. Through this approach, educators can gain a better understanding of students' performance, thereby establishing a solid foundation for instructional decision-making.

Keywords: smart education · machine learning · data mining · density peak clustering · natural neighbors

1 Introduction

With the advancement of globalization and technological progress, smart education has become increasingly popular, and many students have begun to receive education through online platforms. This has led educational institutions to face the challenge of how to effectively manage and analyze a large amount of online learning data [1]. Schools have amassed extensive and intricate data, encompassing students' online learning behaviors, academic performance, major selections, etc. [2]. How to effectively utilize and analyze this vast amount of data, transforming it into valuable knowledge and insights, has emerged as a significant topic in both domestic and international educational data processing [3]. Owing to the swift evolution of internet technology, the adoption of data management technology to address data challenges stemming from the surge of students in the educational sector has significantly contributed to school development [4].

Data mining is a process of latent, patterned, previously undiscovered yet potentially valuable and comprehensible information from extensive, often incomplete, noisy, ambiguous, and random datasets. Cluster analysis stands out as a significant and active evolving field within data mining [5]. Clustering is a basic unsupervised learning algorithm that groups similar instances on the basis of their characteristics. The primary objective of clustering is to identify and assemble analogous instances into clusters, where the similarity among instances within the same cluster is greater than that among those in different clusters. In recent decades, numerous advanced clustering algorithms have been designed for various applications. Clustering algorithms that currently exist can be divided into four primary classifications: partition-based [6, 7], hierarchical-based [8, 9], grid-based [10, 11], and density-based methods [12, 13]. Clustering algorithms play a key role in education by segmenting student groups, identifying similarities and differences, and assisting teachers in developing personalized teaching plans. Furthermore, clustering can also be used for course recommendations, learning path planning, and other purposes to increase educational effectiveness. In summary, the application prospects of clustering algorithms within the educational sector are broad.

In the domain of data mining, researchers have conducted in-depth discussions on clustering algorithms. K-means, proposed by MacQueen, is a prime example of a partition-based clustering algorithm [14]. Through an iterative procedure, the algorithm continuously updates the centroid of each cluster and reallocates objects to the nearest cluster, progressively increasing the accuracy of the clustering outcome. The DPC clustering algorithm suggested by Rodriguez et al. can not only effectively identify cluster centers but also demonstrate robustness in handling clusters of various shapes [15]. Lotfi et al. introduced a new algorithm called DPC-DBFN, which uses fuzzy kernels to enhance cluster separability and mitigate the influence of outliers [16]. Guo et al. proposed density peak clustering with connectivity estimation (DPC-CE), which calculates the connectivity of clustering centers on the basis of a graph-based method and computes sample similarities by incorporating both Euclidean distances and intersample connectivity [17]. Cheng et al. proposed a clustering algorithm (NDP-Kmeans) based on natural density peaks (NDPs), which can discover clusters of arbitrary shapes and overcome the limitations of traditional K-means in identifying nonspherical clusters [18].

Moreover, the applicability of data mining in education is also continuously expanding. In recent years, data mining has been used by many scholars to analyze educational data. Wolbring et al. highlighted that educational evaluation through data collection and analysis not only highlights students' academic achievements but also assesses teachers' instructional effectiveness [19]. Lavelle et al. designed a database that meets the functional requirements of the educational evaluation system and is capable of maintaining basic information, statistical data and other functions [20]. Wang et al. presented an innovative fuzzy clustering algorithm that leverages genetic algorithms for the clustering analysis of data. The algorithm can quickly obtain the global optimal solution and is completely independent of prototype initialization [21].

Currently, the field of education frequently encounters large-scale datasets, presenting new challenges for data analysis and research. Traditional analysis algorithms encounter numerous difficulties when processing these data, including high processing difficulty, lengthy processing times, inefficiency, and poor clustering quality. Additionally, the existing evaluation data tend to be homogeneous in content, and the analysis methods lack depth. Therefore, we need to explore more efficient and accurate data analysis methods to address these challenges and promote deeper educational research. In response to the current situation of educational data analysis, the FDPC-GDNN algorithm is introduced for the analysis of educational assessment data. The innovation of this paper lies in the following:

1. When assessing and classifying students, the attributes of each student are often vague and difficult to classify clearly into a specific category. Therefore, using a local density calculation method based on fuzzy neighborhood relationships can allocate data points more reasonably, making the clustering results closer to the needs of actual application scenarios. To increase the accuracy and reliability of clustering, this paper first removes outliers and employs a K-nearest neighbor propagation mechanism to establish a core clustering area. This ensures that interference factors are eliminated before labels are assigned to noncenter points. Additionally, graph distance (GD) is introduced as an effective tool for measuring the dissimilarity between objects. This approach not only helps improve algorithm efficiency but also significantly reduces time complexity. The application of the above technologies and methods can help educators better understand and analyze students' behavioral characteristics in online learning environments, thereby providing strong support for personalized teaching.
2. On the basis of cognitive learning theory, this paper solves the problems existing in current educational data processing, such as long processing times, low clustering quality, the homogeneity of evaluation data content and the shallowness of analysis methods. We propose an innovative solution to apply the FDPC-GDNN algorithm to educational evaluation data. The experimental results confirm that this method has good applicability in large-scale data mining scenarios. For researchers in related fields, this research not only provides new ideas and methods but also has certain reference and guiding value.

The subsequent sections of this paper are structured as outlined below. Section 2 presents the core concepts of the DPC and NDP-Kmeans algorithms, as well as clustering techniques in educational data mining. The FDPC-GDNN algorithm is provided in Sect. 3. Section 4 analyzes the results of the algorithm on datasets to demonstrate the effectiveness of the FDPC-GDNN. In Sect. 5, the conclusions of this paper are summarized.

2 Related Works

2.1 DPC

DPC is a novel and fast density peak clustering algorithm. It requires fewer input parameters and can effectively identify cluster centers. It efficiently clusters datasets of any shape or dimension. Additionally, DPC boasts advantages such as simplicity of implementation, fast clustering speed, good stability, high clustering efficiency, and insensitivity to noise.

The measurement of the local density of data points can be divided into truncated kernel density and Gaussian kernel density, which are defined by Eqs. (1) and (2), respectively.

$$\rho_i = \sum_{j=1}^{n} \chi(d_{ij} - d_c), \ \chi(x) = \begin{cases} 1, x < 0 \\ 0, otherwise \end{cases} \tag{1}$$

$$\rho_i = \sum_{j \neq i}^{n} e^{-(\frac{d_{ij}}{d_c})^2} \tag{2}$$

Here, n denotes the overall count of points, and d_c denotes the global cutoff distance. D_{ij} represents the Euclidean distance separating data points i and j. For large datasets, the DPC algorithm generally uses truncated kernel density, and for small datasets, it uses Gaussian kernel density. d_c is an important parameter for measuring the point density. The efficiency of DPC often depends on the selection of d_c.

δ_i is the shortest distance from data point i to another data point that has a higher density, defined as follows:

$$\delta_i = \begin{cases} \min(d_{ij}), if \ \rho_i \neq \rho_{max} \ and \ \rho_i < \rho_j \\ \max(d_{ij}), otherwise \end{cases} \tag{3}$$

The DPC algorithm uses δ for the y-axis and ρ for the x-axis to construct a decision graph, aiding in the selection of cluster centers. Those sample points that exhibit both high local density ρ and high relative distance δ are often manually designated as the centers of clusters. When it becomes difficult to determine the cluster centers, the algorithm further calculates the γ value. The decision value γ_i is given by Eq. (4):

$$\gamma_i = \rho_i \times \delta_i \tag{4}$$

After identifying the cluster centers, the algorithm assigns different labels to each identified cluster center. The DPC algorithm subsequently sorts the data points that have not yet been classified in decreasing order of their local density values. Finally, the algorithm will assign the data points to the clusters to which their high-density nearest neighbors belong in this order.

2.2 NDP-Kmeans

The core of the NDP-Kmeans algorithm lies in natural density peaks (NDPs). The natural representative of an object i is the one possessing the greatest density among i and its neighbors, denoted as j. If j is i itself, then i is an NDP.

NDP-Kmeans first calculates the density and selects NDPs from the local neighborhood to replace the original data (density calculation is shown in formula 5). Then, using the neighbor-based distance (formula 6), the GD (formula 7) is calculated. The algorithm subsequently clusters the NDPs through an improved K-means algorithm and uses GDs to update the centers and members. Finally, the clustering results are extended to the original data.

$$Den(o) = \frac{K}{\sum_{j \in KNN(o)} d_{oj}} \tag{5}$$

K is adaptively obtained through the concept of natural neighbors, which combine K-NN and reverse K-NN [28]. d_{oj} is the Euclidean distance between o and j, and KNN(o) is the K-nearest neighbors of object o.

$$ND(i,j) = \begin{cases} \frac{d_{ij}}{|CN(i,j)| \times \sum_{o \in CN(i,j)} Den(o)}, & |CN(i,j)| > 0 \\ \max v \times (1 + d_{ij}), & |CN(i,j)| = 0 \end{cases} \tag{6}$$

$CN(i,j)$ represents the mutual neighboring nodes between NDPs i and j. NNDP(i) denotes the neighbors of NDP i, which are the KNNs of MNDP(i) with a density greater than *DenThr*. *DenThr* is a density threshold used to exclude noise points. MNDP(i) represents the composition of objects represented by i and larger than *DenThr*.

$$GD(i,j) = \sum_{k=1}^{m-1} ND(p_k, p_{k+1}) \tag{7}$$

Given that the Euclidean distance fails to precisely capture the distinctions among objects within manifold clusters, Tenenbaum et al. proposed that the shortest path on the graph can be used to approximate the difference of objects on the manifold, referred to as GD [29]. Equation (7) represents the GD between NDPs i and j.

2.3   Clustering Techniques in Educational Data Mining

The scope of application for data mining in education is continually broadening. In recent years, it has emerged as a crucial tool for many scholars to analyze educational data. Antonenko et al. introduced the application of clusters in educational technology, employing various clustering methods, such as k-means, to analyze students' online learning behavior through mining network server log data [22]. Similarly, item response theory and K-means can be used to successfully identify students' learning abilities in a collaborative learning environment [23]. Anaya et al. proposed an open collaborative learning experience design that infers students' collaboration level through statistical indicators and data mining techniques, helping students and teachers manage the collaboration process and improving learning efficiency [24]. In addition, Cobo et al. used clustering methods to identify different behavioral patterns exhibited by students in online forums [25]. Hooshyar et al. presented an algorithm called PPP to forecast the performance of students with learning difficulties by analyzing their homework submission behavior, with special attention given to the impact of procrastination on grades [26]. Liu calculated the weights of various indicators of students' comprehensive quality through the hierarchical analysis method and proposed an improved sampling technology to process large-scale datasets, achieving higher accuracy [27].

3   FDPC-GDNN Algorithm

To address the issues existing in DPC and its enhanced algorithms to some degree, this paper proposes a fuzzy density peak clustering algorithm based on graph distance and natural neighbors (FDPC-GDNN). First, the FDPC-GDNN uses natural neighbors to define dc and employs a fuzzy neighbor relationship to unify the local density measurement. Second, the algorithm defines core regions and outliers and uses two strategies to assign core points and outlier points. The FDPC-GDNN algorithm consists of three steps: (1) calculating the density and distance of points; (2) allocating core points; and (3) allocating outlier points.

3.1 Calculating Density and Distance

To eliminate the influence of the cutoff distance d_c on clustering outcomes and provide a consistent density measurement for datasets of different sizes, this paper uses natural neighbors to define d_c, aiming to achieve a more stable and universal density calculation. Additionally, this paper considers the introduction of fuzzy neighbor relationships to define local density measurements, thereby taking into account the membership degree of member points to cluster centers in a more comprehensive manner and further enhancing the accuracy and robustness of clustering. The cutoff distance measurement used in this paper is as follows:

$$d_c = \left(\mu^K + \sqrt{\frac{1}{N+1} \sum_{i=1}^{N} \left(\delta_i^K - \mu^K \right)^2} \right) \times \lambda \tag{8}$$

$$\delta_i^K = \max_{j \in KNN(i)} \left(d_{ij} \right) \tag{9}$$

K is the neighborhood parameter adaptively obtained through the natural neighbor method, N denotes the total number of points, δ_i^K represents the distance between point i and its K-th nearest neighbor, μ^K is the average of δ_i^K, and λ is a constant.

This paper employs a fuzzy neighborhood relationship, which replaces the traditional neighborhood relationship by assigning different membership degrees to the distances from points to core points. The neighborhood membership function has been clearly defined. The neighborhood membership function is as follows:

$$\mu'_{(x_i)}(x_j) = \begin{cases} 1 - \frac{d_{ij}}{d_c}, d_{ij} < d_c \\ 0, otherwise \end{cases} \tag{10}$$

The local density is as follows:

$$\rho_i = \sum_j \mu'_{(x_i)}(x_j) \tag{11}$$

This paper uses formula (4) to evaluate the likelihood of each point serving as a cluster center, subsequently selecting the first c points as cluster centers.

3.2 Allocation of Core Points

In the original DPC and its numerous improved versions, incorrect label assignments often have a ripple effect, impacting other unassigned points. To avoid the problem of cluster merging caused by outliers, the FDPC-GDNN first removes outliers before assigning the remaining points and then uses a special strategy to assign outliers.

Before assigning labels to sample points, we first remove outliers to ensure that they do not interfere with the clustering results. The remaining points after removing outliers form dense points. For the set of dense points, the FDPC-GDNN initially assigns a unique label to each cluster center. It then assigns the label of the cluster center to its K-nearest dense points. The label is subsequently further propagated to the neighbors of these K-nearest points. This iterative process continues until each dense point has been assigned the appropriate cluster label.

The definition of outliers is as follows:

$$Outliers = \left\{ o \middle| \delta_i^K > \mu^K \right\} \tag{12}$$

3.3 Allocating Outlier Points

In density peak clustering, the assignment of outliers is a core challenge that is directly related to the results and quality of clustering. Traditional methods often handle this issue inadequately, leading to unsatisfactory clustering outcomes. To address this, we introduce a graph distance method to assign outlier points more accurately, thereby improving the clustering quality and result stability. The algorithm is divided into the following three steps:

First, the algorithm needs to identify and select representative points, which are the points with the highest density within their neighborhoods. To better describe this process, representative points can be analogized to root nodes in a tree. Given two data points x_1 and x_2, if x_2 is a KNN of x_1 and x_2 is the nearest high-density neighbor of x_1, then x_1 is called the child node of x_2, and x_2 is called the parent node of x_1. We denote this relationship as $x_1 \rightarrow x_2$. If $x_1 \rightarrow x_2, x_2 \rightarrow x_3 ..., x_{j-1} \rightarrow x_j$ and there is no point with higher density among the KNNs of x_j, then x_j is the representative point for $x_1, x_2 ...,$ x_{j-1}, and the data points that select x_j as their representative point are members of x_j.

The algorithm subsequently uses GD (Formula (7)) to calculate the distance between each representative point and employs the calculated GD to propagate the labels of already assigned representative points to their nearest representative points. This process continues until every representative point is assigned appropriate labels.

Finally, the algorithm assigns the labels of representative points to their unassigned members.

3.4 Complexity Analysis

The three primary steps determine the time complexity of the FDPC-GDNN: (1) calculating point densities and distances, (2) assigning core points, and (3) allocating outlier points.

In the initial stage, calculating the local density involves determining Euclidean distances between all points, which takes $O(n^2)$ time. Computing the cutoff distance d_c and the corresponding densities requires $O(n)$. Establishing neighborhood memberships also demands $O(n^2)$ time. Consequently, the time complexity for this phase is $O(n^2)$. In the second phase, assigning labels to cluster centers requires $O(c)$ time, where c denotes the number of cluster centers. Subsequently, propagating these labels to dense points involves a process that, in the worst-case scenario, operates at a complexity of $O(n*k)$. Therefore, the time complexity of this part is $O(n)$. In the third phase, during the sample allocation process, scanning all representative points of the samples necessitates $O(n)$. Considering that the number of representative points is significantly less than N, the computational complexity for determining the GD between these representative points is less than $O(n^2)$.

In summary, the FDPC-GDNN algorithm presented in this paper has a time complexity of $O(n^2)$, which aligns with that of DPC.

4   Experiments and Results

To validate the superiority of the FDPC-GDNN algorithm, we selected six synthetic datasets with varying distribution characteristics, as well as six real-world datasets for testing. These algorithms were compared with algorithms such as DPC, DPC-CE, DPC-DBFN, and NDP-Kmeans. The descriptions of these datasets are presented in Tables 1 and 2. The experimental evaluation of the algorithm was carried out on a computing environment equipped with MATLAB R2023a, featuring a Core i7 processor clocked at 3.10 GHz and complemented by 32 GB of RAM.

Table 1. Synthetic datasets.

Datasets	Instances	Attributes	Clusters
Jain	373	2	2
circle	1897	2	3
cmc	1002	2	3
db	630	2	4
cth	1016	2	4
Aggregation	788	2	7

Table 2. Real-world datasets.

Datasets	Instances	Attributes	Clusters
Dna	2000	180	3
Gesture	1747	18	5
Landsat	2000	36	6
Bank note authentication	1372	4	2

(continued)

Table 2. (*continued*)

Datasets	Instances	Attributes	Clusters
Dermatology	358	34	7
Pima	768	8	2

4.1 Experimental Preparation

To assess the clustering algorithms' efficacy, three evaluation metrics are employed: accuracy (ACC), adjusted Rand index (ARI), and adjusted mutual information (AMI). Their upper bound is 1, implying that a higher metric value signifies a superior clustering effect.

ACC [30], AMI [31], and ARI [30] were adopted as evaluation metrics, with their respective definitions outlined as follows:

(1) ACC

Assuming that y_i represents the true label and that z_i represents the predicted label, if $x = y$, then $\delta(x, y) = 1$; otherwise, $\delta(x, y) = 0$. The value range of the ACC is [0, 1].

$$ACC = \sum_{i=1}^{n} \delta(y_i, map(z_i))/n \qquad (13)$$

(2) AMI

$$AMI = \frac{I(U, V) - E\{I(U, V)\}}{\sqrt{H(U)H(V)} - E\{I(U, V)\}} \qquad (14)$$

The AMI measures the similarity between the true labels (U) and the predicted labels (V). Here, H(U) denotes the entropy of U. The higher the AMI score is, the closer the predicted division is to the true classification.

(3) ARI

$$ARI = \frac{RI - E[RI]}{\max(RI) - E[RI]} \qquad (15)$$

The ARI is derived from the Rand index (RI). The higher the ARI index value is, the better the agreement between the predicted division and the real classification.

Before experimenting with the datasets, we conducted parameter tuning for each algorithm to ensure an objective comparison of their optimal performance. For traditional DPC, we select 2% of d_c and apply a Gaussian kernel in the density estimation process. DPC-CE does not require parameter adjustment. For the DPC-DBFN, we adjust the value of K to achieve optimal results. For NDP-Kmeans, we provided the correct number of clusters and adjusted the density threshold to exclude noise. For the FDPC-GDNN, we set the optimal value of λ.

4.2 Synthetic Datasets

For this part, we selected several comprehensive and widely used datasets to evaluate the performance of the clustering algorithms. These datasets encompass various numbers of points and clusters, enabling us to simulate diverse scenarios and compare the performance of various clustering algorithms.

Table 3 presents the clustering outcomes for selected synthetic datasets, including the ACC, AMI, and ARI scores, as well as the parameter Par for each algorithm. For each evaluation metric, the highest score is highlighted in bold. Notably, in most cases, the proposed FDPC-GDNN algorithm achieves the highest scores.

Table 3. ACC, ARI, and AMI of five algorithms on synthetic datasets.

Algorithm	ACC	AMI	ARI	Par	ACC	AMI	ARI	Par
	jain				**circle**			
DPC	0.375	0.233	0.044	-	0.332	0.223	−0.005	-
DPC-CE	**1**	**1**	**1**	-	0.708	0.587	0.326	-
DPC-DBFN	0.938	0.673	0.745	15	0.357	0.021	0.001	6
NDP-Kmeans	**1**	**1**	**1**	0	**1**	**1**	**1**	0
FDPC-GDNN	**1**	**1**	**1**	10	**1**	**1**	**1**	7
	cmc				**db**			
DPC	0.369	0.241	0.157	-	0.415	0.465	0.226	-
DPC-CE	0.677	0.328	0.131	-	0.722	0.713	0.468	-
DPC-DBFN	0.657	0.296	0.219	3	0.423	0.393	0.157	9
NDP-Kmeans	0.871	0.792	0.798	0	**1**	**1**	**1**	0
FDPC-GDNN	**1**	**1**	**1**	10	**1**	**1**	**1**	7
	cth				**Aggregation**			
DPC	0.613	0.582	0.422	-	**1**	**1**	**1**	-
DPC-CE	0.704	0.803	0.715	-	0.998	0.995	0.997	-
DPC-DBFN	0.660	0.558	0.285	25	0.996	0.988	0.987	30
NDP-Kmeans	**1**	**1**	**1**	0	0.996	0.988	0.992	0
FDPC-GDNN	**1**	**1**	**1**	1	0.997	0.992	0.992	2

Figures 1 through 6 illustrate the clustering outcomes obtained by DPC, DPC-CE, DPC-DBFN, NDP-Kmeans, and FDPC-GDNN, respectively.

For the jain dataset shown in Fig. 1, DPC-CE, NDP-Kmeans, and FDPC-GDNN were able to correctly identify all the clusters. The DPC was unable to accurately identify the cluster centers because of the significant density difference between the two clusters. The DPC-DBFN performed poorly. Figure 2 shows that both the NDP-Kmeans and FDPC-GDNN were able to correctly identify the two concentric rings and the spherical dataset in the middle, whereas the performance of the other algorithms was less satisfactory. In

Fig. 3, only the FDPC-GDNN fully recognized the clusters in the cmc dataset. According to the clustering results presented in Figs. 4 and 5, only NDP-Kmeans and FDPC-GDNN correctly detected the clusters within the db dataset. Figure 6 displays the clustering results of FDPC-GDNN, along with those of four other algorithms in the control group, on the aggregation dataset. All five algorithms were able to correctly detect the clusters in this dataset.

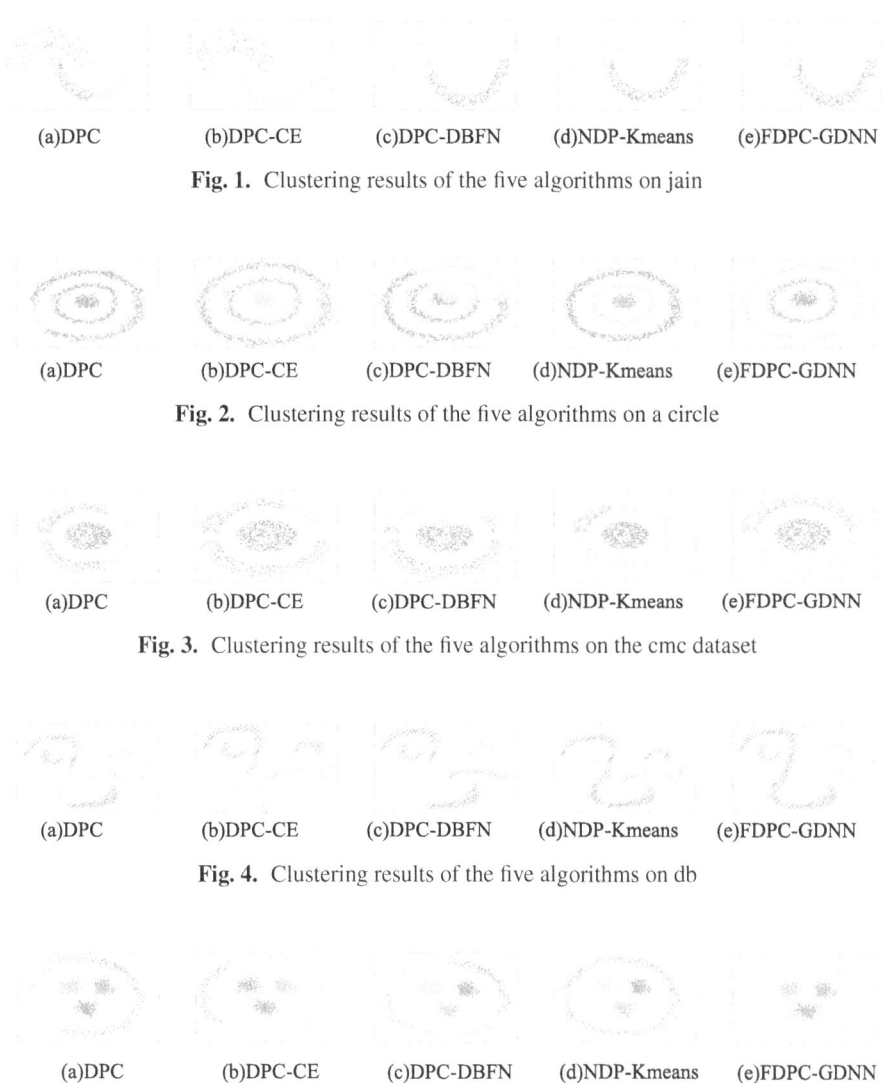

(a)DPC   (b)DPC-CE   (c)DPC-DBFN   (d)NDP-Kmeans   (e)FDPC-GDNN

Fig. 1. Clustering results of the five algorithms on jain

(a)DPC   (b)DPC-CE   (c)DPC-DBFN   (d)NDP-Kmeans   (e)FDPC-GDNN

Fig. 2. Clustering results of the five algorithms on a circle

(a)DPC   (b)DPC-CE   (c)DPC-DBFN   (d)NDP-Kmeans   (e)FDPC-GDNN

Fig. 3. Clustering results of the five algorithms on the cmc dataset

(a)DPC   (b)DPC-CE   (c)DPC-DBFN   (d)NDP-Kmeans   (e)FDPC-GDNN

Fig. 4. Clustering results of the five algorithms on db

(a)DPC   (b)DPC-CE   (c)DPC-DBFN   (d)NDP-Kmeans   (e)FDPC-GDNN

Fig. 5. Clustering results of the five algorithms on the cth dataset

| (a)DPC | (b)DPC-CE | (c)DPC-DBFN | (d)NDP-Kmeans | (e)FDPC-GDNN |

Fig. 6. Clustering results of the five algorithms on aggregation

4.3 Real-World Datasets

In this section, we highlight the potential of the FDPC-GDNN clustering algorithm in the field of education. To validate its performance, six datasets from UCI were used (as shown in Table 2). These datasets differ significantly in the number of samples, attributes, and clusters, providing a diverse testing scenario for the algorithm.

As shown in Table 4, the proposed FDPC-GDNN clustering algorithm performs well on multiple datasets. Specifically, each clustering metric outperforms the other algorithms on the Dna, gesture, bank note authentication, and dermatology datasets. This shows that the FDPC-GDNN is highly adaptable and effective in processing different types of data. Although the AMI metric in the Landsat dataset and the ARI metric in the Pima dataset are not optimal, the remaining two metrics are optimal, which further demonstrates the stability and reliability of the algorithm.

The experimental results indicate that the FDPC-GDNN clustering algorithm has promising potential for broad application in the field of education. For example, in terms of student classification and personalized teaching, teachers can use FDPC-GDNN to group students more accurately to develop more effective teaching strategies for different groups. In addition, the algorithm can also help educational researchers better understand students' learning behaviors and characteristics, thereby providing support for personalized learning. In short, the application of the FDPC-GDNN clustering algorithm in education will help enhance the quality of teaching and students' learning outcomes.

Table 4. ACC, ARI, and AMI of the five algorithms on real-world datasets.

Algorithm	ACC	AMI	ARI	Par	ACC	AMI	ARI	Par
	Dna				**Gesture**			
DPC	0.496	0.005	0.012	-	0.528	0.234	0.127	-
DPC-CE	0.485	0.009	0.019	-	0.493	0.172	0.059	-
DPC-DBFN	0.525	0.017	0.013	4	0.450	0.136	0.039	17
NDP-Kmeans	0.526	0.002	0.000	0	0.439	0.116	0.018	0.1
FDPC-GDNN	**0.591**	**0.129**	**0.126**	1	**0.675**	**0.310**	**0.275**	2
	Landsat				**Bank note authentication**			
DPC	0.495	0.399	0.167	-	0.737	0.341	0.169	-

(continued)

Table 4. (*continued*)

Algorithm	ACC	AMI	ARI	Par	ACC	AMI	ARI	Par
DPC-CE	0.493	0.390	0.155	-	0.459	0.120	−0.001	-
DPC-DBFN	0.567	0.541	0.218	20	0.606	0.073	0.034	9
NDP-Kmeans	0.520	**0.576**	0.238	0.1	0.669	0.130	0.070	0.2
FDPC-GDNN	**0.613**	0.553	**0.306**	1	**0.895**	**0.611**	**0.545**	3
	Dermatology				**Pima**			
DPC	0.293	0.269	0.062	-	0.653	0.005	0.005	-
DPC-CE	0.329	0.304	0.113	-	0.651	0.000	0.000	-
DPC-DBFN	0.561	0.637	0.277	9	0.631	0.008	**0.017**	14
NDP-Kmeans	0.368	0.376	0.095	0.1	0.648	0.002	0.006	0.1
FDPC-GDNN	**0.715**	**0.674**	**0.559**	1	**0.662**	**0.018**	0.016	4

5 Conclusion

Online learning platforms contain a wealth of valuable information, and educators are dedicated to accurately extracting key knowledge from these vast datasets that significantly impacts students' overall quality. On the basis of this requirement, this paper adopts a cognitive learning theory perspective, draws on domestic and international research achievements and practical applications within the realm of educational evaluation data analysis, and proposes the FDPC-GDNN clustering algorithm to analyze educational data. The FDPC-GDNN algorithm is suitable for processing popular datasets and has been experimentally validated on various synthetic and real datasets, demonstrating superior performance compared with other reference algorithms. In this way, this paper not only provides a powerful tool for deep analysis of educational evaluation data but also opens new paths for data mining practices within the education sector.

However, despite the significant achievements of this study, owing to time constraints and research limitations, not all influencing factors and control variables were fully considered during the design process. In the future, we will also introduce datasets with more educational backgrounds to better meet the needs of the education field. Moreover, we strive to improve analysis techniques and continuously improve education evaluation data analysis models, aiming to delve deeper into data value extraction and provide more precise and comprehensive support for educational decision-making.

References

1. Jan, M.A., Khan, F.: Application of Big Data, Blockchain, and Internet of Things for Education Informatization. In: First EAI International Conference, BigIoT-EDU 2021, Virtual Event, 1–3 August 2021, Proceedings, Part I, vol. 391. Springer Nature (2021)
2. Hall, W.A.: Consumerism and consumer complexity: implications for university teaching and teaching evaluation. Nurse Educ. Today **33**(7), 720–723 (2013)

3. Weston, T.J., Hayward, C.N., Laursen, S.L.: When seeing is believing: generalizability and decision studies for observational data in evaluation and research on teaching. Am. J. Eval. **42**(3), 377–398 (2021)
4. Antoci, A., Brunetti, I., Sacco, P., Sodini, M.: Student evaluation of teaching, social influence dynamics, and teachers' choices: an evolutionary model. J. Evol. Econ. **31**, 325–348 (2021)
5. Bergin, C., Wind, S.A., Grajeda, S., Tsai, C.L.: Teacher evaluation: are principals' classroom observations accurate at the conclusion of training? Stud. Educ. Eval. **55**, 19–26 (2017)
6. Lei, T., Jia, X., Zhang, Y., He, L., Meng, H., Nandi, A.K.: Significantly fast and robust fuzzy c-means clustering algorithm based on morphological reconstruction and membership filtering. IEEE Trans. Fuzzy Syst. **26**(5), 3027–3041 (2018)
7. Mazzeo, G.M., Masciari, E., Zaniolo, C.: A fast and accurate algorithm for unsupervised clustering around centroids. Inf. Sci. **400**, 63–90 (2017)
8. Giacoumidis, E., Matin, A., Wei, J., Doran, N.J., Barry, L.P., Wang, X.: Blind nonlinearity equalization by machine-learning-based clustering for single-and multichannel coherent optical OFDM. J. Lightwave Technol. **36**(3), 721–727 (2018)
9. Wu, C., Peng, Q., Lee, J., Leibnitz, K., Xia, Y.: Effective hierarchical clustering based on structural similarities in nearest neighbor graphs. Knowl.-Based Syst. **228**, 107295 (2021)
10. Tao, X., Wang, R., Chang, R., Li, C., Liu, R., Zou, J.: Spectral clustering algorithm using density-sensitive distance measure with global and local consistencies. Knowl.-Based Syst. **170**, 26–42 (2019)
11. Chang, H., Yeung, D.Y.: Robust path-based spectral clustering. Patt. Recogn. **41**(1), 191–203 (2008)
12. Gowanlock, M., Rude, C.M., Blair, D.M., Li, J.D., Pankratius, V.: A hybrid approach for optimizing parallel clustering throughput using the GPU. IEEE Trans. Parallel Distrib. Syst. **30**(4), 766–777 (2018)
13. Chen, Y., et al.: Decentralized clustering by finding loose and distributed density cores. Inf. Sci. **433**, 510–526 (2018)
14. MacQueen, J.: Some methods for classification and analysis of multivariate observations. In: Proceedings of 5-th Berkeley Symposium on Mathematical Statistics and Probability/University of California Press (1967)
15. Rodriguez, A., Laio, A.: Clustering by fast search and find of density peaks. Science **344**(6191), 1492–1496 (2014)
16. Lotfi, A., Moradi, P., Beigy, H.: Density peaks clustering based on density backbone and fuzzy neighborhood. Pattern Recogn. **107**, 107449 (2020)
17. Guo, W., Wang, W., Zhao, S., Niu, Y., Zhang, Z., Liu, X.: Density peak clustering with connectivity estimation. Knowl.-Based Syst. **243**, 108501 (2022)
18. Cheng, D., Huang, J., Zhang, S., Xia, S., Wang, G., Xie, J.: K-means clustering with natural density peaks for discovering arbitrary-shaped clusters. IEEE Trans. Neural Netw. Learn. Syst. (2023)
19. Wolbring, T., Treischl, E.: Selection bias in students' evaluation of teaching: causes of student absenteeism and its consequences for course ratings and rankings. Res. High. Educ. **57**, 51–71 (2016)
20. LaVelle, J.M.: Book review: building evaluation capacity: activities for teaching and training (2018)
21. Wang, W.: Evaluation principles' influence of critical thinking foreign language teaching on German literature classroom learning motivation. Revista de Cercetare şi Intervenţie Socială **73**, 81–94 (2021)
22. Antonenko, P.D., Toy, S., Niederhauser, D.S.: Using cluster analysis for data mining in educational technology research. Educ. Tech. Res. Dev. **60**, 383–398 (2012)
23. Chang, W.C., Wang, T.H., Li, M.F.: Learning ability clustering in collaborative learning. J. Softw. **5**(12), 1363–1370 (2010)

24. Anaya, A.R., Boticario, J.G.: Clustering learners according to their collaboration. In: 2009 13th International Conference on Computer Supported Cooperative Work in Design, pp. 540–545. IEEE (2009)
25. Cobo, G., García-Solórzano, D., Santamaría, E., Morán, J.A., Melenchón, J., Monzo, C.: Modeling students' activity in online discussion forums: a strategy based on time series and agglomerative hierarchical clustering. In: Educational Data Mining 2011 (2010)
26. Hooshyar, D., Pedaste, M., Yang, Y.: Mining educational data to predict students' performance through procrastination behavior. Entropy **22**(1), 12 (2019)
27. Liu, R.: Data analysis of educational evaluation using k-means clustering method. Comput. Intell. Neurosci. **2022**(1), 3762431 (2022)
28. Zhu, Q., Feng, J., Huang, J.: Natural neighbor: a self-adaptive neighborhood method without parameter k. Patt. Recogn. Lett. **80**, 30–36 (2016)
29. Tenenbaum, J.B., Silva, V.d., Langford, J.C.: A global geometric framework for nonlinear dimensionality reduction. Science **290** (5500), 2319–2323 (2000)
30. Yu, D., Liu, G., Guo, M., Liu, X., Yao, S.: Density peaks clustering based on weighted local density sequence and nearest neighbor assignment. IEEE Access **7**, 34301–34317 (2019)
31. Vinh, N.X., Epps, J., Bailey, J.: Information theoretic measures for clusterings comparison: is a correction for chance necessary? In: Proceedings of the 26th Annual International Conference on Machine Learning, pp. 1073–1080 (2009)

Students' Achievement Prediction via MOOC Data

Li'ang Xu, Zuwang He, Shunzhang Chen, Yifan Zhan, and Shaojie Qu[✉]

Beijing Institute of Technology, No. 5 Zhongguancun South Street, Haidian District, Beijing, China

zzmad@163.com

Abstract. Educational data mining is currently a prominent topic. Existing methods such as graph convolutional networks often struggle with high-dimensional complex features and do not effectively utilize the weights and influences between features. To assist teachers in evaluating massive open online courses (MOOCs) and providing timely academic warnings for students. First, we extracted a number of features. Second, we design various feature extraction methods to analyze data from the C programming class on MOOCs. Third, we developed a predictive model incorporating sequence convolution and an improved attention mechanism to enhance the processing of time series features and feature weights. The results indicate that our method outperforms traditional models in terms of prediction accuracy.

Keywords: Machine Learning · MOOC · Educational Data Mining

1 Introduction

To aid teachers in effectively evaluating the performance of students in massive open online courses (MOOCs) and providing timely academic warnings, we designed various feature extraction techniques. These techniques extract multiple features from the C programming MOOC course data. Additionally, we developed a novel predictive model incorporating sequence convolution and an improved attention mechanism to better process time series features and feature weights, resulting in superior prediction outcomes.

Previous approaches [1] usually focus only on student interactions and lack the extraction of more precise and fine-grained features. There has been minimal mining of MOOC student data, and the absence of deep feature extraction makes accurate prediction of complex patterns difficult. Furthermore, the traditional machine learning models used in earlier works had limited effectiveness [2], as these models did not apply constraints on feature weights, treating each feature equally. This approach hinders the accuracy of predictions [3].

K. Zhang et al. (Eds.): CSEI 2024, CCIS 2448, pp. 78–88, 2025.
https://doi.org/10.1007/978-981-96-3738-6_7

In view of the shortcomings of previous works, our contributions are as follows:

(1) By deeply crawling student data from C programming courses in the MOOC of the Beijing Institute of Technology, we extract and calculate a total of 39 features, which increases the richness of features and covers more aspects and dimensions of features.

(2) We summarize and compare the existing basic methods and compare the model effects on the same data and features, including the random forest method [4], the SVM [5] model, the deep learning MLP model, the gradient boosting tree [6] model, the KNN model [7],

(3) We use a 1D ResNet model with an improved attention mechanism to enhance the prediction of student performance in MOOCs. The ResNet architecture captures **temporal dependencies** in student data, whereas the attention mechanism prioritizes key features, increasing accuracy. Additionally, the **CBAM module** was modified with **absolute max pooling** to better handle standardized data. These innovations allow for more precise academic performance predictions, supporting timely interventions by educators. The method outperforms traditional models such as random forest and SVM in handling high-dimensional, time series data, making it a valuable tool for academic monitoring.

Section 2 provides an overview of previous related work. In Sect. 3, we detail the innovative methods, including dataset descriptions, feature extraction and selection, and the principles underlying our model design. Section 4 presents a comparative analysis of the experimental results, and Sect. 5 concludes with a summary and future outlook.

2 Related Work

2.1 Analysis of MOOC Data

Typically, traditional methods such as machine learning are used to model data from MOOC websites, framing the task as a classification problem to evaluate student performance [8]. For data acquisition and feature extraction, manual modeling is often employed to construct effective features, which are then input into the model for training, fitting, and prediction. Previous works usually optimized the traditional process by focusing on three key aspects: feature selection, feature evaluation, and model design [9, 10]. Experiments were conducted to demonstrate the effectiveness of the proposed method. Building on previous work in MOOC data mining, this study further improves the approach of feature extraction.

2.2 Machine Learning

Mainstream machine learning methods, such as random forest [4], KNN [7], SVM [5], and gradient boosting trees (GBTs) [6], are commonly used for classification and regression tasks. While these methods are effective, they have several limitations. For example, random forest can be computationally expensive with large datasets, SVM may struggle with high-dimensional data, KNN is sensitive to irrelevant features, and GBT can be prone to overfitting and is computationally intensive.

3 Methods

3.1 Data

The dataset used in this study comprises student data from an online course platform called massive open online courses (MOOCs), which were collected throughout 2023. MOOCs serve as an educational tool for coding exercises and assessments, providing a comprehensive record of students' performance and progress, which is a successful implementation of the MOOC format by one of the educational unions. The data have been anonymized, with students referred to by IDs instead of names.

We captured several dimensions of information from the MOOC platform: Programming Topic Information, which includes details about programming exercises, such as topics and submission times. Programming Responses: This records the number of user submissions for each topic and includes information on the programming language used, the amount of code, and other related details. Student interactive behavior information: This covers exam scores for online programming questions and user behavior logs, indicating which modules were accessed, at what times, and the specific actions (clicks or browsing) performed by the user.

3.2 Feature Extraction

From the raw data, we extracted 39 features relevant to our analysis. Below are some of the most representative features:

Average Code Lines: This feature measures the average number of code lines per question submitted by a student, considering only the last submission for each question. It helps assess the complexity of the student's solutions.

Discount percentage: This feature calculates the percentage of submissions made after the discount deadline for each question by comparing the submission time with the specified discount deadline. A higher discount percentage may suggest difficulties in managing time effectively.

Activity Hour Mean: This feature calculates the mean active hours spent by each user on the platform, providing an overview of the students' engagement levels throughout the course.

We extracted features not only from single dimensions but also from correlated features across different dimensions. From the behavior log, we focused on interaction frequency, interaction time, and interaction areas on the website. In the dimension of the programming results, we extracted more fine-grained features, such as the number of programming tasks completed by the user, submission times, and late submissions. Features such as the number of submission passes were derived from students' responses to programming questions. Additionally, we included students' mock test scores, obtained from the online mock test scores table, as a critical reference for our feature set.

3.3 Feature Selection

To identify the most relevant features for predicting student performance, we employed several statistical and machine learning techniques. Specifically, we used Pearson correlation coefficients, mutual information, and feature ablation studies to select the most informative features from the dataset. Each method provides different insights into the relationships between the features and the target variable (student performance).

Pearson correlation coefficients: This method measures the linear dependence between two variables. We computed the Pearson correlation coefficient between each feature and the target variable (final exam score). Features with high absolute correlation values were considered strong predictors.

Mutual Information: This technique quantifies the amount of information obtained about one random variable through observing another. We calculate the mutual information between each feature and the target variable to determine the relevance of each feature.

Feature Ablation Study: In this method, we systematically removed one feature at a time and observed a decrease in prediction accuracy to judge the importance of the feature.

These techniques allowed us to select the most significant features for accurately predicting student performance.

3.4   Our Method

The core components of our approach include a 1D ResNet and a modified attention mechanism. The 1D ResNet model [11] is designed to capture temporal dependencies in the data, whereas the attention mechanism allows the model to focus on the most relevant parts of the input sequence. The full schematic of the model is shown in Fig. 1. This method has proven effective in predicting student performance.

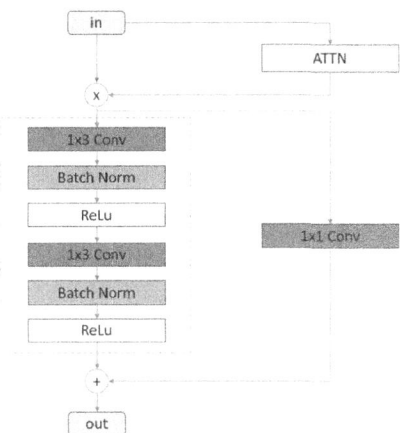

Fig. 1. 1D ResNet model with an **improved attention mechanism**.

Our method adds a residual block before the classic ResNet block. The model can choose to use the original input or add the residual processed by the ATTN module, which is described in detail in the subsequent attention mechanisms section.

ResNet. ResNet evolved from earlier architectures such as AlexNet [12] and VGGNet [13]. Like these models, ResNet [14] employs blocks to build its architecture. The simplified process can be represented by Eq. 1, where F is a generic representation of a function that we explore in detail later.

$$y = x + F(x, \{\mathbf{W}_i\}) \tag{1}$$

where W_i represents the neural network weights, x denotes the feature vector, and where y indicates the output classification. Equation 1 illustrates the principle of residuals.

Inspired by the principles of TextCNN [15], we apply one-dimensional (1D) convolutional networks to our experiment, which can be described as Eq. 2:

$$z = Conv(x) \tag{2}$$

Conv denotes the convolution operation. Applying convolution to the feature vector x produces an intermediate result z.

This approach leverages the power of 1D convolutions to capture local patterns and short-term dependencies within sequences [11]. When dealing with sequential data, the "spatial" dimension of convolution operations transforms into a "temporal" or "sequential" dimension. Sequential convolutions enable the model to detect local patterns and temporal dependencies by applying kernels over contiguous segments of the sequence. Therefore, the modified 1D ResNet architecture can be represented by Eq. 3.

$$y = Conv_n(X_a) + Conv_{1 \times 1}(X_a) \tag{3}$$

where $Conv_{1 \times 1}$ represents the 1D ResNet and where $Conv_n$ represents the convolution operations.

In the equation, X_a is the feature that has been processed through the attention mechanism, and n represents the number of convolutional layers in the model.

Attention Mechanisms. To enhance ResNet's ability to utilize both local and global information, we incorporate attention mechanisms designed to amplify or suppress the weights of certain channels or spatial points, as shown in Fig. 2.

A classical approach for integrating attention mechanisms in convolutional neural networks is the channel and spatial attention module (CBAM) [16], which we have adapted for our purposes.

The channel attention module aims to enable the network to determine which feature channels (filters/channels) are more important, thereby assigning higher weights to them.

However, the original CBAM module is not entirely suitable for our task because of the preprocessing of the input data, which involves standardization to a mean of 0 and a standard deviation of 1. This standardization results in negative values, and using max pooling would discard information about the maximum negative values. Therefore, we propose an adaptation to CBAM by replacing max pooling with absolute max pooling, which retains information about the maximum absolute values. The entire process of CBAM can be represented by Eqs. 4–6. Where X is the feature.

$$X_{CAM} = ChannelAttention(X_{in}) \tag{4}$$

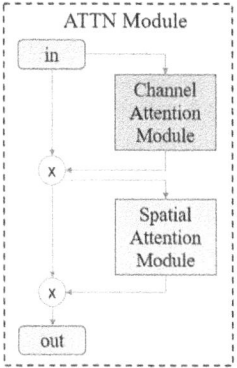

Fig. 2. Illustration of the attention fusion process. The ATTN module consists of two residual blocks connected in series. The channel module provides a channel-level attention matrix, and the spatial attention module provides a pixel-level attention matrix within the channel. The input is partially adjusted here to adjust the importance weights of each element.

$$X_{SAM} = SpatialAttention(X_{CAM}) \tag{5}$$

$$ATTN(X) = X_{in} + X_{CAM} + X_{SAM} \tag{6}$$

The whole attention mechanism includes three parts: X_{in} represents the raw input of the selected features. X_{CAM} represents the channel attention mechanism. X_{SAM} represents the spatial attention mechanism.

In conclusion, the whole process of our method can be seen in Fig. 1, and the formula can be described as Eq. 7:

$$y = Softmax(Conv_n(ATTN(X)) + Conv_{1 \times 1}(ATTN(X))) \tag{7}$$

The main innovations of our experimental method include the following:

1) Applying one-dimensional convolution: We use one-dimensional convolution to process feature information and extract higher-dimensional features.
2) Enhancing Convolution Locality: We improve the locality of the convolution method by incorporating modified attention mechanisms before each convolutional block.
3) Modifying the CBAM method: We adapt the convolutional block attention module (CBAM) by replacing max pooling with absolute max pooling, making it more suitable for our standardized input data.

3.5 Prediction and Evaluation

To evaluate the academic performance of students in the MOOC, we categorized their final grades into three levels on the basis of different score ranges. Specifically, we divided the final exam scores into three categories, as shown in Eq. 8.

$$c(s) = \begin{cases} Low\ Performance & if\ 0 \le s < 60 \\ Moderate\ Performance & if\ 60 \le s < 80 \\ High\ Performance & if\ 80 \le s \le 100 \end{cases} \tag{8}$$

84   L. Xu et al.

By categorizing the scores in this manner, we transform the original continuous outcome into a three-class classification problem. The task can be defined as follows: Given various features X, where $X = [X_1, X_2, \ldots, X_N]$ (with N being the number of features), the goal is to predict class Y, where $Y \in \{0,1,2\}$. We use accuracy, precision, recall, and the F1 score as evaluation metrics to assess how well different features and models predict student performance classification.

4 Experiment

4.1 Feature Analysis

The total score has the strongest positive correlation with the target variable, as it is a component of the final grade. Other features, such as the weighted score, number of scored items, and time rate, also have high correlation coefficients, as shown in Fig. 3. This highlights the effectiveness of the features we have carefully selected.

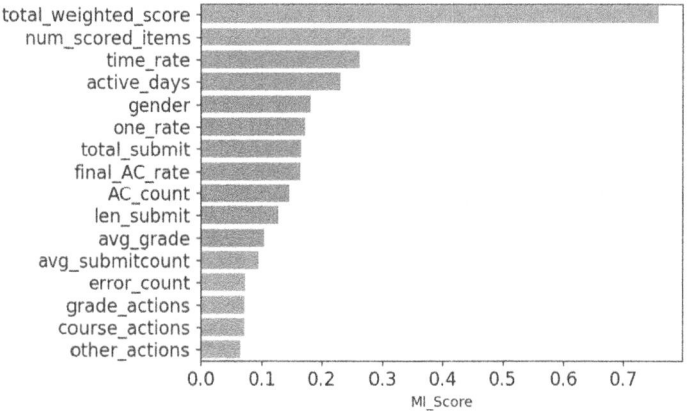

Fig. 3. Pearson correlation coefficients for feature correlation

We also calculate the mutual information score between each feature and the target variable, as shown in Fig. 4. Several areas display high mutual information scores, indicated in red, suggesting a strong relationship with the target variable.

The feature ablation method evaluates the importance of each feature by sequentially removing them and comparing the changes in model performance. The results are shown in Table 1. For brevity, we present only the top ten features by importance. Feature ablation involves training a model with all features and calculating the baseline accuracy. Each feature is subsequently removed one by one, the model is retrained, and the change in accuracy is calculated. The importance of each feature is determined by subtracting the accuracy after feature removal from the baseline accuracy. A greater difference indicates greater importance of the feature.

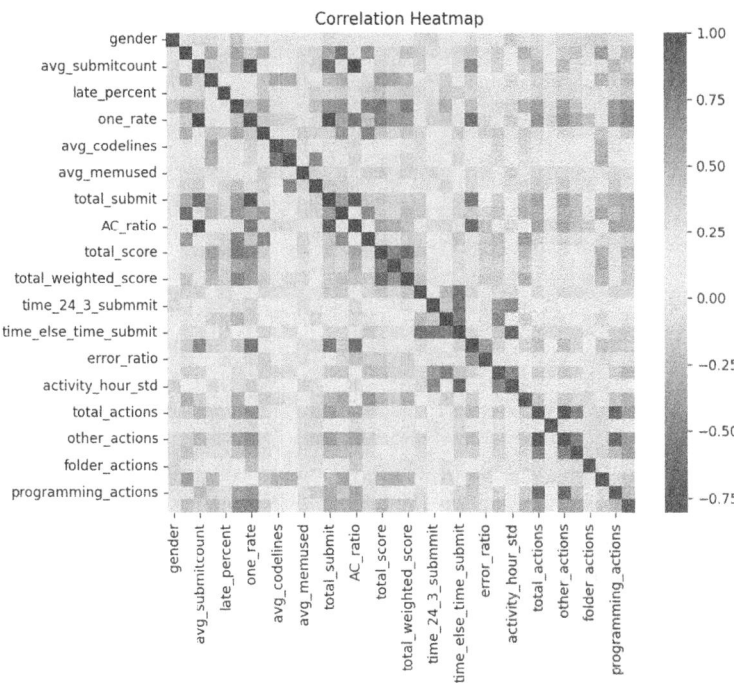

Fig. 4. Mutual Information Scores for Feature Relevance

Table 1. Ablation study of different features

Feature	Importance
total_weighted_score	0.170842
time_rate	0.046862
num_scored_items	0.038838
active_days	0.036350
AC count	0.035589
one_rate	0.030699
avg_grade	0.025789
codesize_ratio	0.018781
len_submit	0.017642
avg_codesize	0.016608

Table 2. Comparison of the results of different models

Model	Accuracy	Precision	Recall	F1-score
Random Forest	0.83	0.80	0.78	0.79
SVM	0.79	0.72	0.70	0.71
KNN	0.79	0.72	0.74	0.73
Gradient Boosting	0.85	**0.82**	0.79	0.80
MLP	0.70	0.63	0.63	0.64
Ours	**0.86**	**0.82**	**0.83**	**0.83**

4.2 Model Comparison

Through our experiments, we can draw the following conclusions. First, the features obtained through manual construction and feature evaluation yielded strong results. Second, the model we used, ResNet with an improved attention mechanism, outperformed the other methods in terms of prediction accuracy.

Our method achieved optimal performance among all the compared methods in terms of accuracy, precision, recall, and F1 score, as shown in Table 2. Specifically, our model improved the accuracy by 3.61% compared with random forest, by 8.86% compared with SVM and KNN, by 1.18% compared with gradient boosting, and by 22.86% compared with MLP. The precision of the proposed method was 2.50% greater than that of random forest, 13.89% greater than that of SVM and KNN, and 30.16% greater than that of MLP. The precision was the same as that of gradient boosting. For the recall, our model improved the recall by 6.41% compared with random forest, by 18.57% compared with SVM, by 12.16% compared with KNN, by 5.06% compared with gradient boosting, and by 31.75% compared with MLP. Finally, with respect to the F1 score, our model improved the F1 score by 3.80% compared with the random forest model, by 15.49% compared with the SVM model, by 12.33% compared with the KNN model, by 2.50% compared with the gradient boosting model, and by 28.13% compared with the MLP model.

4.3 Ablation Analysis

To demonstrate the validity of each component of the model, we designed ablation experiments, and the results are presented in Table 3. The specific steps of our ablation experiments are as follows: First, we divide the model into three components: ResNet, feature selection, and the attention mechanism. We then combined these components in various ways to observe their impact on the final model performance, using the precision, recall, and F1 score as the evaluation metrics.

Table 3. Comparison of different improvements

Components	Precision	Recall	F1-score
1D ResNet	0.75	0.69	0.72
Improved Attention + 1D ResNet	**0.84**	0.75	0.79
Feature Selection + ResNet	0.82	0.79	0.81
Feature Selection + Improved Attention + ResNet	0.82	**0.83**	**0.83**

From the experimental data, we reached the following conclusions:

The data's contribution to model improvement is paramount. Using 1D ResNet alone did not significantly enhance the model's performance. Among the different 1D ResNet variations, feature selection had a more substantial impact on improving the model by streamlining the data than adding the improved attention mechanism. Above all, the elaborated attention mechanism proved extraordinarily effective for this task. After incorporating the improved attention mechanism, the model's performance increased significantly. This improvement occurs because each feature requires global mutual attention, whereas ResNet, which is a convolutional network, can extract only local features.

ResNet can use convolutional networks to capture multiscale feature information, and the attention mechanism can flexibly adjust the model's attention weights and filter out unnecessary noise. Our method combines these two network structures and uses shortcuts to ensure that the two structures promote each other. In addition, we delete collinear features and features with low importance, reducing the risk of model overfitting and improving the generalization ability of the model.

In conclusion, the improved attention mechanism significantly enhances the model's performance by providing the necessary global feature interaction that ResNet alone cannot achieve.

5   Conclusions

In this paper, we focus primarily on feature extraction from MOOC student data, resulting in a total of 39 features. These features were designed from multiple perspectives, including the time dimension, sleep dimension, and problem habit dimension. We enhanced the ResNet model by incorporating sequence convolution and an improved attention mechanism. Consequently, our improved model outperforms several other traditional algorithms.

We hope that this work can assist students by providing study reminders and warnings. Additionally, it aims to help teachers predict student grades more accurately, thereby reducing the administrative burden.

Acknowledgment. This research was supported by the China University-Industry Innovation Fund under the project "Research on the Prediction of University Students' Learning Outcomes Based on Behavioral Models," Project No. 2023 IT 007. We would like to express our sincere gratitude to the Beijing Institute of Technology and the Ministry of Education Higher Education Institutions Research Development Center for their support and funding, which made this study possible.

References

1. Jiang, Z.: Analysisand prediction of learning behavior based on MOOC data. J. Comput. Res. Develop. **52**(3), 1–10 (2015)
2. Chen, X.: Design and research of MOOC teaching system based on TG-C4.5 algorithm. Syst. Soft Comput. **5**(20064), 1–10 (2023)
3. Ma, W., Zhao, Y.: Cascaded knowledge-level fusion network for online course recommendation system. IEEE Trans. Big Data **10**(4), 1–15 (2024)
4. Leo, B.: Random forests. Machine Learning (2001)
5. Vapnik, V., Chervonenkis, A.: The support vector method. In: Statistical Learning Theory, Springer (1995)
6. Jerome, H., Friedman, F.: Greedy function approximation: a gradient boosting machine. Ann. Statist. **29**(5), 1189–1232 (2001)
7. Taunk, K., De, S., Verma, S., Swetapadma, A.: A brief review of nearest neighbor algorithm for learning and classification. In: 2019 International Conference on Intelligent Computing and Control Systems (ICCS), pp. 1255–1260. Madurai, India (2019)
8. Conijn, R., Van den Beemt, A., Cuijpers, P.: Predicting student performance in a blended MOOC. J. Comput. Assist. Learn. **34**(5), 615–628 (2018)
9. Xu, B., Yang, D.: Motivation classification and grade prediction for MOOCs learners. Comput. Intell. Neurosci. **2016**, 1–7 (2016)
10. Nen-Fu, H., I-Hsien, H.: The clustering analysis system based on students motivation and learning behavior. Learn. MOOCS (LWMOOCS) **2018**, 117–119 (2018)
11. He, F., Liu, T., Tao, D.F.: Why resnet works? residuals generalize. IEEE Trans. Neural Networks Learn. Syst. **31**(12), 5349–5362 (2020)
12. Krizhevsky, A., Sutskever, I., Hinton, G.E.: ImageNet classification with deep convolutional neural networks. Commun ACM **60** 6, 84–90 (2017)
13. Simonyan, K., Zisserman, A.: Very deep convolutional networks for large-scale image recognition. Comput. Sci. **2014**, 1–20 (2014)
14. He, K., et al.: Deep residual learning for image recognition. IEEE (2016)
15. Kim, Y.: Convolutional neural networks for sentence classification (2014)
16. Woo, S., Park, J., Lee, J.Y., et al.: Cbam: convolutional block attention module. In: Proceedings of the European Conference on Computer Vision (ECCV), pp. 3–19 (2018)

Methods for Mining the Multiple Intelligences and Character Strengths of College Students via a Fusion Model

Yunfan Fan, Zhengzhou Zhu$^{(\boxtimes)}$, Ziru Fang, and Zichang Yang

School of Software and Microelectronics, Peking University, Beijing, China
zzzmad@163.com

Abstract. The traditional education model focuses on students' test-taking abilities, resulting in students lacking the innovation, internal drive, and qualities required of 'new talents', and not meeting the standards of "new talents". In view of the problem, this paper proposes a method based on students' multiple intelligences and character strengths. The multiple intelligence and character strengths mining algorithm based on the fusion model uses the bagging integrated learning method to fuse the three distributed large language models of ChatGLM-6B, ChatGLM2-6B, and Qwen-7B, and proposes mining students' multiple intelligences and character strengths.

Keywords: Fusion model · large language model · multiple intelligences · character strengths · fine-tuning

1 Introduction

Since China entered the new era of digital education, the drawbacks of traditional exam-oriented education have gradually emerged. Most students trained in exam-oriented education lack internal drive and innovation ability. They are unclear about their own interests and hobbies and do not have outstanding talents and specialties [1].

In September 2023, the general secretary of the Central Committee Xi Jinping proposed the innovative concept of "new quality productive forces" for the first time during his visit to Heilongjiang and noted: "We will integrate scientific and technological innovation resources, lead the development of strategic emerging industries and future industries, and accelerate the formation of new quality productivity [2]". In the formation of new quality productive forces, humans are the most active and vital subjects, playing a decisive role. Without significant improvements in human capital, new quality productivity is out of the question. Therefore, new quality talents are the key factors driving the generation of new quality productive forces [3]. The cultivation of new quality talent should be based on tapping potential and expanding abilities [4]. Only by first discovering students' talents and strengths can we further develop them in a targeted manner. To tap into students' talents and strengths, scientific measurement indicators and effective mining methods are essential.

Multiple intelligences theory [5] was first proposed by Howard Gardner, a famous American educational psychologist, in his book The Structure of Intelligence in 1983. This theory suggests that intellectual talent may exist in areas beyond typical intellectual domains. Intelligence is not limited to traditional language and logical mathematical abilities, but also includes various intelligences such as visual/spatial intelligence, physical movement intelligence, music/rhythm intelligence, and interpersonal intelligence.

Personality strength belongs to the research category of positive psychology. Positive psychology belongs to the positive aspect of personality trait research, which mainly focuses on positive traits in humans, such as talent, aptitude, and personality strength. In 2004, Seligman and Peterson [6] made their first attempt to identify and classify positive psychological traits in humans, identified six types of virtues (i.e. "core virtues") and constructed 24 measurable personality strengths.

With the development of artificial intelligence, natural language processing has entered the era of large language models. The emergence of the large language model represented by ChatGPT has greatly changed the landscape of the education field [7, 8] and brought new possibilities for solving the above problems. To date, there have been attempts to apply the large language model to the field of education, yielding positive outcomes [9]. On the basis of the research background of this field, this paper presents a method grounded in students' multiple intelligences and character strengths.

2   Overseas and Domestic Research Status

2.1   Current Research Status in the Field of Multiple Intelligences

In China and abroad, the research methods used in the field of multiple intelligence include testing scales, expert systems, educational data mining techniques, and machine learning methods. The specific situation is shown in Table 1.

In 1987, the famous developmental psychologist Dr. Branton Shearer developed the Multiple Intelligence Development Assessment Scale (MIDAS) [10], which is used to comprehensively evaluate an individual's intellectual performance and career development potential. In addition, with the popularization of the theory of multiple intelligences in China, some scholars have developed corresponding test scales according to the characteristics of different populations. Wu Wudian et al. developed the Chinese version of the multiple intelligences developmental assessment scales (CMIDAS) [11] system. Sun Qingjun and other researchers from the Multiple Intelligence Research Group at Peking University have elaborately developed a set of multiple intelligence situational assessment scales for children aged 3 to 7 years [12].

Ashraf Alam [13] proposed that educational data mining (EDM) techniques can be used to analyze data on students' interactions with learning materials, such as quizzes, homework, and exams. By analyzing these data, teachers can identify patterns related to the strengths and weaknesses of students with different types of intelligence.

T Kaewkiriya et al. [14] designed a rule base for electronic learning and learning profile recommendation based on multiple intelligences, and compared the performance of various machine learning algorithms (such as ID3, C4.5, NBTree, and naive Bayes.) to select the rule base. Mankad et al. [15] proposed a novel genetic-fuzzy approach to measure and classify students' multiple intelligences. This method combines genetic

Table 1. Main Research Methods for Multiple Intelligence Mines

Main Author	Research Method	Representative Model/Outcome
Branton Shearer	testing scales	MIDAS
Wu Wudian et al	testing scales	CMIDAS
Sun Qingjun et al	testing scales	Multiple Intelligence Situational Assessment Scale
Ashraf Alam et al	educational data mining techniques	/
T Kaewkiriya et al	machine learning	ID3, C4.5, C4.5, NBTree
Mankad et al	machine learning	Genetic-Fuzzy Approach
Fareeha Rasheed et al	machine learning	Support Vector Machine, Random Forest, Decision Tree, Logistic Regression, Naive Bayes
Mankad et al	expert systems	A Fuzzy Expert System
Wulansari R E et al	expert systems	Expert System Based on Howard Gardner's Multiple Intelligence Theory
Fan Fokloung et al	expert systems	Multi Intelligent Expert System Based on Forward Chain Method

algorithms and fuzzy logic to adapt to individual differences among students and provide personalized support for their education and learning. Fareeha Rasheed et al. [16] Various machine learning methods (support vector machine, K-nearest neighbor, decision tree, logistic regression, random forest, linear discriminant analysis, naive Bayes) have been used to predict learning styles on the basis of multiple intelligence theory, and the results revealed that the best performing algorithm among the many machine learning algorithms is the support vector machine, with an accuracy of 75.55%. Asiqur Rahaman [17] proposed the use of NLP and multiple intelligence theory (MI) to enhance the psychological aspects of language education.

Mankad et al. [18] proposed a design of a fuzzy expert system for classifying candidates' multiple intelligences to identify their job performance. Wulansari R E et al. [19] proposed an expert system based on Howard Gardner's theory of multiple intelligences to help students identify their potential and abilities, so that they can make the right choices in the early stages of their careers. The authors also compared expert systems with human experts, emphasizing the strengths of expert systems. Fan Fokloung and Rizki Hardian Sakti [20] designed a multiagent expert system based on the forward chain method to help students identify their potential and abilities, so that they can make wise choices when choosing university majors.

2.2   Current Status of Personality Advantage Research

At present, there are few studies on the mining of personality strengths, most of which focus on the mining of personality traits. Because personality strengths are also personality traits, the following introduces research on personality traits in China and abroad. As shown in Table 2, research on personality trait mining in China and abroad has used methods such as machine learning and deep learning.

Table 2. Main Research Methods for Personality Trait Mining

Main Author	Research Method	Representative Model/Outcome
Cahyani and Faishal	machine learning	Support Vector Machine and Polynomial Naive Bayes
Karanatsiou D et al	machine learning	Regression models (Linear, Support Vector, Gaussian, Random Forest, etc.)
Zuriani Mustaffa et al	machine learning	Artificial Neural Network (ANN)
T.S. Kanchana et al	machine learning	Sentiment A nalysis
Dutta et al	machine learning	Semi Supervised Deep Embedded Clustering (Semi Supervised DEC)
Asad Khattak et al	deep learning	BiLSTM Model
Ilmini W et al	deep learning	Convolutional Neural Network (CNN) And Recursive Neural Network (RNN)
Zhao Jinghua et al	deep learning	Attention Based Neural Network Model
Mehta Y et al	deep learning	BERT, Albert, and Roberta
Ren Z et al	deep learning	BERT
Ahmad H et al	deep learning	CNN and LSTM Hybrid Model
Ramezani M et al	deep learning	CNN, RNN, LSTM, and BILSTM

In Terms of Machine Learning. Cahyani and Faishal [21] used SVM and multinomial naive Bayes (MNB) to analyze Twitter data for Big Five personality trait classification. Karanatsiou D et al. [22] used regression models (linear, support vector, Gaussian, random forest, etc.) from machine learning methods to extract features and predict individual personality traits. The experimental results indicate that the random forest regression model performs better in predicting most personality traits among these methods. Zuriani Mustaffa et al. [23] proposed a personality prediction model based on artificial neural networks (ANNs) and compared three algorithms: naive Bayes, ZeroR, and random forest. The results showed that the prediction accuracy of artificial neural networks is higher than that of the other three algorithms. T.S. Kanchana et al. [24] We started with social media comments; analyzed the emotions in comments through NLP, NLTK, and LSTM; and predicted users' personality traits on the basis of these emotions, with an accuracy rate of up to 92%. Dutta et al. [25] effectively extracted personality features and simultaneously learned feature representations and cluster assignments, by using semisupervised deep embedded clustering (referred to as semisupervised DEC) model, which showed excellent performance on the Kaggle personality dataset, with an accuracy rate of up to 95.90%, providing a new and effective approach for personality feature analysis.

In Terms of Deep Learning. Asad Khattak et al. [26] used the BiLSTM model to explore users' personality traits in depth. In addition, they compared various machine learning models and various deep learning models to validate model performance. The final experimental results showed that the efficiency of the BiLSTM model was improved compared with that of the other models, achieving better results in accuracy, recall, F-measure, and precision. Ilmini W et al. [27] used the CVPR'17 dataset in their study and successfully constructed a personality detection model by combining convolutional neural networks (CNNs) and recurrent neural networks (RNNs). In addition, they also utilized CAM visualization technology to enhance the interpretability and visualization effect of the model. After training deep learning models on the VGG19 and ResNet152 architectures, they used the CAM XAI method to analyze the model results. Zhao Jinghua et al. [28] used Big Five personality trait theory and an attention based neural network model to predict the personality traits of Facebook social network users, achieving better results than currently popular methods do. Mehta Y et al. [29] included BERT, Albert, and Roberta in the fields of personality prediction and traditional psycholinguistic feature research. Ren Z et al. [30] noted that current deep learning based methods lack analysis of emotional information and psycholinguistic features and ignore information about context and polysemy. Therefore, they used transformer (BERT) bidirectional encoder for semantic extraction and a sentiment lexicon for sentiment analysis, and then combined it with a neural network for personality detection. Compared with the most advanced technology, their method improved the average accuracy by 6.91% and 6.04% on the Myers Briggs Type Indicator (MBTI) and Big Five datasets, respectively. Ahmad H et al. [31] proposed a hybrid model of a CNN and LSTM for MBTI personality detection. Kosan M A et al. [32] used semantic structures and LSTM based neural networks to predict personality traits on the basis of a personality dataset retrieved from Twitter. Ramezani M et al. [33] created a knowledge network for automatic personality prediction in their study. This chart was created via DBpedia ontology, the NRC Emotion Intensity Dictionary, and the MRC psycholinguistic database on the basis of input text. Afterwards, they used the generated embedding matrix as input for four DL models (CNN, RNN, LSTM, and BILSTM) to predict personality, and the experimental results revealed that the accuracy of all classifiers improved.

Currently, research on the exploration of character strengths is limited, with most studies concentrating on the analysis of personality traits. To address this issue, this paper introduces a method centered on students' multiple intelligences and character strengths.

3   Experimental Data

3.1   Research Object

This study selected 95 undergraduate students who took software engineering courses at a certain college at Peking University as the research sample; and collected interaction data between students and the big model through a questionnaire survey, as well as the results of students answering psychological test scales. The psychological tests that students answer are divided into the Multiple Intelligence Test Scale and the VIA Personality Strength Test Scale.

3.2   Data Cleaning

For the classification datasets of multiple intelligences and character strengths, two data sources are involved, namely the interaction data between students and large models, and the data from student educational psychology test scales. Before creating the dataset, it is necessary to clean the data collected from these two scales separately, removing any data that do not meet the requirements, such as meaningless characters, garbled characters, and empty data.

The dataset was created by selecting 50 dialog entries for each student. If the experimental data were insufficient (fewer than 50 entries), all available dialog data provided by the student were used instead of being artificially supplemented it. The specific processing methods are shown in Table 3.

Table 3. Cleaning Methods for Multi Intelligence and Personality Advantage Classification Datasets

Data Type	Exception Type	Explanation	Handling Method
Interaction Data Between Students And Large Models	Meaningless Data	The students' questions contain meaningless characters, garbled code	Delete this data item
Interaction Data Between Students And Large Models	Empty Data	The student's question is either empty or contains multiple spaces	Delete this data item
Interaction Data Between Students And Large Models	Insufficient Data	The interaction data between students and the large model is less than 50 pieces	Delete this data item
Student Test Scale Data	Meaningless Data	All answers to the questions on the student test scale are the same	Delete this data item
Student Test Scale Data	Empty Data	There are unanswered questions in the student test scale	Delete this data item

3.3 Dataset Format

For the convenience of conducting experiments, this paper cleaned and organized the collected experimental data into a dataset. When a dataset is created in the format of {"id": id, "name": name, "question": question, "intelligence": intelligence, "character": character}. Where ID is the student ID, name is the student's name, question is the student's question content during the conversation with the big model, intelligence is the student's highest scoring multiple intelligence test scale, and character is the student's highest scoring personality advantage in the VIA personality strength test scale.

3.4 Label Distribution Situation

Statistically analysis of the label distribution of the dataset helps to understand the distribution of multiple intelligences and character strengths in the experimental population. This paper conducted a statistical analysis of the multiple intelligence and personality advantage labels of students in the collected experimental data, and the distribution of the labels obtained is shown in Figs. 1 and 2.

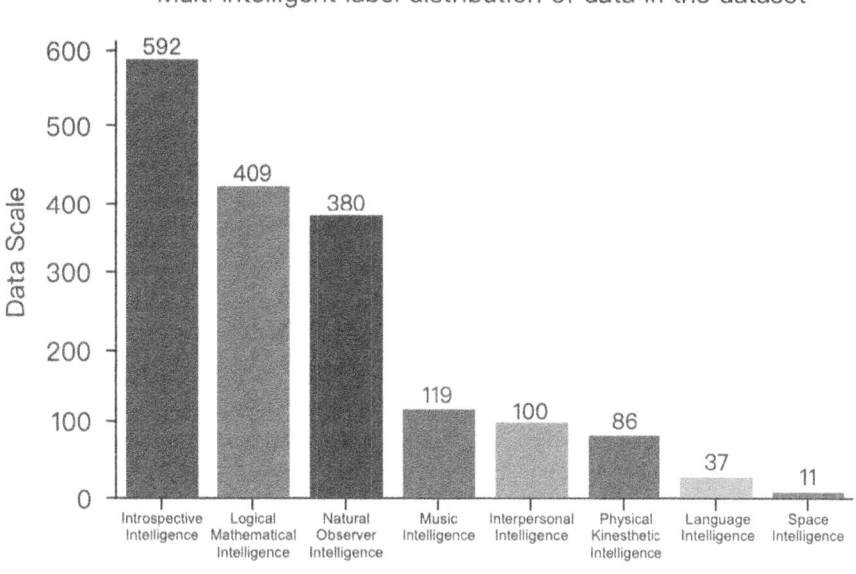

Fig. 1. Distribution of Multiple Intelligence Labels

From the distribution of labels, it can be seen that in the experimental population, introspective, logical mathematical, and natural observer intelligences are relatively prominent in terms of multiple intelligences; In terms of character strengths, humor, appreciation of beauty, and integrity are relatively prominent.

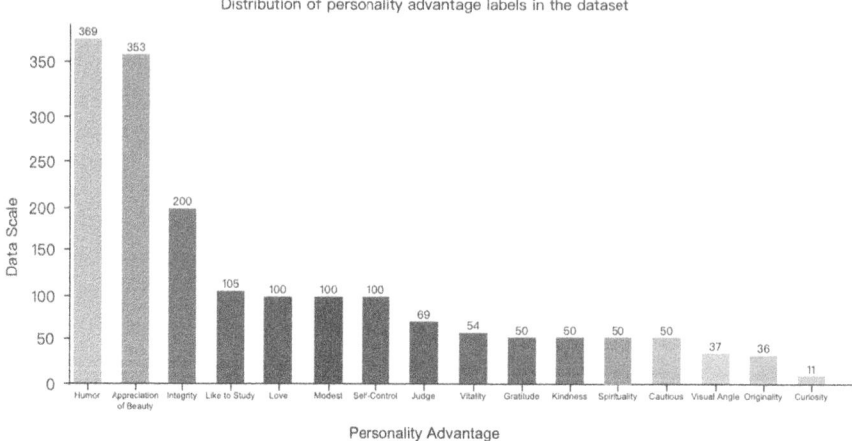

Fig. 2. Distribution of Personality Advantage Labels

4   Fusion Model Design

From the perspective of cultivating talent, it is crucial to accurately tap into students' multiple intelligence and character advantages. As shown in Fig. 3, the fusion model proposed in this paper integrates multiple fine tuned large language models and uses weighted voting to integrate the abilities of each model, to explore students' multiple intelligence and character strengths.

Next, this section introduces the design motivation and principles of the fusion model and the components of the fusion model: the fine-tuning model module, the weight calculation module, the weighted voting module, and the final effect achieved by the fusion model.

4.1   Motivation and Principles for Designing Fusion Models

In the field of education, the importance of personalized learning is increasingly prominent, and the core of achieving personalized learning lies in accurately grasping individual differences among students. The multiple intelligences and character strengths of students are important components of individual differences, but traditional educational assessment methods often struggle to explore this information comprehensively and deeply. With the development of artificial intelligence technology, especially the emergence of large language models, new tools and methods have been provided for personalized education. However, a single model often has limitations, such as data deviation and insufficient generalization ability. Therefore, this paper proposes the design of a fusion model, which aims to improve the accuracy and reliability of mining by integrating multiple models and integrating their respective advantages.

4.2   Fine Tuning Model Module Design

The fine-tuning model module adopts the bagging ensemble learning strategy, which is a commonly used ensemble learning method that improves overall performance by

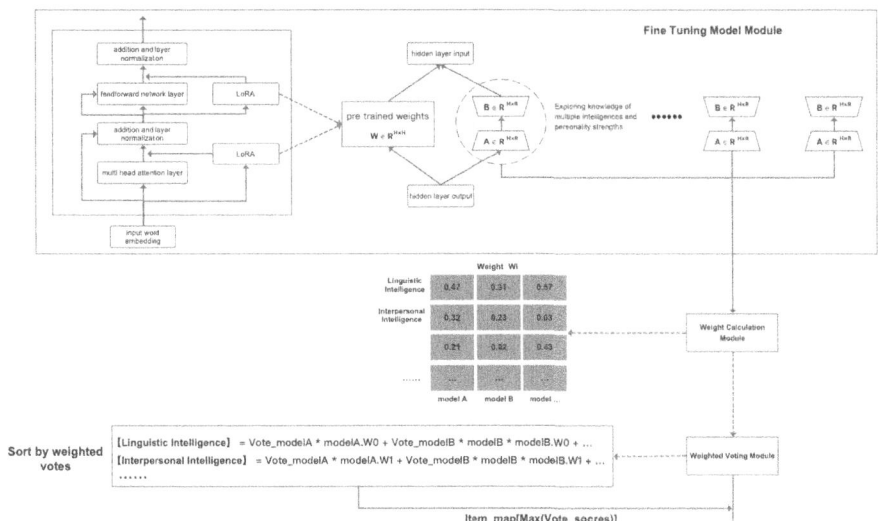

Fig. 3. Fusion Model Design

constructing multiple base models and integrating their results. This paper selects three representative large language models: ChatGLM-6B, ChatGLM2-6B, and Qwen-7B. These models use different datasets and training strategies in the pretraining stage, so they have their own strengths in mining multiple intelligences and character strengths. Through the bagging method, the model is fine-tuned by randomly selecting different subsets from the interaction data between students and large models, and each model is trained on its specific subset of data to learn features and patterns related to that subset.

4.3   Design of the Weight Calculation Module

In the fusion model, weight allocation is a crucial step that determines the contribution of each base model to the final result. This paper assigns weights to each model on the basis of its performance on the validation set, specifically, the prediction accuracy of each model for different categories of multiple intelligences and character strengths is used as weights. This design takes into account the professionalism and accuracy of the model in specific domains, allowing the fusion model to be more focused on the areas of strength of each model.

The weighted voting mechanism is the core of the fusion model decision-making process. In this mechanism, the prediction results of each base model are weighted on the basis of their weights, and the final output is determined by comparing the weighted votes. This process is similar to democratic voting, but introduces the concept of weights to ensure that more accurate models have a greater impact on the results. This mechanism not only improves the robustness of the model, but also enables the fusion model to better adapt to different data distributions and student characteristics.

4.4 Design of the Weighted Voting Module

The weighted voting module is the last step before the output of the fusion model, and the final prediction result of the fusion model is calculated by this module. This module will vote on weighted options predicted by the model according to the weight calculated by the weight calculation module, and then sort them to select the result with the highest number of votes as the final result. For example, suppose that the current fusion model consists of models A, B, and C, which are ChatGLM-6B, ChatGLM2-6B, and Qwen-7B, respectively. For input, if Model A predicts language intelligence, model B predicts interpersonal intelligence, and Model C predicts language intelligence, then the only options for integrating the Model are language intelligence and interpersonal intelligence, where the number of votes for language intelligence is 1 * Model A.W0 + 1 * ModelC.W0, and the vote of interpersonal intelligence is 1 * Model B.W1. The votes for these two options are compared, and the option with the highest number of votes is selected as the final output result.

4.5 The Mining Effect of the Fusion Model

To verify the mining performance of the fusion model proposed in this paper, the mining performance of traditional machine learning methods and a single large model is compared in two dimensions—single data and multiple data—on the validation set (20% of the total dataset).

It is very difficult to mine students' multiple intelligences and character strengths solely through a single piece of data, and the accuracy and reliability are not high; however it greatly tests the model's ability. The mining results obtained from the experiment are shown in Tables 4 and 5.

Table 4. Evaluation Results of Multiple Intelligence Mining Tasks (Single Data)

Model	Accuracy	Precision	Recall	F1 Score
Fusion Model	0.5677	0.4233	0.6282	0.4739
Qwen-7B	0.5418	0.4669	0.329	0.3644
ChatGLM-6B	0.5476	0.4288	0.399	0.4086
ChatGLM2-6B	0.5159	0.6068	0.3046	0.3443
Logistic Regression	0.3948	0.2400	0.1417	0.1008
Stochastic Gradient Descent	0.4006	0.2556	0.1671	0.1413
Naive Bayes	0.4063	0.2415	0.1479	0.1116
Support Vector	0.4063	0.2772	0.1686	0.1419
Random Forest	0.1268	0.3493	0.1656	0.0937
K-NN	0.3804	0.3383	0.1530	0.1128

Table 5. Evaluation Results of Personality Advantage Mining Task (Single Data)

Model	Accuracy	Precision	Recall	F1 Score
Fusion Model	0.5360	0.4553	0.5736	0.4843
Qwen-7B	0.5274	0.5596	0.4658	0.496
ChatGLM-6B	0.4438	0.4122	0.376	0.3588
ChatGLM2-6B	0.4524	0.3693	0.3097	0.3179
Logistic Regression	0.2421	0.1377	0.0866	0.0581
Stochastic Gradient Descent	0.2594	0.4242	0.1306	0.1360
Naive Bayes	0.2392	0.0855	0.0788	0.0465
Support Vector	0.2565	0.3366	0.1192	0.1126
Random Forest	0.1124	0.3663	0.1094	0.0908
K-NN	0.2277	0.2384	0.0994	0.0836

The evaluation results in Tables 4 and 5, indicate that the accuracy, recall, F1 score and other indicators of the proposed fusion model are far higher than those of the traditional machine learning method, and it is also better than those of a single large model, but slightly lower than those of individual single models.

Compared with the use of a single piece of data, the use of multiple dialog data from the same student for predicting multiple intelligences and character strengths has greater accuracy and reliability, and is also a popular prediction method at present. The mining results obtained by the experiment are shown in Tables 6 and 7.

Table 6. Evaluation Results of Multiple Intelligence Mining Tasks (Multiple Data)

Model	Accuracy	Precision	Recall	F1 Score
Fusion Model	0.775	0.6589	0.5927	0.6051
Qwen-7B	0.75	0.5955	0.5146	0.5361
ChatGLM-6B	0.75	0.6156	0.5831	0.5835
ChatGLM2-6B	0.725	0.4734	0.5115	0.4902
Logistic Regression	0.3333	0.0417	0.125	0.0625
Stochastic Gradient Descent	0.359	0.1678	0.1389	0.0887
Naive Bayes	0.359	0.1678	0.1389	0.0887
Support Vector	0.359	0.1678	0.1389	0.0887
Random Forest	0.0513	0.0066	0.125	0.0125
K-NN	0.3333	0.0417	0.125	0.0625

Table 7. Evaluation Results of Personality Advantage Mining Task (Multiple Data)

Model	Accuracy	Precision	Recall	F1 Score
Fusion Model	0.7105	0.7665	0.6406	0.6596
Qwen-7B	0.6842	0.716	0.6094	0.6175
ChatGLM-6B	0.6316	0.4835	0.5234	0.4677
ChatGLM2-6B	0.4474	0.334	0.3047	0.2945
Logistic Regression	0.2308	0.0757	0.0703	0.0356
Stochastic Gradient Descent	0.2564	0.1385	0.1016	0.0778
Naive Bayes	0.2308	0.0757	0.0703	0.0356
Support Vector	0.2308	0.0757	0.0703	0.0356
Random Forest	0.0513	0.0032	0.0625	0.0061
K-NN	0.2051	0.0132	0.0625	0.0217

The above evaluation results, indicate that, compared with mining students' multiple intelligence and character strengths through a single piece of data, mining through multiple pieces of data significantly improves the accuracy, precision, recall, and F1 score. Moreover, compared with traditional machine learning methods and single large models, the fusion model proposed in this paper achieves the highest scores in various dimensions of the evaluation metrics.

5   Conclusion

To solve the problem that the traditional mining algorithm is not ideal for the mining of students' talents and talents, this paper proposes a multi-intelligence and character advantage mining method based on a fusion model from the perspective of students' multiple intelligence and character advantages. This method can be used to mine students' multiple intelligence and character advantages from the dialog between students and large models, and can help educators carry out more accurate and personalized training for students. The experimental results show that compared with traditional machine learning methods and single models, the fusion model proposed in this paper has significant advantages in exploiting students' multiple intelligence and personality advantages. Future work will further explore the application of the fusion model in different educational scenarios, such as learning interventions, career guidance, and cross-cultural education, while continuing to optimize the performance and interpretability of the model to better serve the development of personalized education.

Acknowledgement. This paper is supported by the Humanities and Social Sciences Research Planning Fund Project of the Ministry of Education: "Research on Metacognitive Diagnosis Theory and Technology Driven by Multimodal Learning Data" (23YJA8800091) and The Fundamental Research Funds for the Central Universities. Additionally, we would like to acknowledge the Undergraduate Teaching Reform Project of Peking University in 2024: "Gamified Interactive Experimental Teaching in Softwaree Engineering" (Project No. 7100903145).

References

1. Hu, M., Jing, X.: When the most 'painful' generation enters university. China Sci. Daily (2024)
2. Xi, J.: Firmly grasp the important mission of Northeast China and strive to write a new chapter in the comprehensive revitalization of Northeast China. Construction of old areas in China (2023)
3. Zhu, K.: New quality productivity: the core driving force for promoting new industrialization. Prosecution Storm (2023)
4. Zhu, Z., Dai, L., Zhao, X., Shen, S.: Cultivation of new quality talents: the new mission of education in the digital age. Research on Electronic Education (2024)
5. Gardner, H.E.: Frames of mind: The theory of multiple intelligences. Basic books (2011)
6. Peterson, C., Seligman, M.E.: Character strengths and virtues: a handbook and classification, vol. 1. Oxford university press (2004)
7. Milano, S., Mcgrane, J.A., Leonelli, S.: Large language models challenge the future of higher education. Nature Machine Intelligence (2023)
8. Jeon, J., Lee, S.: Large language models in education: A focus on the complementary relationship between human teachers and ChatGPT. Education and Information Technologies (2023)
9. Zhang, C., Du, L., Zhu, X., Zhao, H.: Research on educational question answering system based on large language model. J. Beijing Univ. Posts Telecommun. (Social Sciences Edition) (2023)
10. Shearer, C.B.: The theory of multiple intelligences, career development and the midas assessment (2011)
11. Wu, W.: Case Analysis and Application of the Multiple Intelligence Scale (CMIDAS). Summary of Papers from the National Conference on Education and Psychological Statistics and Measurement and the 8th Cross Strait Symposium on Psychology and Educational Testing (2008)
12. Sun, Q.: Development of a situational assessment scale for children's multiple intelligences. QUN WEN TIAN DI (2012)
13. Alam, A.: Improving learning outcomes through predictive analytics: enhancing teaching and learning with educational data mining. In: 2023 7th International Conference on Intelligent Computing and Control Systems (ICICCS) (2023)
14. Kaewkiriya, T., Utakrit, N., Tiantong, M.: The design of a rule base for an e-learning recommendation system base on multiple intelligences. Int. J. Inform. Educ. Technol. (2016)
15. Mankad, K., Sajja, P.S., Akerkar, R.: An automatic evolution of rules to identify students' multiple intelligence. In: Advanced Computing: First International Conference on Computer Science and Information Technology, CCSIT 2011, Bangalore, India (2011)
16. Rasheed, F., Wahid, A.: Learning style detection in E-learning systems using machine learning techniques. Expert Syst. Appl. (2021)
17. Rahaman, A.: Empowering language learning: NLP, MI, and Desuggestopedia Strategies for the 21st Century. Vidhyayana-An International Multidisciplinary Peer-Reviewed E-Journal-ISSN 2454-8596 (2024)
18. Mankad, K.B., Sajja, P.S.: A GFA driven framework for classification of multiple intelligence. In: Proceedings of the World Congress on Engineering and Computer Science, vol. 1 (2011)
19. Wulansari, R.E., Sakti, R., Ambiyar, A., et al.: Expert system for career early determination based on Howard Gardner's multiple intelligence. J. Appl. Eng. Technol. Sci. (2022)
20. Folkourng, F., Sakti, R.H.: The design of expert system to determine the university majoring based on multiple intelligence using forward chaining method. J. Eng. Res. Lect. (2022)

21. Cahyani, D.E., Faishal, A.F.: Classification of big five personality behavior tendencies based on study field with twitter analysis using support vector machine. In: 2020 7th International Conference on Information Technology, Computer, and Electrical Engineering (ICITACEE) (2020)
22. Karanatsiou, D., Sermpezis, P., Gruda, D., et al.: My tweets bring all the traits to the yard: Predicting personality and relational traits in Online Social Networks. ACM Trans. Web (2022)
23. Mustaffa, Z., Zaidi, N.A.S.M., Ernawan, F., et al.: Personality predictive analysis based on artificial neural network. In: 2022 6th International Conference on Informatics and Computational Sciences (ICICoS) (2022)
24. Kanchana, T., Zoraida, B.S.E.: A framework for automated personality prediction from social media tweets. In: 2022 IEEE World Conference on Applied Intelligence and Computing (AIC) (2022)
25. Dutta, I., Athilakshmi, R., et al.: Personality prediction using deep learning. In: 2023 Third International Conference on Advances in Electrical, Computing, Communication and Sustainable Technologies (ICAECT) (2023)
26. Khattak, A., Jellani, N., Asghar, M.Z., et al.: Personality classification from text using bidirectional long short-term memory model. Multimedia Tools Appl. (2023)
27. Ilmini, W., Fernando, T.: Explaining the outputs of convolutional neural network-recurrent neural network (CNN-RNN) based apparent personality detection models using the class activation maps. Int. J. Adv. Comput. Sci. Appl. (2023)
28. Zhao, J., Zeng, D., Xiao, Y., et al.: User personality prediction based on topic preference and sentiment analysis using LSTM model. Pattern Recogn. Let. (2020)
29. Mehta, Y., Fatehi, S., Kazameini, A., et al.: Bottom-up and top-down: Predicting personality with psycholinguistic and language model features. In: 2020 IEEE International Conference on Data Mining (ICDM) (2020)
30. Ren, Z., Shen, Q., Diao, X., et al.: A sentiment-aware deep learning approach for personality detection from text. Inform. Process. Manage (2021)
31. Ahmad, H., Asghar, M.U., Asghar, M.Z., et al.: A hybrid deep learning technique for personality trait classification from text. IEEE Access (2021)
32. Kosan, M.A., Karacan, H., Urgen, B.A.: Predicting personality traits with semantic structures and LSTM-based neural networks. Alexandria Eng. J. (2022)
33. Ramezani, M., Feizi-Derakhshi, M.R., Balafar, M.A.: Knowledge graph-enabled text-based automatic personality prediction. Comput. Intell. Neurosci. (2022)

Construction of a Knowledge Graph for State Key Protected Wild Animals Based on the ALBERT Model

KeZhen He[1,2], HaiFeng Wang[1,2(✉)], WenBin Wang[1,2], and He Ning[1,2]

[1] Yazhou Bay Innovation Institute, Hainan Tropical Ocean University, Sanya, China
hfwang@hntou.edu.cn
[2] Hainan Tropical Ocean University, Sanya, China

Abstract. Given that the text paragraphs in the field of wildlife under special state protection are lengthy, the content is fragmented, and the vast majority of the data are unstructured text data. To this end, this paper proposes a knowledge graph construction method for national key protected wildlife based on the lightweight pretrained language model ALBERT, which realizes the construction of the graph while extracting ternary groups from the massive amount of data through a top-down approach. In the self-constructed dataset of wildlife under special state protection, the ALBERT model encodes the features of word vectors, fusing the BiLSTM-CRF and BiLSTM-Attention methods for entity recognition and relation extraction. The experimental results demonstrate that the self-constructed dataset achieves F1 values of 93.72% and 96.04% for entity recognition and relation extraction, respectively. The Neo4j graph database integrates and stores the extracted triples. The constructed knowledge graph can provide an effective information base for subsequent ecological protection research and policy formulation.

Keywords: natural language processing · state key protected wild animals · ALBERT model · named entity recognition · relational extraction

1 Introduction

Biodiversity is essential for establishing a viable and enduring future for the entire planet. China, known for its rich species diversity, has implemented many efforts to support global biodiversity protection [1]. These efforts include the establishment of nature reserves and the classification of wildlife under special state protection. Wildlife, which is under special state protection in China, is categorized into several levels on the basis of the relevant requirements of the Law of the People's Republic of China on the Protection of Wildlife. We prioritize the conservation of valuable and endangered wildlife species through this classification. The List of Wildlife under Special State Protection, released in 2021, represents the first significant revision since its initial release in 1989, significantly enhancing conservation efforts for endangered species and raising public awareness [2].

K. Zhang et al. (Eds.): CSEI 2024, CCIS 2448, pp. 103–115, 2025.
https://doi.org/10.1007/978-981-96-3738-6_9

Massive amounts of data are in the form of unstructured or semistructured data, which contain valuable information that is very difficult to access directly in today's explosive growth of data. How to extract valuable information from unstructured data has become particularly important. In this context, natural language processing (NLP) [3] has emerged as a range of methods and techniques that enable computers to comprehend unstructured text, addressing the human mindset for various tasks. These methods, such as entity recognition and relationship extraction, have become indispensable for accessing structured data from various domains. Additionally, they aid in the construction of subsequent knowledge graphs, laying a solid foundation. Research on NLP encompasses a range of interdisciplinary domains, including fundamental medicine, technical engineering, and earth sciences. However, owing to the characteristics of long text paragraphs, fragmented content, and complex entity features that are difficult to extract in the animal field, little research has been conducted on the use of NLP techniques to obtain structured knowledge and construct knowledge graphs [4].

To address the aforementioned problems, this paper uses a deep learning approach and the Albert pretraining model [5]. It then combines the BiLSTM-CRF and BiLSTM-Attention methods for named entity recognition and relationship extraction [6]. It then uses the trained model to perform ternary extraction on unstructured national key wildlife protection data, with the goal of creating a well-structured knowledge graph of wildlife under special state protection to make the national key protected wildlife data smarter. Compared with existing methods, the main contributions of this study are as follows:

(1) We use a lightweight pretrained language model, ALBERT, for text feature extraction, which not only ensures the accuracy rate but also improves the training speed. We integrate the neural network models BiLSTM-CRF and BiLSTM-Attention.
(2) Simultaneously, named entity recognition and relationship extraction models are trained on data from wildlife under national key protection, and one-step extraction of ternary groups is achieved.
(3) The constructed knowledge graph of wildlife under national key protection covers a wide range, including more than 10,000 entities and 20,000 relationships, which is more comprehensive than those of previous studies.

2 Related Work

In recent years, numerous scholars both domestically and internationally have been delving deeply into the field of natural language, yielding impressive results. These scholars have initiated research utilizing deep learning methods to determine how to extract triples for the purpose of constructing knowledge graphs.

Named Entity Recognition (NER) is the basis for constructing knowledge graphs, which mainly refers to recognizing specific proper nouns from text and classifying them correctly. Collobert [7] et al. used CNN-CRF for feature extraction of sentences, which is an early representative work on NER via neural networks. However, this model does not combine contextual information to train the model, and the phenomenon of multiple meanings of a word may occur. Therefore, Quyang [8] et al. adopted a bidirectional RNN-CRF architecture based on concatenated n-gram representations of characters to obtain considerable contextual information. However, the RNN works well only for short-range dependencies and experiences gradient vanishing or gradient explosion when it is used to address long-range dependencies. The Chinese NER task was performed very well by Yanliang [9] et al., who introduced a hybrid convolutional neural network with a gating filter mechanism to capture local context information and LSTM.

Relationship Extraction (RE) is used to extract the relationship between two entities with the precondition of obtaining entities so that unstructured textual data can be condensed into structured triples. Van-Thuy [10] et al. combined a bidirectional gated recurrent unit model with a piecewise attention mechanism and achieved remote supervised relationship extraction via the bag-level contextual inference method. Graph-state LSTM is a model that Linfeng [11] et al. proposed for a long- and short-term memory network. It uses parallel states to model each word and then refines the state values cyclically through passing messages.

However, natural language processing in the animal domain is limited. Jaskaran [12] et al. used a knowledge-based Intelligent Text Simplification (KITS) approach combined with BioBERT, focusing on the extraction of biological relationships. Lin [13] et al. used the SikuBERT pretraining model to create a named entity recognition model for canonical animals from the point of view of digital humanities. This model is useful for mining knowledge about canonical animals.

3   Data Acquisition and Ontology Construction

Before constructing the knowledge graph, the selection of data sources is crucial and directly affects the accuracy and comprehensiveness of ontology construction and the quality of the final knowledge graph. Therefore, in this work, we selected the "Illustrated Guide to the State Key Protected Wildlife" [14], edited and published by the China Wildlife Conservation Association, the China Animal Theme Database, and the Species Diversity Data Platform, as our main data sources. We also used Baidu Encyclopedia as an auxiliary data source to collect a total of 980 species of key protected wildlife, of which 234 species are first-class national protected animals and 746 species are second-class national protected animals.

The construction of knowledge graphs can be divided into two ways: bottom-up and top-down. In this work, we employ the top-down method to construct a knowledge graph of the wildlife under special state protection. In other words, we construct the schema layer of the knowledge graph using the existing dataset and the structured knowledge base and then extract the entities and relationships from known data sources for filling and matching. By analyzing the existing datasets of protected animals and combining the opinions of Ping et al. [15] on wildlife naming and Wei Fuwen et al. [16] on the classification of Chinese veterinary species as a guide. This led to the definition of 19 wildlife entities and 18 different types of relationships, including scientific names, aliases, orders, families, genera, and species. The specific design is shown in Table 1.

Table 1. Wildlife under special state protection entities

Name of Entity	Account
latin_name	A Latin name unique to each species
another_name	Names other than official legal names
order	The level of biological taxonomy, located between the order and the genus
family	The level of biological taxonomy
genus	The basic unit of biological taxonomy
species	Classification of animals according to their different characteristics
biological_classification	Animals' eating habits
food	Length of life of animals
liftspan	Areas where animals are found on Earth
Distribution_area	Animals choose suitable places to live according to their habits
habitat	Animal body structure, external features
physical_characteristic	Habits formed by animals in the process of adapting to their environment
life_habit	Number of pups per litter
offspring_number	The time of year during which animals are active in reproduction
breeding_season	The period from the beginning of incubation to the breaking of the shell in oviparous animals
hatching_period	Period from fertilization to delivery in mammals
gestation_period	Levels of protection established to protect endangered wildlife
protection_level	Different levels of listing based on the level of threat to the species
endangered_class	The level of biological taxonomy, located between the order and the genus

4   Knowledge Graph Modeling Approach

The process of constructing the knowledge graph of wildlife under special state protection consists primarily of two tasks: named entity recognition and relationship extraction. First, the Albert-BiLSTM-CRF [17, 18] model is trained to identify and predict entities from unstructured text data. Next, the Albert-BiLSTM-Attention [19] model predicts the identified entities and text for interentity relationships. Finally, we use knowledge fusion to obtain the ternary group, which we then store in the Neo4j graph database to form the knowledge graph of the wildlife under special state protection.

4.1   Knowledge Graph Modeling Approach

The named entity recognition model primarily consists of four parts: the input layer for text input, the Albert layer for text feature extraction, the BiLSTM layer for positional sequence annotation, and the CRF layer for sequence optimization. Figure 1 illustrates the structure of the entity recognition model.

The operation steps for each layer are as follows: First, the first layer converts the preprocessed wildlife data into BIO format for the model's input. Second, the Albert layer encodes the input data on the basis of textual features via the trained Albert model. Next, the BiLSTM layer uses the input word vectors to determine the entity label of each entity via contextual semantic feature feature weights. Finally, the CRF layer applies conditional probability constraints on the basis of the feature weights of each entity label, combining the entire sentence to ensure the output of the globally optimal sequence.

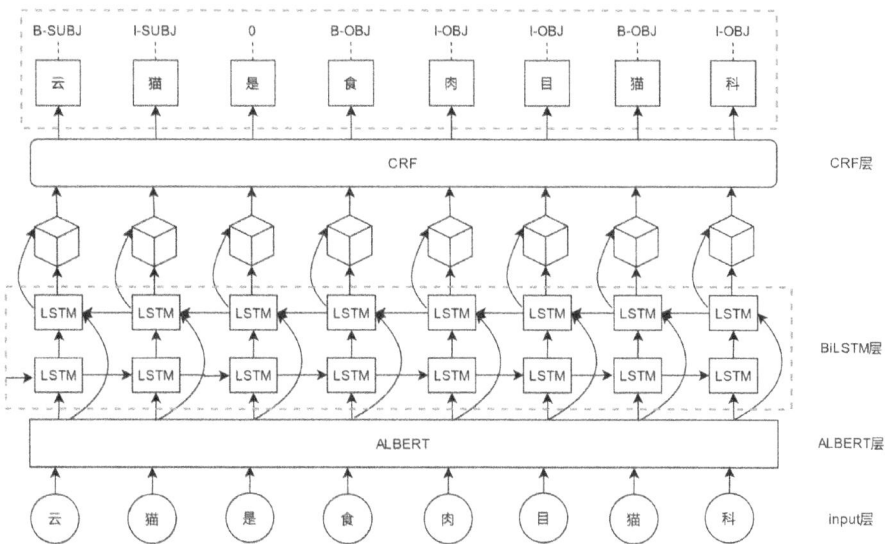

Fig. 1. Albert-BiLSTM-CRF model network structure diagram.

4.2 Relationship Extraction Model

The relationship extraction model for wildlife under special state protection consists of four main parts: the input layer that receives the text input, the Albert layer for text feature extraction, the BiLSTM layer that obtains contextual information, and the attention mechanism layer.

The operation steps for each layer are as follows: Initially, the first layer uses the entity recognition result as input, which is formatted as {'OBJ':object, 'SUBJ':subject, 'text':sentence}, and the subject and object in the sentence are denoted by the # sign. Second, the ALBERT layer receives the processed text and combines it with word vectors and positional information to pretrain text feature vectors. The BiLSTM layer subsequently takes over, offering long-range dependency support for sentences and effectively capturing the semantic features of the context. Finally, it integrates the attention mechanism to sharpen the model's focus on crucial information in the utterance. Finally, it utilizes the full connectivity and Softmax functions to ascertain the type of relationship between the entities.

4.3 Main Methods of Entity Identification and Relationship Extraction

4.3.1 Albert Model

In this paper, we utilize Google's ALBERT (A Lite BERT) as a pretraining model, which is more lightweight than BERT [20] and offers three key improvements:

(4) ALBERT performs a scale transformation on the dimensions of the word vectors by inserting a small dimension E between the length of the word list V and the hidden layer dimension H. The formula is expressed as:

$$O(V * H) \rightarrow O(V * E + E * H) \tag{1}$$

(5) Letting all the layers share all the parameters is equivalent to learning the parameters only in the first layer, with all the other layers using the same set of parameters. In the experimental results, the shared parameters not only compress the total number of parameters but also essentially maintain the same performance.

(6) ALBERT modified BERT's Next Sentence Prediction (NSP) Task to the Sentence Order Prediction (SOP) Task, moving away from the basic topic prediction method and concentrating on intersentence order prediction. The experimental findings indicate an improvement of approximately 1 point in the average model score.

Both ALBERT and BERT are deep learning frameworks that are based on the bidirectional coded representation of the Transformer model. The internal structure of a transformer consists of two components: an encoder and a decoder, as shown in Fig. 2. The fundamental concept involves passing the word vector and positional encoding through the multihead self-attention mechanism layer to determine the contextual connection of each sequence, as illustrated in (2).

$$Attention(Q, K, V) = softmax\left(\frac{QK^T}{\sqrt{d_k}}\right)V \tag{2}$$

The query matrix Q, the characterization context relation matrix K, and the content matrix V are homologous with the word vector matrix X. Furthermore, Q, K, and V are all linear transformations of X, and dk represents the vector dimensions of Q and K.

Given our utilization of the Multi-head Self Attention mechanism, we perform concat splicing by calculating the attention scores of each layer. Next, we perform a dot multiplication on the weight matrix WO to derive the feature vector Z, which has acquired sufficient learning from the contextual information. The calculation formula for this feature vector is shown in (3) and (4).

$$head_i = Attention\left(QW_i^Q, KW_i^K, VW_i^V\right) \tag{3}$$

$$Z = Concat(head_i, \dots, head_h)W^O \tag{4}$$

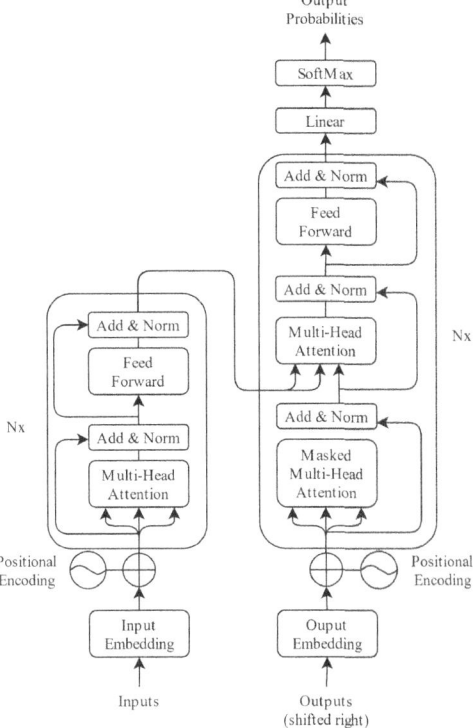

Fig. 2. Transformer Model Structure.

4.3.2 BiLSTM Layer

The bidirectional long short-term memory neural network (BiLSTM) is composed of a pair of LSTM, which is essentially a kind of recurrent neural network (RNN). However, the RNN is only suitable for short-distance dependency and is prone to gradient vanishing or gradient explosion when dealing with long-distance dependency problems, whereas the LSTM can solve the long-distance dependency problem exactly. Three gates comprise the LSTM neuron: the forget gate, the input gate, and the output gate. The forget gate filters out useless information, whereas the input gate preserves useful information. Figure 3 illustrates the internal structure of a single LSTM neuron.

However, LSTM can only perform in one direction to calculate the feature weight of the text. As part of natural language processing, the context and the features of a word work together. To make the most of this contextual information, we use BiLSTM to calculate the feature weight. This adds a line in the opposite direction of the LSTM, so the forward LSTM yields $\overrightarrow{h_L} = \{h_{L1}, h_{L2}, \ldots, h_{Ln}\}$ and the reverse LSTM yields $\overleftarrow{h_R} = \{h_{R1}, h_{R2}, \ldots, h_{Rn}\}$ after vector splicing to obtain the BiLSTM output:

$$h_t = \overrightarrow{h_{Lt}} \oplus \overleftarrow{h_{Rt}} \tag{5}$$

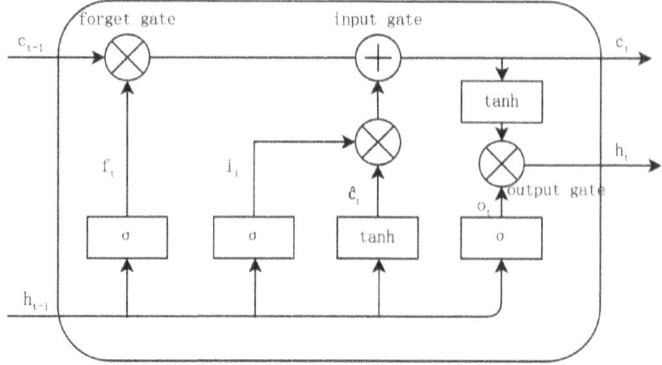

Fig. 3. LSTM cell structure.

4.3.3 CRF Layer

BiLSTM can give the feature weights of each word on the basis of the context, but those feature weights do not affect each other. It can give only the label with the highest probability for each word on the basis of the context. This would result in a situation where the object's nonbeginning label I-OBJ could come after the subject's beginning label B-SUBJ. Therefore, we choose to use Conditional Random Field (CRF) as the output layer, which considers the dependency constraints between each tag to find the optimal tag sequence solution.

Given an input phrase s, after the BiLSTM layer obtains the predicted label sequence $y = (y_1, y_2, \ldots, y_n)$, the CRF will construct a transfer matrix M on the basis of the label sequence, where M_{ij} denotes the probability value from sequence i to sequence j. In this way, the predicted paths can be scored computationally.

$$score(s, y) = \sum_{i=0}^{n}\left(M_{y_i y_{i+1}} + P_{iy_i}\right) \tag{6}$$

P_{ij} denotes the score of word i in sequence j, and n indicates the length of the sentence. The Softmax function normalizes the scores of all the paths with probability, and the optimal labeled sequence solution is the one with the highest predicted score:

$$P(y|s) = \frac{exp^{score(s,y)}}{\sum_{i=0}^{n} exp^{score(s,y_i)}} \tag{7}$$

5 Experiment and Analysis

5.1 Evaluation Indicators

The precision, recall, and F1 value commonly serve as evaluation indices for entity recognition and relation extraction performance in the field of natural language processing, with the F1 value serving as the overall index for experimental evaluation. We utilize three evaluation indices in the subsequent experimental process, and the calculation formula for these indices is provided below.

$$precision = \frac{Number\ of\ correct\ identifications}{Total\ number\ of\ identified\ results} \times 100\% \tag{8}$$

$$recall = \frac{Number\ of\ correct\ identifications}{Total\ number\ of\ samples\ in\ the\ test\ set} \times 100\% \tag{9}$$

$$F1 = 2 \times \frac{precision \times recall}{precision + recall} \tag{10}$$

5.2 Entity Recognition Experiments

5.2.1 Sequence Labeling

There are three common sequence-labeling methods for entity recognition: BIO, BMES, and BIOSE. In this work, the experiment uses the BIO labeling method to sequence label the entities of wildlife under special state protection, where 'B' represents the entity's beginning position, 'I' denotes its middle part, and 'O' denotes the nonentity part. We divide the entity into two parts, the subject and the object, resulting in the design of five entity labels: O, B-SUBJ, I-SUBJ, B-OBJ, and I-OBJ.

5.2.2 Experimental Results and Analysis

We experiment with the ALBERT-BiLSTM-CRF model on the dataset to verify its effect on entity recognition in wildlife under special state protection, and Table 2 shows the recognition results for the subject and the object.

Table 2. Results of recognizing various types of entities.

entity type	precision(%)	recall(%)	F1(%)
SUBJ	99.66	98.33	98.99
OBJ	95.14	90.00	92.50
average	96.01	91.54	93.72

As shown in Table 2, the model designed in this experiment is reasonable and effective, with high accuracy in recognizing both types of entities. The subject's accuracy in entity recognition is better than that of the object, with a precision rate of 99.66%, a recall rate of 98.33%, and an F1 value of 98.99%. This is primarily because this type of entity primarily consists of the animal's name, which consistently appears at the start of the dataset, maintaining a consistent pattern. In contrast, the object, which encompasses more intricate elements such as biological taxonomy, family genus and order, biological characteristics, and numerous other details, lacks a consistent pattern due to its longer length. This is the primary reason for the lower F1 value.

To confirm the efficacy and superiority of this paper's entity recognition model, we compare it with the popular NER model from recent years using the same dataset, and Table 3 displays the recognition outcomes.

Table 3. Different model entity recognition effects.

Model	precision(%)	recall(%)	F1(%)
BERT-BiLSTM-CRF	95.10	86.90	90.82
BERT-BiGRU-CRF	94.84	84.80	89.54
ALBERT-BiLSTM	92.09	90.15	91.11
ALBERT-BiLSTM-CRF	**96.01**	**91.54**	**93.72**

Table 3 reveals that Model 1 and Model 2 use different neural networks to learn contextual semantic information under identical conditions. The BiLSTM layer, when used as the feature vector, outperforms the BiGRU layer, resulting in a 1.43% improvement in the F1 value. By comparing Model 3 and Model 4, we can observe that the CRF layer actively constrains the output labels and finds the optimal solution, resulting in improvements of 4.26% in precision, 1.54% in recall, and 2.86% in the F1 value compared without the CRF layer. Compared with the BERT-BiLSTM-CRF model, the overall F1 value of using ALBERT to extract text feature vectors is improved by 3.19%. Furthermore, the ALBERT-BiLSTM-CRF model is optimal for all three metrics in this experiment, demonstrating its superiority for entity recognition on wildlife under a special state protection dataset.

5.3 Relationship Extraction Experiments

To confirm the superiority of the ALBERT-BiLSTM-Attention model in relationship extraction from wildlife data under special state protection, we conducted comparative experiments using common relationship extraction models from recent years. Table 4 displays the extraction results for each model.

A comparison of Experiments 1 and 4 reveals that the addition of the pretraining model improves the relationship extraction performance, with large improvements in all three metrics, including a 7.76% improvement in the F1 value. Comparing Experiments 2 and 4, replacing the pretraining model from BERT with the lightweight ALBERT

Table 4. Relationship Extraction Effects of Different Models.

Model	precision(%)	recall(%)	F1(%)
BiLSTM-Attention	89.73	88.52	89.12
BERT-BiLSTM-Attention	95.38	95.50	95.42
ALBERT-BiGRU-Attention	95.81	95.82	95.81
ALBERT-BiLSTM-Attention	95.89	96.21	96.04
BiLSTM-Attention	89.73	88.52	89.12
BERT-BiLSTM-Attention	95.38	95.50	95.42
ALBERT-BiGRU-Attention	95.81	95.82	95.81
ALBERT-BiLSTM-Attention	**95.89**	**96.21**	**96.04**

improves the F1 value by 0.64% while increasing the training speed. The change in the feature learning layer between Experiments 3 and 4 results in a 0.24% improvement in the F1 value. Notably, the training time is slightly shortened because of the simplification of the internal network structure by the GRU, but to better address the long sequence of text, LSTM is selected as the feature learning layer in this paper. The experimental results show that the ALBERT-BiLSTM-Attention model is the most effective for relationship extraction for wildlife in the special state protection dataset, with a precision rate of 95.89%, a recall rate of 96.21%, and an F1 value of 96.04%.

5.4   Storage and Visualization of Graphs

Through the aforementioned experimental training, we obtained an entity recognition model consisting of ALBERT-BiLSTM-CRF and a relation extraction model consisting of ALBERT-BiLSTM-Attention. The upper named entity recognition model transfers the subject–object recognition results from the statement about wildlife under special state protection to the lower relation extraction model. The output of the whole model is the result of the statement contained in the ternary. We integrate the output ternary data into CSV-formatted data and store them in the Neo4j graph database, preserving a total of 17405 nodes and 25,269 relations. Figure 4 displays a visualization of the knowledge graph for some key national wildlife.

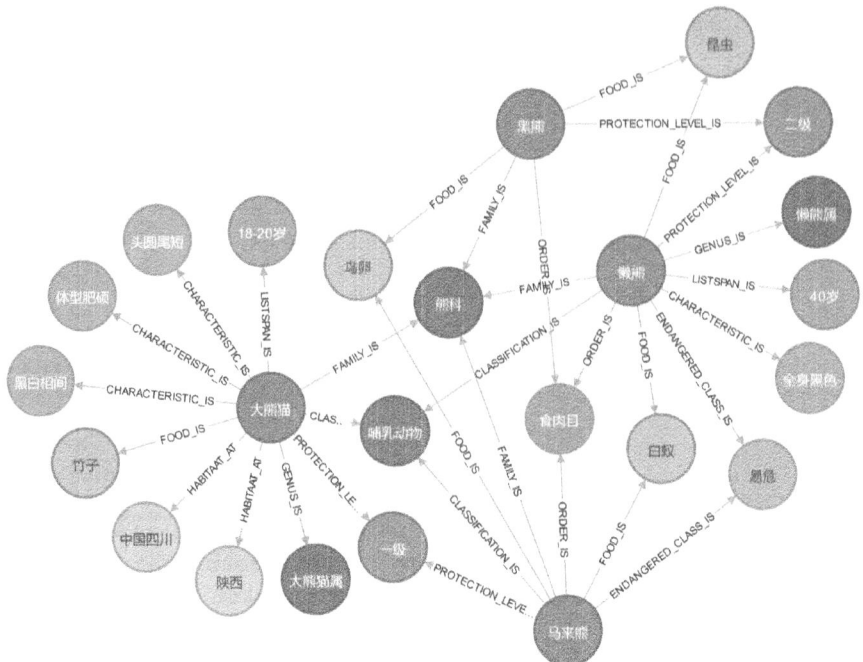

Fig. 4. Knowledge map of wildlife under special state protection (part).

6 Conclusions

We focus on building a knowledge graph of wildlife under special state protection, which primarily consists of the following three aspects: (1) Entity recognition of the dataset through the ALBERTT-BiLSTM-CRF model. (2) The BiLSTM-Attention mechanism facilitates further relationship extraction, which is then combined with the ALBERT model. (3) The model performs ternary extraction on the dataset and stores the results in the Neo4j graph database for graph visualization. The experimental results indicate that we successfully extracted the ternary group model from the dataset of wildlife under special state protection, laying a solid foundation for the construction of a graph store with a comprehensive knowledge system and wide content coverage. Future research efforts will aim to enrich the dataset to broaden the knowledge coverage, enhance the model's generality, and conduct research on an intelligent Q&A system on the basis of the current graph.

Acknowledgments. This research was funded by the Major Science and Technology Program of Yazhou Bay Innovation Institute of Hainan Tropical Ocean University (2023CXYZD001), the Key Research and Development Project of Hainan Province (ZDYF2024SHFZ051) and the University-level Research and Practice Project of New Engineering, New Agriculture and New Liberal Arts of Hainan Tropical Ocean University (RHYxgnw2024).

References

1. Hu, X.J., Lin, Y.Q., Gao, X.L., et al.: Research progress on the connotation of biodiversity value and assessment methods. Acta Ecologica Sinica (20), 1–11 (2024)
2. Chen, J., Wu, X., Lin, H., et al.: Comparative analysis of the list of wildlife under state key conservation and other conservation lists. Biodiversity **31**(06), 190–202 (2023)
3. Xi, X.-F., Zhou, G.-D.: A survey on deep learning for natural language processing. Acta Automatica Sinica **42**(10), 1445–1465 (2016)
4. Pu, F., Zhang, Z.W., Feng, Y., et al.: Knowledge graphs. J. Data Inform. Sci. **7**(2), 84–106 (2022)
5. Lan, Z., Chen, M., Goodman, S., et al.: ALBERT: a lite BERT for self-supervised learning of language representations. CoRR (2019). abs/1909.11942
6. Zhang, X., Liu, L., Wang, H., et al.: Research on the entity-relationship extraction method in knowledge graphs. Comput. Sci. Explor. **18**(03), 574–596 (2024)
7. Collobert, R.,Weston, J., Bottou, L., et al.: Natural language processing (almost) from scratch. CoRR, pp. 2493–2537 (2011)
8. Ouyang, E., Li, Y., Jin, L., et al.: Exploring N-gram character presentation in bidirectional RNN-CRF for chinese clinical named entity recognition (2017)
9. Jin, Y., Xie, J., Guo, W., et al.: LSTM-CRF neural network with gated self attention for chinese NER. IEEE Access **7**, 136694–136703 (2019)
10. Phi, V., Santoso, J., Tran, V., et al.: Distant supervision for relation extraction via piecewise attention and bag-level contextual inference. IEEE Access **7**, 103570–103582 (2019)
11. Song, L., Zhang, Y., Wang, Z., et al.: N-ary relation extraction using graph state LSTM. arXiv: 1808.09101 (2018)
12. Gill, J., Chetty, M., Lim, S., et al.: Knowledge-based intelligent text simplification for biological relation extraction. Informatics **10**(4), 89 (2023)
13. Lin, L., Wang, D., Liu, J., et al.: A study on the recognition of named entities of canonical animals in the view of digital humanities–taking the SikuBERT pretraining model as an example. Lib. Forum **42**(10), 42–50 (2022)
14. China Wildlife Conservation Association. Illustrated Guide to Wild Animals under State Key Protection. Straits Book Publishing House, Fujian (2023)
15. Ping, X., Zeng, Y.: Changes in the nomenclature of species listed in the List of Wild Animals under State Key Conservation and their impact on wildlife conservation. Chin. Sci. Life Sci. **50**(01), 33–43 (2020)
16. Wei, F., Yang, Q., Wu, Y., et al.: List of chinese veterinary species (2021 Edition). J. Vet. Sci. **41**(05), 487–501 (2021)
17. Zhu, Y.: A knowledge graph and BiLSTM-CRF-enabled intelligent adaptive learning model and its potential application. Alex. Eng. J. **91**, 305–320 (2024)
18. An, Q., Pan, B., Liu, Z., et al.: Chinese named entity recognition in football based on ALBERT-BiLSTM model. Appl. Sci. **13**(19) (2023)
19. Ghada, A., Niels, P., Goran, N.: Attention-based bidirectional long short-term memory networks for extracting temporal relationships from clinical discharge summaries. J. Biomed. Inform. **123**, 103915–103915 (2021)
20. Devlin, J., Chang, M.W., Lee, K., et al.: Bert: pretraining of deep bidirectional transformers for language understanding. arXiv preprint arXiv:1810.04805 (2018)

Multi-feature Based Memory-Enhanced Knowledge Tracing

Youwei Sun[1,2,3], Ruyi Liu[1,2,3]($\boxtimes$), Qiguang Miao[1,2,3]($\boxtimes$), Zixiang Lu[1,2,3], Peipei Zhao[1,2,3], and Ronghan Li[1,2,3]

[1] School of Computer Science and Technology,
Xidian University, Xi'an 710071, Shaanxi, China
{ruyiliu,qgmiao}@xidian.edu.cn
[2] Xi'an Key Laboratory of Big Data and Intelligent Vision, Xi'an 710071, Shaanxi, China
[3] Key Laboratory of Collaborative Intelligence Systems, Ministry of Education,
Xidian University, Xi'an 710071, China

Abstract. In the realm of intelligent education, knowledge tracing (KT) has emerged as a crucial tool for enhancing educational efficiency and enabling personalized learning. Traditional KT methods primarily rely on students' historical response data to evaluate their mastery of specific skills and forecast future performance. However, focusing solely on basic interactions, skills and response outcomes, makes it challenging to capture the complexities of real learning environments and accurately reflect students' genuine knowledge states. To address this issue, we propose an innovative multi-feature based memory-enhanced knowledge tracing (MMKT) method. The key innovation of the MMKT model lies in the introduction of '*memory features*' and '*interaction features*'. Memory features account for features such as the interval between repeated responses, the total number of responses, and memory interference during the overall learning process. In contrast, interaction features include response time, number of attempts, and hints. To integrate these features, we employ a self-attention mechanism coupled with a memory enhancement module and a recurrent neural network. This approach effectively uncovers variations in knowledge states while balancing the influence of global and local interactions. Our experimental results from different public datasets emphasize the benefits of the MMKT model in predicting future performance, underscoring the significance of integrating multi-feature and real-world relevant memory improvements.

Keywords: Knowledge Tracing · Memory Features · Interact Features · Memory Enhancement

1 Introduction

The swift advancement of AI has fueled the growth of intelligence across various specialized domains. As a product of the combination of AI and education, intelligent education [1] is gradually subverting the traditional teaching mode. Intelligent education not only improves the efficiency of education [2], but also realizes personalized learning [3], which provides a broad space for the discussion of many scientific research directions.

© The Author(s), under exclusive license to Springer Nature Singapore Pte Ltd. 2025
K. Zhang et al. (Eds.): CSEI 2024, CCIS 2448, pp. 116–130, 2025.
https://doi.org/10.1007/978-981-96-3738-6_10

Knowledge tracing(KT) is a central task in intelligent education [4, 5]. The core value of knowledge tracing is that it can provide customized services for students. The realization of this personalized learning can not only help students identify their own weaknesses, but also recommend corresponding learning resources according to the learning progress and understanding ability of each student. This precise feedback mechanism enables students to learn at a rhythm that suits them, thereby improving learning efficiency. Specifically, by gathering students' historical learning data from online learning platforms like MOOCs[1] and ASSISTments[2], knowledge tracing can effectively analyze students' proficiency in particular skills and track their progression, ultimately allowing for predictions of their future performance.

Generally, the analysis and updating of students' knowledge states rely on their response outcomes, namely whether they are correct or incorrect. This is also the format predominantly captured by most public datasets used in the KT domain. Consequently, the main goal of knowledge tracing methods is to improve the model by minimizing the difference between predicted responses and actual responses. Traditional methods such as Bayesian knowledge tracing (BKT) based on probability model [6, 7] and deep knowledge tracking (DKT) with deep neural network [8] have achieved remarkable results. However, the development of students' knowledge states is complex, and relying solely on response outcomes to assess their mastery of a particular skill is overly simplistic. In recent studies, many KT methods have tried to use other behavioral characteristics recorded by the education system, such as the response time of students in responding a certain exercise, the number of times they use the system prompt, the number of attempts to respond, etc. [9–11], and achieved effective results. In fact, the data dimension and form in the online education system are limited. To more accurately represent students' knowledge states, it is essential to further analyze this data to uncover underlying insights.

We intuitively give a case of a knowledge tracing task through Fig. 1. In the process of responding four exercises of three different skills, in addition to the characteristics recorded by the system, such as response time, we also calculate the effect of the student 's interval between two responses to a skill a and the number of repeated responses on memory changes. It is important to recognize that when students respond incorrectly to e_3 is wrong, the mastery of the skill a contained in it will not necessarily decline, but will deepen the students ' memory of the skill due to repeated exercises. At the same time, the incorrect response may also cause the students to pay special attention to the skill and deepen their understanding through correction and reflection. This also reflects the complexity behind the change of knowledge state and the consistency with the actual scene. In addition, exercise e_2 contains two different skills of b and c, which is also consistent with the actual scene.

From a psychological perspective, the changes in students' skills and memory are considered. It is generally believed that memory naturally decays over time, and new information can interfere with the retention of old information. Therefore, while paying attention to the results of students ' responses to a certain exercise, we should also fully consider the extended development. To address this issue, we introduce a new approach called Multi-feature based Memory-enhanced Knowledge Tracing (MMKT).

---

[1] Https://www.mooc.org.

[2] Https://www.assist.org.

Specifically, the interval time, number of repetitions, and memory interference related to repeated responses for a specific skill in the long-term learning process are defined as memory features. Additionally, behaviors such as response time, number of hints, and number of attempts made by students during practice are categorized as interaction features. Next, a self-attention mechanism is implemented for memory features to effectively extract the overall knowledge state. Furthermore, a recurrent neural network is employed for interaction features to balance both global and local effects. Throughout the iterative updating process, changes in the knowledge state are thoroughly explored, ensuring a certain degree of interpretability. Finally, we aggregate the mined knowledge information. This design idea is different from the combination of historical information and attention mechanism in the literature. On the basis of knowledge aggregation, we highlight the global memory interference, so that the KT model can achieve more accurate prediction and is more suitable for the actual scene. We carried out thorough experiments and analysis on two publicly available datasets. The results indicate that our MMKT model attains new state-of-the-art performance, emphasizing the effectiveness of integrating multiple features and enhancing memory in knowledge tracing methods.

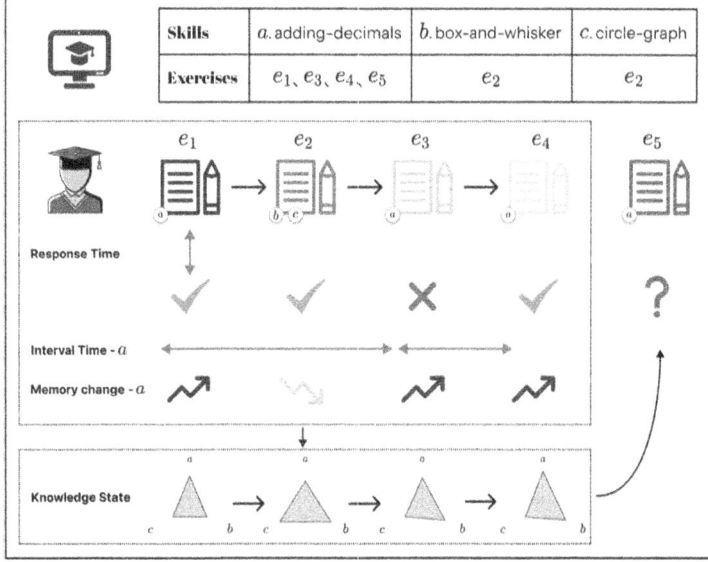

Fig. 1. A simple example of a student's exercise process can be illustrated through a knowledge tracing task. In this scenario, the student completed four exercises involving three skills, along with their corresponding response outcomes. The table above shows the correction between exercises and skills. For skill a, calculate the interval time and the effect on memory change. Repeatedly responding exercises containing skill a will enhance memory, otherwise it may cause a certain degree of weakening. The radar chart below illustrates the student's proficiency in the three skills.

In summary, the main contributions of our work can be highlighted as follows:

- The limited interactive features present in the dataset are fully utilized, with an additional emphasis placed on enhancing the global memory features to enhance the extraction of the knowledge state in the KT method from a real-world perspective.
- A memory enhancement model based on multiple features, MMKT, is proposed to balance the influence of global and local features through mask self-attention mechanism and recurrent neural network, while ensuring a certain degree of interpretability. The knowledge aggregation module that incorporates global memory enhancement is introduced, which ultimately enhances the accuracy of the knowledge tracing model's predictions.

2 Related Works

2.1 Traditional Knowledge Tracing

In the realm of artificial intelligence in education, knowledge tracing has received considerable attention. Traditional knowledge tracing methods primarily rely on machine learning techniques. The earliest knowledge tracing model, Bayesian Knowledge Tracing (BKT) [6], is grounded in the Hidden Markov Model and is utilized to dynamically assess students' knowledge states. BKT combines students' response information through Bayesian reasoning to calculate the probability of students' mastery of specific skills. It is worth noting that BKT assumes that students have only two states of ' mastery ' and ' non-mastery ' for each skill, and updates the knowledge state according to the results of the students' responses (correct or wrong). This method obviously ignores the complexity of knowledge tracing. Although the extended model of BKT takes into account additional factors such as sliding, guess estimation, project difficulty, etc. [7, 14, 15], traditional machine learning methods still face the problems of low computational efficiency and poor generalization ability when dealing with complex educational data.

2.2 Knowledge Tracing Based on Recurrent Neural Network

Deep Knowledge Tracing (DKT) introduces Recurrent Neural Network (RNN) as the core model and pioneers the application of deep learning technology to knowledge tracing. It employs neural networks like RNNs and LSTMs to analyze the interaction sequences between students and skills during the learning process, representing the knowledge state through the updating and iteration of hidden variables. This sequence modeling method effectively captures the time dependence. Compared with traditional machine learning methods, DKT shows significant performance improvement on multiple benchmark datasets. Since then, KT models utilizing deep neural networks have been developed. Notably, Dynamic Key-Value Memory Networks (DKVMN) align students' responses with skills using a key-value memory mechanism, dynamically adjusting the knowledge state to more accurately track students' learning progress and mastery.

In real learning environments, forgetting is an essential factor that cannot be overlooked [13]. Unlike DKT, which views the learning process as one where knowledge is never forgotten, a study [14] takes into account the concept of forgetting over time, suggesting that it decays exponentially [15–17]. In recent studies, many knowledge tracing (KT) models have introduced a variety of time-related learning factors to explore the impact of forgetting on long-term time series. In the learning process consistency knowledge tracing (LPKT) [10], response time is considered a fundamental component of the learning unit. The model comprehensively considers the differences and intervals between historical learning units, and designs a forgetting mechanism to monitor the changes of students' knowledge states. In addition, LBKT [11] combines various learning behaviors and forgetting factors such as response time, attempts, and hints, and explores the impact of these factors on students' knowledge acquisition and the complex dependence patterns behind them.

The recurrent neural network shows good interpretability when updating the knowledge state in sequence, but this update method ignores the long-term dependence between historical interactions and has certain limitations.

2.3 Knowledge Tracing Based on Attention Mechanism

In order to solve the long-term dependence problem of KT model, attention mechanism is introduced. An adversarial training based KT method (ATKT) [18] combines adversarial training and knowledge distillation. By training on adversarial samples, the student model can learn more discriminative features, so as to maintain good predictive ability in the face of input disturbances. At the same time, ATKT introduces the attention mechanism and combines historical knowledge information to effectively consider the long-term dependence between interactions. It is important to note that with the widespread adoption of Transformer [19] in various tasks, knowledge tracing models utilizing self-attention mechanisms have also been introduced. As the first knowledge tracing model to utilize a self-attention mechanism, SAKT [20] establishes a foundation for subsequent knowledge tracing models that integrate Transformer. The context-aware KT model AKT proposed by Ghosh et al. [22], which utilizes a monotonic attention mechanism and applies an exponential decay curve to reduce the impact of past interactions on changes in the current knowledge state. In SAINT [21] and SAINT + [9], the practice and response results are utilized as inputs for both the encoder and decoder, respectively. As an upgraded version of SAINT, SAINT + considers additional learning features and inputs response time and interval time into the decoder, further enriching the embedded representation. HITSKT [23] designs a local interactive encoder and a global session encoder to balance the knowledge acquired by students by hierarchically processing the interaction sequence and taking a student 's session as the core unit, and introduces a power-law attenuation attention mechanism in the session encoder to consider long-term forgetting behavior. These studies have promoted the application and development of Transformer in KT and improved the training efficiency. However, since Transformer is essentially a black box model, its interpretability is obviously insufficient, which poses a certain challenge to the application of KT in real scenes.

In general, we believe that we should make full use of the multiple behavioral characteristics in students' learning records to comprehensively update the changes in knowledge states from both global dependence and local interaction. Thus, we propose a knowledge tracing model that utilizes the efficiency of Transformer to handle global dependencies effectively, the sequential updating and interpretability of recurrent neural networks, and the forgetting theory.

3 Preliminary

In this section, we offer a comprehensive introduction to the MMKT model. First, we define the feature representation of knowledge tracing as it simulates students' learning. Next, we describe the input and output processes, as well as the associated variables of the MMKT model. The symbols utilized in this section and their corresponding meanings are displayed in Table 1.

3.1 Hierarchical Learning Process

Based on the notation in Table 1, we divide the characteristics of students' learning process into two levels, namely memory characteristics and Response characteristics:

Memory Features. Which are expressed as the interval time τ, repetition counts η and memory changes ε of repeated responses to a certain skill in the global learning process. The aim of knowledge tracing is to assess students' mastery of the skills embedded in the exercises. Thus, the interval time discussed in this paper refers to a specific skill, representing the duration between the current response to that skill and the previous response to the same skill. At the same time, the number of repetitions of the same skill in the sequence is recorded as repetition counts. In addition, for the adjacent responses on the time series, if the skills contained are inconsistent, then we believe that this is a kind of interference of the new memory to the old memory, which leads to the memory change of the skill, recorded as $\varepsilon_n \in \{0, 1\}$, where $\varepsilon_j = 1$ if the skills contained in the exercise e_j are inconsistent with the skills contained in the previous sequence, otherwise $\varepsilon_j = 0$.

Interact Features. It is expressed as some attributes such as response time γ, number of attempts α; number of hints β when students respond a certain exercise. This is similar to the design idea in LBKT [11].

3.2 Task Description

Given e_t denotes the practice that the learner responds at time step t, s_t denotes the skill that the practice contains, and r_t denotes the corresponding response results (1 denotes correct, 0 denotes incorrect). We define the student's basic interaction sequence as $I = \{(e_1, s_1, r_1), (e_2, s_2, r_2), \ldots, (e_t, s_t, r_t)\}$. Among them, in order to correspond to the real learning environment, we also define a matrix Q that represents the correspondence between exercises and skills. If the exercise ej contains skill km, then $Q_{mn} = 1$, otherwise $Q_{mn} = 0$. In MMKT, I and Q are used as external basic inputs. In addition, the two features defined in the hierarchical learning process are added to the Transformer and RNN as memory enhancement parts to balance the global and local knowledge state changes.

In general, we define the problem as: given the student interaction sequence and the relationship between practices and skills, in the process of memory enhancement, mine the knowledge state and update the iteration, and predict its learning performance at $t+1$ in the future.

Table 1. Notations and descriptions.

Notaions	Descriptions
I	The Interaction sequence of students
Q	The matrix of the connection between Exercises and Skills
e,s,r	The features of Exercises, Skills and Responses
τ,η,ε	The features of Interval Times, Repeat Counts and Memory Changes
γ,α,β	The features of Response Times, Attempts and Hints

4   The MMKT Model

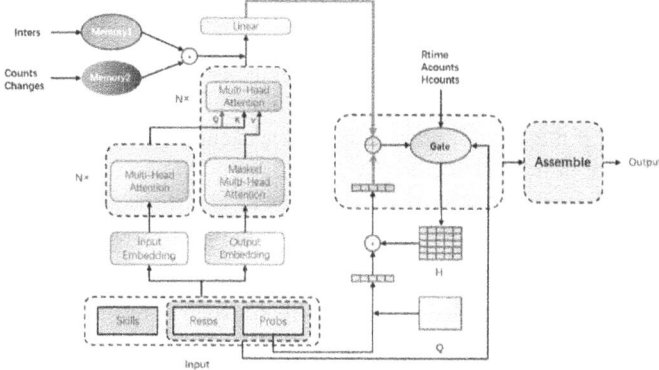

Fig. 2. The framework and details of MMKT.

The overall framework of the MMKT is depicted in Fig. 2. It employs a combination of a masked multi-head self-attention mechanism and a recurrent neural network to effectively balance the global and local knowledge states during students' learning processes. Memory features are integrated into the global module, while interactive features are introduced into the recurrent neural network to simulate the influence of multiple features on knowledge acquisition in a real environment. By sequentially updating the hidden state, the interpretability of the task is achieved.

4.1   Masked Multi-head Self-attention

In the global module, our model is built upon the FKT structure introduced in [24]. Initially, in the encoder, we extract the embedded representation of the interaction sequence.

$$i_t = Encoder(e_t + s_t + r_t) \tag{1}$$

Taking into account the nature of the knowledge tracing task, the current knowledge state is influenced solely by the present interaction and the preceding interactions. Therefore, the impact of future information must be excluded during processing. We employ the masked multi-head self-attention mechanism as the core of the module, replacing the upper triangular portion of the dot product matrix with negative infinity. After softmax processing, the attention weight of the subsequent position can be zeroed.

$$Q = [i_1, i_2, \ldots, i_t] \cdot \mathbf{W}^q \tag{2}$$

$$K = [i_1, i_2, \ldots, i_t] \cdot \mathbf{W}^k \tag{3}$$

$$V = [i_1, i_2, \ldots, i_t] \cdot \mathbf{W}^v \tag{4}$$

$$l_o = Softmax(\frac{Q \cdot K}{\sqrt{d}} + Me) \cdot V \tag{5}$$

where the mapping function is added to the multi-head attention network, and the input I is transformed into Q, K and V using the trainable parameters $\mathbf{W}^q$, $\mathbf{W}^k$ and $\mathbf{W}^v$, respectively. d is the dimension of each head. In addition, Me represents the mask matrix, where all lower triangular and diagonal elements are set to 0, while the upper triangular elements are set to $-\infty$, which indicates that the model only focuses on the interaction information between the current moment and the history. l_o denotes the output of each layer.

The multi-head attention network is used to process the input sequence to obtain different levels of attention mapping to adaptively focus on each part of the input. By aggregating different attention heads, the output of the whole multi-head attention network is obtained through residual connection, normalization and feedforward network.

$$MultiHead(Q, K, V) = Add(l_1, \cdots, l_N)W^o \tag{6}$$

$$O_e = FFN(Norm(MultiHead)) \tag{7}$$

Where W^o denotes the trainable parameters. O_e denotes the output of the encoder.

We use the practice and skill sequence as the input to the decoder, from which we derive V through mapping. Subsequently, the output of the encoder is mapped to obtain the Q and K values for the decoder.

$$I_{t'} = Decoder(e_t + r_t) \tag{8}$$

$$Attention = Softmax(\frac{O_e W^Q \cdot O_e W^K}{\sqrt{d}} + Me) \cdot I_{t'}W^V \tag{9}$$

Similar to the encoder, the decoder also contains an N-layer attention network. We propose two memory modules, memory decline module M_d and memory interference module M_i, which are combined with attention network. Among them, the core factor of Md is skill interval time, and the core factor of M_i is repetition frequency and memory interference.

$$M_d = \frac{\exp(a_1)}{\tau + b_1} + c_1 \tag{10}$$

$$M_i = \sigma\left(\frac{Relu(w^\eta \cdot \eta)}{Relu(w^\varepsilon \cdot \varepsilon) + 1}\right) \tag{11}$$

$$O\prime = \text{FFN}\left(\text{Norm}\left(MultiHead(\text{Attention} \cdot M_d) + w^i M_i\right)\right) \tag{12}$$

where a_1, b_1, and c_1 represent the bias parameters. Equation (10) shows that the memory strength is negatively correlated with the interval time. The longer the interval time is, the less the current historical memory is retained. In Eq. (11), σ represents the sigmoid function, w^η and w^ε are trainable parameters, and the positive effect of η on memory intensity and the negative interference of ε on memory are integrated into the module M_i.

Unlike other transformer-based knowledge tracing models, we do not include a prediction layer at the final output of the decoder. Instead, we treat $O\prime$ as a hidden state that incorporates the global dependencies of the interaction sequence.

4.2 Recurrent Neural Network

To simulate a real learning environment and provide a degree of interpretability, we utilize the Q matrix, which represents the correction between practice and skills, as the skill query matrix for the interaction sequence. Therefore, in this part of the input, skill is no longer considered for embedding representation. Similar to LBKT, we define a knowledge state query matrix $H \in R^{M \times D}$, where M represents the number of skills included in the problem set and D denotes the dimension [11]. Therefore, the students ' mastery of the skill i (or multiple skills i, j, etc.) contained in the current practice can be obtained, and the vector corresponding to line i (i, j) in H can be obtained. Combining the global knowledge state sequence hg obtained in the first stage with the weighted sum of hl obtained by the query, the knowledge state h at the current moment is obtained.

$$I_t^r = Relu(W_1[e_t \oplus r_t] + b_1) \tag{13}$$

$$h_{t-1} = \lambda \cdot O_d[:, t] + (1 - \lambda) \cdot Q[e_t] \otimes H \tag{14}$$

where λ represents the weight parameter, $\oplus$ represents the cascade operation, $\otimes$ represents the matrix multiplication operation, and also represents the query operation. When $t = 1$, h_0 denotes the initialized knowledge state.

Similar to LBKT [11], we add interactive features to the recurrent neural network, use IRT theory [25] to evaluate the impact of each behavior on students' knowledge acquisition, and design it as a gating mechanism to update h.

$$S = \sum_1^n h_t = \sum_1^n h_{t-1} * \sigma(W[h_{t-1} + I_{rt} + IRT[\gamma, \alpha, \beta]] + b) \tag{15}$$

where $IRT[\cdot]$ comprehensively considers the role of three factors in interactive features. Finally, the embedded representation of the exercise is combined to derive the intermediate state S that encompasses historical information and predictions.

4.3 Knowledge Aggregation Module

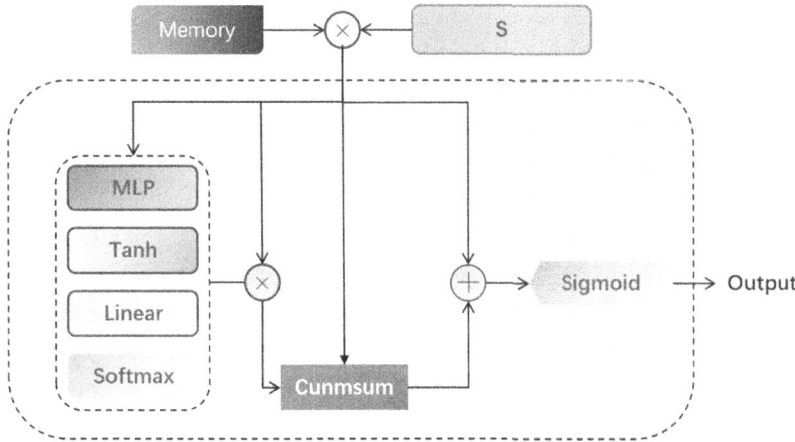

Fig. 3. The framework of knowledge aggregation module.

As shown in Fig. 3, after obtaining all the knowledge states in the current batch, a knowledge information aggregation operation is carried out on the module. The state matrix S obtained by formula (15) is used as the input. Based on the attention module proposed in ATKT [18]:

We first reduce the dimension of the knowledge state considering the global memory feature M_g to aggregate the key information.

$$Att_g = \text{Linear}(\text{Tanh}(\text{Mlp}(S \otimes M_g))) \tag{16}$$

Then, the Softmax function is applied to obtain the weights for different dimensions in the knowledge state.

$$Att_S = \text{Softmax}(W \cdot Att_g) * S \tag{17}$$

We introduce the *Cumsum* function to perform a weighted accumulation operation on the key information, while removing the influence of the initial input and retaining only the transmission state of the information.

$$Sum_S = Cumsum(Att_S) - Att_S \tag{18}$$

Finally, we combine the weight matrix and the initial state matrix, and output the prediction result R through the *Sigmoid*, where r belongs to $\{0, 1\}$, which indicates the probability of answering the question e_{t+1} correctly.

$$R = \sigma(W \cdot cat(Sum_S, S)) \tag{19}$$

5 Experiments

5.1 Datasets

We assess our method using two public datasets: (1) ASSIST2012 and (2) ASSIST2017. The basic statistics for these datasets are provided in Table 2, along with the following descriptions:

- ASSIST2012[3] is gathered from the ASSISTments online tutoring system [26], which tracks the start and end times of the interaction sequence, the correction between problems and skills, as well as recording the *'attempt count'*, *'hint count'* and *'ms first response'*. Data features that align with the requirements of our MMKT model are utilized. Similar to LBKT [11], this approach aims to minimize the influence of data on model performance and to better evaluate the processing outcomes. Empty records in the skill column, student records with less than ten interaction sequences, and practice records with fewer than 10 responses were removed.
- ASSIST2017[4] is also gathered from ASSISTments. We implement the same preprocessing steps that are applied to ASSIST2012.

Table 2. Statistics for all datasets.

Statistics	Datasets	
	ASSISMENT2012	ASSISTMENT2017
Records	2,711,812	934,788
Students	29,018	1,708
Problems	53,019	2,521
Skills	265	97

5.2 Baselines

We compare MMKT with five KT models. The details of these models are as follows::

- **DKT** [8] employs a recurrent neural network to model the interaction sequence, representing the hidden state as the student's knowledge state, which is updated and iterated over time.
- **DKVMN** [12] utilizes a dynamic key-value memory matrix to store and update students' mastery of the corresponding skills.
- **SAKT** [20] introduces the self-attention mechanism into knowledge tracing for the first time to model the global dependence between interaction sequences, and its structure is dominated by transformer.

---

[3] https://sites.google.com/site/assistmentsdata/2012-13-school-data-withaffect.
[4] https://sites.google.com/view/assistmentsdatamining.

- **AKT** [22] introduces a novel monotonic attention mechanism to highlight the impact of historical interactions on students' knowledge states, capturing the long-term dependencies of the interaction sequence. It also proposes the design concept of integrating problem difficulty with skill.
- **LBKT** [11] incorporates the effects of response time, number of attempts, and number of hints on students' knowledge states, designing a gating mechanism to sequentially update the knowledge state matrix in line with the interaction sequence.

5.3 Training Details

We split the preprocessed dataset into training, validation, and test sets in a ratio of 8:1:1. To enhance the effectiveness of information transmission between the global module and the local module, the dimensions of the knowledge state and problem embedding are set to 128, while the dimension of the response embedding in the recurrent network is set to 50. Additionally, in the global module, the encoder and decoder consist of 3 layers, each featuring 4 multi-head attention heads. We use a batch size of 16 and a dropout rate of 0.2, implementing the Adam optimizer with a learning rate of 0.005.

5.4 Experimental Results

To assess the performance of MMKT, we compare it against all baseline models and display the experimental results in Table 3. We utilize commonly employed evaluation metrics in the knowledge tracing (KT) models, specifically the area under the curve (AUC), accuracy (ACC), and root mean square error (RMSE), to assess the model's accuracy in predicting students' future responses. It is not difficult to see that our proposed MMKT model has improved in all three indicators compared with the most advanced model.

Specifically, the AUC of MMKT increased by about 2% on the data set ASSIST2017 and increased by about 4% on ASSIST2012. The results indicate that MMKT significantly enhances the accuracy of predicting future response outcomes. Additionally, it demonstrates that the complexities underlying the interaction sequence can be more effectively uncovered through the integration of multiple features and memory enhancement. Moreover, it is crucial to take into account the impact of historical information and current interactions on the knowledge state. This includes simulating a real learning environment, integrating knowledge tracing tasks with psychological principles, and improving the performance of the model.

5.5 Ablation Experiments

To further investigate the impact of the key parts of the proposed MMKT model on the prediction results, we conducted ablation experiments. The findings are presented in Table 4, based on MMKT, we remove the two key modules of knowledge aggregation and memory enhancement, namely *MMKT w/o agg* and *MMKT w/o me*. *MMKT w/o me* indicates that the global memory enhancement is removed, but the interaction features are still retained. The results show that the two key modules have different degrees of influence on the prediction effect. Among them, *MMKT w/o agg* has almost the

Table 3. The performance of MMKT and all the baselines on four datasets.

Methods	ASSIST2012			ASSIST2017		
	AUC	ACC	RMSE	AUC	ACC	RMSE
DKT	0.7325	0.7354	0.4237	0.7097	0.6881	0.4479
DKVMN	0.7121	0.7254	0.5240	0.6895	0.6917	0.4461
SAKT	0.7787	0.7563	0.4074	0.7571	0.7138	0.4319
AKT	0.7849	0.7603	0.4054	0.7581	0.7152	0.4316
LBKT	0.7847	0.7615	0.4047	0.8123	0.7558	0.4063
MMKT(ours)	**0.8245**	**0.7820**	**0.3875**	**0.8353**	**0.7729**	**0.3937**

lowest performance, indicating that it is necessary to review the influence of historical interaction on the current moment before the prediction layer, which ensures the effective transmission of information in the long term.

Table 4. The ablation experiment results.

Methods	ASSIST2012			ASSIST2017		
	AUC	ACC	RMSE	AUC	ACC	RMSE
MMKT w/o agg	0.7771	0.7568	0.4092	0.8177	0.7590	0.4036
MMKT w/o me	0.8196	0.7786	0.3914	0.8329	0.7701	0.3959
MMKT(ours)	**0.8245**	**0.7820**	**0.3875**	**0.8353**	**0.7709**	**0.3951**

6 Conclusion

In this paper, we address the pressing topic of knowledge tracing in intelligent education through symbolic representation. Through the student question and answer sequence recorded by the education system, the students ' mastery of the predefined skill set is excavated, so as to predict the future performance. From the traditional knowledge tracing methods that only focus on the binary state of students' response results, to the existing methods that introduce students' other behaviors, the complexity and transitivity behind them are not explored in depth. Although considering the influence of forgetting behavior in long-term interaction, the design idea is still too one-sided, and there is still a big gap with the real learning environment. To address this limitation, we propose the MMKT method, which hierarchically defines memory features and interaction features using multi-behavior characteristics, effectively balancing the global and local hidden knowledge states. The effectiveness of our method is verified by experiments, which proves that it narrows the gap with the real learning environment to a certain extent and increases the practicability of the KT method.

However, our model still has some limitations. On the one hand, limited by the design of the education system, multi-feature data does not necessarily exist in all data sets, which leads to the need for additional labeling of more data in practical scenarios. In this regard, future work will focus on expanding data through preprocessing techniques, such as the memory features proposed in this paper, to enhance the model's applicability. On the other hand, the combination of multiple structures, especially recurrent neural networks, increases the complexity of model processing. In the future work, we consider simplifying the model structure. Additionally, for the implementation of large models, we will consider parallel processing to improve the model's efficiency. Ultimately, the advancement of the knowledge tracing (KT) model should prioritize application in real-world scenarios rather than just focusing on accuracy improvement. Therefore, we believe there is still significant potential for exploration in the field of KT in the future.

Acknowledgment. The work was jointly supported by the National Science and Technology Major Project under grant No. 2022ZD0117103, the National Natural Science Foundations of China under grant No. 62272364, the provincial Key Research and Development Program of Shaanxi under grant No. 2024GH-ZDXM-47, the Research Project on Higher Education Teaching Reform of Shaanxi Province under Grant No. 23JG003.

References

1. Chen, L., Chen, P., Lin, Z.: Artificial intelligence in education: a review. IEEE Access **8**, 75264–75278 (2020)
2. Nguyen, T.: The effectiveness of online learning: Beyond no significant difference and future horizons. MERLOT J. Online Learn. Teach. **11**(2), 309–319 (2015)
3. Ayeni, O.O., et al.: AI in education: a review of personalized learning and educational technology. GSC Adv. Res. Rev. **18.2**, 261–271 (2024)
4. Shen, S., et al.: A survey of knowledge tracing: models, variants, and applications. IEEE Trans. Learn. Technol. (2024)
5. M. Khajah, R.V. Lindsey, M.C. Mozer, How deep is knowledge tracing? Int. Educ. Data Min. Soc. (2016)
6. Corbett, A.T., Anderson, J.R.: Knowledge tracing: modeling the acquisition of procedural knowledge. UMUAI **4**, 253–278 (1994)
7. Pelánek, R.: Bayesian knowledge tracing, logistic models, and beyond: an overview of learner modeling techniques. User Model. User-Adap. Inter. **27**, 313–350 (2017)
8. Piech, C., et al.: Deep knowledge tracing. Adv. Neural Inform. Process. Syst. **28** (2015)
9. Shin, D., et al.: Saint+: integrating temporal features for ednet correctness prediction. In: LAK21: 11th International Learning Analytics and Knowledge Conference (2021)
10. Shen, S., et al.: Learning process-consistent knowledge tracing. In: Proceedings of the 27th ACM SIGKDD Conference on Knowledge Discovery & Data Mining (2021)
11. Xu, B., et al.: Learning behavior-oriented knowledge tracing. In: Proceedings of the 29th ACM SIGKDD Conference on Knowledge Discovery and Data Mining (2023)
12. Zhang, J., et al.: Dynamic key-value memory networks for knowledge tracing. In: Proceedings of the 26th International Conference on World Wide Web (2017)
13. Markovitch, S., Scott, P.D.: The role of forgetting in learning. In: Machine Learning Proceedings 1988, pp. 459–465. Morgan Kaufmann (1988)

14. Baker, R.S.D., Corbett, A.T., Aleven, V.: More accurate student modeling through contextual estimation of slip and guess probabilities in bayesian knowledge tracing. In: International Conference on Intelligent Tutoring Systems, pp. 406–415. Springer (2008)

15. Pardos, Z.A., Heffernan, N.T.: Kt-idem: introducing item difficulty to the knowledge tracing model. In: International Conference on User Modeling, Adaptation, and Personalization, pp. 243–254. Springer (2011)

16. Nedungadi, P., Remya, M.S.: Incorporating forgetting in the personalized, clustered, bayesian knowledge tracing (pc-bkt) model. In: 2015 International Conference on Cognitive Computing and Information Processing (CCIP). IEEE (2015)

17. Loftus, G.R.: Evaluating forgetting curves. J. Exper. Psychol. Learn. Memory Cogn. **11.2**, 397 (1985)

18. Guo, X., et al.: Enhancing knowledge tracing via adversarial training. In: Proceedings of the 29th ACM International Conference on Multimedia (2021)

19. Vaswani, A.: Attention is all you need. Adv. Neural Inform. Process. Syst. (2017)

20. Pandey, S., Karypis, G.: A self-attentive model for knowledge tracing. arXiv 2019. arXiv preprint arXiv:1907.06837

21. Choi, Y., et al.: Towards an appropriate query, key, and value computation for knowledge tracing. In: Proceedings of the seventh ACM conference on learning@ scale (2020)

22. Ghosh, A., Heffernan, N., Lan, A.S.: Context-aware attentive knowledge tracing. In: Proceedings of the 26th ACM SIGKDD International Conference on Knowledge Discovery & Data Mining (2020)

23. Ke, F., et al.: HiTSKT: a hierarchical transformer model for session-aware knowledge tracing. Knowl.-Based Syst. **284**, 111300 (2024)

24. Huang, T., et al.: Response speed enhanced fine-grained knowledge tracing: a multi-task learning perspective. Expert Syst. Appl. **238**, 122107 (2024)

25. Cai, L., et al.: Item response theory. Ann. Rev. Statist. Appl. **3.1**, 297–321 (2016)

26. Heffernan, N.T., Heffernan, C.L.: The ASSISTments ecosystem: Building a platform that brings scientists and teachers together for minimally invasive research on human learning and teaching. Int. J. Artific. Intell. Educ. **24**, 470–497 (2014)

Research on Digital Project-Based Learning: An Effective Way to Promote the Construction of New Excellent Classrooms

He Liu[1], Ya Liu[2], Chaoyuan Yu[1(✉)], Jianguo Zhang[3], and Lili Wan[4]

[1] Chongqing Academy of Educational Sciences, Chongqing 400015, China
471857226@qq.com, bjxiexintong@126.com
[2] Chongqing Shizhu County Ethnic Middle School, Chongqing Shizhu 409100, China
[3] Chongqing Changshou Middle School, Chongqing Changshou 401220, China
[4] Chongqing Yuzhong District Majiapu Primary School, Chongqing Yuzhong 400042, China

Abstract. With the rapid development of information technology, digital project-based learning (DPBL), as a new teaching method, is gradually changing the traditional education mode. This paper aims to explore the application strategy and effect of digital project-based learning in the construction of new excellent classrooms. First, this paper clarifies the definition and characteristics of digital project-based learning and emphasizes its importance in cultivating students' innovative thinking, teamwork and problem-solving ability. This paper proposes a strategy for applying digital project-based learning in the construction of new excellent classrooms, including defining learning objectives, selecting appropriate digital tools and resources, designing challenging projects, promoting interdisciplinary integration, establishing collaboration and communication mechanisms, providing real-time feedback and guidance, evaluating and reflecting, cultivating digital literacy, integrating into real-world problems and continuously updating and optimizing. Finally, through case analysis, this paper shows the application effect of digital project-based learning in practical teaching and proves its important role in promoting the construction of new excellent classrooms. Research shows that digital project-based learning helps improve students' learning experience, improve teaching effectiveness, and lay a solid foundation for students' future development.

Keywords: Digital project-based learning · construction of new excellent classrooms · teaching strategies · learning effect · innovation ability

1 Introduction

In the 21st century, the development of information technology has had a profound impact on the field of education. The traditional teaching mode is being replaced by digital and personalized learning methods. As a teaching method that combines modern information technology and the concept of project-based learning, digital project-based

---

H. Liu and Y. Liu—Are the co-first authors of this paper.

K. Zhang et al. (Eds.): CSEI 2024, CCIS 2448, pp. 131–146, 2025.
https://doi.org/10.1007/978-981-96-3738-6_11

learning (DPBL) has become an important direction of education reform. The construction of new excellent classrooms requires educators to explore and innovate teaching methods constantly to meet the educational needs of the new era. This paper discusses the application strategy and effect of digital project-based learning in the construction of new excellent classrooms.

2 Definitions and Characteristics of Digital Project-Based Learning

Digital project-based learning is a student-centered teaching method that emphasizes the promotion of students' active learning and problem-solving ability through practical projects. In this learning mode, students use digital tools and resources, such as online learning platforms, collaborative software, and virtual laboratories, to complete project tasks. Digital project-based learning has the following characteristics:

Student-led: Students constitute the main body of learning, choose the project theme according to their own interests and needs, and dominate the implementation process of the project.

Practice-oriented: Projects are usually designed around real-world problems, and students need to apply theoretical knowledge to solve practical problems.

Interdisciplinary integration: Project-based learning encourages students to consider interdisciplinary approaches and integrate the knowledge and skills of different disciplines into projects.

Teamwork: Project-based learning emphasizes teamwork, and students need to cooperate with others to complete tasks together.

Continuous assessment: In the process of project-based learning, students' performance and achievements are continuously evaluated to adjust their teaching strategies in time.

3 Basic Concept Connotations of the New Excellent Classroom

The new excellent classroom is guided by the cultivation of core literacy in the online and offline learning environments, guided by construction planning and the optimization of teaching design, with the reform of teaching methods and the transformation of learning methods as the core content, with the traction of teaching evaluation and the construction of teachers' ability as the internal driving force, with the improvement of digital empowerment and the deep transformation of teaching and research as important support, to promote the structuralization, integration and ecologicalization of curriculum implementation, resource development, teaching environment, teaching evaluation and other elements, to promote the integration of teaching evaluation, to maximize the efficiency and benefit of teaching and learning, with as little time, energy and investment as possible. To achieve the best possible teaching effect [53].

4   The Application Strategy of Digital Project-Based Learning in the Construction of New Excellent Classrooms

As an innovative educational model, digital project-based learning (PBL) can effectively promote the construction of new excellent classrooms. Current research shows that the application of digital technology in education not only improves the efficiency of teaching but also enhances students' learning experience and teachers' professional development. For example, Matveeva [1] noted that the development of the digital environment requires educators to have modern digital capabilities, which is crucial to the teaching process in higher education. Sancho-Gil [2] emphasized that a narrow digital technology perspective may hinder major improvements in education and therefore requires a diversified technology application strategy.

By integrating various technical means, digital project-based learning can provide more abundant learning resources and more efficient teaching methods in the teaching process. Research by Zimmer [3] shows that the virtual coach model can significantly improve teachers' digital learning ability, which provides strong support for the implementation of digital PBL. Moreover, Gong [4] noted that in the era of education informatization 2.0, college teachers need to continuously improve their informatization teaching ability to ensure the orderly progress of teaching activities.

Digital project-based learning can also enhance the interaction between family and school through technical assistance and promote students' autonomous learning at home. Nazare's [5] research shows that a technology-assisted coaching system can improve parents' participation in and awareness of their children's learning activities, which is highly important for students' growth in the informal learning environment. In addition, a systematic review by Maksimova [6] revealed that the application of educational games and intelligent tutoring systems in language learning can significantly improve students' motivation and learning satisfaction, which provides a reference for the application of digital PBL in other disciplines.

The implementation of digital project-based learning also needs to consider the complexity and diversity of educational technology. Teng [7] noted that the application of multimedia technology can enhance the interactivity and attractiveness of moral education, which is also applicable to digital PBL in other disciplines. Alikarieva [8] emphasized that the application of mathematical modeling methods in the digitization of higher education can provide a scientific basis for the development of the education process, which is highly important for the design and optimization of digital PBL courses.

The future development of digital project-based learning needs to rely on the support of emerging technologies. Ahmad [9] proposed that Education 5.0 can eliminate learning disabilities and enhance personalized learning experiences through the use of technologies such as artificial intelligence, blockchain and virtual reality, which provides technical support for the further development of digital PBL. The research of Ovtsarenko [10] also shows that the combination of a virtual learning environment and building information modeling (BIM) can provide innovative teaching methods for engineering education, which provides a reference for digital PBL in other disciplines.

4.1 Technology Integration and Application of Digital Project-Based Learning

The technology integration and application of digital project-based learning show significant potential in modern education.

Integration of mobile and desktop applications: Yeh et al. [11] proposed a ubiquitous information application that supports project-based learning courses in science, technology, engineering, and mathematics (STEM) education. This application has been practiced in Taiwan for 11 years, helping teachers and students make continuous improvements and cooperate in project work. By analyzing, planning and solving problems, students can apply the knowledge they have learned in the real environment, and the tutor provides timely guidance.

Multimedia teaching and intelligent education system: Cui et al. [12] developed an integrated multimedia teaching model (IMTM) for intelligent education systems. The system leverages smart devices and wireless networks to provide a personalized and seamless learning experience. The experimental results show that IMTM significantly improves students' learning performance and flexibility, especially in listening and oral expression.

Blended learning method: Ghannam et al. [13] combined project-based learning and team learning in an engineering module, aiming to cultivate students' system engineering skills. Through real engineering problems, students develop knowledge in the fields of control systems, image processing, and embedded systems in teamwork while improving decision-making, problem solving, and project planning capabilities.

Computational thinking training for noninformatics students: Hou et al. [14] enhanced the interest of nontechnical students in programming and technology through visual and interactive programming teaching methods such as Scratch and Tableau. Research shows that these methods improve students' acceptance of technology and learning satisfaction.

Teachers' views on the integration of mobile technology: Chen et al. [17] discussed the different concepts and applications of mobile learning through interviews with primary school teachers in Taiwan. These concepts range from 'teacher-centered' to 'student-centered', showing the potential of mobile technology in promoting student-centered learning.

Information-based educational technology in higher vocational education: Lian et al. [18] introduced how to implement a business English education plan through information-based educational technology under the 'school-enterprise dual system' model. This model emphasizes the combination of government policies and enterprise needs and improves students' vocational skills and employability.

Application of virtual technology in civil engineering education: Ovtsarenko et al. [10] discussed the application of building information modeling (BIM) in civil engineering education. The BIM method combines all the parameter information of the three-dimensional object, develops innovative teaching methods through modern technical support, and improves students' basic engineering education.

Web-based database course e-learning application: Dela Rosa [19] developed a web-based e-learning application that focuses on the teaching of database courses. The system provides SQL learning, testing and ERD simulation, which significantly improves students' learning ability and self-assessment ability.

By integrating a variety of technical tools and teaching methods, digital project-based learning has significantly improved students' learning experience and effectiveness and provided teachers with rich teaching resources and support.

4.2 Virtual Coach and Teachers' Professional Development

The application of virtual coaches in teachers' professional development is gradually receiving attention and research.

The application of virtual reality (VR) technology in teacher training has potential for improving teaching practices. Chih-Pu Dai et al. [22] explored the effect of virtual reality-supported simulation learning on improving the teaching practices of graduate teaching assistants (GTAs). The probability of appropriate teaching behavior can be significantly improved by dynamically balancing the simulation scene design of subject knowledge and pedagogical knowledge and prolonging the implementation time of training programs. These findings indicate that well-designed VR scenes and sufficient training time are effective teacher training strategies.

In addition, virtual practice has also proven to be a useful tool in teacher education. H. Theelen et al. [27] reported that virtual internships can significantly reduce the career anxiety of preservice teachers and help them obtain a more realistic picture of teaching. Collaboration in virtual practice and video learning of real classroom events are considered good preparations for the actual teaching environment.

The virtual coaching system has also demonstrated its effectiveness in teacher behavior management training. Delamarre et al. [28] introduced the 3D interactive virtual teacher training system (IVT-T), which allows teachers to interact with virtual students in a virtual classroom, practice behavior management skills, and obtain feedback. Studies have shown that IVT-T graphics and student behavior are very realistic, and its user interface is also confirmed to be effective, efficient and easy to learn.

In the field of vocational training, Heesook Shin et al. [21] presented the application of virtual intervention technology (VI) in virtual vocational training. Studies have shown that VI technology can significantly improve the effectiveness of virtual training and promote the transfer of learning from the virtual world to the real world. This technique is particularly suitable for the training of people with intellectual disabilities or beginners and has higher time efficiency and success rates than traditional methods do.

Finally, online learning provides a new method for teachers' professional development. The study of Lindsay Stoetzel et al. [23] emphasized how learning experiences in online coaching programs promote teachers' professional growth. The study revealed that participants were able to apply what they learned more flexibly to specific school situations by defining and organizing their coaching work and embedding learning in real problems.

Virtual coaching and virtual reality technology have shown a variety of applications and significant effects on the professional development of teachers. These technologies can not only improve teachers' teaching skills and behavior management ability but also reduce occupational anxiety, provide real teaching experience, and promote the practical application of learning.

4.3   Technology-Assisted Home-School Interaction and Students' Autonomous Learning

Research on technology-assisted home-school interactions and students' autonomous learning reveals many achievements and challenges.

Teacher–Student Interaction and Autonomous Learning: Guang Jiang et al. [30] developed NaMemo2, an augmented reality system designed to enhance teacher–student interaction (TSI) and student autonomy in the classroom. Research shows that the system not only improves the interaction between teachers and students but also improves students' attitudes and willingness to interact, thus improving their classroom attention and atmosphere.

The role of parents in the use of digital media: Molly Hammer et al. [31] explored the role of parents in students' digital media self-efficacy. The study revealed that parents' belief in digital media is related to students' self-efficacy, especially the behavior of parents providing smartphones, which plays a mediating role. This finding shows that parents' attitudes and behaviors toward technology use in the family have an important effect on students' autonomous learning.

Digital support in a blended learning environment: Thomas K. F. Chiu et al. [32] studied digital support in a blended learning environment on the basis of self-determination theory (SDT). Research shows that digital support can better meet students' autonomy, relevance and competence than can teacher support to better promote students' participation. This underscores the importance of providing multiple modes of digital support in a blended learning environment.

Technology-assisted family learning guidance: Juliana Nazare et al. [5] studied a technology-assisted human coaching system that provides personalized learning guidance by analyzing children's game data. The results show that this system not only improves parents' understanding of children's learning but also has a more significant effect on families with low education levels and promotes children's autonomous learning.

The impact of technology on classroom interaction: Guofang Li et al. [33] compared teacher–student interaction patterns in EFL classrooms with high and low technology use. The study revealed that high-tech teachers use more display questions and instructions, resulting in a decrease in students' spontaneous output and a decline in the quality of interaction. This shows that teachers' teaching awareness and skills need to be improved in technology-assisted language teaching.

Technical design for visually impaired students: V Gadiraju et al. [34] studied how technology supports classroom and distance learning for visually impaired students. The study suggests that technical designs that integrate behavioral and academic skills, such as audio feedback and progress tracking, can help students succeed in autonomous learning.

The impact of interactive entertainment technology: Wen Li Anthony et al. [35] studied the relationships between the use of interactive entertainment technology and school performance and participation. The results show that the overuse of entertaining interactive technology is related to a decline in academic performance and classroom participation. This suggests that effective guidelines need to be developed to help parents and teachers regulate students' technology use.

Technical support in family language management: Fatma F. S. Said et al. [36] explored the role of technology in family language inheritance. Studies have shown that technology can enhance family language practices, reduce parents' anxiety about children's language development, and support children in developing bilingual identities.

Parents support students' digital learning: Alyssa R. Gonzalez-DeHass et al. [37] discussed the changing role of parents in supporting students' K-12 digital learning. Stressed the importance of two-way communication in the digital space to address parents' concerns and support students' autonomous learning.

Autonomy of mobile-assisted language learning: Gustavo Garcia Botero et al. [38] studied the application of Duolingo in extracurricular language learning. The results show that although apps can provide interesting learning activities, students lack sustained motivation and self-management ability. This shows that in mobile-assisted learning, more encouragement and support are needed to promote students' autonomous learning.

Technology plays an important role in promoting home-school interaction and students' autonomous learning, but its effect depends on the support of teachers and parents, students' self-management ability and appropriate technology design and application.

4.4 Multimedia Technology and Subject Teaching Interactive Enhancement

The application of multimedia technology in subject teaching has significantly enhanced interactivity.

First, the research of Yue Teng et al. [7] noted that the application of multimedia technology in moral education teaching in colleges and universities has greatly increased students' interest and participation. Studies have shown that by using multimedia elements such as music, data interpretation, image and video analysis, and animation, teachers can create a more interactive teaching environment, improve teaching methods, and promote interaction between teachers and students.

Guofang Li et al. [33] explored the application of multimedia technology in primary school English as a foreign language (EFL) classrooms and reported that high-tech classrooms have a certain negative effect on promoting classroom interaction. Although multimedia technology can enrich teaching activities, teachers rely too much on technology to display and instruct, reducing students' opportunities for spontaneous and real language output and resulting in a decline in interaction.

Mercedes Querol-Julian et al. [39] analyzed how to promote students' participation through multimodal interaction in English teaching. Research shows that in the digital environment, lecturers manage and promote interaction through multimodal interactions (such as waiting time and functional diversity in the feedback stage), which help students actively participate in the virtual classroom.

Lianjiang Jiang et al. [40] focused on the participation of teachers in digital multimodal creation (DMC) in EFL courses at Chinese universities. The results show that teachers' participation in DMC affects their way of classroom interaction, and teachers who use multiple resources can significantly enhance students' language use and interaction.

Hayeong Song et al. [41] reported that multimedia content is more helpful to novice users and can improve their usability perceptions and reading efficiency. This finding shows that the proper use of multimedia technology in teaching can help students better understand and master knowledge and enhance classroom interaction.

Manoli Pifarré et al. [42] emphasized the role of interactive technology in creating dialog space and collaborative creation. Research shows that the visibility, responsiveness and multimodality of interactive technology are helpful for improving students' collaboration and interaction.

The research of Colleen Gallagher et al. [43] shows that through multimedia case teaching, preparatory teachers can better grasp the teaching strategies for bilingual students and enhance classroom interaction and teaching effects.

The application of multimedia technology in subject teaching not only enriches teaching methods but also significantly enhances the interaction between teachers and students. However, teachers need to use technology reasonably and avoid excessive dependence to fully exploit the potential of multimedia technology in promoting teaching interactions.

4.5 Support and Future Development of Emerging Technologies for Digital Project-Based Learning

The support and future development of emerging technologies in digital project-based learning can be discussed from many aspects, including the application of technology, the transformation of the education model and the challenges and opportunities in the future.

First, the application of artificial intelligence (AI) and blockchain technology in education has great potential. According to the research of Md Aminul Islam et al. [46], AI and blockchain technology can realize personalized learning, security authentication and decentralized learning networks. These technologies can increase the accessibility, efficiency and security of education and are expected to completely change the field of education. Especially in personalized learning, AI can provide customized learning content according to students' learning progress and needs, whereas blockchain can ensure the security and transparency of academic certification.

Second, the development of digital environments and global networks has led to new requirements for higher education and teachers' career development. Svetlana Valentinovna Matveeva et al. [1] noted that the educational process needs to adapt to modern national and global challenges and provide appropriate teaching tools and courses to cultivate modern digital capabilities. By introducing new teaching techniques and methods, educators can better support digital transformation and improve the quality and effectiveness of education.

In addition, the importance of the hands-on experience of physical technology in students' learning has also been emphasized. Research by Eva Kassens-Noor et al. [49] shows that hands-on experience can help students more easily identify technical challenges, reduce fear of emerging technologies, and increase familiarity with technology. Hands-on experience can not only improve students' technical skills but also enhance their practical application ability of technology, which is particularly important for future career development.

However, digital project-based learning also faces some challenges in future development. Research by Neil Guppy et al. [51] revealed that in the postepidemic era, although blended and online courses will increase, comprehensive revolutionary changes are unlikely to have occurred. Students' expectations for future changes are more conservative, which indicates that students' acceptance and adaptability need to be taken into account in the process of promoting digital learning.

Finally, the research of Shea N. Kerkhoff et al. [52] shows that in low-income countries, the lack of technical resources is the main obstacle to the realization of digital learning. Although teachers accept the student-centered teaching method in theory, it is difficult to fully implement it in practice because of limited technical resources. This suggests that future research and practice need to explore more innovative solutions to overcome the limitations of technical resources and promote digital project-based learning worldwide.

Emerging technologies have shown great potential in supporting digital project-based learning, but their future development still needs to meet the challenges of technical resources, educational model transformation and student adaptability.

4.6 Strategies for Effectively Applying Digital Project-Based Learning in the Construction of New Excellent Classrooms Are Worth Considering

(1) Clear learning objectives

Before starting digital project-based learning, teachers should clarify the learning objectives and expected results. These objectives should be combined with curriculum standards and the development of students' ability to ensure that the design and implementation of the project can achieve the desired educational effect.

(2) Select the appropriate digital tools and resources

The appropriate digital tools and resources are selected according to the learning objectives and the needs of the students. These tools may include online learning platforms, collaboration software, virtual labs, data analysis and visualization tools, etc.

(3) Design challenging projects

The project should be challenging and stimulate students' curiosity and exploration. The project design should take students' age and cognitive level into consideration and provide enough autonomous space for students to develop their creativity and problem-solving ability.

(4) Promotion of interdisciplinary integration

Digital project-based learning should encourage students to think in an interdisciplinary manner and integrate the knowledge and skills of different disciplines into the project. This helps cultivate students' comprehensive ability and innovative thinking.

(5) Establishing collaboration and communication mechanisms

Encourage collaboration and communication among students and establish online discussion groups, shared workspaces or virtual meeting rooms so that students can exchange ideas, share progress and learn from each other in real time.

(6) Providing real-time feedback and guidance

Teachers should provide timely feedback and guidance to help students overcome the difficulties encountered in the implementation of the project. This can be achieved through online scoring systems, video conferencing or instant messaging tools.

(7) Assessment and reflection

After the completion of the project, a comprehensive evaluation and reflection were conducted to collect feedback from students and teachers and to analyze the advantages and disadvantages of the project to improve future projects.

(8) Cultivating digital literacy

In the process of project-based learning, teachers should pay attention to cultivating students' digital literacy, including information retrieval, data analysis and the use of digital tools.

(9) Integrating real-world problems

The project should be designed around real-world problems so that students can link learning content with real life and improve the practicality and significance of learning.

(10) Continuous update and optimization

With the development of technology and the progress of education, the methods and tools of digital project-based learning are continuously updated and optimized to ensure that they are always in line with the latest trend of education development.

5 Analysis of the Application of Digital Project-Based Learning in the Construction of a New Excellent Classroom

The following are some application cases of digital project-based learning in the construction of new excellent classrooms:

5.1 Case 1: Project-Based Learning in STEM Education

In this case, we focus on a science, technology, engineering and mathematics (STEM) education project that aims to increase students' interest and skills in the STEM field through digital project-based learning. The details of the case are as follows:

Background: With the trends of globalization and technological development, STEM education has received increasing attention. To cultivate students' ability to innovate and solve complex problems, schools have begun to adopt project-based learning, especially in the field of STEM.

Project Design: Students are divided into groups, and each group needs to design and build a robot to complete specific tasks, such as navigation and object handling. The design of the project takes into account the age and cognitive level of the students, ensuring the operability and challenge of the project.

Digital tools and resources: Students use a variety of digital tools and resources, including programming software, 3D modeling tools, sensors and actuators. These tools and resources not only support students' design and construction process but also help them understand the science and engineering principles behind it.

Project implementation: The project is divided into several stages, including requirements analysis, design, construction, testing and iteration. At each stage, students need to use scientific knowledge and engineering skills while teamwork and problem solving.

Case analysis:

Learning effect: Through project-based learning, students have made significant progress in knowledge acquisition and skill application in the STEM field. They not only learned how to design and construct robots but also learned how to apply theoretical knowledge to solve practical problems.

Teamwork: The project requires students to work together in a team, which helps them develop their communication skills, collaborative spirit and leadership. Students learn how to coordinate work, assign tasks and resolve conflicts within the team during the project implementation process.

Teacher's role: Teachers play the role of instructor and supporter in the project. They provide the necessary knowledge and skills training to help students overcome difficulties in project implementation.

Challenges and Reflections: In the process of project implementation, students encounter some challenges, such as technical problems, time management and teamwork. Through reflection and adjustment, students learn how to face challenges and learn from them.

5.2   Case 2: Project-Based Learning in Social Science Courses

In this case, we explored project-based learning in a social science course that aims to help students understand social issues and develop critical thinking skills.

Background: Social science courses usually involve the understanding and analysis of social phenomena. Through project-based learning, students can study specific problems more deeply and connect them with the real world.

Project design: Students were asked to study a specific social issue, such as the impact of urbanization on the local community. They need to collect data, analyze problems, and design solutions.

Digital tools and resources: Students use digital tools and resources such as online databases, social media, questionnaires, and geographic information systems (GISs) to support their research.

Project implementation:

Learning effect: Students improve their research ability, data analysis ability and critical thinking ability through project-based learning. They are able to better understand the complexity of social problems and develop innovative solutions.

Autonomous learning: The project encourages students to learn autonomously. They need to set their own research goals, choose research methods and explain the research results.

Teacher support: Teachers provide necessary guidance and feedback in the project to help students overcome difficulties in the research process.

Continuing Learning: After the project, students remain interested in the issues studied and continue to explore relevant social phenomena.

These two cases demonstrate the application effect of digital project-based learning in the construction of new excellent classrooms. Through actual project implementation, students not only improve the learning effect but also cultivate teamwork, critical thinking and autonomous learning abilities. These skills are valuable assets for future learning and careers.

6 Summary

The future development direction of digital project-based learning can be considered from multiple dimensions. The following are some possible development trends and directions.

(1) Technological innovation and integration

Application of emerging technologies: With the development of emerging technologies such as artificial intelligence, big data, and cloud computing, digital project-based learning will integrate these technologies to provide a more personalized and intelligent learning experience.

Interdisciplinary integration: Digital project-based learning promotes the integration of different disciplines, such as the integration of science, technology, engineering and mathematics (STEM) education and the intersection of art and science.

(2) Teaching mode innovation

Blended teaching: Combining the advantages of online and offline teaching, digital project-based learning promotes the development of blended teaching modes to adapt to the learning needs and environments of different students.

Student-centered teaching: Digital project-based learning continues to emphasize the student-centered teaching model, encouraging students to actively explore, practice and create, rather than passively accepting, knowledge.

(3) Teachers' professional development

Changes in teachers' role: Teachers will change from knowledge transmitters to guides, collaborators and designers and need to continuously improve their digital teaching ability.

Continuous professional training: Teachers need to receive continuous professional training, including technical training and teaching strategy updates, to adapt to changes in the digital education environment.

(4) Policy and institutional support

Policy formulation: The government will formulate more policies to support digital project-based learning, including capital investment, resource allocation and education reform measures.

Evaluation system reform: To adapt to the development of digital education, the evaluation system needs to be reformed to evaluate students' learning outcomes and abilities more comprehensively.

(5) International cooperation and communication

Cross-border cooperation: Digital project-based learning promotes cross-border educational cooperation and exchanges, shares educational resources, and improves the quality of global education.

The formulation of global education standards: With the deepening of international education cooperation, it will be possible to form a global education standard and quality certification system.

(6) Combinations of research and practice

Empirical Research: More empirical research is needed in the future to verify the effectiveness of digital project-based learning and its application in different cultural and educational environments.

Case sharing: Through the sharing of case studies and best practices, educators can learn from each other and continuously optimize the implementation strategies of digital project-based learning.

(7) Sustainable development and ethical considerations

Sustainable development: Digital project-based learning focuses on sustainable development, including environmental education, resource conservation and recycling.

Ethical considerations: With the application of technology, digital project-based learning will pay more attention to ethical issues, such as data privacy and intellectual property protection.

The future development direction of digital project-based learning will be diversified, and it will constantly adapt to technological progress, educational needs and global development trends to promote the innovation and development of education.

In short, as an effective teaching method, digital project-based learning can play an important role in the construction of new excellent classrooms and promote the process of educational modernization.

Acknowledgments. This paper presents the phased research results of the Chongqing Education Comprehensive Reform 2024 research topic "Research on the Strategy and Path of New Excellent Classroom Teaching Reform in Basic Education" (project no. 24JGY37), the key project of Chongqing Education Commission Science and Technology Research Plan "Brain-like Network Theory and Key Technology Research for Smart Education" (project approval no. KJZD-K202114401), the special project of Chongqing Research Institute Performance Incentive Guidance "Spiking Neural Network Theory and Method Research for Smart Education" (acceptance no. cstc2022jxjl0214), Chongqing Education Science Planning Project "Promoting Teaching Improvement with Wisdom Education" (Project No.: 2019-04-616), and the project of Chongqing Academy of Educational Sciences "Application of Brain-like Network Theory in Smart Education."

References

1. Svetlana, V.M., Natalia, S.A., Yuriy, I.S., Nadezhda, V.F., et al.: Digitalization of higher education and professional development of educators: technologies and new opportunities. Artif. Intell. **9**(29), 77–86 (2020)

2. Sancho-Gil, J.M., Rivera-Vargas, P., Mino-Puigcercos, R.: Moving beyond the predictable failure of Ed-Tech initiatives. Learn. Media Technol. **45**(1), 61–75 (2020)
3. Zimmer, W.K., Matthews, S.D.: A virtual coaching model of professional development to increase teachers' digital learning competencies. Teach. Teach. Educ. **109** (2022)
4. Gong, L.: Cultivation and improvement of college teachers' informatization teaching ability in the era of education informatization 2.0. Lifelong Educ. **9**(5), 117–117 (2020)
5. Juliana, N., et al.: Technology-assisted coaching can increase engagement with learning technology at home and caregivers' awareness of it. Comput. Educ. **188**, 104565 (2022)
6. Maksimova, A.: A systematic review of research on the use and impact of technology for learning chinese. Int. J. Cybern. Inform. **11**(4), 67–78 (2022)
7. Teng, Y., Jiang, P.-X., Wang, K.: Moral education teaching in colleges and universities based on the application of multimedia technology. Int. J. Electric. Eng. Educ. **60**(2_suppl), 251–265 (2020)
8. Alikarieva, A.: Using mathematical modeling methods in digitalization of higher education. Ižtimoij tadkikotlar žurnali **7**(3), 30–39 (2020)
9. Shabir, A., Sabina, U., Ghulam, M., Muhammad, S.A., Taegkeun, W., et al.: Education 5.0: requirements, enabling technologies, and future directions. CoRR, abs/2307.15846 (2023)
10. Ovtsarenko, O., Makuteniene, D., Timinskas, E.: Virtual technologies possibilities for improving background knowledge of civil engineering education. Headache 509–517 (2020)
11. Yeh, C.-T., Chen, M.-C.: A mobile/desktop application to integrative science, technology, engineering, and mathematics project-based learning curriculum for continuous improvement. Int. J. Electr. Eng. Educ. **59**(1), 3–19 (2019)
12. Cui, Q.: Multimedia teaching for applied linguistic smart education system. Int. J. Hum.-Comput. Interact. **39**(1), 272–281 (2022)
13. Ghannam, R., Chan, C.: Teaching undergraduate students to think like real-world systems engineers: a technology-based hybrid learning approach. Syst. Eng. **26**(6), 728–741 (2023)
14. Hou, H.-Y., Agrawal, S., Lee, C.-F.: Computational thinking training with technology for non-information undergraduates. Think. Skills Creat. **38** (2020)
15. Taghizadeh, M., Yourdshahi, Z.H.: Integrating technology into young learners' classes: language teachers' perceptions. Comput. Assist. Lang. Learn. **33**(8), 982–1006 (2019)
16. Wang, L., Chiang, F.-K.: Integrating novel engineering strategies into STEM education: APP design and an assessment of engineering-related attitudes. British J. Educ. Technol. **51**(6), 1938–1959 (2020)
17. Chen, C.-H., Tsai, C.-C.: In-service teachers' conceptions of mobile technology-integrated instruction: tendency toward student-centered learning. World Culture **170**, 104224 (2021)
18. Lian, Y.: Research and practice on the application of esp informatizational education technology in higher vocational education based on the college-enterprise dual system integration mode. Lethaia **9**(4), 118 (2020)
19. Aaron, P.M.D.R., Luigi, M.M.V., John, M.R.S.M., John, E.B.Q., et al.: Web-based database courses e-learning application. Turkish Online J. Qualit. Inquiry **12**(6), 5414–5421 (2021)
20. Zhong, J., Jiang, L.: Professional development of CLIL teachers. System **101** (2021)
21. Heesook, S., Sungjin, H., Hyo-Jeong, S., Seong-Min, B., Cho-Rong, Y., Youn-Hee, G., et al.: Effect of virtual intervention technology in virtual vocational training for people with intellectual disabilities: connecting instructor in the real world and trainee in the virtual world. Int. J. Hum.-Comput. Interact. **40**(3), 624–639 (2022)
22. Chih-Pu, D., Fengfeng, K., Zhaihuan, D., Mariya, P., et al.: Improving teaching practices via virtual reality-supported simulation-based learning: scenario design and the duration of implementation. Br. J. Edu. Technol. **54**(4), 836–856 (2023)
23. Stoetzel, L., Shedrow, S.: Coaching our coaches: how online learning can address the gap in preparing K-12 instructional coaches. Teach. Teach. Educ. **88** (2020)

24. Oagaz, H., Schoun, B., Choi, M.-H.: Real-time posture feedback for effective motor learning in table tennis in virtual reality. Int. J. Hum Comput Stud. **158**, 102731 (2022)
25. Wan, F.W.M.R., Mydin, A.A., Ismail, A.: coaching pengajaran sebagai pembelajaran profesional guru: satu tinjauan. Astrophys. J. **3**(2), 50–61 (2020)
26. Seth, A.P., Amy, C.H., Leigh, A.H., Allison, W.P., Samantha, T.I., Alicia, B.L., et al.: US teachers' perceptions of online professional development. Teach. Teach. Educ. **82**, 33–42 (2019)
27. Theelen, H., et al.: Virtual internships in blended environments to prepare preservice teachers for the professional teaching context. British J. Educ. Technol. **51**(1), 194–210 (2019)
28. Delamaree, A., et al.: The Interactive Virtual Training for Teachers (IVT-T) to practice classroom behavior management. Int. J. Hum. Comput. Stud. **152**, 102646–102646 (2021)
29. Woulfin, S.L.: Coach professional development in the urban emergent context. Urban Educ. **55**(10), 1355–1384 (2017)
30. Guang, J., Jiahui, Z., Yunsong, L., Pengcheng, A., Yunlong, W., et al.: NaMemo2: facilitating teacher-student interaction with theory-based design and student autonomy consideration. Educ. Inf. Technol. **29**(6), 7259–7279 (2023)
31. Hammer, M., Scheiter, K., Stuermer, K.: New technology, new role of parents: how parents' beliefs and behavior affect students' digital media self-efficacy. Comput. Hum. Behav. **116**, 106642 (2021)
32. Chiu, T.K.F.: Digital support for student engagement in blended learning based on self-determination theory. Comput. Hum. Behav. **124**, 106909–106909 (2021)
33. Li, G., Sun, Z., Jee, Y.: The more technology the better? A comparison of teacher–student interaction in high and low technology use elementary EFL classrooms in China. System **84**, 24–40 (2019)
34. Gadiraju, V., Doyle, O., Kane, S.K.: Exploring technology design for students with vision impairment in the classroom and remotely. In: ACM Conference on Human Factors in Computing Systems, pp. 1–13 (2021)
35. Wen, L.A., Zhu, Y., Nower, L.: The relationship of interactive technology use for entertainment and school performance and engagement: evidence from a longitudinal study in a nationally representative sample of middle school students in China. Comput. Hum. Behav. **122**, 106846–106846 (2021)
36. Said, F.F.S.: 'Ba-SKY-aP with her each day at dinner': technology as supporter in the learning and management of home languages. J. Multilingual Multicultural Develop. **42**(8), 747–762 (2021)
37. Alyssa, R.G., Patricia, P.W., Jillian, R.P., Ann, T.M., et al.: Parental involvement in supporting students' digital learning. Educ. Psychol. **57**(4), 281–294 (2022)
38. Botero, G.G., Questier, F., Zhu, C.: Self-directed language learning in a mobile-assisted, out-of-class context: do students walk the talk? Comput. Assist. Lang. Learn. **32**(1–2), 71–97 (2018)
39. Querol-Julian, M.: Multimodal interaction in English-medium instruction: How does a lecturer promote and enhance students? participation in a live online lecture? J. Engl. Acad. Purp. **61**, 101207 (2023)
40. Jiang, L., Shulin, Y., Zhao, Y.: Teacher engagement with digital multimodal composing in a Chinese tertiary EFL curriculum. Lang. Teach. Res. **25**(4), 613–632 (2021)
41. Hayeong, S., Jennifer, H., Alexa, F.S., Curtis, W., John, S., et al.: Experts prefer text but videos help novices: an analysis of the utility of multimedia content. CHI Extend. Abst. abs/2304.11565, pp. 1–9 (2023)
42. Pifarré, M.: Using interactive technologies to promote a dialogic space for creating collaboratively: a study in secondary education. Think. Skills Creat. **32**, 1.0–16.0 (2019)
43. Gallagher, C.: The use of a multimedia case to prepare classroom teachers of emergent bilinguals. Teach. Teach. Educ. **84**, 17.0–29.0 (2019)

44. Mohammed, H., Mokhtar, E., Ahmed, A., Abdulkrim, Z., Hatem, A., et al.: Smart interaction and social TV used by Jordanian University students. Technol. Soc. **71**, 102110 (2022)
45. Suvi, K., Hanni, M., Teemu, S., Marjatta, T., et al.: I still miss human contact, but this is more flexible - Paradoxes in virtual learning interaction and multidisciplinary collaboration. British J. Educ. Technol. **51.0**(4.0), 1101–1116 (2020)
46. Islam, M.A.: AI & Blockchain as sustainable teaching and learning tools to cope with
 the 4IR. Blockchain and AI abs/2305.01088, pp. 123–153 (2023)
47. Ma, Q., Yan, J.: How to empirically and theoretically incorporate digital technologies into language learning and teaching. Bilingualism (Cambridge, England) **25**(3), 392–393 (2022)
48. Wenjing, L., Jin, L.: Artificial intelligence and emerging digital technologies in the energy sector. Appl. Energy **303** (2021)
49. Eva, K., Noah, D., Travis, D., Jake, P., et al.: Experiencing autonomous futures: Engaged learning with next generation technology. Act. Learn. High. Educ. **24**(1), 21–36 (2023)
50. Higinio, M., Francisco, A.P., Julio, C.M., Mario, R.M., et al.: An education-based approach for enabling the sustainable development gear. Comput. Hum. Behav. **107**, 105775 (2020)
51. Neil, G., Dominique, V., David, B., Lin, L., Joanna, T., Silvia, B., et al.: The post-COVID-19 future of digital learning in higher education: views from educators, students, and other professionals in six countries. Br. J. Edu. Technol. **53**(6), 1750–1765 (2022)
52. Kerkhoff, S.N., Makubuya, T.: Professional development on digital literacy and transformative teaching in a low-income country: a case study of rural Kenya. Read. Res. Q. **57**(1), 287–305 (2022)
53. Xinhuanet. A five-year plan for the construction of new excellent classrooms in primary and secondary schools aimed at core literacy (2024).http://www.cq.xinhuanet.com/20240403/ce3 be2c058f240f189977d5d942e8c00/c.html

An Analysis of the Application of Education Informatization in Addressing the Unique Needs of Macao Students for National Conditions Education

Lijun Tang[1], Lue Li[1(✉)], and Xuan Zhuang[2] ⓘ

[1] Faculty of Humanities and Social Sciences, Macao Polytechnic University, Macao, China
lli@mpu.edu.mo, 68614155@qq.com
[2] Sanya Aviation and Tourism College, Hai Nan Sheng, China

Abstract. With the increase in exchanges between mainland China and Macao, an increasing number of Macao students choose to study mainland China. This study, which analyzes the unique needs of Macao students studying in mainland China in terms of national education conditions, explores the feasibility and effectiveness of education informatization in addressing these needs. This article first summarizes the basic status of Macao students studying in mainland China and the importance of national education conditions and then analyzes the unique needs of Macao students in terms of national education conditions on the basis of the data. On the basis of briefly explaining the distinctive strengths of education informatization, this study proposes recommendations to meet the unique needs of Macao students for national education conditions through education informatization to provide a helpful reference for improving national education conditions for Macao students.

Keywords: Education informatization · Macao students studying on the mainland · National conditions education · Unique needs

1 Introduction

National conditions education, with national identity and patriotism at its core, is a "compulsory course" in education worldwide to promote a noble virtue shared by all mankind. For Macao students studying in the mainland (hereinafter referred to as Macao students), national conditions education bears on carrying forward the core value of loving the country and Macao, on fully implementing the principle of "patriots administering Macao" and on passing down the cause of One Country, Two Systems. It is therefore an important mission of mainland universities to make education a success. However, owing to the significant differences in cultural backgrounds, values, and living habits between Macao and mainland China students, it is necessary for mainland China universities to consider Macao students' unique needs when carrying out education under national conditions. Education informatization, as a crucial force in advancing the modernization of education, offers new perspectives and pathways to meet the unique needs

K. Zhang et al. (Eds.): CSEI 2024, CCIS 2448, pp. 147–157, 2025.
https://doi.org/10.1007/978-981-96-3738-6_12

of Macao students for national education. As a result, in-depth research on the application of education informatization in national conditions education for Macao students is highly important for ensuring their overall development and enhancing their national identity. This research also helps promote the reform and innovation of the mainland's education system and improve education quality.

2 Introduction of Macao Students

2.1 The Mainland has Become the Main Choice for Macao Students who Further their Studies Outside Macao

In the 1980s, mainland universities resumed the acceptance of Macao students. Since 1993, the Hong Kong, Macao and Taiwan Affairs Office and the Department of Students of Higher Education of the Ministry of Education have organized several key universities under the Education Ministry to hold the "China Mainland University Education Exhibition" in Macao every year to carry out admission consultation and publicity. As Macao has been increasingly integrated into overall national development since its return to the motherland in 1999, an increasing number of young people in Macao have chosen to pursue higher education in the mainland. The main ways for them to enter mainland universities include recommended examinations, national joint admissions, applying for mainland universities with Macao's "Four Schools Joint Examination" scores, and independent admissions by individual universities. By analyzing data from the "Briefing on the Destinations of Macao High School Graduates' Further Studies" conducted by the Education and Youth Development Bureau of the Macao Special Administrative Region, since the 2017/2018 academic year, the number and proportion of Macao students going to the mainland for further studies have increased annually (see Fig. 1 for details). The number stood at 1,679 in the 2022/2023 academic year, far exceeding the number of students going to other regions for further studies and almost equal to the number of students going to local universities in Macao. As of 2024, the number has exceeded 8,000.

2.2 Macao is the Main Way for Macao Students to Find Employment

In August 2021, the Education and Youth Development Bureau of the Macao SAR Government, on the basis of the registration information of the 2020 "College Student Learning Supplies Subsidy" program, conducted a survey on the intention of Macao college graduates to further their studies or enter the workforce. The Bureau expected that there would be a total of 9,983 graduates (including Macao students) from various college degree programs in 2021. An online questionnaire was sent to all the above students, and a total of 2,695 questionnaires were collected, of which 2,465 were valid. The results revealed that for "employment destinations for fresh graduates who intend to enter the workforce", the vast majority choose to work in Macao. (See Table 1 for details.)

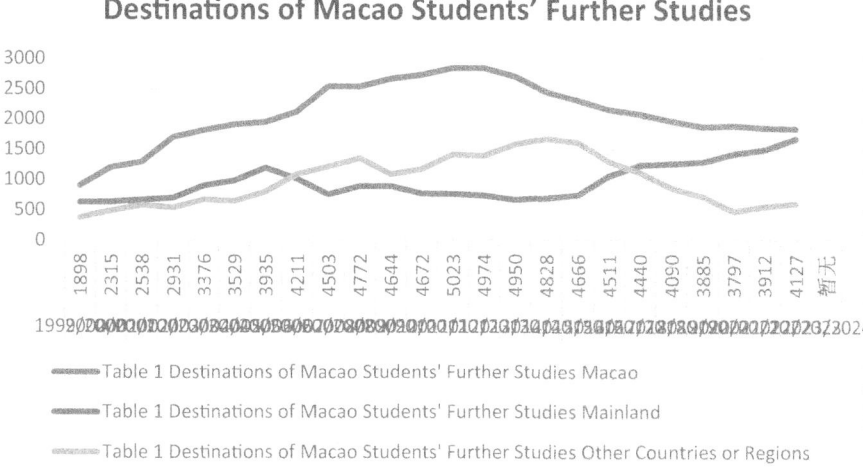

Fig. 1. Destinations of Macao Students' Further Studies

Table 1. Employment Destinations and Salary Expectations of Macao College Graduates.

Category	Destinations	Proportion	Category	Destinations	Proportion
Employment Destinations for Fresh Graduates Who Intend to Enter the Workforce	Macao SAR of China	89.8%	Employment Destinations for Fresh Graduates Who Intend to Enter the Workforce	the United States	0.8%
	the mainland of China	3.2%		Australia	0.7%
	Hong Kong SAR of China	2.6%		the United Kingdom	0.5%
	the Taiwan region of China	1.6%		other countries or regions	0.8%

2.3 The Importance of Cultivating Macao Students has Been Highlighted

Macao will thrive only when its young people thrive. According to 2023 population statistics, the total population of Macau is 683700, of which 72600 yuan is for people aged 15--24, accounting for 10.6%; the number of people aged 25--34 is 114200 yuan, accounting for 16.7% (see Table 2 for details), and the shortage of talent is a long-standing issue. The number of Macao students who choose to study on the mainland has been growing steadily. These students generally enter renowned universities, such as Peking University, Tsinghua University, Zhongshan University, and Wuhan University. They develop in a well-rounded way, possess outstanding professional capacity, are familiar with both Macao and the mainland, and have a strong sense of national identity. This means that both the "quality" and "quantity" of these students should not be ignored. Moreover, these students are generally willing to return to Macao for employment and are therefore strategic reserve talents for the development of Macao. As Macao practices a capitalist system, it is common for Macao students to feel unfamiliar with and alienated from the socialist system in the mainland during their growth years. Under the influence of Western ideological hegemony, some Macao students have also experienced "spiritual loss". "Once people feel that they are between two worlds and that they are rootless in society, they will not be able to have the kind of firm sense of identity necessary to build a stable and modern nation-state." [1] Therefore, it is even more necessary to use the training platform of mainland universities to strengthen national education conditions for Macao students.

Table 2. Age Group Statistics of the Macau Population.

Age group	Number of people (in 10000)	Proportion%
Under 15 years old	9.01	13.2
15–24 years old	7.26	10.6
25–34 years old	11.42	16.7
35–44 years old	12.63	18.5
45–54 years old	9.44	13.8
55–64 years old	9.05	13.2
65 years old and above	9.56	14
total	68.37	100

3   Analysis of the Unique Needs of Macao Students for National Conditions Education

The theory of singularity was innovatively proposed by Leckwitz, a well-known sociologist active in Germany today, in his 2019 book, The Society of Singularities: The Structural Transformation of the Modern World. It emphasizes the uniqueness and distinctiveness of individuals and holds that each individual has his or her unique value and contribution [2]. In the field of education, the application of this theory helps teachers pay more attention to students' individual differences and, in this way, provide personalized educational services. In regard to Macao students, the application of this theory means that educators need to have a deep understanding of the students' cultural backgrounds, values, lifestyles, etc., respect their individual differences and needs, and provide them with more tailored national education in both content and methodology.

In 2022, an institution sent a questionnaire to 316 Hong Kong and Macao students in mainland China through "golden data", a data collection and management tool. Among the surveyed students, 96.8% were Macao students, and 91.1% were undergraduates.

Therefore, the results basically reflect the perspectives of Macao students and are highly relevant. The data revealed that the vast majority of Macao students had received national conditions education in Macao, but more than 70% of Macao students said that the national conditions education they had received in Macao was still at a relatively basic stage, with more general and abstract impressions and concepts. Moreover, 80% of the Macao students believed that after studying in mainland China, "their understanding of national conditions had been significantly or relatively significantly improved." However, as shown in the survey, the mismatch between the national education conditions of mainland universities and the unique characteristics of Macao students was also quite obvious (see Table 3 for details).

Table 3. Mismatch problems between the national education conditions of mainland universities and the unique characteristics of Macao students and recommendations

Category	Content/Option	Number	Proportion
What do you think are the problems of national conditions education of mainland universities for Hong Kong and Macao students?	National conditions education for Hong Kong and Macao students is similar to that for mainland students, not taking the unique circumstances of Hong Kong and Macao students into consideration	211	66.80%
	The course is relatively traditional and unitary in form, and not that appealing to students	194	61.40%
	Some Hong Kong and Macao students are not very familiar with national conditions education, having difficulty understanding what is taught	179	56.60%
	Some Hong Kong and Macao students resist national conditions education and are therefore not willing to take the course	121	38.30%
	There are not enough teachers dedicated to carrying out targeted education	91	28.80%
	Other problems	9	2.80%
How do you think national conditions education for Hong Kong and Macao students can be improved?	Develop more diverse forms of activities attractive to students	223	70.60%
	Design textbooks tailored to Hong Kong and Macao students	174	55.10%

Data analysis revealed that there were at least four reasons for the unique needs of Macao students in national education.

3.1 Differences in Cultural Backgrounds Lead to Unique Needs

As a place where Chinese and Western cultures blend, Macao has unique cultural backgrounds and values. During their growth years, Macao students are not only influenced by traditional Chinese culture but also exposed to elements of Western culture. This multicultural background sometimes produces a sense of confusion and conflict in cultural identity when students receive national education in mainland China. Since most universities use the same textbooks for Macao students as they do for mainland students, Macao students generally feel that what is taught is too abstract or theoretical and find it hard to understand many concepts. Quite a few Macao students feel that, as the content of the course is out of touch with the environment in which they grow up, they lack the sense of history and reality that can produce empathy. The questionnaire revealed that 67% of the respondents thought that national conditions education in mainland China did not consider the special circumstances of Hong Kong and Macao students and that 55% of them hoped that the curriculum and textbooks of national conditions education could be improved.

3.2 Differences in Values Bring About Unique Needs

Macao students place more emphasis on personal freedom, rights protection and the spirit of the rule of law, whereas mainland students attach more importance to collectivism, national interests and moral codes. Differences in values have led to resistance among some Macao students to national education. The data show that 38% of the respondents were resistant to education in national conditions. The main reason is that the internet environment and public opinion environment to which Macao students have been exposed since childhood are different from those in mainland China. Some students believe that they can get to know more than what they are taught in class through foreign websites and thus do not believe in what their teachers tell them. They even fall prey to false claims made by some foreign websites that stigmatize China's national conditions education as "a brainwash project" and "political propaganda" and come to believe in the smearing accusations against China's democracy and human rights situation made from the perspective of so-called Western "universal values" [3].

3.3 Differences in Educational Methods Lead to Unique Needs

The education system in Macao focuses on the development of students' personalities and the cultivation of the ability to put what they learn into practice, whereas the education system in mainland China places more emphasis on the acquisition of basic knowledge and the ability to obtain high scores on exams. These differences can make it difficult for Macao students to adapt to the learning methods and educational environment in mainland China. Since many universities focus on concepts in the examination of political courses, Macao students cannot but memorize them by rote. This can be counterproductive to a certain extent, making the students feel afraid or even regret taking national conditions courses. The data show that 61% of the surveyed respondents believed that inadequate interaction and inappropriate teaching methods had weakened the appeal of national conditions education and that as many as 70.6% of the respondents suggested developing more ways to practice what they have learned in class and carrying out innovative activities welcomed by students.

3.4 Differences in Political Systems Bring About Unique Needs

As Macao practices the policy of one country, two systems, its political and legal systems are different from those in mainland China. During their studies on the mainland, Macao students need to understand and adapt to the mainland's political system and social environment. Since they lack direct understanding and experience of the mainland's political system and social development, they have certain difficulty in empathy. It is therefore necessary to guide them to understand and identify with the country's political system through national conditions education and, in this way, to promote mutual understanding and respect between the two systems. The data indicate that "Moral Codes and the Rule of Law" and "Outline of Modern Chinese History" were the two main national conditions taken by Macao students, and the percentages of students opting for these two courses were 60.5% and 48.0%, respectively. In comparison, only 27% of the students took "Basic Tenets of Marxism", "Introduction to Mao Zedong Thought and the Theoretical System of Socialism with Chinese Characteristics" and "Introduction to Xi Jinping Thought on Socialism with Chinese Characteristics for a New Era", mainly because "the foundation of national conditions education in primary and secondary schools was weak and it was difficult for them to keep up with the pace of teaching."

4 Strategies to Apply Education Informatization to Meet Macao Students' Unique Needs for Education Under National Conditions

Education has entered an information era. Education informatization aims to make information and information technology a basic component of the education system and apply it to various fields of education to promote the comprehensive reform of education [4]. Education informatization has distinctive strengths in addressing the unique needs of Macao students in terms of national education conditions. For example, a large number of resources for education in national conditions can be integrated through digitalization, networking and other technical means. It can increase time and space constraints in traditional teaching to provide more possibilities and flexibility for teaching and greatly enhance students' sense of participation and interaction. It can also realize personalized teaching and tutoring according to students' learning characteristics and needs through technologies such as big data analysis and artificial intelligence and provide a more convenient way for home-school cooperation and communication. Thus, it is necessary for mainland universities to make good use of these distinctive strengths to better meet the unique needs of Macao students for education in national conditions.

4.1 We Need to Develop New Educational Resources and Teaching Models

First, we can put in place a targeted curriculum system for national conditions education. It is helpful to use big data technology to further explore the needs and characteristics of this special group of Macao students and design a targeted curriculum system of national education conditions on the basis of the students' cultural backgrounds, cognitive needs and especially the historical reality of Hong Kong and Macao. It is necessary to make full use of information technology to present what is taught in a digital and networked manner to make students more interested and improve the effectiveness of education. Second, emphasis must be placed on the application of virtual reality (VR) and augmented reality (AR) technologies. VR technology enables students to visit historical sites, revolutionary memorials and other important places in an immersive way and obtain a better understanding of the country's history and culture, whereas AR technology can integrate virtual information into real scenes, enabling students to obtain multidimensional information about buildings, attractions, historical backgrounds, etc., in real time during their visits to mainland cities [5]. Applications such as the "Virtual National Conditions Tour" can be developed to allow students to experience China's major historical events, important cultural attractions and celebrations of traditional Chinese festivals in a virtual environment by wearing VR equipment. Third, we can focus on the design and application of gamified learning. By setting tasks, challenges and reward mechanisms, gamified learning can stimulate students' learning motivation and enhance their sense of participation. This is an application of the theory of "comprehension-based teaching" [6]. The hugely popular domestic video game "Black Myth: Wukong", which is impressive for its unique narrative techniques and profound cultural connotations, is a stellar example worth learning from. We can design immersive games such as "National Conditions Explorer", "Red Script Killing", and "Revolutionary History Board Game" [7]. The sense of uncertainty created by these games can satisfy young people's pursuit of uniqueness and novelty so that their patriotic feelings can be awakened and their value system reshaped through rigorous reasoning and immersive role-playing. Fourth, we need to focus on the customization of personalized learning paths. Providing personalized learning paths is an important innovation to meet the needs of Macao students for education in national conditions. We can use big data analysis to analyze the learning behavior and performance of Macao students, determine their learning preferences and weaknesses, and recommend suitable learning resources and paths for them. In this way, Macao students can independently choose learning content and methods according to their own needs and interests and thus improve the pertinence and effectiveness of learning.

4.2   We Need to Increase Home-School Cooperation and Platform Development

First, parents can participate in the design and teaching of relevant courses. Since parents play an important role in the education of students, they can be invited to participate in the design and teaching of national education through information technology to increase the depth and breadth of home-school cooperation. For example, we can grasp parents' expectations and suggestions for national education through means such as online parent meetings and questionnaires. We can also invite parents to put forward their opinions and suggestions in the process of course design so that there can be more suitable teaching materials. Second, we should strengthen the development of an interactive platform for students, schools, and parents. We can build a three-in-one interactive platform through education informatization to facilitate efficient communication and exchanges between students, schools, and parents. For example, WeChat groups and QQ groups can serve as channels for communication. Online learning platforms can also be used to help parents understand their children's learning progress and enhance home-school interaction and cooperation. Such interactive platforms can not only improve the efficiency and effectiveness of communication but also enhance students' and parents' understanding of and support for school education. Third, we need to strengthen the development of online teaching platforms. Teaching activities on online platforms can lift geographical restrictions and allow Macao students to participate in national education anytime and anywhere. Take the "Jinan University Continuing Education Cloud Classroom", a platform aimed at students from Hong Kong and Macao, as an example. By adding courses such as "Introduction to Traditional Chinese Culture", "Outline of Modern Chinese History", and "Introduction to Chinese Social Development" to the teaching plan and adopting a model of online plus offline teaching, it has enhanced the Chinese cultural identity and sense of national pride of Hong Kong and Macao students[8].

4.3   We Need to Establish a Diversified Mechanism for Evaluation and Feedback

First, evaluations in the process and evaluations in the end should be combined. We should focus not only on the students' final scores but also on their learning process and attitudes. Specifically, we can evaluate students' learning process and attitudes by informing them of their learning records, sense of participation and homework completion and evaluate their learning outcomes and mastery of knowledge through exams, project reports, papers, etc. second, we can combine self-evaluations with mutual evaluations. Through Information Technology, we can introduce a mechanism that combines self-evaluation and mutual evaluation, allows students to participate in the evaluation process, and enhances their ability to self-reflect and cooperate. For example, students can be asked to evaluate their own learning and determine their own strengths and weaknesses. They can be organized to conduct mutual evaluations and learn from each other. In this process, teachers can also understand the effectiveness of learning and what students think and provide timely guidance and help. Third, it is necessary to ensure the timeliness and pertinence of the feedback mechanism. A mechanism that provides timely and effective feedback is important for improving students' performance. Through education informatization, this goal can be achieved. For example, online learning platforms can be used to provide real-time feedback on students' learning, helping them find and correct problems in a timely manner. At the same time, data analysis can be utilized to analyze students' learning data, find weak links in learning, and provide them with targeted guidance and help. this timely and effective feedback mechanism can not only improve students' performance but also enhance their confidence and interest in national education.

5   Conclusion and Prospects

5.1   A Subsection Sample

On the basis of the theories of singularity and education informatization, this article explores the unique needs of Macao students in terms of national education conditions and proposes corresponding educational methods to improve national education conditions for Macao students. With the continuous development and improvement of education informatization, we believe that national education conditions for Macao students will usher in broader development prospects. Future research can focus more on how to better apply education informatization in national conditions education, how to develop a more complete national conditions education curriculum system, how to strengthen the in-depth cooperation between the mainland and Macao in education, and how to adapt to the trend of globalization to enhance the international competitiveness and cross-cultural adaptability of Macao students.

In short, national education for Macao students is a long-term and arduous task that requires continuous exploration, practice, improvement and innovation. Only in this way can we cultivate better talent that can help Macao develop and prosper and contribute more to building China into a great nation and realizing national rejuvenation.

References

1. Pye, L.W.: Aspects of Political Development. Tianjin Renmin Press, Tianjin, Translated by Xiao Ren and Yuan Wang (2009)
2. Reckwitz, A.: The Society of Singularities: The Structural Transformation of the Modern World. Social Sciences Academic Press, Beijing (2024)
3. Jie, C.: Study on Challenges Facing "National Identity Education" For Hong Kong People Since Hong Kong's Return and Countermeasures. Education Sciences in China, **4**, p. 40 (2021)
4. Tong, X.: Informatization of Higher Education Management. China Commerce Press Ltd, Beijing (2023)
5. Li, H.: Big Data on Education: Ushering in Era 2.0 of Education Informatization, chapter 7. Chongqing University Press, Chongqing (2018)
6. Chen, L. Application and Innovation of Education Technologies in the Era of Informatization. Publishing House of Electronics Industry, Beijing (2009)
7. Csikszentmihalyi, M.: Flow : The Psychology of Optimal Experience. Translated by Dingqi Zhang. CITIC Press Corporation, Beijing
8. Case Study (80), Innovation and Practice of Online Teaching Models of Continuing Higher Education in the Guangdong-Hong Kong-Macao Greater Bay Area from the Jinan Extension School. CEDU Media. 2023.06.05
9. Xu, J.: Research on the Use of Information Technology in Education and Teaching. The Road to Success (19), 65–66 (2016)
10. Wang, Z.: Research on the development path of higher education informatization in the era of "Intelligence+5G". Theoretical Observation (11), 156–158 (2021)
11. Wang, Y., Huang, R., Liu, Y., et al.: In the era of big data, the informatization construction of teaching management in universities. Journal of Shanxi University of Finance and Economics **43**(S2), 99–102 (2021)
12. Liang, D.: Research on the informationization construction of higher education management. Tech Wind (22), 82–84 (2021)
13. Zhou, Z., Ma, J., Chen, Z.: Research on the Development Effectiveness of Higher Education in Macau. Macau Institute of Technology, Macau 55 (2018)
14. Zou, S.: The concept and achievements of elite education in Hong Kong universities. Journal of Southern University **13**(6), 113–116 (2011)
15. Ding, Y., Ge, P.: Research on the practical path of integrating excellent traditional chinese culture into college art education work. Art Education Research (21), 140–142 (2023)
16. Hu, R.: National Education in Primary and Secondary Schools in Macau since the Return: Development and Experience Contemporary Chinese History Research **27**(02), 63–76 (2020)

17. Guo, X., Xie, A., Zhu, S., Wang, M.: Experience of strengthening education governance since Macao's return. Hong Kong and Macau Studies (03), 49–58 (2020)
18. Liu, F.: Value Analysis of Education Policy. Education Science Press, Beijing (2003)
19. Chai, Y.: Macao: Persistently Innovating National Education Practices. People's Daily Overseas Edition (004) (2022)
20. Huang, S.: Review of the development direction of civic education in macau after the return. Journal of Basic Education (2), 108 (2008)
21. Zhu, Z., Hu, J.: The practical logic and development opportunities of digital transformation in education. Research on Electronic Education **43**(1), 5–15 (2022)

Innovative Application for the Deeper Integration of Education Practice and Information Technology

Visual Research Trend Analysis of International Students Utilizing Short Videos Learning Based on CiteSpace

Ting Liu🆔, Patrick Cheong-Iao Pang(✉)🆔, Yiming Luo🆔, Ziqi Chen🆔, and Yuanze Xia🆔

Faculty of Applied Sciences, Macao Polytechnic University, Macao 999078, China
mail@patrickpang.net

Abstract. Learning through short videos (SVs) is an effective medium for international students (ISs). This active learning method allows students, particularly those from abroad, to quickly and conveniently gain knowledge about life and study through short video content. Using Web of Science (WOS) data, CiteSpace analyzes the spatial patterns, trends, and hotspots within research studies on ISs utilizing SVs for learning. Results: 1) ISs and SVs initially increased in the first half of the study period, reaching a peak before experiencing a decline over the next five years. This trend indicates a predominant focus on the ISs & SVs field from the perspectives of education and sociology. 2) This research has formed a complex international collaboration network, particularly among the United States, Spain, and China. 3) Educational studies examining the adaptability of ISs and issues such as culture shock, particularly those concerning SVs based on digital technologies and tools, have emerged as a primary focus area. 4) With the relaxation of study abroad policies in various countries and the further development of short video platforms, research on ISs and SVs is likely to regain momentum. Conclusion: This study provides a comprehensive and objective research analysis of ISs and SVs. This highlights the role and impact of SVs as a form of digital educational technology on the learning experiences of ISs.

Keywords: Short videos · International students · CiteSpace

1 Introduction

The rapid advancement of multimedia technology has given rise to a diverse array of we-media, fundamentally transforming the landscape of information dissemination and educational practices. In the context of the internet era, students are presented with an unprecedented array of learning resources that extend beyond conventional classrooms and traditional computer-based learning environments. The proliferation of portable electronic devices, such as mobile phones and tablets, enables learners to access information with increased ease and flexibility. Among the various forms of new media, short videos (SVs) have emerged as particularly effective and engaging educational tools, garnering significant attention within academic settings [1]. College students represent a

© The Author(s), under exclusive license to Springer Nature Singapore Pte Ltd. 2025
K. Zhang et al. (Eds.): CSEI 2024, CCIS 2448, pp. 161–175, 2025.
https://doi.org/10.1007/978-981-96-3738-6_13

primary audience for SVs, and this demographic is notably prevalent among international students (ISs). The appeal of SVs to this group can be attributed to several factors: these video formats provide a wide range of information, facilitate convenient methods for knowledge acquisition, and afford high levels of creative freedom and engagement. ISs, which are often faced with numerous challenges in both academic and personal contexts, encounter significant obstacles in obtaining accurate and timely information—obstacles that traditional class-room settings and standard online searches may not adequately address. The utilization of SVs for learning constitutes an active learning strategy that enables ISs to efficiently acquire relevant information regarding their studies and life in unfamiliar educational environments. By engaging with SVs, these students can enhance their comprehension of academic material and navigate the complexities associated with their new surroundings more effectively. Consequently, this paper aims to investigate the research trends and current landscape regarding the utilization of SVs as educational resources among ISs.

This study uses data from the Web of Science (WOS) database. The research objectives and structure are outlined: the first section details the data sources and methodologies, offering an overview of the analytical framework. The second section explores the publication characteristics of the selected samples, examining factors such as trends over time, publication patterns, and highly cited works, with the analysis categorized by country, institution, and author. All relevant data were systematically extracted from the WOS database.

In the third section, this study evaluates critical research hotspots and trends associated with ISs and SVs by employing keyword clustering and analyzing mutation terms. This method offers valuable insights into prominent themes and emerging topics in the field. The fourth section synthesizes the dominant research trends and provides an overview of the current knowledge landscape regarding the integration of SVs in ISs. Furthermore, CiteSpace software was used to visually analyze the literature included in the study, enhancing the comprehension of intricate data.

The primary research questions guiding this investigation are as follows:

1) What are the temporal evolution features of research concerning ISs and SVs?
2) What spatial distribution characteristics can be observed in this body of research?
3) What specific research hotspots exist within the intersection of ISs and SVs?
4) What are the emerging developmental trends related to research on ISs and SVs?

By addressing these questions, this study aims to contribute substantively to the literature by providing a comprehensive analysis of the intersection between ISs and SVs. This area has previously received limited scholarly attention. Employing advanced bibliometric methods and visual analysis tools such as CiteSpace, this research aims to identify key trends and hotspots and deepen our understanding of how SVs can serve as effective learning tools for ISs. The findings of this study are expected to offer valuable insights for educators and policymakers seeking to leverage multimedia technologies to enhance educational experiences and outcomes related to ISs. Ultimately, this research aims to inform future educational practices and contribute to the effective integration of technology into learning environments tailored for ISs.

2 Methods

2.1 Data Collection and Processing

The data for this study are derived from the WOS Core Collection, supplemented by a curated selection of reputable academic journals. The WOS database is recognized as a comprehensive and authoritative resource for academic information and is characterized by its extensive citation network. This network assists researchers in identifying the latest advancements in research and gaining insights into the connections among scholarly publications [2]. Figure 1 illustrates the data retrieval process adopted in this research, providing a visual representation of the methodological framework used for data collection. To maximize the potential of the WOS database, a well-defined search strategy was meticulously designed, incorporating targeted keywords and topic criteria aligned with the study's objectives. This approach aimed to guarantee the inclusion of the most relevant literature for subsequent analysis. The search was conducted in English on August 30, 2024, and was executed with precision to ensure the reliability of the data retrieval process.

Following the initial search, irrelevant and duplicate entries were systematically excluded to refine the datasets. This process involved manual correlation screening of a total of 656 papers, which allowed for a targeted approach to identifying relevant literature in the context of the study's focus on the intersection of ISs and SVs. Leveraging the advanced functionalities of CiteSpace, data cleaning was conducted to ensure that the selected papers met the stringent criteria outlined in the methodological framework. After the thorough screening and data cleaning processes, a total of 565 papers were retained for further analysis. These papers underwent a formatting conversion process facilitated by CiteSpace, resulting in the selection of 515 valid papers that were deemed suitable for in-depth examination. Importantly, all the data retrieval and cleaning processes were conducted with precision, adhering strictly to the predefined timeline and established search parameters. This meticulous approach aims to guarantee the reliability and accuracy of the findings reported in this study.

2.2 Methods

This study employed CiteSpace, an advanced visualization tool developed by Dr. Chaomei Chen, a professor at Drexel University in the United States. CiteSpace has become widely recognized within the academic community for its powerful ability to measure and analyze data derived from scientific literature. The software excels in producing knowledge maps, which visually depict the characteristics of knowledge within particular academic domains, as well as in pinpointing emerging research hotspots and trends within the literature [3]. In this study, data extracted from the WOS database were exported in two distinct formats: plain text files and the RefWorks format. This dual-format approach ensures compatibility with CiteSpace, allowing seamless integration of data into the software for subsequent analysis. By utilizing CiteSpace's visualization mapping capabilities, this study conducted a thorough exploration of both spatial and temporal distribution characteristics within the research focused on ISs and SVs.

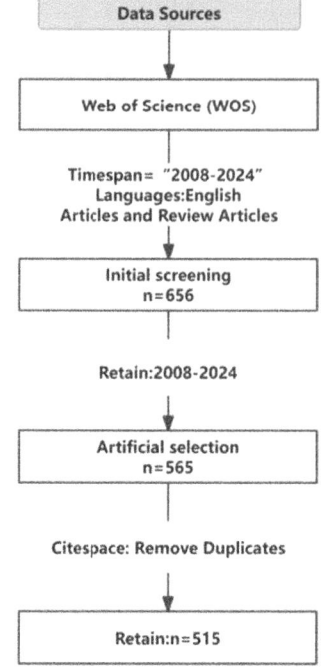

Fig. 1. Flowchart of paper data retrieval.

To provide a comprehensive analysis of the literature, coword analysis was employed, which facilitates the examination of research trends by categorizing publications on the basis of associations among countries, institutions, and authors. This method enables researchers to identify collaborative networks and key contributors in the field, offering insights into the global landscape of IS and SV research.

The visualization capabilities of CiteSpace were further employed to create keyword cluster maps, which facilitate the identification of prominent themes within the literature. By analyzing the relationships between keywords, the study was able to discern significant clusters that represent areas of focused inquiry within the domain of ISs and SVs. Additionally, explosive word visualization techniques were used to highlight emerging trends, providing insights into how specific topics gained prominence over time.

Through these various analytical methods, this study aimed to systematically delineate the research landscape related to ISs and SVs. By visualizing the complexities inherent in the data, CiteSpace allows for a nuanced understanding of the underlying patterns that characterize this body of literature. Ultimately, this approach is expected to yield valuable findings regarding the interplay between ISs and SVs, shedding light on the evolving dynamics of educational practices in a multimedia context.

In summary, using CiteSpace enhances the analytical depth of the research while improving the clarity of findings concerning ISs and SVs. By harnessing software features, this study aims to provide a thorough overview of research trends and hotspots, thereby deepening the understanding of how SVs can be effectively employed as educational tools for ISs. The visualization of complex datasets through CiteSpace further amplifies the interpretative power of the research, allowing for informed conclusions and implications to be drawn that are highly relevant to educators, researchers, and policymakers in the domain of international education.

3   Descriptive Analysis

3.1   Spatial and Temporal Distributions

The analysis of spatial and temporal distributions involves two aspects: 1) the number of annual publications and 2) highly cited references.

Figure 2 illustrates the annual research trends in ISs and SVs derived from the WOS database. Between 2008 and 2024, publication trends in this field show notable shifts and developments. a) Growth phase (2008--2016), during which the number of publications related to IS&SV demonstrated a steady increase, averaging 18 per year, gradually attracting the attention of more researchers; b) peak phase (2017--2019), reaching a summit in 2018--2019, with an average annual number of 55 papers; c) decline phase (2020--2024), in which the number of publications began to gradually decrease over the following five years, averaging 36 per year, indicating a waning interest and activity in this research area. The number of published papers related to ISs and SVs is closely linked to the rise of SVs and advancements in media technology. In 2008, the acceleration of globalization and the increased mobility of ISs marked the beginning of this research area. The years 2017--2019 experienced a peak in research quantity related to ISs and SVs, driven by the rapid emergence of various short video platforms, such as TikTok and Instagram Stories, which became mainstream social media outlets. During this period, researchers actively began to explore the impact of SVs on different demographics, including ISs. However, approximately 2020, the global outbreak of the COVID-19 pandemic significantly affected education, social interactions, and media consumption patterns worldwide. As a result, more researchers have shifted their focus toward pandemic-related topics, such as online education for ISs. With the gradual reopening of the pandemic situation starting in 2023 and the easing of restrictions on IS mobility in various countries, research in the field of ISs and SVs is expected to regain momentum in the future.

Using data from the WOS database, Table 1 lists the top 10 most highly cited references in studies related to ISs and SVs. The literature has focused primarily on the fields of educational technology, mental health, and learning methodologies.

In the realm of educational technology, the literature highlights the integration of multimedia resources through digital technology (DT). For example, Chang et al. examined the use of digital technologies, including social media and online games, and conducted in-depth discussions on their roles and impacts on college students, as well as the relationships between these technologies and psychological factors [4]. Hawi et al. investigated the effects of online gaming on adolescents' mental health and academic performance, focusing on how DT influences behavior and psychological well-being [5]. Tamura et al. analyzed the correlation between excessive mobile phone use and adolescents' mental health, further exploring the connection between DT and mental

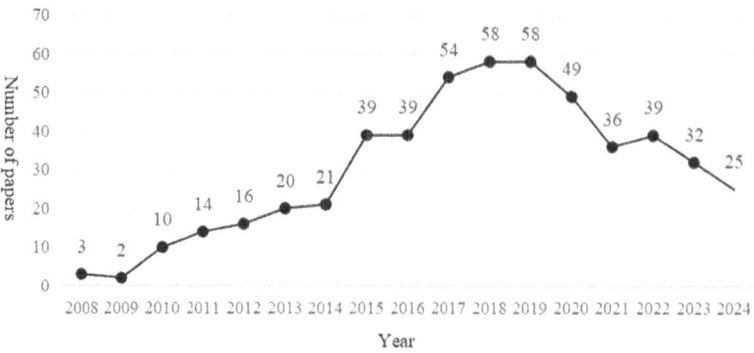

Fig. 2. ISs & SVs research annual publication trends.

states [6]. Additionally, Moon et al.'s study addresses the effects of smartphone usage, primarily concentrating on health, while also acknowledging the potential risks that DT poses to children's well-being [7].

This paper examines various learning methods, including video feedback and classroom reversal, and analyzes their impact on students' learning behaviors. Diwanji et al. investigated the influence of content, format, and interactivity on learning outcomes, emphasizing the importance of the appeal and educational value of online instructional videos during their design [8]. Research by Mi et al. on online learning methods and student engagement strategies offers valuable insights for optimizing educational practices [9]. Hew et al. focused on the implementation of the flipped classroom model in a fully online environment, analyzing the teaching strategies and learning outcomes associated with this approach under uncertain conditions [10]. Zainuddin et al. explored the adoption of flipped classrooms and students' cognitive experiences, assessing the acceptance of this learning method among Malaysian students and its practical implications [11]. Yan et al. conducted a direct comparison of the learning outcomes between flipped classrooms and traditional classrooms [12]. Additionally, Scaffidi et al. examined how video feedback as a learning method influences learners' self-assessment abilities, incorporating techniques related to skill acquisition and reflective learning [13].

3.2 Spatial Distribution

By utilizing data extracted from the WOS database, CiteSpace generated a "knowledge map of national collaboration networks" (Fig. 3) on the basis of the "country" criteria, highlighting the top 10 countries in terms of publication volume (Table 2). As depicted in Fig. 3, the research network of ISs and SVs reflects international collaboration across 82 countries and regions, including the United States, Spain, China, the United Kingdom, Japan, Germany, Malaysia, Australia, Italy, Switzerland, and Canada. Notably, the United States has established strong collaborative relationships with Australia, China, and the United Kingdom, whereas Australia has formed solid partnerships with Spain, Switzerland, Italy, and other countries. Table 2 lists the top 10 countries, including the United States, Spain, China, the United Kingdom, Japan, Germany, Malaysia, Australia, Italy, and Canada. The higher publication output from these countries is largely attributed

Table 1. The Top 10 Most Highly Cited References in IS & SV Research.

S/N	Citations	Year	Title	Author
1	154	2015	Temporal Models for Predicting Student Dropout in Massive Open Online Courses	Fei Mi. et al
2	150	2016	Smartphone use is a risk factor for pediatric dry eye disease according to region and age: a case control study	Jun Hyung Moon. et al
3	112	2018	Internet gaming disorder in Lebanon: Relationships with age, sleep habits, and academic achievement	Nazir S. Hawi. et al
4	86	2017	Association between Excessive Use of Mobile Phone and Insomnia and Depression among Japanese Adolescents	Haruka Tamura. et al
5	77	2020	Transitioning to the "new normal" of learning in unpredictable times: pedagogical practices and learning performance in fully online flipped classrooms	Khe Foon Hew. et al
6	70	2016	Malaysian students' perceptions of flipped classroom: a case study	Zamzami Zainuddin. et al
7	26	2022	Relationships Between Problematic Social Media Use, Problematic Gaming, and Psychological Distress Among University Students: A 9-Month Longitudinal Study	Ching-We Chang. et al
8	19	2014	Success Factors of Online Learning Videos	Prajakta Diwanji. et al
9	18	2018	A Comparison of Flipped and Traditional Classroom Learning: A Case Study in Mechanical Engineering	Jing Yan. et al
10	13	2019	Influence of video-based feedback on self-assessment accuracy of endoscopic skills: a randomized controlled trial	Michael A Scaffidi. et al

to the United States, Spain, China, and the United Kingdom, which maintain robust educational collaborations with other nations and offer ISs an environment conducive to learning, along with superior educational resources. Additionally, the greater penetration of DTs in these countries offers excellent equipment and environmental support for the utilization of SVs. An open and supportive social environment further facilitates the dissemination and development of SVs. Collectively, these conditions have propelled research on ISs and SVs in these nations.

Fig. 3. Country cooperation network for IS and SV research.

Table 2. Top 10 countries in terms of the number of papers.

Rank	Countries	Count
1	USA	92
2	SPAIN	70
3	CHINA	60
4	ENGLAND	40
5	JAPAN	23
6	GERMANY	21
7	MALAYSIA	20
8	AUSTRALIA	19
9	ITALY	16
10	CANADA	15

Using data from the WOS database, CiteSpace generated a "knowledge map of institutional collaboration networks" (Fig. 4) on the basis of the "institution" parameter. In this map, each node represents an institution, with the size of the node indicating the number of publications associated with that institution. The connections between the nodes highlight the degree of collaboration between these institutions. As shown in Fig. 4, the institutional collaboration network has a density of 0.0043 and is composed of several small clusters, indicating that the interactions among institutions are both widespread and significant. This suggests that stronger collaboration between institutions enhances knowledge integration and fosters innovation within the field. According to Table 3, the top 10 universities on the basis of their international publication output include Nottingham Trent University, Universidad Politécnica de Madrid, University of Zaragoza, Complutense University of Madrid, and De Montfort University. This study examines the institutional characteristics of these universities and their role as leading research institutions in the field. These universities typically possess a strong academic background and research focus in fields such as media, communication, educational technology, cultural studies, and information systems. This foundation provides robust support for related research endeavors. Additionally, these institutions attract many ISs from diverse countries and cultural backgrounds. This diversity among the student body offers a wealth of case studies and data sources for research on SVs, particularly in areas such as comparative culture, language, and learning methods.

Fig. 4. Institutional network.

In the author collaboration network, each node represents an individual author, with the size of the node reflecting the total number of publications associated with that author. The degree of collaboration between authors is indicated by the number of links between nodes. Larger nodes with denser connections highlight the prominent role of these authors in the research landscape. Using the WOS database and the "Author" function, a knowledge map of the author collaboration network was created (Fig. 5) for international research on ISs and SVs, with the network density calculated at 0.0042. The network shows moderate density, suggesting a relatively compact overall structure. The top three authors on the basis of citation count are Pena-Fernandez A, Acosta L, Gonzalez M C, Benito S, and Palmero D.

Table 3. Top 10 institutions.

Rank	Institutions	Count
1	Nottingham Trent University	7
2	Universidad Politecnica de Madrid	7
3	University of Zaragoza	6
4	Complutense University of Madrid	5
5	De Montfort University	5
6	Universidade de Vigo	5
7	Centre National de la Recherche Scientifique (CNRS)	4
8	Chinese University of Hong Kong	4
9	State University System of Florida	4
10	Carnegie Mellon University	4

Fig. 5. Author cooperation network.

4   Hotspot and Trend Analysis

4.1   Hotspot Analysis

By using CiteSpace to analyze coword clustering maps, we can identify the research interests of scholars in the field. A co-occurrence clustering map related to IS and SV research was created through coword clustering analysis with data from the WOS database (Fig. 6). The log-likelihood ratio (LLR) algorithm was applied to cluster and analyze keywords (Table 4). In Fig. 6, the coword clustering map for IS and SV research shows a modularity Q value of 0.8627 (greater than 0.3) and a silhouette S value of 0.9091 (greater than 0.5). These values suggest that the results are reliable and provide a clear representation of the current research landscape. This analysis identified 10 core clusters: #0 Collaborative Learning, #1 Mathematics Teachers, #2 Blended Learning, #3 Problematic Social Media Use, #4 Active Learning, #5 Video, and #6 Flipped Classroom. Research on ISs and SVs has focused primarily on digital and technological tools, educational and learning methods, psychological and social-emotional aspects, and educational innovation and assessment. This suggests that when examining how ISs utilize SVs for learning, current related research emphasizes the integration of digital technologies and tools to achieve effective teaching and learning processes.

Table 4. Coword clustering.

Cluster number	N	Clustering S values	Year	Clustering content
0	35	0.955	2015	collaborative learning (13.57, 0.001); physical education (6.73, 0.01); digital storytelling (6.73, 0.01); higher education (6.72, 0.01); social-emotional orientation (3.35, 0.1)
1	27	0.971	2019	mathematics teachers (4.48, 0.05); productive vocabulary knowledge (4.48, 0.05); video evaluation (4.48, 0.05); transportation (4.48, 0.05); surgical training (4.48, 0.05)
2	26	0.923	2015	blended learning (20.67, 1.0E-4); mobile learning (8.15, 0.005); soft skills (4.06, 0.05); mobile applications (4.06, 0.05); asynchronous learning (4.06, 0.05)
3	26	0.962	2021	problematic social media use (9.57, 0.005); problematic gaming (9.57, 0.005); gaming addiction (9.57, 0.005); internet gaming disorder (5.94, 0.05); adolescents (4.76, 0.05)
4	25	0.969	2019	active learning (12.03, 0.001); short video (12.03, 0.001); flipped learning (7.99, 0.005); padlet (3.97, 0.05); teaching innovation (3.97, 0.05)
5	24	0.961	2020	video (6.43, 0.05); short-term learning (5.01, 0.05); videos (5.01, 0.05); addiction tendency (5.01, 0.05); science achievement (5.01, 0.05)
6	23	0.981	2016	flipped classroom (18.2, 1.0E-4); experiential learning (7.75, 0.01); e-learning (7.75, 0.01); autonomous learning (7.75, 0.01); application (7.75, 0.01)

4.2 Trend Analysis

This study employs the burst detection feature of CiteSpace to analyze changes in keywords. Figure 7 presents the top 20 keywords with the strongest citation bursts in the

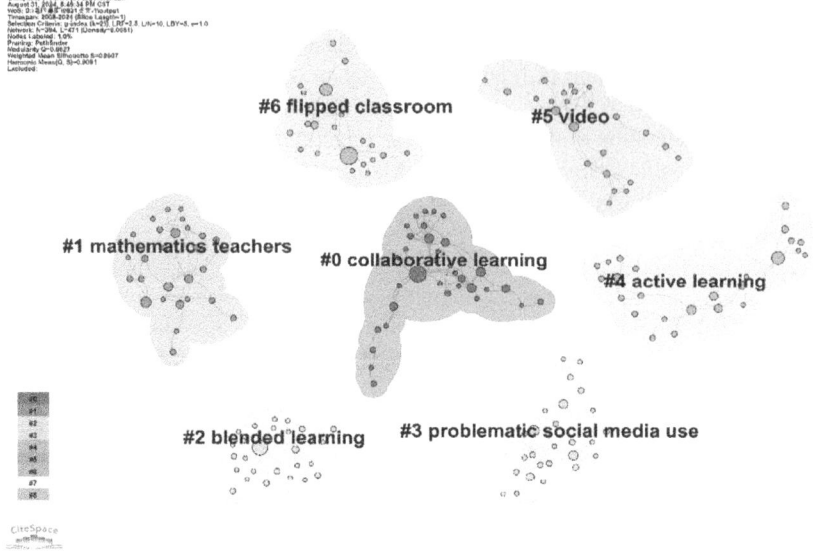

Fig. 6. Coword clustering map.

research on ISs & SVs from 2008--2024. The blue lines indicate time intervals, whereas the red lines denote the periods during which the keywords emerged.

Figure 7 also illustrates the trends in research on ISs and SVs, highlighting keywords such as collaborative learning, educational videos, distance education, cooperative learning, flipped classrooms, flipped teaching models, higher education, blended learning, and advanced instructions. Beginning in 2011, keywords such as collaborative learning, educational video, and distance education emerged as critical focal points within this research domain. This development coincided with the rapid proliferation of DTs during this period, characterized by an increasing number of individuals possessing smartphones and the emergence of various forms of media. Consequently, collaborative learning, educational videos, and distance education have become prominent research hotspots. Since 2016, the growth of various video media has increased dramatically, with short video formats becoming prevalent not only in entertainment but also in the realm of education. However, beginning in 2020, the onset of the global COVID-19 pandemic posed significant obstacles for ISs studying abroad, resulting in a decline in research intensity within this area. The COVID-19 pandemic has significantly influenced the global adoption of digital technology in education [14].

5   Discussion

The rise of research on ISs and SVs is closely linked to advancements in media technologies and platforms. Since 2008, the proliferation of smartphones and high-speed internet has facilitated the production and consumption of video content, leading to increased engagement with SVs. Before 2008, platforms such as YouTube, though established, did

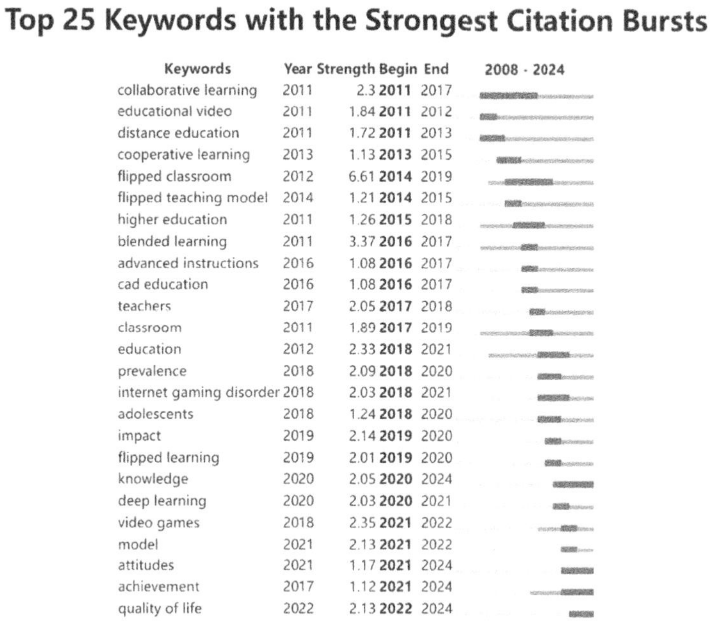

Top 25 Keywords with the Strongest Citation Bursts

Keywords	Year	Strength	Begin	End	2008 - 2024
collaborative learning	2011	2.3	2011	2017	
educational video	2011	1.84	2011	2012	
distance education	2011	1.72	2011	2013	
cooperative learning	2013	1.13	2013	2015	
flipped classroom	2012	6.61	2014	2019	
flipped teaching model	2014	1.21	2014	2015	
higher education	2011	1.26	2015	2018	
blended learning	2011	3.37	2016	2017	
advanced instructions	2016	1.08	2016	2017	
cad education	2016	1.08	2016	2017	
teachers	2017	2.05	2017	2018	
classroom	2011	1.89	2017	2019	
education	2012	2.33	2018	2021	
prevalence	2018	2.09	2018	2020	
internet gaming disorder	2018	2.03	2018	2021	
adolescents	2018	1.24	2018	2020	
impact	2019	2.14	2019	2020	
flipped learning	2019	2.01	2019	2020	
knowledge	2020	2.05	2020	2024	
deep learning	2020	2.03	2020	2021	
video games	2018	2.35	2021	2022	
model	2021	2.13	2021	2022	
attitudes	2021	1.17	2021	2024	
achievement	2017	1.12	2021	2024	
quality of life	2022	2.13	2022	2024	

Fig. 7. Top 20 keywords.

not attract substantial research interest because of their nascent stage [15]. The emergence of platforms such as Vine (2013) and TikTok (2016) marked a pivotal shift, making SVs more influential and warranting academic scrutiny. From 2017 to 2019, short video platforms increased in popularity, establishing themselves as significant trends in social media. As consumption habits related to SVs solidified, researchers began exploring their impacts on diverse demographics, including ISs [16]. During this period, globalization accelerated, prompting a greater number of ISs to study abroad, which in turn led to investigations into the social, cultural, and educational implications of these experiences. Issues such as cultural adaptation, culture shock, and mental health have become prominent research topics, reflecting the changing landscape of educational challenges faced by ISs [17]. However, the emergence of the COVID-19 pandemic in 2020 significantly altered the focus of research. Before the pandemic, studies on ISs and SVs were thriving, and the urgency of addressing pandemic-related challenges redirected attention toward online education, mental health, and social isolation [18]. This shift can be attributed to several factors: the sudden need for effective online learning solutions, the psychological impacts of isolation on students, and the limitations imposed on traditional research methodologies due to travel and interaction restrictions. Consequently, the relative decline in research on ISs and SVs after 2020 is not merely a temporal fluctuation but reflects broader societal changes and the pressing need for adaptive strategies in educational research [19].

Moreover, the characteristics of short video technology, such as its interactive nature, real-time engagement, and visual storytelling capabilities, offer unique advantages in educational scenarios. These features facilitate active learning, enhance student engagement, and support diverse learning styles [20]. Integrating SVs into educational practices can transform traditional learning environments, making them more dynamic and responsive to students' needs.

In summary, this discussion highlights the complex interplay between technological advancements, societal shifts, and research trajectories. Understanding these dynamics is crucial for future studies, which should further explore the integration of short video technology in education and its implications for ISs. As researchers navigate the post-pandemic landscape, reassessing the role of SVs in enhancing educational outcomes and addressing the evolving needs of students is essential.

6 Conclusion

This study investigates the trends and current status of ISs in the utilization of SVs for educational purposes. Through a visual analysis of the WOS database, we identify three developmental phases: a growth phase from 2008--2016, a peak phase from 2017--2019, and a decline phase from 2020--2024. Notably, the COVID-19 pandemic has shifted the focus toward online learning and mental health, influencing research interest in SVs.

Spatial distribution analysis reveals that institutions in the United States, Spain, and China frequently collaborate, fostering research on integrating SVs with ISs. Keyword analysis shows a concentration on digital tools, educational methodologies, and psychosocial aspects of learning.

This research makes a significant contribution to the field by shedding light on the evolving relationship between media technology and educational trends, emphasizing the importance of adaptive educational practices. As the global situation stabilizes, we expect a resurgence of interest in ISs and SVs, providing fresh perspectives on innovative learning tools in various educational contexts. Future research should focus on exploring the practical applications of SVs in different learning environments and evaluating their long-term impact on educational outcomes.

References

1. Guo, Q.: The influence of short video on college students' values from the perspective of new media. In: 2020 5th International Conference on Mechanical, Control and Computer Engineering (ICMCCE) (2020)
2. Birkle, C., Pendlebury, D.A., Schnell, J., Adams, J.: Web of science as a data source for research on scientific and scholarly activity. Quantitative Science Studies 1, 363–376 (2020)
3. Chen, C.: CiteSpace II: detecting and visualizing emerging trends and transient patterns in scientific literature. J. Am. Soc. Inform. Sci. Technol. 57, 359–377 (2005)
4. Chang, C.-W., Huang, R.-Y., Strong, C., Lin, Y.-C., Tsai, M.-C., Chen, I.-H., et al.: Reciprocal relationships between problematic social media use, problematic gaming, and psychological distress among university students: A 9-Month longitudinal study. Frontiers in Public Health 10 (2022)
5. Hawi, N.S., Samaha, M., Griffiths, M.D.: Internet gaming disorder in Lebanon: relationships with age, sleep habits, and academic achievement. J. Behav. Addict. 7, 70–78 (2018). https://doi.org/10.1556/2006.7.2018.16

6. Warren, E., Melendez-Torres, G.J., Viner, R., Bonell, C.: Using qualitative research to explore intervention mechanisms: findings from the trial of the learning together whole-school health intervention, Trials. **21** (2020). https://doi.org/10.1186/s13063-020-04688-2

7. Moon, J.H., Kim, K.W., Moon, N.J.: Smartphone use is a risk factor for pediatric dry eye disease according to region and age: a case control study. BMC Ophthalmology **16** (2016)

8. Diwanji, P., Simon, B.P., Marki, M., Korkut, S., Dornberger, R.: Success factors of online learning videos. 2014 International Conference on Interactive Mobile Communication Technologies and Learning (IMCL2014) (2014)

9. Fei, M., Yeung, D.-Y.: Temporal models for predicting student dropout in Massive open online courses. In: 2015 IEEE International Conference on Data Mining Workshop (ICDMW) (2015)

10. Hew, K.F., Jia, C., Gonda, D.E., Bai, S.: Transitioning to the "New normal" of learning in unpredictable times: pedagogical practices and learning performance in fully online flipped classrooms. International Journal of Educational Technology in Higher Education **17** (2020)

11. Zainuddin, Z., Attaran, M.: Malaysian students' perceptions of flipped classroom: a case study. Innov. Educ. Teach. Int. **53**, 660–670 (2015)

12. Yan, J., Li, L., Yan, J., Niu, Y.: A comparison of flipped and traditional classroom learning: a case study in mechanical engineering. Int. J. Eng. Educ. **34**, 1876–1887 (2018)

13. Scaffidi, M., Walsh, C., Khan, R., Parker, C., Al-Mazroui, A., Abunassar, M., et al.: Influence of video-based feedback on self-assessment accuracy of endoscopic skills: a randomized controlled trial. Endoscopy International Open **07** (2019)

14. Liu, T., Pang, P.C.-I., Xiong, Q.: Visualized analysis of research trends of digital technology and public health based on CiteSpace. Frontiers in Artificial Intelligence and Applications (2024)

15. Katz, J.E., Aakhus, M.: Perpetual Contact: Mobile Communication, Private Talk, Public Performance. Cambridge University Press, Cambridge (2002)

16. Wang, Z.: An analysis on the use of video materials in college english teaching in China. International Journal of English Language Teaching **2**(1), 23–28 (2015)

17. Singh, H.P., Das, J.R.: The impact of social media on student engagement and academic performance. European Journal of Innovation in Nonformal Education **2**(7), 110–113 (2022)

18. Tess, P.A.: The role of social media in higher education classes (real and virtual) – a literature review. Comput. Hum. Behav. **29**(5), A60–A68 (2013)

19. Ivala, E., Gachago, D.: Social media for enhancing student engagement: the use of Facebook and blogs at a University of Technology. South African Journal of Higher Education **26**(1), 152–167 (2012)

20. Vuta, D.R.: Augmented reality technologies in education – a literature review. Bulletin of the Transilvania University of Brasov. Series V: Economic Sciences 35–46 (2020)

A Personalized Teaching Assistant Platform Driven by Large Language Models of Artificial Intelligence

Fei Guo[1], Junwen Duan[1(✉)], Xiaoqing Peng[2], and Cheng Liang[3]

[1] School of Computer Science and Engineering, Central South University,
Changsha 410083, China
{guofei,jwduan}@csu.edu.cn

[2] Center for Medical Genetics and Hunan Key Laboratory of Medical Genetics,
School of Life Sciences, Central South University, Changsha 410083, China
xqpeng@csu.edu.cn

[3] School of Information Science and Engineering, Shandong Normal University,
Jinan 250358, China
ALCS417@sdnu.edu.cn

Abstract. Artificial intelligence (AI) is a pivotal technology driving the next industrial revolution and shaping the future of education. This research focuses on developing a learner-centered educational environment that leverages AI to provide personalized, lifelong learning experiences. In response to the evolving educational landscape, we propose an innovative approach that integrates "Internet + Education" principles with AI-driven technologies. Our study explores the deep integration of information technology and education, emphasizing the creation of a new educational paradigm centered on individual learners. By harnessing the power of big data analytics and AI, we aim to revolutionize the teaching environment, enabling truly individualized instruction. The concept of "AI + X" is introduced as a framework for nurturing multidisciplinary talent, combining expertise in AI with knowledge from two or more additional fields. This approach places particular emphasis on programming education across various majors and disciplines, recognizing it as a crucial component of AI integration in education. Our research on programming pedagogy contributes significantly to the broader "AI + X" teaching model, offering valuable insights and methodologies applicable to AI education in interdisciplinary contexts. This study lays the groundwork for a more adaptive, responsive, and personalized educational system that prepares learners for the challenges and opportunities of an AI-driven future.

Keywords: Personalized Teaching Assistant Platform · Large Language Model · Artificial Intelligence

1   Introduction

In accordance with the "New Generation of Artificial Intelligence Development Plan", intelligent technology was used to speed up the reform of talent training methods and teaching methods, and a new education system integrating intelligent learning and interactive learning was built. The Ministry of Education clearly stated in the "Education Informationization 2.0 Action Plan" that, at present, it is necessary to adapt to the development of new education in an intelligent environment, promote internet + education, take informationization as its guide, create a new education ecology centered on learners, adhere to integration and innovation, and promote a deep integration of information technology and education and teaching. Through the analysis of a large amount of teaching data, artificial intelligence can provide personalized learning resources, strategies, and feedback to ensure accurate diagnosis and effective guidance for learners. Data analysis applied to curriculum personalized assisted teaching is an important research field in the field of education, as well as an important symbol of education modernization. Personalized assistant teaching is an important research direction in the field of education, and it is also a symbol of modernization in education.

The purpose of artificial intelligence teachers is to use artificial intelligence techniques [1], such as natural language processing, machine learning and knowledge representation. Through virtual teachers, teachers can communicate with students in natural language and provide feedback and guidance to students individually. In artificial intelligence-assisted systems, artificial intelligence technologies, such as data mining, recommendation systems, and sentiment analysis, are used to provide auxiliary functions, such as curriculum design, resource recommendations, and emotional support, to teachers and students. Using artificial intelligence technology, such as semantic analysis, image recognition, and speech recognition, artificial intelligence evaluation systems evaluate and analyze students' assignments, exams, performance, etc., automatically or semiautomatically, thus improving the efficiency and quality of evaluation. Personalized assisted teaching utilizing artificial intelligence is being researched and implemented both domestically and internationally through various approaches [2]. In foreign countries, the emphasis is primarily on system-level developments, including the creation of AI teachers, AI assistant systems, and AI evaluation frameworks. Moreover, in China, artificial intelligence is applied directly to course content to facilitate personalized learning.

ChatGPT can help teachers design course syllabuses and lesson plans and provide ideas for course design [3, 4]. In the classroom, ChatGPT might serve as an artificial intelligence assistant, providing instant feedback for teachers and students and increasing classroom interest, attraction, and fun. After class, ChatGPT can help teachers generate homework questions and exam questions, providing teachers with a better understanding of how well students have mastered knowledge. By applying ChatGPT and other digital technologies to education, it is possible to make a personalized diagnosis for students. ChatGPT can help students identify their weaknesses and shortcomings in the dialog process to further bridge this gap and achieve improvement. Additionally, ChatGPT can also be used as a tool to help teachers improve their teaching quality after training and improvement. As far as programming practice is concerned, artificial intelligence is relatively rare at home and abroad. Despite the OJ platform's ability to compile, run, and test, it cannot deliver heuristic teaching. ChatGPT can guide and improve students' programming processes heuristically through the collaboration of humans and models. While ChatGPT supports multiple languages, it can be widely used in the teaching of programming across a variety of disciplines, majors, and programs [5].

2   System Design Concept

A personalized teaching assistant platform is built using the big language model of artificial intelligence to complete course design and teaching application for a computer major, using the big language model of artificial intelligence [6]. Exploring the application value of digital technology in the field of education can improve students' learning interest and learning effects in undergraduate teaching. To guide students in solving programming problems independently, cultivate their interest in programming, and improve their programming learning efficiency and ability, a programming teaching assistant based on an artificial intelligence big language model is constructed. The application value of artificial intelligence technology in the field of education should be explored, related teaching applications using the "Artificial Intelligence + X" core should be explored, and personalized teaching assistant platforms driven by artificial intelligence big language models should be applied to computer professional courses [7–9] to increase the quality and efficiency of education and teaching through positive exploration and contribution.

2.1   Designing Personalized Learning with Artificial Intelligence

Personalized teaching assistants play an important role in instructional design. The rapid development of artificial intelligence technology has also led to new opportunities and challenges in the field of education. In addition to providing new opportunities for personalized education, artificial intelligence is reshaping the traditional learning path. Computer science course education can be personalized through artificial intelligence models, which creates a learning method that is more flexible and efficient for students. First, the personalized teaching assistant platform can design personalized education on the basis of the learning situation and characteristics of the students. As the teaching assistant platform analyzes big data and students' learning trajectories, it can provide targeted teaching resources and feedback on students' learning progress. Thus, students can receive more personalized and targeted education and learn more effectively. Furthermore, a personalized teaching assistant platform can be used by teachers to assist in the creation and teaching of courses. Students' learning situations and feedback can be analyzed by teachers, and courses can be adjusted and optimized accordingly. Through the use of a teaching assistant platform, teachers can also access teaching aids and resources, thereby improving their teaching efficiency.

2.2   Diversified Learning Strategies with Big Data

The personalized teaching assistant platform also plays an important role in learning applications. While taking advantage of the advantages of big data education, it is also necessary to face the challenges brought by big data to education and to exploit the advantages of big data through diversified forms of education. To enhance traditional classroom teaching with the rich and diverse educational methods offered by big data, we need to do a good job of identifying, analyzing, mining, and other aspects of data technology, as well as adhering to principles of student-centeredness, value-leadership, emotional penetration, etc.,etc., to improve students' learning effects. First, students can access more convenient and abundant learning resources through personalized teaching assistant platforms. With the teaching assistant platform, students can access a variety of learning materials and resources, and their educational needs can be met through personalized learning. As a result, students can choose their own learning resources on the basis of their own interests and needs, improving their initiative and enthusiasm for learning. Additionally, the platform can provide students with feedback about their learning progress. Students can receive learning suggestions and guidance through the teaching assistant platform by analyzing their learning situation and performance. In this way, students can obtain timely feedback and evaluations, understand their progress and problems, and adjust their learning strategies and methods accordingly.

2.3 Programming Teaching Assistants with Large Language Models

A hybrid teaching mode is used to teach computer programming courses on the basis of a personalized teaching assistant platform, where the assistant teaching system is combined with traditional teaching methods. Students' active participation and independent exploration are encouraged, and teaching quality and efficiency are improved. The teaching strategy of hierarchy, stage, and type is implemented. Students receive exercises, questions, and feedback on their level, progress, and interest through the assistant teaching system. During class discussion, case analysis and project practice were used to promote students' understanding and application of what was learned. Artificial intelligence provides after-class assistance for programming instruction, improving students' interest in learning, cultivating students' independence in programming, and exploring how artificial intelligence technology can be applied to education. To evaluate the advantages and disadvantages of the assisted teaching system in terms of interactivity, intelligence, personalization, and learning effects, an experimental comparison method was employed. A questionnaire survey, student performance, and teacher feedback were used to assess the effectiveness of the system. First, an artificial intelligence-based programming teaching assistant is based on a large language model. In addition to providing teaching content, answering questions, administering exercises, and evaluating feedback, the assistant uses natural language interaction with students. By optimizing and improving the assistant system, the system's intelligence and interactive performance improve continuously, and more accurate teaching services are provided for students. As a second step, the programming teaching assistant is realized and promoted. An AI-based programming teaching assistant can be used in both traditional classroom teaching and online education platforms, programming learning apps, and other teaching tools. It can continuously improve teaching effectiveness and personalize services through continuous interaction with learners. Programming assistants can also provide real-time coding suggestions and bug fixes for programmers, helping them write codes and solve problems more efficiently. Programming teaching assistants based on big language models of artificial intelligence has become a key part of future programming education, enabling more learners to experience high-quality programming learning.

3   Teaching Strategy Implementation

From three perspectives, this study examines a personalized teaching assistant platform based on artificial intelligence big language models: an artificial intelligence model for personalized teaching design, big data technology for improving diversified learning strategies, and a large language model for teaching programming. Figure 1 shows the overall research content and logical connections.

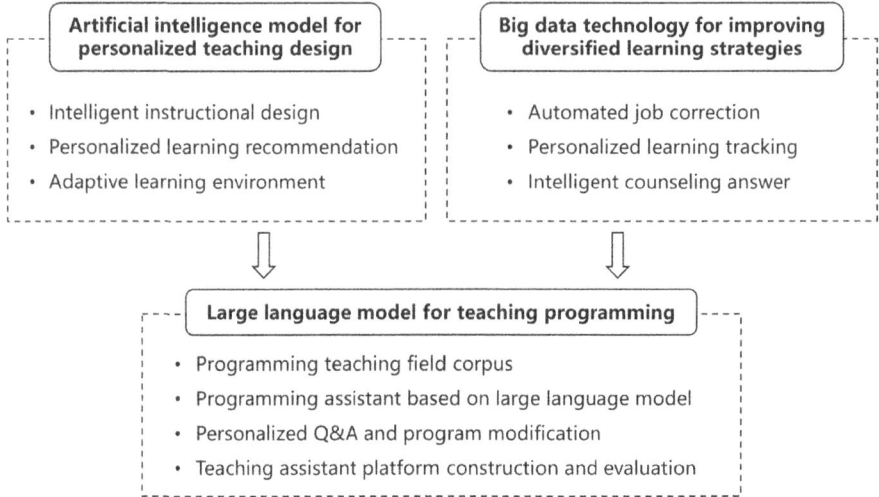

Fig. 1. An illustration of the framework for a personalized teaching assistant.

3.1   Collecting Data Both Online and Offline

A key element of personalized teaching is the effective collection and processing of students' learning data. With the help of big data technology, it is possible to collect and analyze students' massive amounts of learning data and to track and record the students' learning data throughout the learning process. Two aspects need to be considered when collecting students' learning data. First, enough data must be collected to ensure that the analysis is credible. Second, data collection must be effective since invalid data generate incorrect analysis guidance.

Data Collection and Analysis. Accurately understanding student information is the cornerstone of personalized education. The use of artificial intelligence technology can assist educational institutions in collecting and analyzing academic performance, study habits, interests, and hobbies of students. To provide students with more targeted education programs, teachers can analyze these data in depth to better understand each student's learning characteristics.

Intelligent Instructional Design. **Big** data technology can be used to customize intelligent instructional **designs on the basis of** a learner's learning data and personality characteristics. AI models can rapidly identify students' weaknesses and strengths on **the basis of** learning algorithms and models and tailor learning content and teaching methods accordingly. In contrast to one-size-fits-all teaching methods, this personalized approach allows students to master knowledge more efficiently.

3.2 Accurate Learning Resource Matching

To achieve personalized learning, artificial intelligence technology must be used to diagnose teaching problems accurately. Using knowledge graphs and machine learning, each student's learning characteristics were identified, their mastery of subject knowledge points was assessed, and dynamic subject knowledge graphs were created to meet their individual needs. To assist students in scientifically planning their learning paths on the basis of the knowledge map and blind spot diagnosis of subject knowledge, the system can match the learning resources to students' personalized difficulty and rhythm and avoid many questions.

Personalized Learning Recommendations. Artificial intelligence recommends learning resources and auxiliary materials on **the basis of** students' learning data and interests. With the help of intelligent recommendation systems, students can more easily find learning materials that suit their needs, improving their enthusiasm and initiative for learning. Furthermore, intelligent teaching can adjust learning content and difficulty on **the basis of** students' learning progress and personal situations to help them establish a more scientific learning plan.

Adaptive Learning Environment. Learning environments can be personalized **via** artificial intelligence technology on **the basis of** students' learning habits and personalities. Using **an** intelligent system, students' learning content, style, and pace can be automatically adjusted to meet their individual needs and stimulate their interest and motivation in learning. As a result of this adaptive learning environment, students are able to study in a more comfortable and appropriate way.

3.3 Assisting with Personalized Learning

Individual students cannot develop personalized education unilaterally, nor can teachers. Teachers and students must cooperate to complete the work of three links before class, during class, and after class. To achieve the learning before teaching effect, teachers optimize the teaching design according to preclass preview data and preset the teaching emphasis and difficulty.

Automation of Homework. The traditional homework process is tedious and time-consuming, and artificial intelligence technology can automate it. Learning algorithms and natural language processing can be used to assess and provide detailed feedback and suggestions on student work. In addition to reducing teachers' workloads, this can guide students to correct errors in a timely manner and improve learning outcomes.

Personalized Learning Tracking. Real-time tracking of students' learning progress and performance and generation of learning reports. These reports help teachers gain a clear understanding of each student's learning situation, detect problems in time, and take appropriate action. Additionally, the learning tracking system allows parents to know their children's learning status, better communicate with teachers, and jointly monitor their children's learning progress.

Intelligent Tutoring and Q&A. Intelligent tutoring and Q&A services can be provided by artificial intelligence. Educators provide their students with an intelligent system that they can use if they encounter problems while learning. According to the description of the problem and the learning data, the intelligent system can provide accurate answers or solutions and assist students in overcoming difficulties.

3.4 Platform Construction and Evaluation for Teaching Assistants

Continuous evaluation and improvement are needed for the implementation of personalized education. By collecting feedback data from students and analyzing learning outcomes and effects, educational institutions can evaluate and adjust personalized education programs. Additionally, the continuous development of artificial intelligence technology provides more opportunities and innovation points for personalized education. Personalized education must be continuously promoted by the education community to keep up with the times.

Data processing and analysis capabilities enable personalized teaching assistant platforms to customize intelligent teaching content on the basis of students' learning situations. With the help of learning and analyzing a large amount of data, as well as combining syllabuses, subject knowledge points, and other related resources, each student is presented with the best learning materials and content on the basis of their needs and interests. It uses speech recognition, natural language processing, and other technologies to help students solve problems, ask questions, and receive responses. In addition to providing students with real-time help and guidance, it enables real-time dialog and communication. Artificial intelligence technology is used in personalized teaching assistant platforms to assess student learning. During the learning process, performance can be monitored and analyzed to evaluate outcomes and effects. In addition to recording students' learning process and results, educational assistants can provide targeted evaluations and suggestions.

3.5 Implementation and Application of Programming Teaching Assistants

The collection of corpora in the field of programming benefits the teaching of programming. Among these corpora are curriculum-related concepts, definitions, theoretical knowledge, practice cases and programming cases, which are derived from textbooks, academic papers, websites, etc. A programming teaching domain corpus is created by collecting and collating knowledge points, which serves as a basis for fine-tuning an open source model and developing a system.

By designing a programming teaching assistant using artificial intelligence large language models, we are able to create a teaching assistant that can be fine-tuned via instructions or via the API interface of the existing large language model for programming teaching. Using natural language interaction, the assistant can provide personalized content, answer questions, conduct exercise tests, provide feedback and evaluate student learning progress. To achieve these functions, artificial intelligence large language models are trained via instruction fine-tuning technology to improve their understanding of programming. Moreover, this study also optimizes and improves the existing large language model's API interface to improve its intelligence level and interactive performance.

With personalized question answering and real-time program modification functions, students are provided with instant and accurate question answering and program modification services. As a result of the artificial intelligence language model, the system can automatically understand student questions and respond accordingly. The knowledge base is also constructed and optimized to improve the system's understanding and application capability in programming education.

4   Assessment and Analysis of Effectiveness

Through feedback from students and teachers, the software program is applied to the teaching process. Teaching resources are shared publicly for reference and use by other teachers.

4.1   Number of Students

This program is open to all students in courses related to "AI + X", and at least 4000 students are anticipated to participate each year. In this program, students gain a better understanding and mastery of course content, improve their learning efficiency, and improve their academic performance.

4.2   Effects of Teaching

Artificial intelligence-assisted teaching is intended to increase students' interest in learning and autonomous learning ability. By implementing this program, the teaching effect is enhanced, and students' needs are better met. Moreover, students can learn in a variety of teaching modes, master the course content more comprehensively, and enhance the quality of teaching through the use of artificial intelligence and traditional methods.

4.3   Influence of Social Factors

In addition to providing a reference for the "AI + X" teaching reform, the results of this research contribute to the advancement of education and teaching. As new technologies and models are applied in education, they help promote the application and promotion of artificial intelligence technology. In addition, they promote the development of educational information.

5 Future Directions

The existing problems and shortcomings in computer science teaching are analyzed. Using big data technology, it is possible to collect and analyze students' massive amounts of learning data, track their progress throughout the learning process, and conduct effective monitoring and feedback.

By using artificial intelligence technologies such as knowledge graphs and machine learning, we can identify each student's learning characteristics, diagnose their mastery of subject knowledge points, and create a dynamic subject knowledge graph unique to them. Using the blind spot diagnosis results of students' subject knowledge helps students scientifically plan their learning paths, meets the needs of students' personalized learning, and accurately matches the learning resources to the level of difficulty and rhythm of the student.

To provide personalized assistant teaching and adjust teaching strategies and learning methods. Through personalized teaching assistants, teaching and learning methods can be gradually changed, and education can be reconstructed. Personalized teaching guidance can be provided by teachers on the basis of students' feedback and learning situations to help students master knowledge and better understand it.

6 Conclusion

In conclusion, new technologies are being developed, and classroom teaching methods are being modified to meet the needs of students for personalized learning. By combining global online learning with localized classroom teaching, students can benefit not only from high-quality teachers and academic content but also from localized learning communities and learning support services. It has a powerful impact on curriculum teaching by transforming teacher-centered and knowledge-input-based teaching modes into a student-centered and autonomous internalization model. In addition, it promotes the transition from static and closed knowledge teaching to dynamic and open intelligence education in school. A fundamental change in teachers' teaching methods and students' learning methods will accelerate the reconstruction of classroom ecology [10].

Acknowledgments. This work is supported by the Central South University Graduate Education and Teaching Reform Research Project (No. 2023--102), the Central South University Graduate Education and Teaching Material Development (No. 2024--3), the Central South University Education and Teaching Reform Research Project (Grant No. 2023iy139), and the Shandong Normal University Undergraduate Education and Teaching Reform Research Project (2021BJ081).

References

1. Alqahtani, T., et al.: The emergent role of artificial intelligence, natural learning processing, and large language models in higher education and research. Research in Social and Administrative Pharmacy **19**(8), 1236–1242 (2023)
2. Bhutoria, A.: Personalized education and artificial intelligence in the United States, China, and India: a systematic review using a human-in-the-loop model. Computers and Education: Artificial Intelligence **3**, 100068 (2022)
3. Chen, J., et al.: When large language models meet personalization: perspectives of challenges and opportunities. Worldwide Web **27**(4), 42 (2024)
4. Bonner, E., Lege, R., Frazier, E.: Large language model-based artificial intelligence in the language classroom: practical ideas for teaching. Teaching English with Technol. **23**(1), 23–41 (2023)
5. Jeon, J., Lee, S.: Large language models in education: a focus on the complementary relationship between human teachers and ChatGPT. Educ. Inf. Technol. **28**(12), 15873–15892 (2023)
6. Sajja, R., Sermet, Y., Cwiertny, D., Demir, I.: Platform-independent and curriculum-oriented intelligent assistant for higher education. Int. J. Educ. Technol. High. Educ. **20**(1), 42 (2023)
7. Abd-Alrazaq, A., et al.: Large language models in medical education: opportunities, challenges, and future directions. JMIR Medical Education **9**(1), e48291 (2023)
8. Kang, K., Yang, Y., Wu, Y., Luo, R.: Integrating large language models in bioinformatics education for medical students: opportunities and challenges. Annals of Biomedical Engineering, pp. 1–5 (2024)
9. Zhong, T., Cai, C., Zhu, G., Ma, M.: Enhancing the analysis of interdisciplinary learning quality with GPT Models: fine-tuning and knowledge-empowered approaches. In International Conference on Artificial Intelligence in Education, pp. 157–165. Springer Nature Switzerland, Cham (2024)
10. Kim, J.: Leading teachers' perspective on teacher-AI collaboration in education. Educ. Inf. Technol. **29**(7), 8693–8724 (2024)

Deep Integration of Generative Artificial Intelligence and Higher Education: Contents, Potential Risks, and Solutions

Xiuxi Wei and Xingqiong Wei[✉]

College of Artificial Intelligence, Guangxi Minzu University, Nanning, China
wxq@gxmzu.edu.cn

Abstract. Amid the rapid development of generative artificial intelligence (GAI), it is essential to recognize, prevent, and mitigate the educational risks that the GAI poses to higher education. This paper begins by examining the integration of the GAI within higher education, focusing on areas such as classroom teaching, extracurricular activities, and online learning. It further investigates the closed-loop teaching process, including objectives, resources, methods, and evaluation. Additionally, the paper explores a human-centered approach that prioritizes students' core competencies, teachers' digital literacy, and administrators' effective leadership. However, the GAI presents risks such as diminished academic integrity, threats to student privacy and security, challenges to the education of core societal values, reduced student innovation, strained teacher–student relationships, and disruptions to the job market for university graduates. In response, this paper proposes strategies to address these issues: fostering a strong academic spirit, advancing AI-related legal frameworks, innovating pedagogical approaches in ideological and political courses, establishing a human-centered framework for cultivating innovation, enhancing collaboration among teachers, AI-assisted educators, and students, and reforming higher education disciplines. Collectively, these measures aim to mitigate the potential risks that the GAI introduces to higher education.

Keywords: Generative artificial intelligence (GAI) · Higher education · Educational risks · ChatGPT

1 Introduction

The rapid development of generative artificial intelligence (GAI) has transformed knowledge production models in the digital era, providing new momentum for educational innovation and reform. GAI, an AI technology utilizing deep learning models, generates human-like content in response to complex prompts [1]. Common GAI tools include ChatGPT, Google Bard, ERNIE Bot, and Tongyi Qianwen. The direct integration of GAI, represented by ChatGPT, into education has triggered a "chain reaction" among various system elements [2], with higher education being notably affected. Consequently, educational risks from this technological integration are emerging. For example, an article in the Atlantic titled "College Essays Are Already Dead" raised concerns about increased cheating in university assignments [3]. Additionally, ChatGPT may produce fake references [4] and fabricate historical information [5], potentially misleading students.

As GAI applications deepen within higher education, recognizing, preventing, and mitigating the risks posed by the GAI to the education system is imperative. This study explores three dimensions: content, risk early warning, and risk mitigation strategies. It addresses three questions: What specific educational risks does the GAI introduce to higher education? How can these risks be proactively managed? How can they be effectively resolved? The goal is to facilitate the safe integration of this new generation of AI technology in higher education.

2   The Content of Deep Integration Between Gai and Higher Education

Yu Shengquan posits that the digital transformation of education involves three key levels: technology, business, and human-centeredness [6]. Education in the era of artificial intelligence requires changes in contexts, systems, and ideologies to address technological impacts effectively. Building on these insights, this study establishes an analytical framework focused on educational scenarios, teaching processes, and human-centered thinking paradigms. On the basis of educational ecology theory, educational scenarios are divided into three categories: classroom teaching, extracurricular activities, and online learning. Using teaching system element theory, educational and teaching processes are organized into four categories: teaching objectives, teaching resources, teaching methods, and teaching evaluation. Finally, human-centered thinking paradigms are classified into three categories according to the primary actors in higher education: student thinking paradigms, teacher thinking paradigms, and administrator thinking paradigms, as shown in Fig. 1.

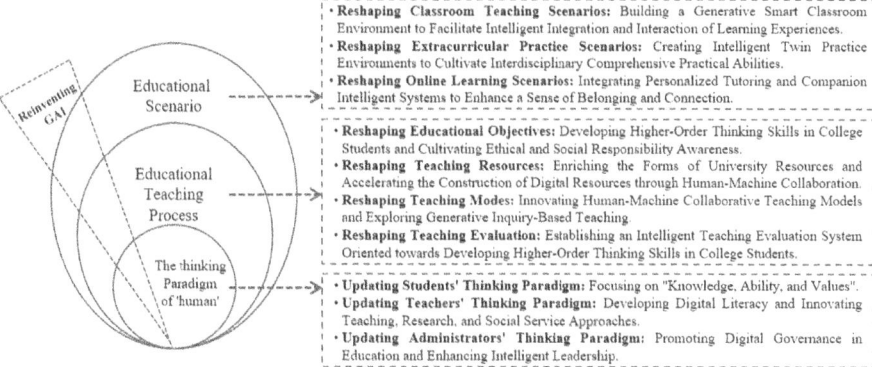

Fig. 1.   Specific Content of the GAI Reshaping the Form of Higher Education.

2.1   Reshaping Higher Education Scenarios

Higher education scenarios, characterized by dynamism and flexibility, integrate both the physical and virtual dimensions of time and space, as well as the certainty and uncertainty of social life. This integration creates a multidimensional educational landscape comprising a fixed time space represented by "physical classrooms," a semifixed time space represented by "extracurricular activities," and an indefinite time space represented by "online learning," as shown in Fig. 2.

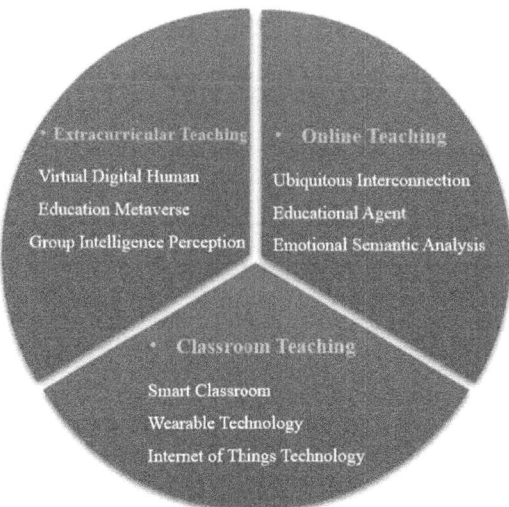

Fig. 2.   GAI Reshaping Higher Education Scenarios.

2.1.1   Reshaping Classroom Teaching Scenarios

Classroom teaching scenarios refer specifically to offline teaching environments at universities. Traditional university classrooms often experience one-way knowledge transmission and inadequate interaction between teachers and students, as well as among students themselves, which significantly hinders the cultivation of innovative talent. GAI creates an immersive smart classroom environment that dismantles barriers between information and physical spaces, facilitating the intelligent integration of university students' learning experiences. By incorporating virtual digital personas, such as learning partners and expert panels, and utilizing speech recognition and wearable technologies, students can engage in immersive experiences that enhance their classroom involvement. This approach strengthens students' inquiry consciousness and abilities, fostering research-oriented thinking. For example, Zhejiang University's smart teaching ecosystem, which leverages AI-generated speech, video technology, and cloud computing services, has established various teaching service modes, including "seamless remote teaching," "borderless classrooms," and "fully immersive interconnected classrooms," effectively promoting immersive, research-based learning among students [7].

2.1.2   Reshaping Extracurricular Practice Scenarios

Extracurricular practice scenarios refer specifically to blended online and offline practical learning environments for university students. In the ongoing reform of the talent cultivation model focused on competency enhancement, universities often prioritize theory over practice, resulting in deficiencies in student learning. Strengthening extracurricular practices can cultivate students' interdisciplinary innovation and entrepreneurship capabilities. By integrating large language models, video models, brain–computer interfaces within the metaverse, digital twins, and other technologies, we can intelligently enhance and translate content from the real world. This integration facilitates ubiquitous interconnectivity on the basis of data among diverse groups and objects, extending into intelligent learning spaces. Central China Normal University has combined the National Smart Education Platform, GAI, and education metaverse technologies to create immersive "AI-empowered Teaching Analysis Workshops" and "Autonomous Learning Rooms for Biology Virtual Simulation Experiments." These initiatives help teacher trainees refine their teaching skills and foster practical innovation capabilities among university students.

2.1.3   Reshaping Online Learning Scenarios

Online learning scenarios refer specifically to autonomous online learning environments for university students. The human-like information generation capabilities of large language model technologies enable the creation of more realistic educational agents. By leveraging chain-of-thought technologies, these agents can engage in real-time interactions with students, providing personalized responses and explanations to their inquiries. On the one hand, educational agents infused with GAI act as mentors, overseeing students' learning and offering personalized tutoring services. For example, in postclass online reading scenarios, question-answering robots can provide targeted feedback and examples in response to students' queries, deepening their understanding of the reading material [8]. On the other hand, these agents serve as companions, providing emotional and mental support to learners. Research by Rudolph et al. indicates that the immediate feedback offered by the GAI can fulfill university students' needs for affection, dignity, and self-actualization, thereby enhancing their sense of belonging and connection [9].

2.2   Reshaping the Teaching and Learning Processes in Higher Education

Only when educational technology prompts us to rethink and innovate the educational system can education and technology truly intersect. The reshaping of the educational system is more profound than that of spatial scenarios. By constructing a set of educational and teaching processes compatible with the development of the GAI, we can ensure that this transformation penetrates from the overt outer layer to the implicit inner layer. On the basis of the findings of a systematic literature review and the theory of teaching system elements, the GAI reshaped educational and teaching processes, as shown in Fig. 3.

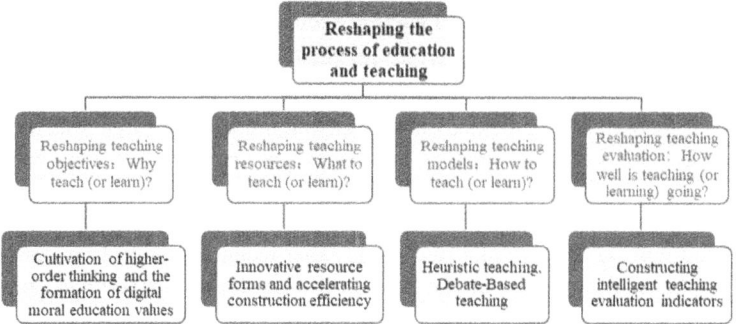

Fig. 3. GAI Reshaping the Teaching Process of Higher Education.

2.2.1 Reshaping of Teaching Objectives

With the development of the GAI, numerous industries reliant on mental labor may be displaced, necessitating a reorientation of higher education's teaching objectives toward areas where the GAI struggles to excel. Unlike previous intelligent technologies, students must first learn to flexibly utilize prompts when engaging with GAI. In this context, educators should prioritize fostering students' problem awareness and prompt-organizing skills to facilitate human–machine collaboration. Additionally, cultivating critical thinking is essential, as GAI's propensity to generate false content can disrupt students' cognition. By emphasizing critical thinking, students can grasp the essence of issues, develop independent thinking and decision-making abilities, discern false content, and effectively navigate the pitfalls of GAI technology. For example, erroneous legal regulations generated by the GAI in law studies may pose ethical and professional risks, potentially violating laws and regulations. Students equipped with critical thinking skills can identify false information, competently perform professional tasks, and mitigate technological risk. Last, fostering awareness of ethical and social responsibility is paramount. GAI has raised numerous educational ethical issues, such as the potential for students to cheat on exams or plagiarize assignments using tools such as ChatGPT. Therefore, universities must prioritize digital ethics education, instructing students to use GAI ethically and responsibly [10].

2.2.2 Reshaping of Teaching Resources

Research indicates that universities often lack the awareness and ability to develop digital and intelligent course resources, resulting in a significant shortage of high-quality educational materials [11]. GAI can enhance the creation of multimodal teaching resources, and collaborative human–machine resource development can expedite this process. First, the GAI can generate personalized multimodal resources. Cognitive resources, such as virtual experiments and 3D videos, enable students to gain practical experience and skills through scenario-based experiments and simulated operations. Second, emotional resources, including virtual teachers and virtual peers, can be developed through virtual human video generation and real-time interaction. Third, metacognitive resources—encompassing plans, strategies, and adaptive feedback—can be utilized for the logic design of nonplayer characters in educational games and for providing personalized feedback in educational assessments. Furthermore, human–machine collaboration accelerates resource development, which is defined as the synergistic creation of content by humans and machines [12]. Teachers can leverage GAI to quickly retrieve teaching resources related to specific knowledge points or themes, construct interdisciplinary knowledge maps, dismantle disciplinary barriers, and expedite the development of digital textbooks.

2.2.3 Reshaping of Teaching Modes

Traditional university classroom instruction, which relies primarily on teacher-led lectures, hinders the development of creativity and critical thinking among college students. By leveraging GAI, educators can transform traditional teaching methods and actively explore collaborative human–machine teaching approaches, as well as generative inquiry-based instruction aimed at cultivating higher-order thinking skills.

First, innovative human–machine collaborative teaching modes can be implemented. Prior to class, the GAI can generate diagnostic reports on student learning, equipping teachers with pretest questionnaires and relevant teaching cases. During class, educators can guide students in formulating questions for GAI to obtain precise information, thereby broadening their problem-solving perspectives and sparking new ideas. Post-class, GAI can assist in creating personalized assignments, helping teachers reduce their workload and enhancing efficiency.

Second, generative inquiry-based teaching can be explored. Educators can utilize educational AI assistants, such as Khanmigo, developed by Khan Academy, to facilitate enlightening dialogs through the Socratic method, guiding students toward discovering answers and deepening their critical thinking [13]. Furthermore, Guo et al. employed the debate chatbot argumate to enable students to assess their argumentation skills before debates, evaluating indicators such as structural complexity and argument quality [14].

2.2.4 Reshaping of Teaching Evaluation

For a long time, teaching evaluation in higher education has struggled with an overemphasis on "knowledge" at the expense of "ability" and has relied on simplistic evaluation indicators. GAI is transforming teaching evaluation in higher education by facilitating the development of an intelligent evaluation system. First, it reshapes the philosophy of teaching evaluation. The new philosophy, influenced by GAI, centers on students and places greater emphasis on higher-order thinking skills, including human–machine collaboration literacy and critical thinking. Second, it reshapes the content of teaching evaluation. The GAI can generate scenario-based and innovative test items by leveraging extensive training data and deep learning technologies. By incorporating specific prompts from teachers or students, the GAI can produce diverse and creative test questions, thereby enhancing the efficiency and quality of question generation. Third, it reshapes the methods of teaching evaluation. GAI compiles a diverse chain of learning evidence, utilizing predictive analytics, system modeling, and other techniques to integrate and analyze both process-oriented and outcome-oriented data collected from learners. This approach enables a comprehensive evaluation of student innovation and enhances the precision of teachers' decision-making [15].

2.3 Updating the "Human" Thinking Paradigm in Higher Education

Thinking is the most fundamental quality of education, and the transformation of cognitive processes is both personal and profound. The influence of the GAI on higher education should focus on the core objective of talent development, addressing the pressing question of "what type of individuals to cultivate" in today's context, while embracing the new mission of nurturing talent with contemporary qualities.

2.3.1 Updating Students' Thinking Paradigm

The updating of students' thinking paradigms should prioritize "knowledge as the foundation, ability as the key, and values as the guiding principle." First, students' thinking paradigms are rooted in foundational knowledge. While AI intervention in knowledge production accelerates knowledge growth and renders rote memorization seemingly unnecessary, basic knowledge and skills remain essential for cultivating higher-order thinking. Higher-order thinking can be fostered only by establishing connections between foundational knowledge and other skills [16]. Second, students' thinking paradigms emphasize higher-order abilities. College students develop human–machine symbiotic thinking and strong AI integration skills, enabling them to overcome their original thinking inertia and acquire innovative problem-solving abilities. Finally, students' thinking paradigms are guided by values rooted in digital moral education. College students should cultivate values that are truthful and benevolent, solidify their foundation in digital humanities, shape emotional attitudes and value orientations that respect others, care for society, and show concern for their country. They should actively integrate with the international community, adopt a global perspective, and ultimately contribute to an international digital moral education system that fosters both human and technological progress, leading to harmonious coexistence between humans and technology [17].

2.3.2 Updating Teachers' Thinking Paradigm

Currently, many university instructors remain at a superficial level of technology adoption. In the era of GAI, educators should prioritize developing digital literacy and innovating collaborative teaching, research, and service methods. First, the GAI functions as an "assistant," helping alleviate educators' instructional burdens. Tailored to teaching objectives and student learning contexts, the GAI can prepare lesson plans and case studies for instructors. Additionally, it can assist in generating test questions, with educators determining which prompts the GAI to support and review the accuracy and contextual relevance of the generated questions. Second, the GAI serves as a "mentor," enhancing instructors' research and innovation capabilities. For example, Dr. Markel at Stanford University developed GPTeach, a teacher training tool that simulates various student roles to engage in one-on-one interactions with trainee teachers, thereby promoting their professional development [18]. Finally, the GAI operates as a "facilitator," empowering educators in social services. University instructors engage in social service activities, such as academic reporting and science communication, to disseminate university research achievements and enhance the institution's social impact.

2.3.3 Updating Administrators' Thinking Paradigm

In the era of GAI, higher education administrators must transform their paradigms and focus on enhancing intelligent leadership to drive systematic changes in higher education across three dimensions: self-leadership, leading others, and organizational leadership. First, self-leadership involves managing one's thoughts, emotions, and actions. In the GAI era, administrators should adopt a growth mindset, recognize the practical value of the GAI in education, and demonstrate the willingness and courage to experiment with new strategies aimed at improving institutional performance. Second, leading others pertain to how individuals collaborate with and influence their colleagues. Administrators must foster effective collaboration between humans and machines, clarify the distinct roles of machines and educators, and leverage their respective strengths to enhance the overall capabilities of their teams. Finally, organizational leadership pertains to how individuals facilitate the achievement of institutional goals. Administrators must develop a clear vision, establish a resource allocation mechanism, and implement an incentive system for GAI in education, thereby steering the direction of reforms in GAI applications within the educational landscape.

3 Risk Early Warning for the Integration of Gai into the Higher Education Ecosystem

The integration of the GAI into the higher education ecosystem presents numerous risks, necessitating the establishment of early warning risk mechanisms to ensure its safe operation and sustainable development. The purpose of these mechanisms is to predict and alert stakeholders to educational risks associated with the GAI, focusing on four key questions: "Who will conduct the early warning?", "What should be warned about?", "How can it be ensured?", and "How should the early warning be implemented?". This study constructs a risk early warning mechanism comprising four modules: risk early warning subjects, risk early warning content, risk early warning safeguards, and risk early warning processes, as shown in Fig. 4. Specifically, this mechanism designates universities as the primary subjects of early warning, supplemented by governments, educational administrative departments, families, and society. It targets risks at four levels: ecological subjects, ecological media, ecological environments, and ecological functions. The safeguards include organizational development, institutional construction, technology application, and talent cultivation, following a risk early warning process of "risk identification → risk analysis → risk assessment → risk warning → risk tracking → risk identification…", to preemptively alert against educational risks arising from the GAI.

3.1 Risk Early Warning Subjects

In the context of implementing risk early warning systems, the key participants include governments, educational administrative departments, universities, families, and society.

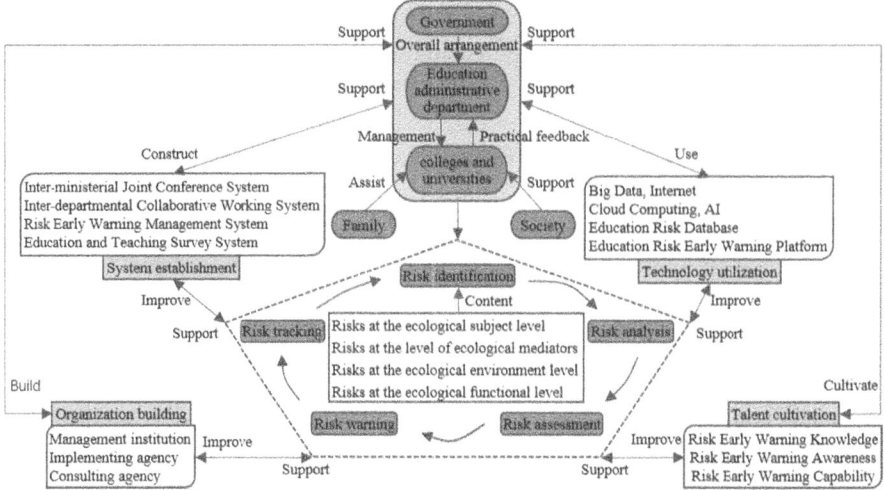

Fig. 4. Risk early warning mechanism for the integration of the GAI into the higher education ecosystem.

Among these, universities play a direct role in risk early warning activities and serve as the primary actors. Other stakeholders contribute indirectly through collaboration and interaction with universities:

(1) **Government:** As the "overall coordinator," the government is primarily responsible for the comprehensive planning of risk early warning efforts. This includes establishing a GAI education risk early warning system, promoting the development of normative documents for GAI risk prevention and control, providing policy support to universities for educational risk early warning and prevention, mobilizing various functional departments to participate in risk early warning, and clarifying their respective responsibilities.

(2) **Educational Administrative Departments:** Serving as "Direct Managers," these departments are tasked with formulating specific policies, regulations, and plans related to early risk warning. They determine the fundamental processes for early risk warning and guide and manage the early warning efforts of universities.

(3) **Universities:** As "Key Actors," universities undertake specific risk early warning tasks as dictated by the requirements of the government and educational administrative departments. They identify, analyze, assess, warn of, and track educational risk. Moreover, universities promptly report specific risk early warning situations encountered in educational and teaching practices to higher-level education authorities, considering both universal educational risk frameworks and their unique characteristics.

(4) **Families:** Acting as "important assistants," families maintain close ties with universities and primarily collaborate in conducting relevant educational risk surveys or actively reporting observed educational risk factors to universities, thereby enhancing risk early warning efforts.

(5) **Society:** Serving as "Strong Supporters," various sectors within society, such as industry associations, technology enterprises, and major media outlets, can provide support to universities in conducting related risk early warning work. For example, industry associations can offer intellectual support for the formulation of GAI standards and norms, technology enterprises can provide technical support for establishing educational risk early warning platforms, and major media outlets can facilitate the widespread dissemination of educational risk early warning information through promotional efforts.

3.2 Risk Early Warning Content

The integration of GAI into the higher education ecosystem has introduced various risks, including the erosion of teacher–student sovereignty, distortion of knowledge content, disruption of safety and inclusiveness, and alienation of talent cultivation. Additionally, it has prompted an evolution in the structure (comprising subjects, mediators, and environments) and functions of the higher education ecosystem. Consequently, the content of risk early warning must not only address four major risk manifestations at the micro level but also adopt a macro perspective to consider risk across four dimensions:

(1) **Risks at the Ecological Subject Level:** These risks pertain to the threats posed by the GAI to educational stakeholders, including departments, universities, administrators, teachers, and students. They encompass infringements on, weakening, and changes to educational rights, functions, and roles.

(2) **Risks at the Ecological Mediator Level:** These risks involve the harm inflicted by the GAI on the content, methods, and media of higher education, which impacts interactions among ecological subjects and between subjects and their environments. Universities, as critical hubs for education, technology, and talent, rely on knowledge as a foundational pillar of their missions. Consequently, the risk of distorted knowledge content within the higher education ecosystem warrants special attention.

(3) **Risks at the Ecological Environment Level:** These refer to the disruption of the multidimensional spaces and environments that facilitate or constrain higher education development due to the GAI. The advancement of GAI technology may not only compromise safety and inclusiveness but also subject the educational environment to the influence of capital interests [19], prioritizing commercialization over public good and humanistic values.

(4) **Risks at the Ecological Function Level:** These represent disruptions to educational functions within the higher education ecosystem caused by the GAI. In addition to alienating talent cultivation functions, the GAI poses threats to the academic research roles of higher education institutions, including the dispersion of academic responsibilities and the fostering of academic discrimination. Overall, these risks are intricately linked to higher education, characterized by complex and diverse sources, dynamic changes in risk types, and profound, lasting impacts.

3.3 Risk Early Warning Safeguards

The early warning system for educational risk associated with the GAI represents a comprehensive and systematic effort that necessitates an intelligent and holistic approach.

The concept of "holistic smart governance" emphasizes leveraging digital technologies to enhance integrated governance by consolidating organizational departments, reshaping institutional systems, adopting digital tools, and strengthening the capabilities of key stakeholders. To fortify the early warning system, four primary dimensions should be emphasized: organizational construction, the institutional framework, technological application, and talent cultivation.

(1) **Organizational Construction:** Governments, education administration departments, and universities must establish dedicated or integrated management, execution, and advisory bodies for early warning of educational risk. These bodies should be responsible for organizing and implementing relevant measures. Universities can take inspiration from the Massachusetts Institute of Technology (MIT), which has established risk steering groups to provide strategic guidance, risk advisory teams composed of experts from various fields to identify and assess risks, and risk management committees to oversee risk warning activities and promote a risk management culture [20]. Additionally, universities can create risk warning research centers to provide intellectual support for mitigating educational risks arising from digital technologies.

(2) **Institutional Framework:** A three-tiered risk warning system should be established, spanning the "national (central government and Ministry of Education) - local (local governments and education administration departments) - university" levels. This system should prioritize the establishment of interministerial joint conference systems for consultative decision-making on GAI educational risk, departmental collaboration mechanisms to ensure unified execution and effective implementation of risk warning measures, risk warning management systems to clarify responsibilities, standardize processes, establish information reporting mechanisms, and educational investigation systems to assess the application of the GAI in universities regularly and identify potential risks.

(3) **Technological application:** Universities should leverage their research strengths and collaborate with relevant enterprises to develop an educational risk database and a risk warning platform utilizing big data, the internet, cloud computing, and artificial intelligence technologies. By applying machine learning, intelligent statistical engines, and image recognition technologies, universities can detect, identify, qualify, analyze, and assess risks within educational data.

(4) **Talent Cultivation:** Universities and education administration departments should organize educational and training activities related to GAI risk warnings. This includes developing risk warning courses, employing scenario-based teaching methods, constructing risk warning training platforms, organizing specialized lectures, implementing risk competence assessments, and enhancing collaboration between universities and enterprises in talent cultivation. These efforts aim to increase the risk warning awareness of students, teachers, education administrators, and technical personnel, consolidate their knowledge of risk warning, and continuously enhance their risk management capabilities.

3.4 Risk Warning Process

Risk warning is a fundamental component of risk management. According to the International Organization for Standardization (ISO) in its 2018 publication "Risk Management - Guidelines," the risk management process encompasses activities such as communication and consultation, establishing context, risk assessment (which includes risk identification, risk analysis, and risk evaluation), risk treatment, monitoring and review, and recording and reporting. Furthermore, effective communication of warning information is crucial in risk warning and represents a key aspect of the process. On the basis of this framework, this study has designed a cyclical risk warning process comprising the following stages: risk identification → risk analysis → risk evaluation → risk warning → risk tracking → risk identification. This continuous and iterative process involves multiple stakeholders collaborating to implement risk warning procedures, supported by risk mitigation measures. At its core, this approach emphasizes the application of human–machine collaboration methods and tools, integrating human expertise in risk perception and judgment with machines' capabilities in data collection, analysis, evaluation, and monitoring. This integration enables agile responses to early signs of risk and facilitates the rapid dissemination of warning information within the higher education ecosystem.

3.4.1 Risk Identification

The initial step in educational risk warning involves identifying educational risks associated with the adoption of the GAI. This process requires pinpointing the specific educational issues that pose risks and analyzing their types. To facilitate this, the Ministry of Education should establish a universal AI educational risk indicator system (hereinafter referred to as the "Universal Indicator System") to serve as a reference point for universities in their risk identification efforts. Universities should subsequently integrate their unique characteristics, leverage the Universal Indicator System, and employ big data technology to collect and analyze relevant information comprehensively for real-time screening and identification of educational risk. Traditional methods, such as interviews and questionnaires, can also be utilized to uncover potential risks. Ultimately, a human–machine collaboration approach should be adopted for educational risk identification, which encompasses two primary aspects:

(1) **Identifying the Existence of Educational Risks:** Universities can identify existing risks by reviewing relevant documents and analyzing available data. Regular feedback can be obtained from students, teachers, parents, and other stakeholders through interviews and questionnaires to understand the challenges encountered in the application of the GAI. Additionally, expert seminars and technical forecasts can be organized to anticipate and confirm potential risks in advance.

(2) **Identifying the Types of Educational Risks:** Universities should classify identified educational risks on the basis of the Universal Indicator System issued by the Ministry of Education. However, it is important to note that this system may not encompass all types of educational risk across universities. Therefore, institutions with varying levels, types of education, and security classifications must further develop tailored educational risk indicator systems to address their unique circumstances and

identify individualized educational risks. Subsequently, universities should record corresponding risks in risk registers and promptly upload them to educational risk databases.

3.4.2 Risk Analysis

After identifying educational risks, the subsequent step involves analyzing these risks, which includes the following components:

(1) **Analysis of Educational Risk Sources:** The origins of educational risks can be examined from multiple perspectives, including the GAI technology itself, the digital literacy of educational stakeholders, and the application of technology in teaching and learning. In this analysis, universities can collaborate with enterprises and utilize technical testing platforms, such as the "GAI Content Security and Model Safety Testing Platform," developed by Xinhua News Agency in partnership with the Institute of Computing Technology at the Chinese Academy of Sciences and other industry institutions. This collaboration enables comprehensive testing of the GAI, conducting interviews and surveys with educational stakeholders, and employing risk consultation teams to scientifically evaluate risk sources.

(2) **Analysis of Educational Risk Probability:** Universities can engage in consultations with internal risk consultation teams and third-party risk assessment agencies, gathering insights from experts and technicians across various fields to estimate the likelihood of educational risks occurring. Additionally, universities, in collaboration with the Ministry of Education, can establish an educational risk information-sharing platform that connects educational risk databases and aggregates relevant data. This collaboration facilitates the analysis of risk probabilities through the application of big data, AI, and other technologies.

(3) **Analysis of Educational Risk Impacts:** Universities can assess the potential hazards posed by the GAI to higher education ecosystems by focusing on elements such as ecological subjects, ecological mediators, ecological environments, and ecological functions. In this context, universities can leverage risk consultation teams and utilize machine learning, deep learning, and other technologies to develop educational risk prediction models. This approach allows for a detailed analysis of the impacts of educational risks, taking into account their scale, scope, and timeliness. Special emphasis should be placed on the long-term effects of the GAI on educational ethics.

3.4.3 Risk Evaluation

The objective of educational risk evaluation is to assess the level of educational risk associated with the GAI on the basis of findings from the educational risk analysis and to evaluate the institution's risk appetite and tolerance. This process encompasses the following:

(1) **Evaluation of Educational Risk Levels:** The educational risk level indicates the severity of potential risk and can be categorized into four levels: low risk, moderate risk, substantial risk, and critical risk. By considering both the probability and impact of these risks, the risk matrix method can be employed, in consultation with experts,

to calculate a numerical risk level. This value is then compared against established risk standards to determine the educational risk level. Currently, there are no unified evaluation standards in China that specifically address GAI-related educational risk. To facilitate a scientific assessment of these risks, the government and the Ministry of Education urgently need to establish evaluation standards for the GAI in education, clarify classifications of risk levels, provide guidance on evaluation methodologies, and offer support to local educational administrative departments and universities in conducting risk assessments.

(2) **Evaluation of Educational Risk Appetite and Tolerance:** Risk appetite refers to the level of risk that a university is willing to accept, whereas risk tolerance represents the degree of variability in outcomes that the university is prepared to accept when managing these risks, thereby quantifying the risk appetite. Universities should establish varying risk appetite statements that clarify the risk levels they are willing to accept to achieve early warning objectives, as well as define corresponding risk-bearing capacities. This guidance will assist university risk managers in making decisions that align with the institution's degree of risk tolerance. In the context of GAI-driven teaching innovations, universities may need to adopt a greater risk appetite; however, concerning data privacy and security issues arising from technology, they may need to adopt a lower risk appetite or even declare a lack of risk appetite.

3.4.4   Risk Warning

Educational risk warning is a pivotal component of the early warning system for educational risk and is implemented through a combination of hierarchical dissemination and networked communication. The content of these warnings encompasses the probability of occurrence, impact, and severity of educational risk. Specifically, educational administrative departments at all levels, universities, and relevant media collaborate within a top-down, hierarchical risk warning information reporting system, leveraging the internet to disseminate educational risk warning information promptly and ensuring that all stakeholders are informed:

(1) **Educational administrative departments** primarily issue risk warnings through various means, such as notifications, recommendations, public announcements, and reminders. For example, the Ministry of Education publishes a list of educational risk warnings related to the GAI, alerting universities to potential widespread educational risks within a specified timeframe and urging them to take proactive risk prevention measures.

(2) **Universities** utilize online platforms to disseminate warning information, ensuring that relevant faculty, staff, and students across departments, grades, majors, and classes are promptly notified. This enables them to guard against educational risks while utilizing the GAI in teaching and learning. In addition to disseminating the general educational risks associated with the GAI, universities must also account for their unique institutional circumstances and provide additional warnings for specific risks faced by their institution.

(3) **Relevant media outlets** should actively share educational risk warning information issued by the government, educational administrative departments, and other entities, thereby broadening the reach of these warnings. It is crucial for major media organizations to prioritize the authenticity and reliability of their information sources to avoid the dissemination of false information. In this process, authoritative official educational media play an indispensable role.

3.4.5   Risk Tracking

As the internal and external environments of the higher education ecosystem evolve, educational risks may emerge, change, or dissipate, necessitating dynamic tracking to add, adjust, or remove relevant educational risk warnings. To facilitate this, universities must establish an educational risk review system through their risk steering groups and risk management committees, which will record risks in real time and convene regular meetings for comprehensive risk assessments. The primary components of risk tracking include the following:

(1) **GAI Technology and Its Application Systems:** Following the release of ChatGPT-3.5, OpenAI promptly introduced ChatGPT-4. The rapid evolution of GAI technology may introduce new risks to higher education ecosystems. Therefore, universities must stay informed about GAI advancements and conduct timely assessments of their technical capabilities.
(2) **Relevant laws, regulations, and regulatory requirements:** In July 2023, the Cyberspace Administration of China and six other departments jointly issued the "Interim Measures for the Administration of GAI Services." Universities must align their identification of educational risk with the normative requirements outlined in these interim measures, providing a foundation for reassessing the nature and severity of risk.
(3) **The application of the GAI in** teaching: universities should establish a comprehensive educational and instructional survey system to monitor the evolution of educational risk, including the emergence of new risk. In this context, collaboration with technology enterprises is essential for developing educational risk monitoring systems that leverage big data, AI, and other technologies for large-scale and continuous monitoring and risk reassessment.

4   Risk Mitigation Strategies for Integrating Gai into the Higher Education Ecosystem

In light of risks such as the erosion of teacher–student sovereignty, distortion of knowledge content, disruption of security and inclusivity, and alienation of talent cultivation, prevention should not be confined solely to risk early warning mechanisms. Instead, universities, as key actors, must collaborate with governments, education administrative departments, and other stakeholders to effectively manage and mitigate these risks. This collaboration should involve activating stakeholder awareness, critically evaluating knowledge content, optimizing digital environments, and innovating talent cultivation strategies.

4.1 Innovating Digital Governance Policies and Tools to Mitigate the Risk of Academic Misconduct

In response to academic misconduct, including student plagiarism, exam cheating, and the unauthorized appropriation of papers due to the application of the GAI in higher education, it is essential to innovate governance policies and tools at the national, institutional, and corporate levels. At the national level, regulations governing GAI usage must be established, actively exploring universal technical quality standards, contingency plans for significant issues, and risk response strategies. It is crucial to delineate the rights and responsibilities of diverse support alliances and the contributions of each entity to technology governance, thereby guiding the effective harnessing of the GAI's potential. At the institutional level, policies for campus access to the GAI and its educational applications should be developed to facilitate its use in specific educational contexts. Finally, at the corporate level, tools for early warning of academic misconduct risk should be created, employing predictive models to analyze the teaching behaviors of learners and educators during educational activities, along with the construction of a visual warning system.

4.2 Driving Evaluation Reform to Foster Student Creativity and Critical Thinking

To address concerns that the misuse of GAI may hinder the development of students' higher-order thinking skills, educators must reform assessment systems to foster creativity and critical thinking. First, it is essential to establish evaluation task norms. Before instruction begins, educators should define a comprehensive evaluation framework that incorporates contextualized and authentic assessment tasks, supported by diverse types of learning evidence. Second, educators should assign multimodal tasks that require students to complete work independently or significantly modify GAI-generated content. Finally, strengthening process-oriented evaluation is important. Educators can conduct regular reviews of students' interim essays and research outputs, prompting students to reflect on the insights gained throughout the completion process.

4.3 Enhancing Teachers' Human–Machine Collaborative Teaching and Research Capabilities to Address Role Crises

In response to the challenges that teachers encounter while navigating multiple role transitions in the era of GAI, enhancing their competencies in human–machine collaborative teaching and research to facilitate professional development is crucial. First, at the individual level, teachers should familiarize themselves with GAI-related knowledge and operational skills, cultivating a greater awareness of how to leverage new technologies to transform education. Second, at the institutional level, schools should establish policies governing campus access to and the application of intelligent tools, incorporating teachers' smart education literacy into their professional evaluation criteria to intrinsically motivate them to utilize the GAI to enhance their teaching practices. Finally, at the national level, the government should implement a comprehensive mechanism for cultivating smart education talent, focusing on creating diverse platforms and key projects to nurture university teachers' smart education literacy, refining evaluation index systems, and systematically promoting this initiative in a scientific and orderly manner.

5   Conclusions

The integration of GAI promises to reshape the higher education ecosystem, enhancing teaching and learning, academic research, social services, and educational governance. However, it also introduces potential educational risks to this ecosystem. This study analyzes these risks from three perspectives, namely, risk manifestation, early warning, and risk mitigation, providing theoretical guidance for governing GAI-related educational risks and reinforcing the foundation for the digital transformation and high-quality development of higher education. To facilitate the deep integration of the GAI into this ecosystem, the following approaches are recommended: (1) Prioritize safety as a fundamental principle, adhere to the core framework of trustworthy AI, and develop secure and reliable large educational models tailored to the needs and application scenarios of higher education, with a focus on foundational capabilities, professional competencies, and application services. (2) Address the ethical risks posed by the GAI in the higher education ecosystem by establishing ethical principles for the GAI's educational applications, conducting ethics education in science and technology, and promoting the ethical use of GAI tools among faculty and students. (3) Integrate GAI with the metaverse to create an embodied intelligent higher education environment, develop dynamically adaptive immersive learning resources, explore new models of human–machine collaboration, enable university students to master professional knowledge, cultivate higher-order thinking, enhance ethical awareness, and ultimately achieve intellectual growth through deep dialog, embodied experiences, and effective empathy.

Acknowledgements. This work is supported by the Key Topics of Guangxi Science and Technology Think Tank (Gui Science Association (2024) K-19) and the Innovation Project of Guangxi Graduate Education (JGY2022104, JGY2023116).

References

1. Lim, W.M., Gunasekara, A., Pallant, J.L., et al.: Generative AI and the future of education: Ragnarök or reformation? A paradoxical perspective from management educators. The International Journal of Management Educ. **2**, 1–13 (2023)
2. Zhan, Z., Ji, Y., Niu, S., et al.: The intrinsic mechanism, representation form, and risk mitigation of embedding chatGPT into the educational ecosystem. Modern Distance Educ. **4**, 3–13 (2023)
3. Marche, S.: The college essay is dead. The Atlantic **6**, 1–4 (2022)
4. Zhou, H.-Y., Li, Y.-Y.: The Impact of ChatGPT on education ecology and strategies to cope with it. Journal of Xinjiang Normal University (Edition of Philosophy and Social Sciences) (4), 102–112 (2023)
5. Shen, L.-P., He, C.-F., Cao, D.-X., et al.: Evaluation and analysis of large language models application in of historical discipline middle schools. Modern Educational Technology (2), 62–71 (2024)

6. Yu, S.: Levels of digital transformation in education. China Educational Technology (2), 55–59,66 (2023)
7. Shen, L.-Y., Li, M., Zhang, Z.-H., et al.: The construction and application in practice of intelligent teaching ecosystem in colleges and universities based on AI technology——taking zhejiang university as an example. Modern Educational Technol. **32**(12), 85–92 (2022)
8. Liu, M., Zhang, J.X., Nyagoga, L.M., et al.: Student-AI question cocreation for enhancing reading comprehension. IEEE Transactions on Learning Technologies (17), 815–826 (2023)
9. Rudolph, J., Tan, S., Tan, S.: ChatGPT: bullshit spewer or the end of traditional assessments in higher education? Journal of applied learning and teaching (1), 1–22 (2023)
10. Zhang, L., Llu, X., Chang, J.: Ethical issues of artificial intelligence education and its regulations. e-Education Research **42**(8), 5–11 (2021)
11. An, G., Zhao, X.: Research on the problems of outstanding talents training under the background of "double world-class" construction. Journal of Henan University (Social Sciences) **62**(1), 117–125, 155 (2022)
12. Wan, L., Du, J., Xiong, R.: Human–machine co-creation: a new paradigm for the development of digital educational resources based on AIGC. Modern Distance Education Res. **35**(5), 12–21 (2023)
13. Dong, Y., Xia, L., Li, X., et al.: Analysis of the path to empowering student learning with ChatGPT. e-Education Research **44**(12), 14–20,34 (2023)
14. Guo, K., Zhong, Y.C., Li, D.L., et al.: Effects of chatbot-assisted in-class debates on students' argumentation skills and task motivation. Comput. Educ. **203**, 1–19 (2023)
15. Emerson, A., Cloude, E.B., Azevedo, R., et al.: Multimodal learning analytics for game-based learning. British J. Educational Technology **51**(5), 1505–1526 (2020)
16. Gu, X., Hao, X.: Viewing future education based on the ai-reshaped concept of knowledge. Educational Research **43**(9), 138–149 (2022)
17. Zhu, Z., Dal, L., Hu, J.: Higher consciousness generative learning: innovation of learning paradigm enabled by AIGC technology. e-Education Research **44**(6), 5–14 (2023)
18. Markel, J.M., Opferman, S.G., Landay, J.A., et al.: GPTeach: interactive TA training with GPT based students. In Proceedings of the Tenth ACM Conference on Learning @ Scale (L@S'23), Copenhagen, Denmark. ACM, New York, NY, USA, pp. 1–11 (2023)
19. Luo, F., Ma, Y.-X.: The impact of artificial intelligence generated content on academic ecology and countermeaures——discussion and analysis based on ChatGPT. Modern Educational Technology (6), 15–25 (2023)
20. Zhao, L., Zhang, L., Dal, R.: The risk governance of education data in the era of intelligence: real dilemma and practical path. Journal of Educational Science of Hunan Normal University (6), 94–102 (2021)

Evolutionary Test Data Generation for Automatic Defect Detection in Teaching Environments

Shuping Fan[1], Jiahang Li[2], Haiwei Pan[3], Kejia Zhang[3], Baoying Ma[4(✉)], and Jun Xing[1]

[1] School of Computer and Information Technology, Mudanjiang Normal University, Mudanjiang 157011, China
[2] School of Public Health and Emergency Management, Southern University of Science and Technology, Shenzhen 518000, China
[3] School of Computer Science and Technology, Harbin Engineering University, Harbin 157000, China
[4] School of Health Administration, Mudanjiang Medical University, Mudanjiang 157011, China
myj@hrbeu.edu.cn

Abstract. In the process of automated program defect detection in software, the importance of different statements without test data coverage is often neglected when test data are generated via a genetic algorithm (GA), which affects the efficiency of generating target data and the performance of defect detection. In this paper, the program key statements are defined first, and then, the importance of the key statements and their calculation methods are proposed. On this basis, the fitness function of the GA is given to increase the fitness of individuals corresponding to the data covering high statement importance. The goal is to improve their probability of being retained during evolution and generate the target data quickly. Finally, the proposed method is tested on benchmarks and industrial programs and compared with existing methods. The results show that the proposed method can generate data efficiently and improve the efficiency of defect detection compared with existing methods. In addition, this method is suitable for automatic defect detection in the program writing process and can provide support for intelligent programming teaching.

Keywords: Generating Test Data · Evolutionary Algorithms · Defect Detection · statement importance · software testing

1 Introduction

The goal of software testing is to detect errors to ensure software quality, which accounts for more than half of the total costs for software development [1]. Traditional test data design is often performed manually. It has the disadvantages of a long development cycle, high cost, and low efficiency. With the emergence of large-scale and complex software, traditional manual data design methods often cannot meet these requirements.

K. Zhang et al. (Eds.): CSEI 2024, CCIS 2448, pp. 204–220, 2025.
https://doi.org/10.1007/978-981-96-3738-6_16

Automated testing has been widely used because it can effectively improve the quality of software products while saving human resources and costs [2]. In addition to random testing, existing automated test data generation techniques also include symbolic execution testing as well as testing via evolutionary algorithms. Search-based testing enables the automatic generation of test data via intelligent optimization technology. At present, genetic algorithms [3], artificial immune algorithms [4], differential evolution algorithms [5] and other algorithms have been widely used to search for and generate target data in the program input domain. Researchers [6] have shown that the most frequently used optimization algorithm for test data generation is the GA. The study also revealed that cover-age testing is more often used in programs than functional testing is [7].

The coverage criterion affects the effectiveness of the data generation [8]. We study the automatic generation of test data on the basis of path coverage criteria in this paper. The contributions of this paper include the following:

- We emphasize the importance of different program statements for generating test data. We also consider program key statements and propose a method to generate data to increase the efficiency of defect detection.
- We consider the difficulty of different program statements being covered by test data and focus on different branches of program branch statements without data coverage. We design a calculation method for the weights of program statements and compute the importance of different statements.
- We design a new fitness function for the genetic algorithm and verify its effectiveness and running efficiency through benchmark and industrial program experiments.

2   Related Works

To date, many scholars have applied genetic algorithms or other algorithms or combined them to generate test data.

2.1   Generating Test Data via Evolutionary Algorithms

In the work of combining a genetic algorithm with other optimization algorithms, Singla et al. [9] proposed a method using a GA and a particle swarm optimization algorithm, which achieves target data that meet path coverage standards, and analyzed the efficiency by using programs of different scales and complexities. Singh et al. [10] introduced a particle swarm algorithm into the operator of a genetic algorithm. To cover different paths of the program, they use the transformation relationship of the program and derive new data from the generated data. Similarly, Ji et al. [11] also used two algorithms to enhance the test case generation of intelligent contract data stream testing. Compared with the baseline method, it achieves greater coverage. For object-oriented software, Arcuri and Yao [12] further apply the hybrid algorithm in [10] to achieve target data. In addition, Fraser et al. [13] first combined a genetic algorithm with a hill climbing algorithm to obtain test data that met the program functions. The results prove that the hybrid algorithm is better than using any of the algorithms alone, and Mann et al. [14] used a GA and a simulated annealing algorithm to generate target data. Evolutionary algorithms have been increasingly used in the generation of test data.

2.2 Generating Test Data via Evolutionary Algorithms

In terms of using a GA to generate test data, Qian et al. [15] combined key point probabil-ity with path similarity, which improved individual fitness according to the individual's contribution to generating test data. Esnaashari et al. [16] proposed a memetic popula-tion size algorithm that uses reinforcement learning in a genetic algorithm to provide better coverage with fewer evaluations. Mann et al. [17] studied the impact of early populations on the efficiency of a GA and designed a method for generating data. To further solve the problems of falling into local minima and premature convergence of the genetic algorithm, Zhang et al. [18] used a multipopulation genetic algorithm. The method uses two subpopulations as well as one main subpopulation to ensure that the subpopulations run simultaneously.

2.3 Structured Testing

Structured testing ensures that test cases can cover all parts of software code, includ-ing statements, branches, loops, etc.,, ensuring that test cases meet complete coverage criteria. For test data generation in structured testing, McMinn [19] combines the layer proximity of the path to generate test data covering multiple target paths. Zhang et al. [20] considered the dynamic capture of rare data to generate test data. They adjust the fitness by calculating the contributions of individuals. To quickly generate target data, Fan et al. [21] use the balance degree of crossing the various branches of programs by individuals in the population.

Actual software often has a large code size and contains many complex statements, and how to set weights for different program statements and retain test data covering important statements during data generation is crucial. We propose a method to generate test data on the basis of the importance of program key statements. The goal is to increase the individual weight of test data covering high-importance statements.

3 Basic Concepts

For convenience, the program in Fig. 1(a) and its control flow graph are shown in Fig. 1(b). We define the basic concepts [22] as follows.

3.1 Program Path

A program path P is a set of node sequences in a control flow graph that includes an initial node and an end node [23]: $P = \{s, n_1, n_2, \cdots n_k, e\}$, where $n_i \in N (i = 1,2, \cdots , k)$ and $< s, n_1 > \in E, < n_i, n_{i+1} > \in E (i = 1, 2, ..., k\text{-}1), < n_k, e > \in E$. As shown in Fig. 1 (b), one path in a control flow graph is $p_1 = \{s, n_1, n_2, n_5, n_6, n_8, e\}$.

3.2 Sequence Structure

Sequence statements usually include expression statements, compound statements, and empty statements. We define an ordered statement set consisting of the most consecutive statements as a sequence structure. As shown in Eq. (1):

$$SE_i = \left\{ s_i \ldots s_j \middle| \max(j) \wedge (i \leq j) \wedge (s_i \rightarrow \cdots \rightarrow s_j) \right\} \qquad (1)$$

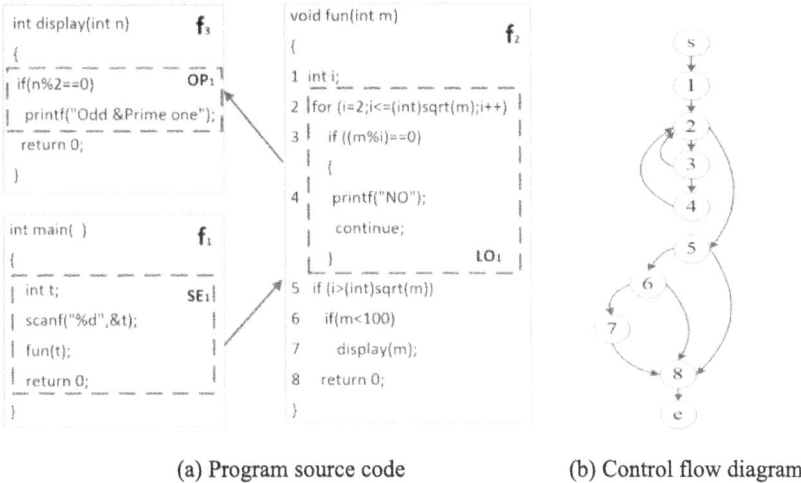

(a) Program source code   (b) Control flow diagram

Fig. 1. Sample program and control flow graph

where s_i and s_j represent the ith row and the j th row ($i \leq j$) program statement, respectively. $s_i \ldots s_j$ is the continuous code fragment from the i th to the j th row. $\max\{j\}$ Represents the maximum value of j; that is, the i th sequential structure SE_i contains the maximum number of continuous statements starting from statement s_i, and the sequential structure ends with statement s_j. $s_i \rightarrow \cdots \rightarrow s_j$ Shows that if and only if the statement s_i is executed, each intermediate statement from the beginning statement s_i to the end statement s_j will be executed in sequence. For example, SE_1 in Fig. 1(a) is a sequential structure.

3.3 Option Structure

The option structure is used to select a compound statement when the statement expression is satisfied, and it is defined as follows:

$$OP_i = Option(\rho)Compound(s_i) \tag{2}$$

where *Option* is a selection structure keyword, including *if* and *switch*. ρ is a predicate expression, and its value is true or false. *Compound*(s_i) is a compound statement block, s_i shows the ith statement, and it can be a sequential structure, a selection structure, a loop structure, or their combination. *Compound*(s_i) will be executed if and only if ρ is true. For example, OP_1 in Fig. 1(a) is a selection structure.

3.4 Loop Structure

When the loop expression is true, the loop executes the region $Region(s_i)$. The expression is shown in Eq. (3).

$$LO_i = \big(Loop(\rho)Region(s_i)\big)_n \tag{3}$$

Loop represents the keyword for the loop structure, including for, while do…while, etc. If and only if ρ is true, $Region(s_i)$ will be executed. $(\cdots)_n$ indicates that the loop is executed $0\sim n (n \geq 0)$ times. For example, LO_1 in Fig. 1(a) is a loop structure.

3.5   Program Key Statements

On the basis of the number of times the loop body is executed, we represent the loop structure as a double-branch structure [21]. For ease of explanation, branch and loop structures are collectively referred to as branch structures. The statements in these two structures on the target path are called key statements. The nodes corresponding to these two structures in the control flow graph are defined as branch nodes. For example, statement 3 in Fig. 1(a) is a key statement of f_2, and n_3 and n_5 in Fig. 1(b) are both branch nodes.

3.6   Child Node

In the control flow graph, for nodes n_i and n_j on the target path, if n_j exists, ensuring that n_j controls dependent node n_i, then n_j is called the child node of n_i, recorded as $n_j \in sub(n_i)$. For example, n_6 is the child node of n_5 in Fig. 1(b).

3.7   Programme Statement Weights

The number of branch or loop structures nested outside a statement is called the level of the statement. The ratio of the level of the statement j to the largest statement level on the target path is called the statement weight of the statement j. The calculation method is shown in Eqs. (4) and (5) in Sect. 4.1.

3.8   Statement Importance

The product of the difference in test data covering each branch of a statement and the weight of that statement is the statement importance of the branch statement. The calculation method is shown in Eq. (6) in 4.2.

4   The Proposed Method

We first consider the weights of the program statements, then calculate the importance of the statements, and finally, we obtain the fitness of each individual in the GA.

4.1   Calculation of Program Statement Weights

As seen from the control flow graph in Fig. 1(b), compared with the sequential structure, the statements in the branch and loop structures are more difficult to traverse with individuals. Therefore, to reduce the algorithm cost, our method considers the statement importance in the branch structure. According to the correspondence between the code and control flow graph (see Fig. 1), finding the weights of statements can be converted into finding the levels of their corresponding nodes in Fig. 1(b). According to the definition in Sect. 3, if $n_j \in sub(n_i)$, that is, n_j is the child node of n_i in the control flow graph, then the weight of the statement j corresponding to node n_j can be expressed as $weight_j$:

$$weight_j = 1 + level_j/max(level_1, level_2, \cdots , level_N) \tag{4}$$

The level of statement j in Eq. (4) is defined as $level_j$:

$$level_j = \begin{cases} level_i + \sum_h(1), & n_j \text{ is a branch or loop node} \\ 0, & else \end{cases} \tag{5}$$

In the above equation, $level_i$ represents the level of the node corresponding to the statement i in the control flow graph, and N represents the node number on the target path, that is, the number of target statements. $max(\cdots)$ Represents the maximum value, which here refers to the maximum value at the statement level corresponding to all nodes on the target path. h in $\sum_h(1)$ represents the number of branches or loops nested in n_j. For calculation of the statement levels, when n_i is the node corresponding to a branch or loop structure statement, $level_j > 0$. Otherwise, when n_i is the node corresponding to a sequential structure statement, $level_j = 0$. For example, in Fig. 1(a), assuming that the target path is $p_1 = \{s, n_1, n_2, n_5, n_6, n_8, e\}$, the weight of key statement 6 can be found. Since n_6 corresponding to statement 6 is the child node of n_5, n_5 is the node corresponding to a branch structure statement, and its parent is the node corresponding to a sequential statement. Therefore, the level of n_5 is $level_5 = 1$, and the level of n_6 is $level_6 = 2$. Assuming that the loop structure executes a true branch once, the level of statement n_6 is the maximum level on the target path, that is, $max(level_1, level_2, level_5, level_6, level_8) = 2$. Then, according to (4), we obtain the weight of statement 6 as $weight_6 = 3/2$.

4.2 Calculation of the Importance of Key Statements

Existing methods consider the balance of test data coverage of each program branch [21] or rare data that traverse difficult-to-cover nodes to generate data [20]. However, they do not consider the true branches or false branches of program branch nodes, which are not covered by test data, and lack the measure of difficulty of program statements themselves being covered by test data. As seen from the control flow graph, when a branch node is not traversed by test data, its corresponding branch node is also not traversed by data. In other words, at this time, no test data cover the subsequent descendant nodes of the branch node. If the target path contains these nodes, no data can be found to cover the target path. If the difference in test data crossing program branch nodes is considered in the process of test data generation, the weights of different statements are calculated for the target path. The influence of individual corresponding data on the importance of statements is designed and calculated so that individuals with a large influence on the importance of statements have greater fitness to improve the efficiency of target data generation. As shown in Fig. 1(b), if no individual traverses n_6, then if the target path contains n_6, it is difficult to quickly generate target data covering the required path. Therefore, it is important to further increase the weight of test data covering such key statements in test data generation.

Assuming that there are N' branches of key statement j, after the test data run the program, it is possible to calculate whether x_k corresponding data cover the t th ($t \leq N'$) branch of key statement j, represented by $tra_{jt}(k)$. When x_k covers the t th branch of statement j, $tra_{jt}(k)$ is 1; otherwise, $tra_{jt}(k)$ is 0.

If the population size of the genetic algorithm is M, after all test data run the program, the total test data number covering the t th branch of statement j can be obtained, expressed as $\sum_{k=1}^{M} tra_{jt}(k)$. Note that $max_{jN'}$ is $max(\sum_{k=1}^{M} tra_{jt}(k))$, that is, the maximum value among the N' branches covering statement j. We represent the importance of the j th key statement as $diff_j$, as shown in (6).

$$diff_j = weight_j * \sum_{t=1}^{N'} \frac{1 + max_{jN'} - \sum_{k=1}^{M} tra_{jt}(k)}{1 + max_{jN'} + \sum_{k=1}^{M} tra_{jt}(k)} \qquad (6)$$

In the above equation, $weight_j$ represents the weight of the j th key statement, and $\sum_{t=1}^{N'} \frac{1+max_{jN'}-\sum_{k=1}^{M} tra_{jt}(k)}{1+max_{jN'}+\sum_{k=1}^{M} tra_{jt}(k)}$ reflects the j th statement, which is the difference between the number of data covering the t th branch and the branch with the most data coverage. It is used to represent all the data covering the overall balance of each branch of the j th statement.

4.3 Design Fitness for Individuals

To further compute the individual fitness of the genetic algorithm, the importance of key statements is calculated before and after deleting a specific individual. If $\sum_{k=1}^{M} tra_{jt}'(k)$ is used to represent, in addition to the corresponding data of individual x_k, the total number of corresponding data of other individuals in the population covering the t th branch of the key statement j. Correspondingly, $max_{jN'}'$ is $max(\sum_{k=1}^{M} tra_{jt}'(k))$ in the N' branches covering statement j. $diff_j'$ shows the importance of the key statement j after deleting x_k. Following the same method as in Sect. 4.2, $diff_j'$ is defined as follows:

$$diff_j' = weight_j * \sum_{t=1}^{N'} \frac{1 + max_{jN'}' - \sum_{k=1}^{M} tra_{jt}'(k)}{1 + max_{jN'}' + \sum_{k=1}^{M} tra_{jt}'(k)} \qquad (7)$$

The meaning of the variables in (7) is consistent with that in (6), but it represents the corresponding variable value after the individual x_k is deleted. Assume that $m = \sum_{j=1}^{|branch|} diff_j$ and that $m' = \sum_{j=1}^{|branch|} diff_j'$. After x_k runs the program, by calculating the impact of x_k on the importance of the key statements, the fitness function of x_k is defined as follows:

$$f(x_k) = \begin{cases} m - m', m > m' \\ 0, else \end{cases} \qquad (8)$$

In the above equation, $|branch|$ is the number of branch nodes on the target path. For the calculation of the fitness of x_k, if $m > m'$, the importance of the key statement is less than the original importance without considering x_k. This means that x_k better reflects the importance of statement j. Therefore, the fitness of the current individual x_k should be improved, and the greater the difference between m and m' is, the greater the individual fitness should be. Otherwise, x_k cannot effectively represent the importance of j, and its fitness is set to 0.

4.4   The Algorithm Flow of the Proposed Method

The algorithm is shown in Algorithm 1. First, parameter initialization is performed (Lines 1--2), which includes instrumenting the program, assigning various pa-rameter values and initializing the population data of the genetic algorithm. After that, the target path of the program is selected, and the program is run using the initial population data as input. Then, the iterative process is started (Lines 3--15). The weights of the key statements are calculated according to the required path. The importance of the individual to the corresponding statements of each node on the required path is obtained, thereby obtaining the individual fitness. The selection operation, crossover operation and mutation operation are sequentially run on the data to obtain offspring population data. If the algorithm termination condition is reached (Lines 11--13), the target data corresponding to an individual are saved, and the algorithm ends.

Algorithm 1: The process of generating test data

Input: $x_1, x_2, \cdots, x_n$, initial population, P_i: the target path,
G_{max}: maximum of iteration times, p_c: crossover probability,
   p_m: mutation probability, T: iterations number,
   Cov: the coverage for target path

Output: Test data covering target path

1 $Initialize()$;
2 $DataSet = \emptyset$
3   **WHILE**($ite \leq T \&\& ov == 0$)
4       $iter \leftarrow iter + 1$;
5       $Simportance_j = diff_j$;
6       $Simportance'_j = diff'_j$;
7       $fitness(x_k) = \max(0, Simportance_j - Simportance'_j)$;
8       $population \quad \leftarrow Selection()$;
9       $population' \quad \leftarrow Cross(x_i, x_j)$;
10      $population'' \quad \leftarrow Mulatation(x_k)$;
11   **IF**($path(x_k) == P_i$) THEN
12          $DataSet \leftarrow x_k$;
13   break;
14   **END**
15   **END**
16 **return** $DataSet$

---

5   Experiments

5.1   Problems to Be Verified

To better verify the effectiveness of the test data, time validity, and algorithm running cost, the simulation experiments use five metrics. They are the success rate, runtime, evaluation time, number of defect detection generations, and defect detection rate. There are three problems to be verified.

Q1: Can the proposed method generate target data effectively?
Q2: How is our method in terms of time?
Q3: How efficient is the genetic algorithm when generating data via our method?
Q4: What is the fault detection performance of our method?

5.2   Comparison Methods and Selection of Tested Programs

The experimental results of each group are compared and analyzed with those of similar methods. The comparison methods selected include the method of rare data capture in [20] (denoted as RDC), which considers capturing rare data, and on this basis, the layer proximity and branch distance are used to form an individual fitness function. This is also a common comparison method. In the method in [21] (denoted as BOT), by calculating the program balance, the fitness of individuals is set by preserving the effect on the program balance degree. In the experiment, our method is based on key statement importance, so it is denoted as KSI. We propose a type of method. It is suitable for the evolutionary generation technology of test data under path coverage conditions. First, two typical programs, triangle and maxmin, which contain sequence, option, and loop structures, are selected. In addition, the industrial program space [20, 21] is selected for the experiments.

In the experiment, different fitness functions are applied to each method. Except for the parameter values specified, all three methods use the same experimental parameters. The basic control parameters of the genetic algorithm used in our method and the comparative methods are also the same: individuals are all encoded in binary, using roulette wheel selection, single-point mutation and single-point crossover. The crossover and mutation probabilities are 0.95 and 0.25, respectively. The evaluation time is used to measure the number of times an individual is evaluated during the running of the genetic algorithm. The more generations a genetic algorithm runs, the greater the number of evaluations, which reflects that the efficiency of the genetic algorithm is not high. The success rates in generating data are also compared. To further verify the defect detection performance of different methods, mutation testing is applied to inject defects into the source programs to simulate actual defects in the software, and mutation operators in MuClip are used to generate different variants [23]. Finally, the defect detection rate and number of defect detection generations are used to measure the defect detection performance of the different methods.

5.3 Experimental Results

For convenience, the best experimental results are represented in a thickened manner. In the tables below, "Size" and "Maxg" represent the size of the population and the maximum evolutionary generation of the GA, respectively. "Range" means the data range. In Table 1, [1,128] shows the data range between 1 and 128, and 128 is used to represent it in the tables.

Experimental Results for a Triangle. In this section, the most typical program of triangle classification is used. There are the same experimental parameter settings in each method: the data range of individuals is [1,128]–[1,8192]. The maximum number of generations of the GA is between 300 and 1000. The number of defects in the program is 38. To reflect the randomness of the experimental results, each group of data in the experiment has different ranges, maximum generations and population sizes. The experimental results of the different methods are shown in Table 1.

Table 1. Comparison of different methods (triangles)

Experimental setup			success rate/%			Average runtime/s			Evaluation times		
Range	Size	Maxg	KSI	BOT	RDC	KSI	BOT	RDC	KSI	BOT	RDC
128	30	300	**100**	95	89	**0.89**	1.59	1.72	**1793.7**	3399.6	3545.7
256	50	400	**100**	100	81	**1.6**	3.09	4.08	**3318**	5476.5	9098.5
512	70	500	**99**	98	61	**3.5**	4.41	9.4	**7174.3**	8416.8	21369.6
1024	90	800	**100**	97	60	**5.48**	9.51	21.93	**11413.8**	17609.4	41111
2048	120	1200	**100**	97	55	**18.9**	21.94	52.43	**22970.4**	33351.6	89907.6
4096	150	1500	**100**	100	66	**14.39**	23.46	65.42	**22539**	31981.5	108639
8192	200	2000	**100**	100	76	**18.45**	28.45	92.89	**24538**	35668	143320

In Table 1, the success rates of the three methods in generating target test data are compared under different data ranges, population sizes, and maximum evolutionary generations. Except for a set of conditions with a data range of [1,512], the success rate of the proposed method is 99%. In all other cases, the success rate of the proposed method is 100%, which is better than those of the other two methods. Under various conditions, the success rate of the BOT is better than that of the RDC, which also verifies Q1. The proposed method can effectively generate target test data. Compared with the other two methods. It is more effective at generating test data that cover the target path.

The runtime data are shown in Table 1. Under seven different experimental conditions, our method requires less runtime than the other methods do. Both methods have higher runtimes than our method does. This is because our method considers not only the coverage of program branches by data but also the importance of program statements when calculating fitness, so the algorithm has higher time efficiency and less runtime. By comparing runtimes, problem Q2 is verified. Our method has better time effectiveness in generating test data than the other two methods do.

In terms of evaluation times, as shown in Table 1, the times of the other two methods are significantly greater than those of our method. In addition, the required evaluation times for our method vary less with the population size. This also verifies problem Q3: the proposed method has fewer average evaluation times and higher efficiency when generating target data.

Table 2. Defect detection generations (triangle)

Experimental setup			success rate/%			Average runtime/s			Evaluation times		
Range	Size	Maxg	KSI	BOT	RDC	KSI	BOT	RDC	KSI	BOT	RDC
128	20	500	**99**	98	**99**	**0.56**	0.76	0.67	1496.8	1694.4	**1306.6**
256	50	600	**100**	**100**	**100**	**0.48**	0.56	1.77	**981.5**	1397.5	2854.5
512	70	800	**100**	**100**	**100**	0.66	**0.63**	4.12	**1594.6**	1607.2	7802.9
1024	90	1000	**100**	**100**	91	0.96	**0.88**	14.12	2223.9	**2113.2**	27826.2
2048	120	1500	**100**	**100**	98	1.01	**0.97**	14.84	**2194.8**	2220	28486.8
4096	150	2000	**100**	**100**	99	**0.97**	1.13	18.1	**2139**	2367	34101
8192	200	3000	**100**	**100**	**100**	**1.12**	1.24	19.68	**2268**	2648	35490

To compare the defect detection performance of the target data, the data range of the three methods is set to [1,16384], with a maximum evolutionary generation of 500. The defect detection rates of the three methods are compared, and the experimental results are shown in Fig. 2. As the test data in the population increase, the defect detection rates of BOT and RDC gradually increase. However, at different population sizes, our KSI method can detect all defects. A further comparison is made on the total evolutionary generations required for detecting all defects via different methods. The smaller the value is, the earlier the defects in the program are detected. A comparison of the defect detection generations of different methods is shown in Table 2. The number of defect detection generations required by our method is less than those required by the other two methods. This finding also verifies that for Q4, the proposed method has better defect detection capability.

Experimental Results of Maxmin. To further illustrate the effectiveness of our method, the maxmin program is selected for the experiments. In addition, it is compared with the BOT and RDC. There are the same experimental parameters in each method: the range of test data is [1,128]–[1,8192], the maximum evolutionary generation is between 500 and 3000, the population size is between 20 and 200, and the tested program contains 26 defects. The experimental results of the three methods are shown in Table 3. Since the maxmin program is small in scale, the runtime of the three methods is not long, and the difference in runtime is not large. Table 3 shows that under different conditions, the evaluation times and runtime of our method do not change much, and the performance is stable. However, the change range of the RDC is more obvious. However, when the data range is [1,128] and [1,1024], the evaluation time of our method is greater than those of the RDC and BOT methods. Under other conditions, the evaluation times of our method

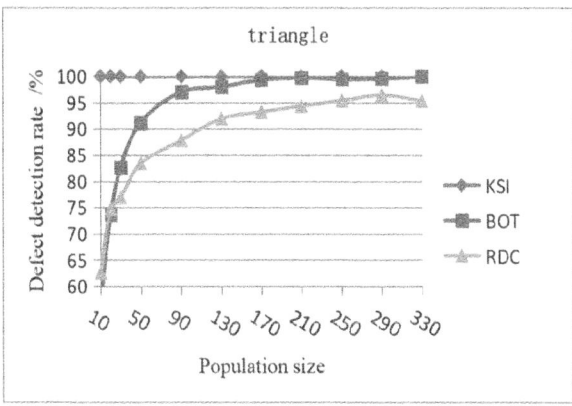

Fig. 2. Defect detection rate of triangles

are the lowest. The experimental results of this group show that the proposed method has advantages in terms of success rate, runtime, and evaluation times.

Table 3. Comparison of maxmin

Size	Defect detection generations		
	KSI	BOT	RDC
50	**4683.2**	6344	15716
100	**1728.2**	2038.8	24061.5
150	1810.5	**1718.1**	18809.9
200	**857.3**	1303.2	5036.3
250	**587.7**	830.9	5837.5
300	**575.7**	718	3552.7
350	**504**	670.5	1637.1
400	**323.1**	496.5	4313.2
450	**412.8**	430.7	1147
500	**357.5**	437.1	3154.1

Furthermore, the maximum evolutionary generation is set to 200, and the test data range is set to [1,200]. The defect detection results of the three methods are compared, as shown in Table 4 and Fig. 3. We can obtain the same conclusion as that in Sect. 5.3.1. In Table 4, when the population sizes are 10, 70, and 80, the total number of evolution generations of all the defects detected by our method is slightly greater than that of BOT but significantly less than that of RDC. In other cases, our method requires fewer defect detection generations than the other two methods do. In terms of the defect detection rate, compared with those of the other two methods, except for the population size of 20 in Fig. 3, the defect detection rate of our method is slightly lower than that of BOT; under other experimental conditions, the defect detection efficiency of the proposed method is greater.

Table 4. Defect detection generations (maxmin)

Size	Defect detection generations		
	KSI	BOT	RDC
10	163.66	**145.53**	215.7
20	**74.15**	75.63	130.5
30	**38.91**	52.25	68.06
40	**34.86**	35.19	53.12
50	**28.57**	31.29	44.13
60	**25.53**	29.53	38.3
70	26.7	**24.63**	31.06
80	24.87	**23.91**	25.37
90	**23.58**	24.15	25.45
100	**21.71**	23.71	21.89

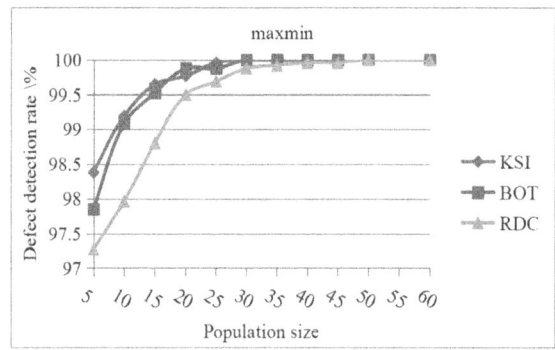

Fig. 3. Defect detection rate of maxmin

Space Experimental Results. For the space program, the three methods in the experiment share the same parameters. The range of individual corresponding data for the genetic algorithm is [1,80]–[1,500], and the maximum range of evolutionary generation is 500–3000. The population size is 50–500, and the tested program contains 67 defects. Table 5 shows the experimental results. For different experimental settings, the success rate of the proposed method in generating target data is higher. The proposed method requires less runtime and evaluation.

To compare the defect detection results of the three methods, we set the test data range to [1,50] in the experiment, and the maximum number of evolutionary generations is

Table 5. Comparison of different methods (spaces)

Experimental setup			success rate/%			Average runtime/s			Evaluation times		
Range	Size	Maxg	KSI	BOT	RDC	KSI	BOT	RDC	KSI	BOT	RDC
80	50	500	**100**	86.67	86.67	**11**	102	82	**510**	5100	5270
100	70	600	**100**	86.67	93.33	**6**	228	52	**298.67**	11606	3187.33
100	100	1000	**100**	**100**	**100**	**10**	200	54	**320**	10220	2940
150	120	2000	**100**	**100**	**100**	**10**	435	80	**440**	22768	4640
300	200	2500	**100**	**100**	**100**	**24**	1215	534	**800**	61613.3	29893.3
350	300	2800	**100**	**100**	**100**	**19**	1069	284	**720**	53480	14260
500	500	3000	**100**	**100**	**100**	**20**	50	39	**1000**	2733.3	1600

1000. The experimental results are shown in Fig. 4. When the population size is between 10 and 1000, the defect detection rate of the proposed method is higher than that of the other two methods, and the defect detection rate of RDC is significantly higher than that of BOT. Furthermore, while the test data range remains unchanged, the maximum evolutionary generation is set to 20,000, and the sum of the evolutionary generations required by the three methods to detect all defects is compared in Table 6. The defect detection generations of the three methods are quite different, and our method requires fewer detection generations. This is because our method not only considers the weights of different statements in the program but also considers the nodes without test data coverage and their branches. The result is that the data evenly cover all the program branches; therefore, the defect detection performance is better.

Table 6. Defect detection generations (space)

Size	Defect detection generations		
	KSI	BOT	RDC
100	**252.2**	27251.6	12414.8
150	**196.6**	26486.8	15031.6
200	**120.6**	22353.8	4095.4
250	**131**	16828.2	4354
300	**112.8**	16215.4	3705.6
350	**104**	9890.6	2272.6
400	**102**	8906.4	3217
450	**102.4**	1968.8	1517
500	**96.2**	3944.6	1404.4

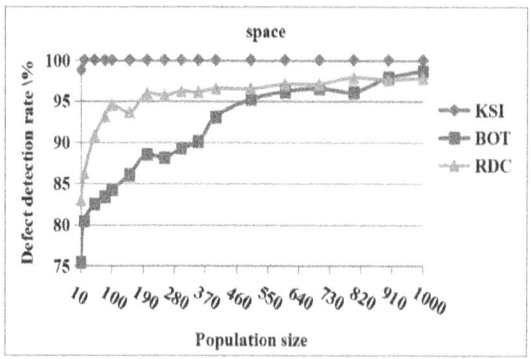

Fig. 4. Space defect detection rate

6 Conclusion

At present, there are many studies on test data generation for path coverage, but few studies consider the weights of program statements when generating test data and processing program statements without test data coverage. In this paper, the importance of key statements is quantified, and the weights of key statements are set. On this basis, the fitness function of the genetic algorithm is designed by considering statements without data coverage to optimize the evolution process of the genetic algorithm. Compared with similar methods, the results show that the proposed method has good performance in terms of evaluation times, success rates, runtimes and defect detection. It can improve the efficiency and quality of generating test data.

However, our work is limited. The proposed method is suitable for the evolutionary generation of single-path test data. How to apply it to the data generation of multiobjective paths is a problem that we will study in the future. In addition, the scale of the program targeted by this experiment is limited, and the next step is to apply it to more industrial programs with more codes to further verify the effectiveness of our method.

Acknowledgment. This work was supported in part by the Higher Education Institutions Basic Research Business Fee Research Project of Heilongjiang Province under Grants 1452ZD009 and 1452CXY006; in part by the Research Projects of Mudanjiang Normal University under Grant YB2022008; in part by the Natural Science Foundation of Heilongjiang Province under Grant LH2023F037; in part by the Higher Education Institutions Basic Research Business Fee Research Project of Heilongjiang Province under Grant 1451TD018; and in part by the Research Team Project of Mudanjiang Normal University under Grant 1451TD003.

References

1. Gao, L., Bai, S., Liu, M., et al.: Automated test case generation for path coverage using hierarchical surrogate-assisted differential evolution. Appl. Soft Comput. **158**(111586), 1–14 (2024)
2. Hui, Z., Wang, X., Huang, S., Yang, S.: MT-ART: a test case generation method based on adaptive random testing and metamorphic relation. IEEE Trans. Reliab. **70**(4), 1397–1421 (2021)
3. Wang, K., Zhu, Y., Li, G., et al.: Test case generation method based on particle swarm optimization algorithm. Second International Symposium on Computer Applications and Information Systems (ISCAIS 2023). SPIE, pp. 12721, 393–399 (2023)
4. Liu, F., Huang, H., Yang, Z., et al.: Search-based algorithm with scatter search strategy for automated test case generation of NLP toolkit. IEEE Transactions on Emerging Topics in Computational Intelligence **5**(3), 491–503 (2019)
5. Li, L., Weng, Q.: Research on adaptive differential evolution algorithm for test data generation. J. Chinese Computer Syst. **39**(02), 292–296 (2018)
6. Xiang Juan, Y., Tian, T., Xiang Ying, D., et al.: Review on the application of intelligent optimization in software testing. Control and Decision **37**(02), 257–266 (2022)
7. Xu, D., Xu, W., Kent, M., Thomas, L., et al.: An automated test generation technique for software quality assurance. IEEE Trans. Reliab. **64**(1), 247–268 (2015)
8. Wang, L., Zhai, Y., Hou, H.: Genetic algorithm and its application in software test data generation. In: Proceedings IEEE Int. Conference Computer Science and Electronics Engineering **2**, 617–620 (2012)
9. Singla, S., Kumar, D., Rai, H., et al.: A hybrid PSO approach to automate test data generation for data flow coverage with dominance concepts. International Journal of Advanced Science and Technol. **37**, 15–26 (2011)
10. Singh, A., Garg, N., Saini, T.: A hybrid approach of genetic algorithm and particle swarm technique to software test case generation. International Journal of Innovations in Engineering and Technology **3**(4), 208–214 (2014)
11. Ji, S., Zhu, S., Zhang, P., et al.: Test-case generation for data flow testing of smart contracts based on improved genetic algorithm. IEEE Trans. Reliab. **72**(1), 358–371 (2022)
12. Arcuri, A., Yao, X.: A memetic algorithm for test data generation of object-oriented software. In: Evolutionary Computation, 2007. CEC 2007. IEEE Congress on, IEEE, pp. 2048–2055 (2007)
13. Fraser, G., Arcuri, A., McMinn, P.: A memetic algorithm for whole test suite generation. J. Syst. Softw. **103**, 311–327 (2015)
14. Mann, M., Sangwan, O.P., Tomar, P., et al.: Automatic goal-oriented test data generation using a genetic algorithm and simulated annealing. International Conference-Cloud System and Big Data Engineering (Confluence). IEEE, 2016, pp. 83–87 (2016)
15. Qian, Z.S., Zhu, J., Zhu, Y.M., et al.: Multipath coverage strategy combining key point probability and path similarity. Journal of Software **33**(2), 434–454 (2022)
16. Esnaashari, M., Damia, A.H.: Automation of software test data generation using genetic algorithm and reinforcement learning. Expert Syst. Appl. **183**, 115446 (2021)
17. Mann, M., Tomar, P., Sangwan, O.P.: Test data generation using optimization algorithm: an empirical evaluation. Soft Computing: Theories and Applications: Proceedings of SoCTA 2016, Volume 2. Springer Singapore, pp. 679–686 (2016)
18. Zhang, N., Wu, B., Bao, X.: Automatic generation of test cases based on multipopulation genetic algorithm. Int. J. Multimedia Ubiquitous Eng. **10**(6), 113–122 (2015)
19. McMinn, P.: Evolutionary Search for Test Data in the Presence of State Behavior [Ph. D. dissertation]. University of Sheffield, England (2005)

20. Zhang, Y., Gong, D.W.: Evolutionary generation of test data for paths coverage based scarce data capturing. Chinese Journal of Computers **36**(12), 2429–2440 (2013)
21. Fan, S.P., Zhang, Y., Ma, B.Y.: Evolutionary generation of test data for paths coverage based on balance optimization theory. Acta Elect Ronica Sinica. **48**(7), 1303–1310 (2020)
22. Sun, C., Xue, F., Liu, H., et al.: A path-aware approach to mutant reduction in mutation testing. Inf. Softw. Technol.Softw. Technol. **81**, 65–81 (2017)
23. Zhang, G.J., Gong, D.W., Yao, X.J.: Test case generation based on mutation analysis and set evolution. Chinese Journal of Computers **38**(11), 2318–2331 (2015)

Incorporating Design Thinking in the Exploration of a New Teaching Paradigm for Game Design Course

Juncong Lin(✉), Chenkang He, Shihui Guo, Dewen Wu, Cheng Wang,
and Minghong Liao

School of Informatics, Xiamen University, Fujian, China
jclin@xmu.edu.cn

Abstract. Promoting educational innovation and cultivating creative learners are currently the focus of attention in the field of education. How to cultivate innovative talent in software engineering is an important mission for software engineering majors in universities. Design thinking is in line with the current global demand for innovative talent cultivation, and introducing the concept of design thinking into software engineering teaching and training can help achieve a paradigm shift. This article takes the game design and development course, which has been practiced for many years, as a carrier to explore how to apply the concept of design thinking to the cultivation of software innovation talent. Games are a typical large-scale software applications, and their development involves the design of the game software development cycle. Games also contain a large amount of artistic creation, which has extremely high requirements for learners' design innovation. It is precisely the perfect integration of technology and art that makes game design and development courses particularly suitable as good carriers for introducing design thinking concepts in teaching reform of the major. The authors have comprehensively innovated the teaching mode, content, and tools of the course, developed an artificial intelligence (AI) enhanced design thinking tool, and finally conducted a systematic evaluation of the teaching effectiveness.

Keywords: Innovative talent cultivation · Design thinking · Game design

1 Introduction

Increasing attention has been given to cultivating learners' innovative abilities today. The "Education for All Global Monitoring Reports" released by UNESCO, the "21st Century Skills" of the United States, the "Eight Core Competencies" of the European Union, the "Melbourne Declaration on Educational Goals for Youngs" of Australia, the "21st Century Competencies" of Japan, and the "Core Competencies for Chinese Student Development" of China all attach great importance to the cultivation of learners' creative and innovative abilities. Innovative talent in software engineering is the foundation of independent innovation in the software industry. How to cultivate innovative talent in software engineering is an important task for software engineering majors in universities.

© The Author(s), under exclusive license to Springer Nature Singapore Pte Ltd. 2025
K. Zhang et al. (Eds.): CSEI 2024, CCIS 2448, pp. 221–232, 2025.
https://doi.org/10.1007/978-981-96-3738-6_17

Software technology requirements change rapidly, with obvious diversity, flexibility, and coordination, and software development models are also developing rapidly. Software engineers need to have practical skills, engineering application abilities, comprehensive application abilities for complex problems, and innovative application abilities. They also need to develop comprehensive application abilities in software engineering through cross-industry and interdisciplinary integration, combined with domain backgrounds and specific application scenarios. However, in the process of exploring teaching modes, there are generally problems such as too-coarse mode design and insufficient focus on refining and cultivating students' higher-level thinking abilities. Specifically, there is no relatively mature method for enhancing the higher-level thinking ability, especially innovative thinking ability, of college students. The current practice of innovative education still faces problems such as the simple coexistence of old and new paradigms, teachers' one-sided understanding of evaluation, and narrow understanding of the "dual subject" model, which to some extent constrains learners' thinking breadth and depth, and is not conducive to the substantive reform of education. Following the original educational methods, it is evident that they are no longer able to meet the demands of the times for talent. Reforming education requires not only changing the content and form of education, but also changing the path of cultivating people, strengthening the cultivation of human thinking, and guiding students to learn how to design and create. However, innovation requires guiding tools, and design thinking is an innovative tool that promotes deep thinking among learners. Design thinking reflects a series of continuous thoughts and actions undertaken by designers to explore design challenges and creatively solve design problems. Compared with general thinking concepts, design thinking emphasizes more on helping learners construct a knowledge and ability system while guiding them to discover the relationships between knowledge and ability and real-world problems, forming the ability to create new knowledge and solve more complex problems. However, the cultivation of design thinking requires a specific carrier, and design activities such as game design are the most intuitive way to cultivate design thinking. Computer games are a cultural products that combine technology and art. From a technical perspective, computer games are a new form of entertainment that is achieved through human-computer interaction and reflects the high level of current computer software and hardware technology. Owing to the complexity of electronic games, game technology, which refers to software and hardware technologies that directly serve or provide support for game development and operation, involves materials science, information science, mathematics, physics, psychology, and humanities. From the perspective of software engineering, computer games are a rich, complex, and often large-scale software applications. They are an important, interesting, and highly attractive field of software application research in the discipline of software engineering. Game design and development have extremely high requirements for learners' innovation. It includes the design of the game software development cycle, in which students need to understand and examine the entire development and production process of the game from a macro perspective, involving the division of labor and role allocation of personnel throughout the process, and mastering how to arrange the game's production schedule and reasonable budget. The Incorporation of design thinking concepts into game design education can help students better understand the design process, serve as a communication language to cultivate collaborative skills in the design process, and aid in developing students' innovative and critical thinking abilities. Introducing design thinking into the process of school education is not only a response to the questioning of education by the times, but also a natural demand for cultivating people's inner laws. In particular, the design thinking philosophy perfectly fits project-based learning (PBL), to provide practical guidance when students conduct their projects.

2   Teaching Paradigm of a Game Design Course Integrating Design Thinking Concepts

2.1   Design Thinking Concept

With the increasing application of design practice in different fields, decision-makers are increasingly attempting to combine the thinking processes and methods behind design practice to solve some of the chaotic and pathological problems they encounter. In 1969, Simon, H. proposed the concept of design as a way of thinking, and Rowe, P. first used the concept of design thinking. Narrowly speaking, design thinking is the process in which designers mobilize various relevant materials and accumulated experience in their minds on the basis of commissioned design projects; integrate natural, technological, social, and cultural factors to form an understanding of future works; and weigh various constraining factors to conceive design solutions. In a broad sense, design thinking starts from the end user and utilizes creative thinking to establish goals or directions through observation, exploration, definition, brainstorming, model design, storytelling, etc., and then seeks practical and creative solutions. Design thinking is fundamentally different from the analytical and linear problem-solving methods widely used in the fields of science and engineering. The analytical method emphasizes the principles of planning and optimizing goals and predetermined objectives. This method is most suitable when the problem is clearly defined, relevant data are available, and the future can be predicted well from the past. On the other hand, design thinking is suitable for uncertain and complex situations, especially those where people are the key evaluators of "good or bad" solutions. The process and method of design thinking help to quickly learn and understand the situations and personnel involved while allowing for iterative generation and testing of possible solutions (Fig. 1).

Although there are still different opinions on what design thinking is, there are some commonalities among different expressions, such as observing design challenges; establishing connections between ideas and solutions; and reflecting on and improving design. Taking the representative IDEO model [7] as an example, the entire model includes five stages: discovery, interpretation, conceptualization, experimentation, and evolution. Design thinking reflects a series of continuous thoughts and actions taken by designers to explore design challenges and creatively solve design problems. It has the characteristics of being based on meeting needs, being behavior oriented, and aiming to develop innovative abilities. Design thinking is a double helix structure composed of design and thinking, which are interdependent and mutually reinforcing. Design activities such as graphic design and game design are the best carriers for cultivating design thinking.

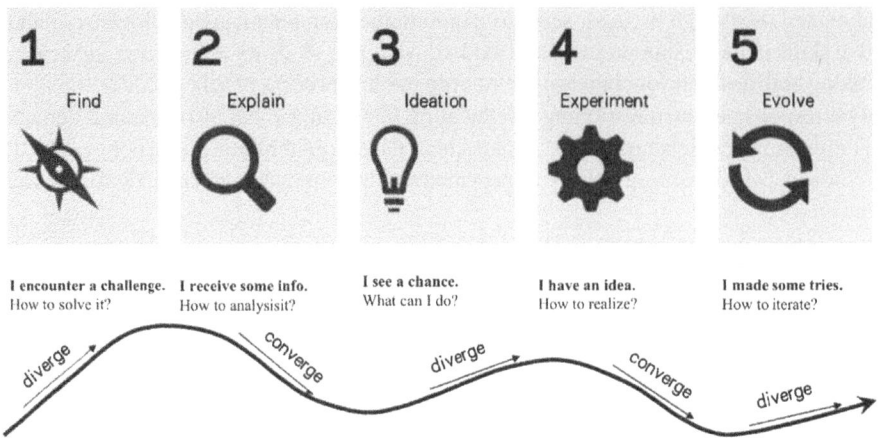

Fig. 1. IDEO design thinking model

2.2 Construction of the Teaching Paradigm

Currently, an increasing number of design courses are adopting project-based teaching models. This is consistent with the increasing use of project-based and problem-based teaching frameworks in fields such as engineering, medicine, and even business and law. The introduction of design thinking concepts can also promote a shift in teaching paradigms from overly relying on passive teaching methods to more proactive, problem-based approaches. Especially for game design courses, tasks such as game conceptualization, character or world creation, prototype-level production, and game development and design are all in line with the process of design thinking. As a practical course for design thinking reform, it can greatly reduce the challenges of integration and the threshold for constructing teaching paradigms. However, design thinking projects also face unique challenges. One of them is how to provide the relevant experiences, iterations, cycles, and other practical opportunities needed to develop practical skills, while meeting the structured needs of students and teachers. Design thinking is not composed of a series of rigid, predefined, and orderly steps. As ideas are refined, projects typically benefit from cycles of early processes. Although some structuring is indeed necessary, design thinking also requires a phased development process to achieve repeated practice in multiple cycles.

On the basis of the above understanding and combined with the characteristics of game design courses, we propose a core framework for guiding teachers to teach students the steps and principles of design thinking on the basis of the IDEO model. As shown in Fig. 2, the entire framework consists of five stages: problem discovery, problem definition, conceptualization, prototyping, and iteration. At each stage, the project team, which is composed of students completes specific tasks and challenges through a small cycle of "action perception thinking". Moreover, the teacher provides targeted guidance at each stage to help the student team overcome stage challenges:

- Problem finding. The key to this stage is to develop empathy toward the target player. The most powerful way for students to cultivate empathy is through direct, face-to-face observations and interviews of the target player's life or work background, until they immerse themselves in the user's world. However their observation ability may be relatively weak, and they may feel that the entire process is very time-consuming, uncertain, and ambiguous, which can make them feel frustrated. Teachers can remind students to conduct reasoning and analysis after completing observations while also informing them that there may be some sense of frustration at this stage.

- Problem definition. The team will develop a problem statement on the basis of the given design challenge. The main challenge at this stage is that it does not have a reliable formal process like analytical methods, and there is a risk of team stagnation. In addition, progressive problems will gradually mask fundamental issues. At this stage, teachers can guide student teams to first identify areas where they have an "observational advantage", and then require them to present four to five problem statements before finalizing a final problem statement.

- Ideation. The team brainstormed, recorded fragmented ideas, and pieced them together into a new 'complete idea', and finally voted on the best idea to narrow down the list. The main challenge at this stage is that brainstorming and voting may lead to "atomization". This process is prone to becoming stuck, leading to frustration and withdrawal. Rhythm is important and requires strong guidance and/or leadership. Teachers can help teams adhere to a highly structured process to prevent losing direction. At the same time, it is important to constantly remind the team of the dangers of locking in or falling in love with a single solution.

- Prototyping. Create prototypes or storyboards for "low fidelity" games (levels, characters, worlds, etc.) to facilitate communication with target players. Observe users through prototypes to form new insights and prototypes. Prototypes usually need to be created in a very short period of time, and team members may have a strong attachment to the initial prototype idea, resisting the formation of new insights. Teachers should encourage students to develop a few rough prototypes, using charts and storyboards in addition to physical models, and remind students that their goal is to have a deeper conversation with the target player rather than to prove how good their ideas are.

- Iteration. On the basis of completing the product prototype, the team will observe the target players' experience of their prototype, collect feedback, and further update and improve the prototype based on the basis of the results of testing and feedback. Throughout the cycle of testing feedback iteration, testing is the key to the iterative process (Fig. 2).

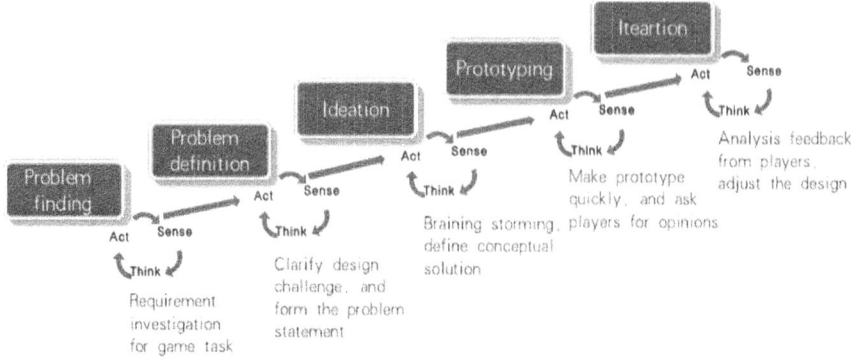

Fig. 2. Teaching framework of a game course on the basis of design thinking.

3 Teaching Implementation

On the basis of the above teaching paradigm, the teaching team has innovated in terms of teaching content, teaching methods, and teaching tools for the course. The course adopts a hybrid online and offline approach, with online courses teaching relevant theories of game design and design thinking. The offline course consists of design practice and experimental components. In the design practice section, students will practice the entire design thinking process according to the corresponding design tasks, and ultimately complete the corresponding design scheme. Students form a design and development team of 4–6 people on the basis of voluntary principles at the beginning of the course. Notably, the design thinking process is not simply applied to the entire game development at the macro level, but can be refined to various aspects of the game, such as game conceptualization, game world and character design, and game interaction design. Below are the specific contents of each section.

3.1 Innovation in Teaching Content

Relevant courses are designed and developed from the perspective of learners, and the teaching theory of game development courses is updated with design thinking concepts as the core. A modular and project-based approach is adopted to arrange course content, and organically integrate course knowledge, information technology applications, and problem-solving. We introduce the relevant theories of design thinking in online courses, while in offline flipped classrooms, a design task (game concept design, game world design, and game level design) is set according to the teaching progress of online theoretical courses.

3.2 Innovation in Teaching Methods

The traditional workshop style design education paradigm requires learners to comprehend implicit knowledge on their own during interactions with mentors, which has problems such as motivation barriers, insufficient guidance in the design process, and low learning efficiency. Its effectiveness also depends on the personality traits, experiences, and cognitive styles of mentors and learners. Therefore, in terms of game design classroom teaching, we have incorporated more of the characteristics of design thinking concepts, which are based on meeting needs, guided by behavior, and aimed at developing innovative abilities. On the basis of the design tasks assigned during offline classes, we designed diverse classroom activities, guided student teams to adopt the concept of design thinking, and organically combined knowledge learning with practical activities such as design and exploration, effectively promoting classroom teaching innovation and improving students' immersion.

3.3 Innovation in Teaching Techniques

Design thinking is a human-centered design philosophy that focuses more on the relationship between people and design objects, as well as the relationship between nature and the social environment, but considers technology itself less. Design thinking cannot be applied in teaching and learning without the support of various types of learning methods and information technology tools. We provided a detailed introduction to the tools that can be used in various stages of design thinking in our online theoretical class (Table 1) and taught their usage with specific examples. The offline flipped classroom combines design tasks to guide students in completing various stage tasks. In addition, we introduced specialized tools tailored to the characteristics of the game design course itself, such as Machinations, a rapid prototyping tool for game mechanics. As shown in Fig. 3, it abstracts the game mechanism as the flow of various resources and constructs it via a graphical approach similar to UML. Users can select various basic components used to describe the resources and flows in the core mechanism of the game from the upper right corner area of the tool, set their properties in the lower right corner, and combine these components to draw on the canvas on the left. The play button in the upper left corner can simulate the flow of various resources.

4   AI-Enhanced Design Thinking Tool

Finally, we developed our own design thinking tool, LLGLinkography, which is used to track various ideas effectively during the ideation phase and help teams converge their thinking. The system targets the ideation stage of the design thinking model, which is usually accompanied by warm and possibly noisy discussions and can easily go out of control. Linkography was proposed to track, visualize and analyze the ideation process [8]. Although some mathematical tools (such as clustering and entropy) have been introduced to enhance linkography, the tedious manual management of linkography is still a heavy burden for the user. This paper presents AI-enabled computational linkography, with large language models (LLM) introduced to automatically analyze the voice-captured ideas proposed by the user and propose new ideas for inspiration. Coarse-to-fine visual analysis manner is introduced to provide the freedom for the user to either obtain an overview of the whole process or go into detail in some special moments. In-context visual stimuli are generated with the guidance of LLM and displayed in a compact manner.

Table 1. Common Methods and Tools for Design Thinking at Various Stages.

Stages	Related methods and tools
Problem finding	• Questionnaire Investigation • User interviews • KWHL table • Character chronicles storyboard
Problem definition	• Journey analysis method • 5Why analysis method • Transference diagram • Fish bone analysis chart
Design	• Brainstorming • Mind map • Value chain analysis method • Miro • LLGLinkographics
Prototyping	• Machinations • Mockplus • AxureRP • 3D printing
Iteration	• Usability testing • AB Test • Internal testing • Public beta testing

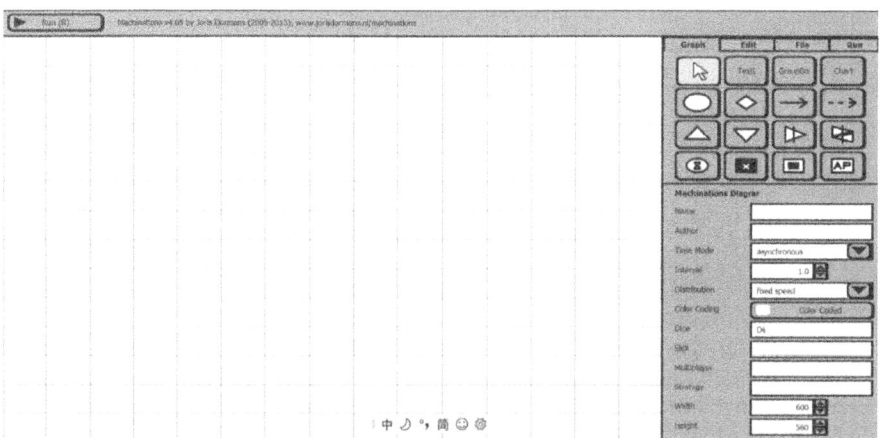

Fig. 3. Game prototype design tool-Machinations.

The user interface of the system is presented in Fig. 4. The middle area of the software (Fig. 4②) displays a link notation structure used to track all ideas in the discussion. The area above (Fig. 4⑤⑥) displays data related to the brainstorming state, such as entropy values and the behavioral characteristics of each member during the brainstorming process. The bottom left corner (Fig. 4④) is an image provided on the basis of the discussion process as a visual stimulus. Our system also introduces a large language model to assist in the analysis of ideas (Fig. 4①③), and the bottom right corner (Fig. 4⑦) displays the interactions between users.

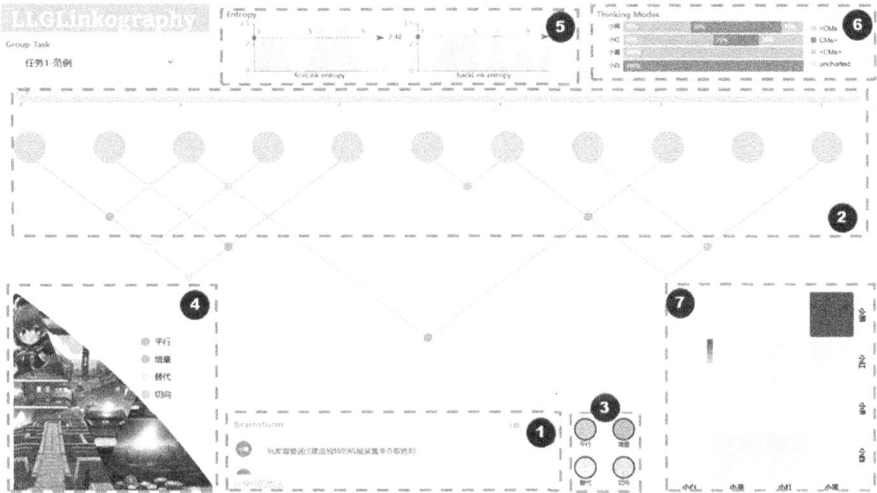

Fig. 4. User interface of our AI-empowered design thing tool.

5 Teaching Effectiveness Evaluation

The effectiveness of teaching reform needs to be tested through systematic evaluation. However, there is currently limited research on design thinking from a scientific perspective, and related studies still carry strong humanistic colors such as subjectivity, experientiality, introspection, and abstraction, especially with insufficient empirical research. Existing empirical research has focused mainly on the perspective of designers, with less research from the perspective of users. The acceptance level of design thinking theory achievements is still relatively low, one of the reasons being that existing research results lack application and do not reflect their guiding effect on design practice. On this basis, we design a targeted evaluation system, as shown in Table 2. Our system values both results and processes; there are both quantitative and qualitative indicators. There are two main dimensions in the evaluation system: process and results. For the process dimension, we set various indicators in each stage of the design thinking model according to the main mission of each stage, whereas for the result dimension, there are general evaluation metrics for projects (such as novelty and design quality) and specific metrics for games (such as playability). In summary, the evaluation system is both comprehensive and specific.

We focused on exploring the effects of introducing some information tools at different stages of design thinking. For example, in the ideation stage, we introduced Miro and our

Table 2. Common methods and tools for design thinking at various stages.

Evaluation perspective	Evaluation dimension	Evaluation method
Process	Problem finding	The number of questionnaires distributed and collected, and the standardization of KHWL forms
	Problem definition	The correctness of problem explanation and the standardization of empathy diagram
	Design	The activity level of team members, the quantity and diversity of ideas, and the quality of the final ideas
	Prototyping	Prototype production time and tool usage
	Iteration	Usability testing score, players' evaluation of interaction mode, difficulty, and balance, etc
Result	Novelty	Including originality, whether third-party materials, especially code, have been used, specific usage methods and degrees
	Playability	Mainly considering the richness of playable modes, with appropriate consideration for game balance, etc
	Technical difficulty	The depth of some technologies and algorithms involved
	Design quality	The degree of implementation of design thinking concepts and the richness of game design documents
	Presentation	Time control, smooth and clear presentation, etc

own LLGLinkography. Although both tools are designed for the ideation stage, their roles are different. The former focuses on helping brainstorming members record and present various ideas, whereas the latter is committed to preventing the entire brainstorming process from being too divergent. We asked the student project team to rate their creativity on the basis of the five dimensions of creativity (Table 3) after using the tool via a five point Likert scale.

Table 3. Rating table for design thinking tools.

Dimension	Description
Q1	Can gain more inspiration
Q2	It is easy to explore many different ideas and choices
Q3	The generated creativity is more diverse
Q4	Can generate results that meet or even exceed expectations
Q5	Make brainstorming experience more enjoyable

As shown in Fig. 5, compared with the situation without using any tools, Miro and LLGLinkgraphics provided better creativity support to the project team during brainstorming in all aspects, especially LLGLinkgraphics. In terms of result evaluation, we asked users to score the five-level Likert scale from the five dimensions listed in Table 2, and compared it with the completion status of course projects that did not use design thinking models in previous years. In the interviews after user study, many participants agreed that the tool helped them to focus more on the discussion topic, advance the progress of the discussion and avoid stalling. From Fig. 6, it can be observed that the introduction of design thinking models has improved project quality in various aspects, especially in novel aspects. In terms of sexual indicators, especially in terms of novelty, playability, and design standards of the project. In particular, design quality has been improved greatly with the design thinking philosophy.

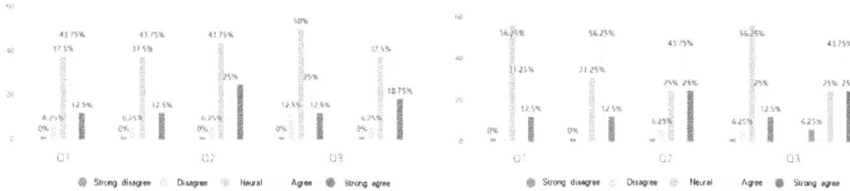

Fig. 5. The promoting role of design thinking tools, Miro (Left) and LLGLinkogrpics (Right), in brainstorming.

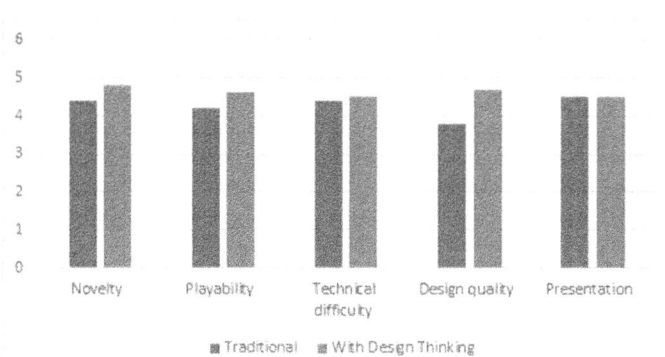

Fig. 6. Evaluation of course reform (course projects).

6 Conclusions

Cultivating creative talent has become a focus of attention in the field of education both domestically and internationally and is also an important goal of China's education reform. The design thinking approach is a special case that emerged in the movement of education from excessive reliance on passive teaching methods to more proactive problem-based learning. Design thinking guides students to expand and utilize knowledge in a positive way. At the same time, it requires teachers to develop a more proactive and relevant curriculum based on traditional emphasis on subject content, emphasizing behavioral skills. Participating in design thinking projects not only builds confidence in handling complex problems, but also provides tools and helps develop perspectives that support these efforts. Based on the game design courses taught by the author for many years, this article explores a path that can make the allocation of learning content more reasonable, allowing learners to establish an inline relationship between textbook knowledge and the real world in the process of building new knowledge and ability structures, and form a new structure for using learned knowledge to solve complex problems. We also focused on exploring how to teach students how to use various design thinking tools reasonably in the process of educational reform. In addition, we have developed our own design thinking tools. The relevant teaching evaluation shows that the author's efforts have achieved initial results. In the future, we would like to explore the spread of the design thinking philosophy in other courses under a project-based learning framework. We may also explore the use of the AI-assisted design thinking tool, LLGLinkography, in other areas involving ideation.

Acknowledgement. This project is partially supported by the National Natural Science Foundation of China (62077039).

References

1. Zhang, J., Feng, X.: Research and practice on the cultivation of software engineering application ability under the new engineering department. High. Educ. J. **16**, 146–149 (2024)
2. Shi, Z., Liu, Y., Ye, L., Dan, J., Liu, Y.: Exploring blended learning with a focus on cultivating design thinking from a methodological perspective. Comput. Educ. **8**, 165–170 (2024)
3. Lin, L., Shen, S.: The conceptual connotation and cultivation strategies of design thinking. Modern Distance Educ. **6**, 18–25 (2016)
4. Simon, H.: The Sciences of the Artificial. MIT Press, Cambridge, MA (1969)
5. Rowe, P.: Design Thinking. MIT Press, Cambridge, MA (1987)
6. Hu, X., Zhu, L.: Design thinking model and case study for cultivating creativity. Modern Distance Educ. Res. **3**, 75–82 (2018)
7. Brown, T.: Design Thinking for Educators. IDEO Corporation, New York (2011)
8. Goldschmidt, G.: Linkography: Unfolding the Design Process. MIT Press (2014)

Research on Methods of Online Education Learning Early Warning in the Era of Digital Intelligence

Chunqiao Mi[1], Yunlong Mi[2], Qingyou Deng[3(✉)], Bo Tang[1], and Changhua Zhao[1]

[1] School of Computer and Artificial Intelligence, Huaihua University,
418000 Hunan, People's Republic of China
[2] School of Business, Central South University, Changsha 410083,
Hunan, People's Republic of China
[3] School of Physics, Electronics and Intelligent Manufacturing, Huaihua University,
Huaihua 418000, Hunan, People's Republic of China
dengqingyou@163.com

Abstract. Online education has become a new popular educational mode, but its quality issues are also becoming increasingly evident, so effective diagnosis and personalized interventions for online learning are crucial. This paper first reviews and analyzes the current research status and development trends from five perspectives: learning status perception and recording, learning risk cognitive diagnosis, learning crisis grading and warning, learning improvement interventions, and learning early warning information technology tools. Most current early warning methods remain at the measurement level and have not delved into the cognitive level, and the results obtained often focus on presentation rather than prediction, which makes it challenging to implement personalized interventions. Then, on the basis of modern cognitive diagnosis theory and generative AI technology, this paper proposes the concept of an artificial intelligence agent for learning early warnings in online education, which can integrate the efficiency of data-driven models, the interpretability of knowledge-driven models, and the scale benefits of new technologies. The findings of this research can provide insights into the current shortcomings of learning early warning methods and propose an innovative early warning AI agent tool that integrates knowledge, behavior, and emotional monitoring with academic improvement, which is valuable for improving online learning quality and enhancing the effectiveness and efficiency of early warning management.

Keywords: Learning early warning · Cognitive diagnosis · Online education · Digital intelligence

1 Introduction

In the era marked by digitalization and intelligence, online learning has become the new normal [1]. Currently, the number of online education users in China has reached 423 million [2]. However, with rapid development, the quality of online learning has

K. Zhang et al. (Eds.): CSEI 2024, CCIS 2448, pp. 233–249, 2025.
https://doi.org/10.1007/978-981-96-3738-6_18

also become increasingly problematic. Issues such as poor learner autonomy, inadequate monitoring and management, shallow teacher–student interactions, declining levels of emotional engagement, overly mechanical teaching methods, and difficulty in ensuring effective learning outcomes have become prominent [3]. Learning early warning in online education involves real-time monitoring, diagnosis, warning, and improvement of learners' knowledge acquisition, learning behaviors, and social-emotional states. It is a crucial approach to enhancing the quality of online learning and has become a significant focus of online education research. The advent of the digital intelligence era has made it possible to use new intelligent technologies for learning quality management. In particular, the emergence of the large language model (LLM) in recent years has provided feasible technical pathways for constructing and implementing various artificial intelligent agents. Therefore, the construction of intelligent agents based on LLM has garnered increasing attention in the field of artificial intelligence and across various vertical domains. However, there is still a lack of systematic designs and comprehensive discussions in the field of early warning. Therefore, researching methods and AI agents for learning early warnings in the era of digital intelligence is vital. Such research can significantly contribute to enhancing the quality of online education, promoting the connotative development of online education, and providing substantial insights for the systematic improvement of learning early warning mechanisms.

2   Analysis of Current Research Status

Learning early warning in online education involves five key aspects: the perception and recording of learning status, the cognitive diagnosis of learning risks, the grading and warning of learning crises, interventions for learning improvement, and the development of early warning information technology tools. The current state of research in these areas is as follows.

2.1   Methods for Perception and Recording of Learning Status

Rich foundational data on online education learning conditions constitute the essential starting point for conducting risk analysis and monitoring early warnings. Research in this area can be divided into four categories. The first method involves manual observation and recording. This method can be traced back to learning condition survey studies that emerged in the 1980s [4]. It involves offline data collection, which uses manually designed scales and hand-recorded data. The key features of this method are its strong targeting ability and ease of operation, but it is low in efficiency and limited in data volume. The second method involves information system recording with manual data transfer. This approach leverages intelligent tutoring systems and electronic learning platforms, such as Sakai, Blackboard, Moodle, Learning Metaplatform, and social network visualization tools [5]. It collects data on students' online learning activities and teachers' online teaching behaviors. This method is characterized by high efficiency and low cost but lacks customizability. The third method uses automatic recording through information tracking and mirroring technologies. For example, the learning dashboard introduced by Khan Academy uses information tracking and mirroring technologies to track learners' online behaviors precisely, recording and integrating vast amounts of learning information [6]. This method is highly efficient but requires professional software development technology support. The fourth method employs associative recording through semantic association technologies. For example, Professor Shengquan Y.'s team fully utilizes semantic association technologies in the Learning Metaplatform Knowledge Community to interconnect learners, activities, resources, and tools, facilitating data interaction and flow [7]. Similarly, Professor Xianmin Y.'s team proposed methods that combine comprehensive semantic genes, rule-based reasoning, and association rule mining to achieve dynamic semantic associations of resources [8]. This approach is beneficial for the rapid expansion of data volume but demands high technical expertise and lacks numerous mature practical cases, indicating significant potential for exploration.

Thus, current research on methods for perceiving and recording learning status has made significant progress in terms of data sources, indicators, collection, and recording techniques. However, several shortcomings persist. First, with respect to the data source, current early warning research focuses primarily on student learning behavior data, with insufficient attention given to the data on teacher teaching effectiveness and environmental media efficacy. Second, with respect to the data indicators, there is a heavy emphasis on the cognitive content related to subject knowledge, with an inadequate focus on social-emotional and learning emotion aspects. The collection of cognitive data by current early warning tools is far more advanced than that of emotional data. Third, with respect to data collection tools, there is a notable absence of mature and generalized tools for automated perception and recording of learning status. With the development of new AI technologies, enhancing the emotional recognition capabilities of teaching tools and improving the efficiency of automated perception and recording of learning status data are emerging trends. For example, using generative AI combined with web scraping technologies to automatically collect emotional state data during human–machine interactions is an important future research direction.

2.2 Methods for the Cognitive Diagnosis of Learning Risk

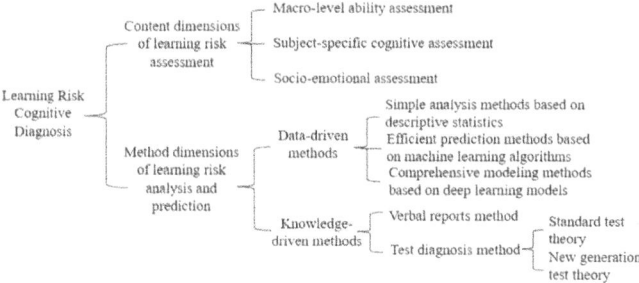

Fig. 1. Hierarchical structure of research on the cognitive diagnosis of learning risk

The cognitive diagnosis of learning risks is crucial for accurate early warning and serves as the basis for implementing learning improvement interventions. Existing research has focused primarily on two dimensions: the content of learning risk assessment and methods of risk analysis and prediction. Each dimension can be further divided into different directions, as illustrated in Fig. 1.

Content Dimensions of Learning Risk Assessment. Macrolevel ability assessment involves evaluating the overall ability levels of students via aggregate scores from tests, with a focus on general cognitive capabilities. The most typical approach is to use the total score obtained by students on a test to measure their overall ability level. The theoretical foundation for this is classical test theory (CTT), also known as true score theory, which is one of the earliest and most extensively developed psychometric theories and is widely known and applied in practical work [9]. A typical study by Gaixiao Z. et al. deeply analyzed how to integrate CTT techniques to improve the quality of academic monitoring tools [10]. Another study by Xiaoling F. et al. applied CTT in test score equating research and concluded that the linear equating method is superior to the equipercentile equating method [11]. CTT-based studies are built on weak assumptions, require minimal implementation conditions and rely on simple mathematical models. They are easy to understand and accept, offering clear concepts, simple calculations, and broad applicability[9]. However, this approach focuses on measuring and assessing macrolevel abilities, failing to reflect the finer details of the internal psychological processing and response mechanisms of the subjects [12]. As a result, the explanatory power of the findings and their guidance for subsequent improvements are limited.

Subject-specific cognitive assessment refers to the evaluation of students' mastery of specific subject knowledge, identifying areas where students struggle to understand or apply concepts. Current research in this area mainly assesses learning risks and academic crises on the basis of students' mastery of subject-specific knowledge. Some studies use course attendance, homework, and classroom test performance to reflect students' cognitive states, whereas others predict students' course grades to determine cognitive mastery. A typical study by Dan S. et al. conducted course performance prediction and early warning research using multisource data from professional courses, unit tests, mobile teaching data, and virtual simulation experimental data, thus determining subject-specific cognitive states [13]. Another study by Zhijia M. et al. reported that cognitive analysis in learning analytics tools should present task completion, learning performance, learning participation, and learning behaviors [14]. These studies are characterized by a direct correlation between cognitive factors and students' academic performance, making identification and operation straightforward and making the results easy to understand. However, they do not comprehensively address the deeper driving factors and mechanisms behind learning risks, such as the significant impact of emotions.

Socioemotional assessment involves evaluating the emotional and social aspects of students' learning experiences, identifying emotional issues such as anxiety and a lack of motivation that may impact learning outcomes. In recent years, research on early warning of emotional states in online learning has emerged. Emotions are critical implicit learning characteristics that are crucial for maintaining academic persistence, efficiency, and resilience; the absence of social-emotional support can lead to academic burnout, goal confusion, and even psychological health risks[15]. For instance, a study by Vilkova K. revealed that social–psychological interventions have heterogeneous effects on different demographic variables in a MOOC platform teaching experiment [16].

Dexin C. et al. proposed a deep learning model for emotion classification that is capable of monitoring and warning learners about emotional changes [17]. Gatebox by Line Corporation uses hybrid sensors to recognize human expressions and voices, analyze users' emotional states and provide social-emotional support through virtual characters [15]. These studies are beneficial for deeply analyzing learning risk and improving learning outcomes from the perspective of intrinsic motivation. However, the precision of emotion data recognition, the efficiency of emotion data collection, and the integration of emotional and cognitive assessments need further improvement.

In summary, learning risk assessment has become increasingly refined with increasing attention given to the intrinsic motivational role of emotional states in learning. Online learning early warning is shifting toward noncognitive research. However, further exploration is needed on how to integrate and accurately apply ability, cognitive, and emotional assessments for subsequent learning remediation and improvement.

Method Dimensions of Learning Risk Analysis and Prediction

Data-Driven Methods. The first category is simple analysis methods based on descriptive statistics. These methods primarily use basic statistical techniques to identify correlations between external factors and learning performance, providing a straightforward analysis of learning behaviors and outcomes, with a focus on identifying factors that affect learning quality. Various statistical models are used to analyze students' learning behaviors and performance. Examples include using factor analysis to identify the characteristics of students at academic risk [18], stage prediction models for identifying struggling students [19], logistic regression to reveal indicators of academic crises [20], random forest and logistic regression for predicting student performance [21], multiple linear regression to analyze performance characteristics [22], and mixed-effect linear regression models for predicting student academic performance [23]. These methods are characterized by simple calculations, ease of use, and relatively low technical barriers, but they lack high accuracy and often provide static, descriptive conclusions that offer limited guidance for future learning quality improvements.

The second category consists of efficient prediction methods that are based on machine learning algorithms. These methods usually apply algorithms such as support vector machines, Bayesian methods, and decision trees to quantitatively predict learning performance on the basis of complex pattern relationships extracted from data. Examples include the use of support vector machines to predict student grades [24], Bayesian methods for predicting student course performance [25], and decision trees to predict online learner behaviors and outcomes [26]. Additionally, Karalar H. et al. proposed an optimal ensemble model based on machine learning algorithms, which monitored and supervised the academic performance of over 2,000 learners in a higher education setting[27]. The key features of these methods are their predictive and generalization capabilities, their suitability for modeling nonlinear relationships, and their ability to perform incremental learning. However, they require high-quality and large quantities of sample data, and their computational processes are often difficult for educators to interpret and customize.

The third category comprises comprehensive modeling methods that are based on deep learning models. These methods effectively utilize deep learning neural networks to analyze large, heterogeneous datasets, effectively capturing multilayered structural relationships between data and learning outcomes for precise predictions. Owing to the rapid development of deep learning technology and its advantages in handling multidimensional data, research on online learning early warnings using deep learning neural networks has increased. For example, Biya X. constructed a BP neural network-based prediction model for learning performance on the Chaoxing online education platform, enabling the prediction of university students' grades[28]. Chuping S. et al. innovatively proposed an improved RBF neural network algorithm to achieve early warning of university learning crises, considering the multiple causes of learning crises [29]. Deep neural network models with multilayer structures have stronger feature extraction capabilities for large amounts of input data, resulting in more accurate and reliable outputs [17]. However, similar to machine learning algorithms, their computational processes are still "black boxes", making interpretability of the results a challenge.

In summary, data-driven methods leverage external behavioral data to predict potential learning crises and hidden dangers, which is characterized by high computational efficiency. However, they generally suffer from poor interpretability, necessitating the complement of knowledge-driven methods to enhance their practical application in education.

Knowledge-Driven Methods. The first category is the verbal reports method. This method involves researchers asking testees to report their thought processes while attempting to solve problems or answer test questions, either during the experiment or as a recall after the experiment [12]. This makes the testee's internal cognitive processes explicit through verbalization. By analyzing these reports, researchers can explore internal processes of artificial information processing that cannot be directly observed. Studies such as those by Leighton J. P. and Gierl M. J. use verbal report data as a basis for cognitive diagnosis [30]. Xuefeng W. et al. conducted an empirical study using verbal reports to diagnose and intervene with primary school students who have difficulties in mathematics [31]. The advantage of this method is that it fully leverages the teaching experience of educators, allowing for detailed observation of students' cognitive processes and deviations, ultimately enabling one-on-one cognitive diagnosis and intervention. However, it lacks strong theoretical support and heavily relies on the personal experience and knowledge of the observer, leading to issues with objectivity, low operational efficiency, and a limited audience of students.

The second category consists of test diagnosis methods. This method involves associating subject knowledge and expert experience with test items and then using students' performance on these items to classify and diagnose their abilities and knowledge structures. The development of its foundational theories can be divided into two stages: standard test theory and new generation test theory.

In the standard test theory stage, the most representative theories include classical test theory (CTT), generalization theory (GT), and item response theory (IRT). IRT, for example, was developed in the mid-20th century, building on the creative research of American scholar Lord and Danish scholar Rasch. IRT focuses on test items rather than the entire test and uses probabilistic models to explore the relationship between observable external variables and unobservable internal traits of the testee. Studies such as those by Yansu W. on multitrait knowledge tracing models [32] and Xueling S.

et al. on the quality evaluation of graduate entrance examination items via IRT [33] illustrate its application. These methods have greatly impacted educational assessment and teaching diagnosis, contributing to the development of computerized adaptive testing and enhancing the scientific basis of measurement models, test construction, and item banks. However, they primarily offer testees' macrolevel trait evaluations, neglecting the diagnosis of microlevel cognitive processes involved in answering questions.

The new generation test theory stage is marked by the publication of "Test Theory for a New Generation of Tests" by Frederiksen et al. in 1993. This stage integrates cognitive variables into measurement models, known as cognitive diagnosis models (CDMs), which provide both macrolevel ability evaluations and microlevel cognitive structure and process diagnostics. Examples include the rule space model (RSM) [34], the attribute hierarchy model (AHM) [35], and deterministic inputs, noisy "and" gate model (DINA) [36]. Studies such as those by Wenjia B. on cognitive diagnosis in chemistry via RSM [37], Lidong W. on the diagnostic evaluation of mathematical achievements via AHM [38], and Dongmei L. on English reading ability diagnosis via DINA [39] illustrate their application. Recent advancements include extending models with diagnostic factors related to learning conditions and integrating AI technologies with CDMs, such as considering the importance of knowledge points [40] and combining knowledge graphs [41] and neural networks [42]. These methods not only assess students' overall performance but also quantify their cognitive strengths and weaknesses, facilitating targeted remediation and improvement. However, they often focus solely on knowledge points, neglecting emotional and behavioral factors. Additionally, the complexity of these models limits their practical application to small-scale studies, with insufficient exploration in large-scale online education contexts.

In summary, knowledge-driven methods leverage expert experience to diagnose learners' strengths and weaknesses by analyzing the underlying principles, mechanisms, and causes of learning quality. These methods are highly interpretable and easily guide subsequent improvement actions. However, the results are often descriptive and rely on the experts' level of expertise, lacking objectivity and scientific rigor. The efficiency of automated knowledge reasoning also needs improvement. As data science and knowledge engineering mature, combining the efficiency of data-driven methods with the interpretability of knowledge-driven methods to develop deep cognitive methods for learning risk in large-scale online education is a critical area for future research.

2.3   Methods for Grading and Warning Learning Crises

Risk Grading Methods. Risk grading involves categorizing the various levels of risk present in learning conditions to help learners understand their current risk status and facilitate subsequent improvement measures. Notable studies in this area include Arnold K. E. et al.'s Course Signals system, which categorizes students into green, yellow, and red levels to indicate the severity of learning risk [43]. Xiaoli C. et al. developed a five-level warning method based on negative records and mental health issues, with a table providing the criteria, warning colors, and intervention measures for each level [44]. Yifu J. et al. established a two-category, six-level learning warning signal system on the basis of the frequency of outlier behaviors in students [45]. Chunqiao M. et al. used a combination of the quantile method, coefficient of variation method, expert experience method, and analytic hierarchy process to classify learning risk into two categories (normal and abnormal) and four levels (no risk, low risk, medium risk, and high risk) [46]. Additionally, Meng Y. et al., in designing a network learning resource evolution warning system from a high-quality development perspective, defined the evolution states of network learning resources as initial, growth, stable, decline, and death to improve the quality and management efficiency of these resources [47]. Current research is characterized by qualitative grading methods based on expert experience, which can be subjective and lack a high degree of automation. These methods focus on knowledge mastery risks and often neglect behavior anomalies and emotional vulnerabilities. Future research should aim to combine qualitative and quantitative methods to increase the objectivity and scientific rigor of learning risk grading.

Crisis Warning Methods. Once risks are graded, they form specific crisis events. Crisis warning involves presenting these crisis states in an attention-grabbing format across various dimensions, such as knowledge, behavior, and emotions, to alert learners. There are three main mature types of methods currently in use. The first type is text-based alerts. These include emails, text messages, desktop pop-ups, and notifications within learning management systems. Examples include the starfish early alert module in the starfish enterprise success platform and the predictive warning application system developed by the University of Electronic Science and Technology of China [3]. The second type is graphical-based alerts. These use line charts, bar charts, radar charts, and other graphical formats to visualize the dynamic evolution and comparative analysis of risks. A representative example is the learning dashboard developed by Khan Academy [6]. The third type is symbol- and color-based alerts. These use noticeable symbols and various colors, such as red flags, traffic lights, and signal lights, to visualize risks. The Course Signals system developed by Purdue University is a notable example [43]. These methods are simple, easy to use, and easy to understand, and they have relatively low technical requirements. However, they are often static rendering methods with limited variety and lack voice or video reminders, which could provide more emotional encouragement and a sense of connection to the students, thus promoting timely improvements. Additionally, learners can only passively receive information without an active feedback interface. Future trends will involve leveraging integrated multimedia technologies, such as WeChat API interfaces, to provide warnings to learners in text, image, audio, and video formats, thereby increasing the reachability, diversity, and feedback effectiveness of risk alerts.

In summary, research on methods of learning risk grading and crisis warning has made significant strides in categorizing learning risks and presenting crisis states. However, challenges remain in integrating qualitative and quantitative approaches, improving the objectivity and automation of risk grading, and developing more interactive and emotionally engaging warning methods. Future efforts should focus on these areas to increase the effectiveness and responsiveness of learning crisis management systems.

2.4   Methods for Learning Improvement Interventions

Manually Written Improvement Comments Based on Expert Experience. Teachers and administrators manually write learning assessment reports and improvement suggestions on the basis of the pushed early warning information, recommending personalized learning resources suitable for learners. For example, Black P. and Wiliam D. conducted an in-depth analysis of how teachers use expert experience for personalized guidance in classroom assessments and discussed how teachers' direct involvement can enhance learning outcomes [48]. Similarly, Xuefeng W. et al. used verbal reports to observe students with difficulties in mathematics learning and implemented one-on-one personalized improvement interventions on the basis of expert experience[31]. This method's advantages include strong targeting, allowing for one-on-one on-site guidance for learners and facilitating emotional encouragement. However, it is characterized by low operational efficiency, limited coverage, and high subjectivity, with the scientific nature of the interventions varying from person to person and being difficult to ensure.

Interventions are Provided on the Basis of a Fixed Strategy Library with Predefined Matching Rules. The early warning system contains a comprehensive library of learning intervention strategies, storing specific strategies for various problems. On the basis of preset matching rules, the system can automatically recommend appropriate learning strategies to learners. For example, Safsouf Y. et al. designed the TaBAT tool on the basis of an e-learner success assessment model, which provides corresponding interventions according to preset rules. The specific intervention modules include platform login notifications, resource access notifications, social participation reminders, course incompletion warnings, and test and assignment notifications, thus improving intervention efficiency to some extent [49]. This method's advantages lie in its ability to respond quickly to learners' needs, high intervention efficiency, and ease of large-scale application. However, the effectiveness of the intervention is directly influenced by the quality and comprehensiveness of the strategy library. The application of fixed strategies may overlook individual differences among learners, leading to suboptimal intervention outcomes.

Combining Systemic and Manual Interventions. The system generates personalized suggestions and resources for students on the basis of the pushed early warning information and adaptive engines, which are then manually refined. For example, Shuixing H. et al. designed an online learning intervention framework based on intelligent educational agents, which can select the most appropriate options from six types of intervention strategies: visual charts, instant message notifications, social support services, learning resource recommendations, academic advice planning recommendations, and interactions with learning stakeholders, on the basis of indicators such as the scenario, type, and quantitative level of the learner's problem. These are then combined with teacher decisions and assistance to form the final intervention strategy [15]. This method balances the efficiency of system recommendations with the effectiveness of manual interventions, making it a relatively safe intervention method, although the overall level of intelligence needs improvement.

Automated Intervention Methods Based on Artificial Intelligence. These methods use intelligent algorithms to analyze learners' learning data and automatically generate personalized learning improvement suggestions and resource recommendations. For example, Khosravi H. et al. proposed an artificial intelligence intervention scheme based on online analytical processing, data mining, and process mining technologies, helping educators identify, explore, and select appropriate intervention measures, with instructions presented via a dashboard [50]. The significant advantages of this method are its efficiency and broad coverage, ability to process large amounts of data in a short time and ability to provide real-time, personalized interventions to a large group of learners. However, this method also faces challenges, including issues of algorithm interpretability and ensuring that AI-generated suggestions align with learners' actual needs and contexts. Therefore, constructing new intelligent dialog intervention systems using LLMs, which interact with students in a more natural and emotionally conscious manner, dynamically adjust personalized intervention strategies on the basis of students' feedback and learning progress, and achieve continuous optimization and improvement, is an important future research trend.

In summary, research on methods for learning improvement interventions has evolved significantly, ranging from manually written comments based on expert experience to automated AI-based interventions. Each method has its own strengths and limitations, and the future trend lies in integrating the efficiency of automated systems with the personal touch of manual interventions. This integration aims to develop more intelligent, adaptive, and emotionally supportive intervention systems to effectively enhance learning outcomes.

2.5   Information Technology Tools for Learning Early Warning

Visualization Tools for Learning Monitoring and Early Warning. This is currently the mainstream approach, including tools such as learner profiles, learning growth archives, and learning analytics dashboards [51], with the learning analytics dashboard being the most typical example. The advantages of these tools are their high technological maturity and ease of integration with existing teaching systems. Numerous studies, both domestic and international, have confirmed their practical utility in enhancing the understanding of academic crises, improving learners' self-monitoring and reflection, and increasing intrinsic motivation [15]. However, there are also several shortcomings. First, there is a lack of mature learning theory support, which limits the tools' ability to explain variations in learner behavior, leading to situations where learners may know what is happening but not why, thereby limiting the promotion of metacognition [52]. Second, there is a lack of effective support for human–computer collaboration; most tools focus solely on data presentation without providing valuable insights for educators and overlook the value of educators' involvement in assessments, making it difficult for inexperienced teachers to benefit from these aids [53]. Third, the emotional regulation functions need improvement; the absence of self-assessment mechanisms can lead to calculation anxiety and negative emotions related to statistical data. When learners face confusion or crisis, tools should offer appropriate feedback channels to optimize emotional regulation functions [51].

Learning Diagnosis and Tutoring Subsystems in Intelligent Teaching Platforms. This approach is gradually gaining popularity. For example, Nathan M. J. et al. developed the ANIMATE intelligent diagnosis and tutoring system, which diagnoses errors and helps students form problem-solving strategies by incorporating mathematical schemata [54]. Shihua H. et al. analyzed the design of cognitive student models within intelligent teaching systems and achieved favorable experimental results [55]. Additionally, systems such as Purdue University's Course Signals [43], Desire2Learn's Student Success System [56], the Starfish Early Alert System within the Starfish Enterprise Success Platform [3], and the learning early warning plugin developed for Moodle by the University of the South Pacific [57] all provide early warning functionalities based on course learning, helping students better complete their academic tasks. These systems effectively diagnose and intervene in knowledge transfer and skill development, but most exist as modules, subsystems, or plugins within online learning platforms, limiting their standalone functionality, portability, and general applicability.

Simulation Models of Virtual Agent Roles for Learning Monitoring and Assistance Based on Pedagogical Agent. The concept of a pedagogical agent (PA) originates from Skinner's principles of programmed instruction and teaching machines. The intelligent tutor systems in the 1970s represented the early prototype system of the concept [15]. In recent years, propelled by advancements in AI and other technologies, PAs have evolved from intelligent tutor systems to hypermedia teaching systems, intelligent learning robots, and educational intelligent agents. Pioneers in this field, such as Ross, define PAs as virtual assistant roles within learning systems that dynamically perceive the learning environment, analyze and synthesize learner information, and proactively or reactively provide assistance on the basis of needs [58]. Research in this domain focuses on three main areas: a) Theoretical foundations: Studies, such as those by Castro-Alonso J. C. et al., have confirmed the support of cognitive load theory, the cognitive theory of multimedia learning, and social agency theory for PA through meta-analyses [59]. Zhengguo X. et al. highlighted that current PAs often combine multiple roles, such as companions, encouraged, supervisor, and evaluator [60]. b) Technical support: Most research is in the model framework design stage, where researchers explain the PA's model structure, decision paths, and adaptive algorithms while also exploring future directions in self-quantification, affective computing, emotional design, and teaching agents [61]. c) Practical applications: There have been initial explorations into the interactive applications of PAs in online video teaching [62], their use in training children's questioning skills [63], and their impact on student attention in multimedia learning environments [64]. Therefore, PAs, leveraging the rapid development of the IT industry, are quickly expanding their applicability and intelligence, offering vast potential for transformative online learning interventions. However, most current research remains at the level of teaching agents, operating passively to execute instructions without autonomous decision-making and planning capabilities in learning early warnings.

In summary, research on learning early warning information technology tools encompasses visualization tools for learning monitoring, intelligent teaching platform subsystems, and simulation models of virtual agent roles. Each approach has advantages and limitations, with a common need for further development in theoretical support, human–computer collaboration, and emotional regulation functionalities. Future research should aim to integrate these tools more deeply, leveraging advanced AI technologies to increase their ability to provide effective, personalized, and emotionally supportive learning interventions.

3 Discussion and Propose

In summary, current research on learning early warnings in online education has made notable progress in areas such as learning status perception and recording, cognitive diagnosis of learning risks, grading and warning of learning crises, and learning improvement interventions. However, despite years of practice both domestically and internationally, several deficiencies remain. These include the following: a) Incomplete data sources and low automation in data collection: The foundational data for learning status are not comprehensive, and the degree of automation in data collection is insufficient. b) Lack of focus on microcognitive structures and processes in risk diagnosis: Current cognitive diagnosis methods do not adequately address the intricacies of learners' cognitive structures and processes and struggle to balance efficiency and interpretability. c) Monolithic crisis grading and warning methods: Existing methods are often static and lack exploration into feedback-driven, multimedia-integrated approaches. d) Weak social-emotional support in intervention plans: The personalization of improvement plans is limited, and social-emotional support in early warning interventions is inadequate. e) Low degree of tool intelligence: early warning tools are not sufficiently intelligent, and there is a lack of specialized AI agent research tailored for learning early warnings. Therefore, leveraging the interdisciplinary strengths of education, psychology, learning sciences, and information science, and on the basis of cognitive diagnosis theory and generative AI technology such as LLM, it is imperative to develop a comprehensive AI agent system for early warning learning. This system should integrate automatic perception and recording of learning status, precise cognitive diagnosis of learning risks, intelligent grading and warning of learning crises, and personalized generation of learning improvement interventions. Such a holistic AI-driven approach could provide a novel pathway to significantly enhance the quality of online learning and improve the effectiveness and efficiency of early warning management.

With advancements in cognitive psychology and educational measurement, the new generation of test methods centered around cognitive diagnosis theory emphasizes both the assessment of individual macrolevel abilities and the diagnosis of internal microcognitive structures and processes. This provides a robust theoretical foundation for more precise monitoring and diagnosis of learning conditions. Concurrently, the rapid development of information science and intelligent technologies, exemplified by generative AI technologies such as ChatGPT, enables the automatic generation of personalized learning improvement resources. Additionally, the recent emergence of AI agent frameworks based on LLM offers immense potential for developing highly intelligent early warning tools capable of autonomous perception, planning, action, and evolutionary expansion. In this context, on the basis of cognitive diagnosis theory and AI technologies, particularly LLM, developing an artificial intelligence agent for early warning is feasible, with the aim of achieving real-time monitoring, precise diagnosis, effective warning, and personalized intervention for students' learning through techniques such as multimodal perception, retrieval-augmented generation, reasoning and planning, and interactive evolution. It can fully automate data collection and integration, perform in-depth analysis and prediction via advanced algorithms, formulate personalized intervention strategies, and realize continuous feedback and iterative optimization. It can also identify and support struggling students, optimize course teaching, and support large-scale personalized autonomous learning. This intelligent agent encompasses capabilities such as self-perception, autonomous planning, automatic decision-making, and self-expansion to adapt dynamically to students' needs in educational environments and provide intelligent solutions for early warning.

4   Conclusion

The advent of the digital and intelligent era has accelerated the widespread adoption of online education while also imposing higher quality standards on online learning. In this context, early warning is becoming crucial for ensuring the quality of online education. This paper first conducts an in-depth analysis of the current research status of learning early warnings in online education, revealing that most existing early warning methods remain at the measurement level rather than delving into the cognitive level. The results obtained are often descriptive rather than predictive, with a focus on statistical and mining techniques rather than generative approaches, making it difficult to achieve truly personalized interventions for each student.

The fundamental reason is that existing data-driven models, while effective in predicting potential learning crises via external learning data and characterized by high computational efficiency, suffer from poor interpretability. Conversely, existing knowledge-driven models, which guide external learning improvement behaviors through the analysis of deep-seated principles, mechanisms, and causes of learning conditions, are highly interpretable but currently face challenges in achieving automated knowledge reasoning efficiently. Moreover, new intelligent technologies, while significantly enhancing the scale and efficiency of early warning, risk becoming rigid technical tools if used without modification to align with early warning business needs.

In response, in the current era of digitalization and intelligence, which leverages interdisciplinary advantages, modern cognitive diagnosis theories, and generative AI technologies, it is feasible and significant to construct and implement an artificial intelligence agent for early warning, which can lead to new progress in the research and practice of early warning. This study provides insights into the development of new methods for early warning by integrating knowledge, behavior, and emotional monitoring and diagnosis with academic improvement. This study provides new perspectives for governing learning quality in large-scale online education and offers valuable references for future developments.

Acknowledgment. This study is supported by the Hunan Provincial Natural Science Foundation (Grant No. 2023JJ50455), the Scientific Research Project of Hunan Provincial Department of Education (Grant No. 24A0562) and the general program of Humanities and Social Sciences Research of the Ministry of Education of China (Grant No. 19YJC880064). This work is also supported in part by the Aid Program for Science and Technology Innovative Research Team in Higher Educational Institutions of Hunan Province (Information Processing and Control Technology for

Intelligent Agriculture in the Wuling Mountain area), the Key Laboratory of Intelligent Control Technology for Wuling-Mountain Ecological Agriculture in Hunan Province, and the Huaihua University Double First-Class Initiative Applied Characteristic Discipline of Control Science and Engineering.

References

1. Huang, R., Hu, Y., Liu, M., Wang, H., Tursenali, B.: Seven facts about online learning—the implications of superscale online education. Modern Distance Educ. Res. **33**(3), 3–11 (2021)
2. Chen, E., Liu, Q., Wang, S., et al.: Key techniques and application of intelligent education oriented adaptive learning. CAAI Trans. Intell. Syst. **16**(5), 886–898 (2021)
3. Wang, L., Ye, Y., Yang, X.: Design of online learning early-warning model based on big data—the learning early-warning of "research and practice column about big data in education." Mod. Educ. Technol. **2016**(7), 5–11 (2016)
4. Zheng, S.: An investigation and analysis of college English students' learning situation in our college. J. Huiyang Teach. Coll. (Soc. Sci. Ed.) **1988**(3), 86–92 (1988)
5. Zhao, H., Jiang, Q., Zhao, W., Li, Y., Zhao, Y.: Empirical research of predictive factors and intervention countermeasures of online learning performance on big data-based learning analytics. e-Education Res. **38**(1), 62–69 (2017)
6. Zhang, Z., Liu, W., Han, Z.: Learning dashboard: a novel learning support tool in the big data era. Modern Distance Educ. Res. **2014**(3), 100–107 (2014)
7. Yu, S., Wang, Q., Wang, F., Wan, H.: Designing an organization and description framework for ubiquitous learning resources: a study of international standards for learning cell. Chinese J. Distance Educ. (7), 1–9, 76 (2021)
8. Yang, X., Yu, S., Zhang, F.: Design and implementation of dynamic semantic association of learning resources. China Educ. Technol. **2013**(1), 70–75 (2013)
9. Liu, Q.: The Application Research of Rule Space Model in Diagnosing and Remedying Chemistry Knowledge on Junior High School Students. Jiangxi Normal University, 1–37 (2008)
10. Zhou, G., Liu, E.: Integrating CTT and IRT to improve the quality of monitoring tools—taking primary science examinations as an example. J. Capital Norm. Univ. (Natl. Sci. Ed.) **39**(04), 54–61 (2018)
11. Fan, X., Ouyang, S., Lu, X., Qu, W., Qin, B.: Comparative study on equivalent methods of mathematics test papers in college entrance examination. Educ. Measur. Eval. **2018**(10), 47–55 (2018)
12. Tu, D., Cai, Y., Ding, S.: Cognitive Diagnosis Theory. Beijing Normal University Press, Beijing (2021)
13. Song, D., Liu, D., Feng, X.: Course performance prediction and course early warning research based on multisource data analysis. Res. High. Educ. Eng. **2020**(01), 189–194 (2020)
14. Mou, Z., Wu, F.: Research on the function of learning analytics tools based on educational data. Mod. Educ. Technol. **2017**(27), 113–119 (2017)
15. Hu, S., Jing, Z.: New developments in online learning interventions: from learning analysis dashboard to pedagogical agent. J. Dist. Educ. **40**(05), 83–92 (2022)
16. Vilkova, K.: The promises and pitfalls of self-regulated learning interventions in MOOCs. Technol. Knowl. Learn. **27**(3), 689–705 (2022)
17. Chen, D., Zhan, Y., Yang, B.: Analysis of applications of deep learning in educational big data mining. e-Educ. Res. (2), 68–76 (2019)

18. Campbell, J.P.: Utilizing Student Data within the Course Management System to Determine Undergraduate Student Academic Success: An Exploratory Study. PhD thesis, Purdue University (2007)
19. Chen, Y., Zheng, Q., Ji, S., et al.: Identifying at-risk students based on the phased prediction model. Knowl. Inf. Syst. **62**(3), 987–1003 (2020)
20. Yakubu, M.N., Abubakar, A.M.: Applying machine learning approach to predict students' performance in higher educational institutions. Kybernetes **51**(2), 916–934 (2021)
21. Oku, A.Y.A., Sato, J.R.: Predicting student performance using machine learning in fNIRS data. Front. Hum. Neurosci. **15**, 1–12 (2021)
22. Yang, S.J.H., Lu, O.H.T., Huang, A.Y.Q., et al.: Predicting students' academic performance using multiple linear regression and principal component analysis. J. Inf. Process. **26**, 170–176 (2018)
23. Jovanovic, J., Saqr, M., Joksimovic, S., et al.: Students matter the most in learning analytics: the effects of internal and instructional conditions in predicting academic success. Comput. Educ. **172**(1), 104251 (2021)
24. Sandeep, M.J., Erik, W.M., Eitel, J.M.L., et al.: Early alert of academically at-risk students: an open source analytics initiative. J. Learn. Analy. **1**, 6–47 (2014)
25. Hamoud, A.K., Humadi, A.M., Awadh, W.A., et al.: Students' success prediction based on bayes algorithms. Int. J. Comput. Appl. **7**, 6–12 (2017)
26. Wang, G., Fu, G.: Prediction of online learning behavior and performance and design of learning intervention model. Chin. J. Distance Educ. **2019**(2), 39–48 (2019)
27. Karalar, H., Kapucu, C., Gürüler, H.: Predicting students at risk of academic failure using ensemble model during pandemic in a distance learning system. Int. J. Educ. Technol. High. Educ. **18**(1), 1–18 (2021)
28. Xu, B.: Research on early warning methods of college students' achievements based on BP neural network. Comput. Knowl. Technol. (21), 7–8, 16 (2021)
29. Song, C., Li, S., Cai, B.: Application of an improved RBF neural network algorithm in learning early warning of colleges. Comput. Appl. Softw. **2020**(8), 39–44 (2020)
30. Leighton, J.P., Gierl, M.J.: Verbal report as data for cognitive diagnostic assessment. In: Leighton, J.P., Gierl, M.J. (eds.) Cognitive Diagnostic Assessment for Education: Theory and Applications, pp. 146–172. Cambridge University Press, Cambridge (2007)
31. Wei, X., Cui, G.: Research on one to one cognitive diagnosis and intervention for students with learning difficulties in primary school mathematics. e-Educ. Res. **37**(02), 75–81 (2016)
32. Wei, Y.: Research of Multifeature Knowledge Tracing Model Based on Item Response Theory. PhD thesis, Central China Normal University 2023, 1–58 (2023)
33. Song, X., Liang, Z.: The evaluation of the quality of postgraduate entrance examination based on IRT. Stud. Psychol. Behav. **21**(02), 253–259 (2023)
34. Tatsuoka, K.K.: Rule space: an approach for dealing with misconceptions based on item response theory. J. Educ. Meas. **20**(4), 345–354 (1983)
35. Leighton, J.P., Gierl, M.J., Hunka, S.M.: The attribute hierarchy method for cognitive assessment: a variation on tatsuoka's rule-space approach. J. Educ. Meas. **41**(3), 205–237 (2004)
36. De, L., Torre, J.: DINA model and parameter estimation: a didactic. J. Educ. Behav. Stat. **34**(1), 115–130 (2009)
37. Bao, W.: The Cognitive Diagnosis of High School Students Based on Rule Space Model—Taking "Acid and Alkali Salt" as an Example. PhD thesis, Harbin Normal University 2023, 1–57 (2023)
38. Wang, L., Guo, K., Meng, M.: Application of cognitive diagnose model in mathematics educational assessment. J. Math. Educ. **25**(06), 15–19+55 (2016)
39. Lv, D.: A Study of Senior High School Students' English Reading Ability Based on DINA Cognitive Diagnostic Model. PhD thesis, Guangxi Minzu University 2022, pp. 1–54 (2022)

40. Liu, Y., Zhang, L.: Cognitive diagnosis model integrating forgetting and importance of knowledge points. J. South China Univ. Technol. (Natl. Sci. Ed.) **51**(5), 54–62 (2023)
41. Huang, M., Liu, C., Du, H., Liu, J.: Research on cognitive diagnosis model based on knowledge graph and its application in teaching assistant. Comput. Sci. **48**(6A), 644–648 (2021)
42. Wang, F., Liu, Q., Chen, E., et al.: Neural cognitive diagnosis for intelligent education systems. In: Proceedings of the AAAI Conference on Artificial Intelligence, vol. 34, no. 4, pp. 6153–6161 (2020)
43. Arnold, K.E., Pistilli, M.D.: Course signals at purdue: using learning analytics to increase student success. In: LAK12. In: Proceedings of the 2nd International Conference on Learning Analytics and Knowledge, pp. 267–270. ACM, Vancouver (2012)
44. Chen, X., Zhu, J.: A discussion of carrying out "5-level prewarning" methodology for college students management. J. Guangxi Youth Leaders Coll. **2007**(05), 56–58 (2007)
45. Jin, Y., Wu, T., Zhang, Z., et al.: Design and analysis of learning alert system in big data condition. China Educ. Technol. **2016**(02), 69–73 (2016)
46. Mi, C., Deng, Q., Peng, X., et al.: The business process optimization of early warning education in colleges and universities—taking H college for example. Mod. Educ. Technol. **28**(03), 92–98 (2018)
47. Yuan, M., Yang, X., Li, K.: Design of early warning system for online learning resource evolution from the perspective of high-quality development. Chin. J. Distance Educ. **43**(11), 50–59 (2023)
48. Black, P., Wiliam, D.: Assessment and classroom learning. Assess. Educ. Principles Policy Pract. **5**(1), 7–74 (1998)
49. Safsouf, Y., Mansouri, K., Poirier, F.: TaBAT: design and experimentation of a learning analysis dashboard for teachers and learners. J. Inf. Technol. Educ. **20**, 331–350 (2021)
50. Khosravi, H., Shabaninejad, S., Bakharia, A., et al.: Intelligent learning analytics dashboards: automated drill-down recommendations to support teacher data exploration. J. Learn. Analyt. **8**(3), 133–154 (2021)
51. Yousef, A.M.F., Khatiry, A.R.: Cognitive versus behavioral learning analytics dashboards for supporting learner's awareness, reflection, and learning process. Interact. Learn. Environ. **12**, 2–17 (2021)
52. Matcha, W., Uzir, N.A., Gasevic, D., et al.: A systematic review of empirical studies on learning analytics dashboards: a self-regulated learning perspective. IEEE Trans. Learn. Technol. **13**(2), 226–245 (2020)
53. Keuning, T., Geel, M.V.: Differentiated teaching with adaptive learning systems and teacher dashboards: the teacher still matters most. IEEE Trans. Learn. Technol. **14**(2), 201–210 (2021)
54. Nathan, M.J., Kintsch, W., Young, E.: A theory of algebra-word-problem comprehension and its implications for the design of learning environments. Cogn. Instr. **9**, 329–389 (1992)
55. Huang, S., Han, H., Lu, Z.: Design of students' cognitive model in intelligent tutoring system. J. Guangzhou Open Univ. **14**(2), 30–34 (2014)
56. Essa, A., Ayad, H.: Improving student success using predictive models and data visualizations. Res. Learn. Technol. **20**, 58–70 (2012)
57. Jokhan, A., Sharma, B., Singh, S.: Early warning system as a predictor for student performance in higher education blended courses. Stud. High. Educ. **5**, 1–12 (2018)
58. Liu, Z., Fang, C., Liu, S., et al.: A review of physical learning spaces oriented learners' emotion perception research. J. Dist. Educ. **37**(2), 33–44 (2019)
59. Castro-Alonso, J.C., Wong, R.M., Adesope, O.O., et al.: Effectiveness of multimedia pedagogical agents predicted by diverse theories: a meta-analysis. Educ. Psychol. Rev. **33**(3), 989–1015 (2021)
60. Xu, Z., Liu, Z., Dang, T., et al.: Development, application and prospect of pedagogical agents. e-Educ. Res. **42**(11), 20–26+33 (2021)

61. Tulli, S.: Explainability in autonomous pedagogical agents. In: Proceedings of the AAAI Conference on Artificial Intelligence, vol. 34, no. 10, pp. 13738–13739 (2020)
62. Li, H.: Interactive Online Video Teaching System Based on Educational Agent. Shandong University, pp. 1–63 (2023)
63. Abdelghani, R., Wang, Y.H., Yuan, X., et al.: GPT-3-driven pedagogical agents to train children's curious question-asking skills. Int. J. Artif. Intell. Educ. **2023**, 1–36 (2023)
64. Pirouzmand, R., Rostaminezhad, M., Mohammadhasani, N., et al.: The effect of animated pedagogical agent visual signaling on the attention of students in a multimedia learning environment: an eye-tracking approach. Technol. Educ. J. **2024**, 465–478 (2024)

CNFPRNet: Innovative Fusion of GPT-2 Language Model and Natural Language Generation Model for Personalized Educational Recommendations

Chao Li⬤, Zixuan Xu⬤, and Weipeng Jing$^{(\boxtimes)}$⬤

College of Computer and Control Engineering, Northeast Forestry University,
Harbin 150040, China
{lichaonefuzyz,xzx0306,jwp}@nefu.edu.cn

Abstract. In this paper, we propose a novel AI-based model that combines a GPT-2 language model with a natural language generation component to generate Customized Narrative Fragments for Personalized Recommendations(CNFPR) in education. Our approach builds on the existing literature on AI-based learning content generation and learning pathway augmentation, but introduces a new component that leverages the power of GPT-2 and an innovative Conceptual Definition Extractor to generate high-quality natural language text. By integrating this component into our model, we aim to create a more personalized and engaging learning experience for students, one that is tailored to their individual needs and preferences. Experimental results show that compared with the Zero-shot evaluation with GPT-2, our CNFPRNet model demonstrates a 23.5% increase in ROUGE scores. This improves the accuracy of recommended content and enables teaching resources to better meet the individual needs of users.

Keywords: AI-based · Customized Narrative Fragments · Conceptual Definition Extracto · Individual needs and preferences

1 Introduction

1.1 A Subsection Sample

In the contemporary landscape of education, the infusion of artificial intelligence (AI) into pedagogical strategies has become an imperative pursuit [1]. The last decade has witnessed an explosion in the number of web-based learning systems due to the increasing demand in higher-level education, the limited number of teaching personnel, advances in information technology and artificial intelligence, and, more recently, COVID-19. Therefore, the utilization of AI, particularly in the domain of personalized recommendations, addresses a crucial need for educational systems to cater to the diverse learning styles, preferences, and capabilities of individual students [2]. As the educational landscape becomes increasingly digitized, the potential for AI to enhance the efficacy of learning experiences is more evident than ever.

K. Zhang et al. (Eds.): CSEI 2024, CCIS 2448, pp. 250–265, 2025.
https://doi.org/10.1007/978-981-96-3738-6_19

The rationale behind employing AI in personalized educational recommendations lies in its inherent capacity to process vast datasets and discern intricate patterns within the multifaceted realm of learning [3]. In the past few years, to enhance the conventional classrooms, to bridge the constraints of time and distances, and to improve Individualized needs by making high-quality education accessible, most primary and secondary schools have integrated Massive Open Online Course (MOOC) platforms such as the edX [4] consortium in their education systems. Moreover, schools are leveraging online labs as an innovative approach to personalized learning. These virtual laboratories serve as invaluable alternatives, particularly for students facing challenges accessing physical labs. Here, personalized recommendations play a pivotal role, tailoring experiments and practical learning experiences to the unique needs and preferences of individual learners. Additionally, there has been a notable surge in the development of various online educational tools designed to streamline the learning process. Examples include software dedicated to text summarization across different domains, as well as tools for generating questions and tests [5]. These resources, coupled with effective evaluation mechanisms, not only benefit students by enhancing their learning experiences but also provide valuable support to educators in delivering personalized instruction.

However, the current state of personalized recommendations in education is not without its challenges. Existing systems often grapple with issues of limited contextual understanding and struggle to capture the subtleties of individual learning journeys [6]. The conventional algorithms employed in educational recommendation systems often fall short in discerning the nuanced preferences and aptitudes that characterize a student's educational profile. The currently available online teaching platforms also have significant limitations. One fundamental difference between existing recommender systems and personalized education is the optimization objective: The former focuses on some form of user engagement to maximize profit, which is system-centric and relatively easy to quantify, whereas the latter focuses on some form of learning outcomes, which is student-centric and hard to define. Consequently, the recommendations generated tend to lack the depth and personalization required to facilitate optimal learning outcomes.

In the global landscape of educational technology research, national and international endeavors are actively exploring the integration of AI into personalized educational recommendations [7]. Countries and institutions worldwide are investing in research initiatives aimed at enhancing the adaptability and responsiveness of educational technologies [8]. Recent national and international studies showcase the diversity of methodologies employed, reflecting the global commitment to harnessing AI for educational enrichment [9]. Some initiatives emphasize the integration of learner analytics, while others explore the potential of reinforcement learning in tailoring educational content [10]. The consensus emerging from these efforts is a shared acknowledgment of the transformative potential of AI in personalizing educational experiences, and a recognition of the need for innovative solutions to overcome the existing limitations in the field [11].

In this context, our research presents a distinctive contribution by introducing the integration of OpenAI's GPT-2 language model and an innovative Conceptual Definition Extractor in the creation of a "Definer." This novel framework aims to not only address the current shortcomings in personalized recommendations but also to push the boundaries of adaptability, responsiveness, and enrichment in educational AI systems. Through a meticulous exploration of this integration, we aim to not only contribute to the global discourse on AI in education but also to offer a tangible and innovative solution to the persistent challenges in personalized learning experiences.

2 Related Works

2.1 Adaptive Learning Based Method

Since the 20th century, scholars have delved profoundly into the integration of machine learning for the purpose of tailoring personalized recommendations within the realm of education. This expansive exploration forms a confluence of artificial intelligence and pedagogical methodologies, aspiring to craft educational experiences finely tuned to the distinctive needs and preferences of individual learners. The emergence of machine learning algorithms represents a watershed moment, providing the analytical prowess to distill intricate patterns from extensive datasets that encapsulate the nuances of students' learning behaviors [12]. Far transcending conventional didactic approaches, the ambition is to cultivate adaptive learning environments where algorithms undergo a symbiotic evolution with the intellectual journey of the learner. Chen et al. [13] propose a mathematical framework for which decisions are made based on the current knowledge of the learner and that of the learning materials, two plain vanilla systems are introduced in his fremework for which the optimal recommendation at each stage can be obtained analytically. Embarak et al. [14] build a recommendation model for predicting at-risk students to provide direct system-based coaching to such students to remediate the fragmentation in their knowledge and skills. Bian C L et al. [15] creates a learner-centred concept map using graph theory based on the features of the learners and concepts, then generates a linear concept sequence from the concept map and learn objects (LOs) to model it as a multi-objective combinatorial optimization problem to achieve adaptive learning path recommendation.

These methods content to the individual needs and progress of each students, ensures that learners receive personalized instruction, addressing their unique strengths and weaknesses. Also, they can accommodate diverse learning styles, ensuring that content delivery aligns with the preferences and cognitive approaches of each student. This adaptability contributes to a more inclusive and effective learning environment. However, adopting adaptive learning technologies may involve significant upfront costs, including software development, training, and infrastructure. Institutions must weigh the initial investment against the long-term benefits. The algorithms driving adaptive learning systems may inadvertently introduce biases. Ensuring fairness and equity in recommendations and assessments is an ongoing challenge, requiring careful scrutiny and refinement of the underlying algorithms.

2.2 Artificial Intelligence Based Method

With the advancement of intelligent information processing technology, artificial intelligence (AI) is progressively finding application in personalized recommendations within the realm of education. This convergence marks a pivotal moment where the capabilities of AI are harnessed by researchers and educators to revolutionize how learning experiences are tailored for individual students. Utilizing artificial intelligence technology, Gao et al. [16] simulate the intelligent behavior of users in resource searches to identify words with higher frequency. Subsequently, teaching resources exhibiting high similarity are designated as the recommendation targets, and the recommendation format is chosen to implement the resource recommendation. Wei et al. [17] propose a LinUCB-based learning resource recommendation algorithm to extract features of learning resources such as difficulty degree, a personalized exploration coefficient is carefully constructed in this algorithm according to student's ability and attention scores. Zheng et al. [18] use a hybrid framework of artificial intelligence to focuses on the way to provide targeted recommendations for the implementation of integrated standard lesson plans, which will be the main tool for creating flexible differentiated pedagogical programs that will perfectly meet the personal needs and particularities of each student.

The application of AI in personalized recommendations not only signals a technological evolution but also underscores a paradigm shift in pedagogical approaches [19]. These methods focus on AI-driven content creation and memory science. They utilize algorithms to generate personalized quiz questions, learning materials, and assessments. The emphasis is on tailoring content to individual learning needs while incorporating memory-enhancing strategies. Compared to traditional adaptive learning methods, the AI-powered approach enables highly personalized educational content creation, tailoring learning experiences to individual student needs and preferences. This adaptability enhances engagement and comprehension. However, While AI excels at pattern recognition and data analysis, it may struggle with generating truly creative or innovative educational content. The ability to foster critical thinking, creativity, and originality might be challenging for AI algorithms. Furthermore, the dependence of AI on historical data for making predictions and recommendations raises concerns. This reliance has the potential to perpetuate biases inherent in historical educational data, possibly reinforcing stereotypes or perpetuating inequities.

3 Methodology

3.1 CNFPRNet

In our exploration, CNFPRNet serves as a pioneering framework, seamlessly merging advanced linguistic technologies to articulate and refine definitions across a spectrum of concepts. At its core, CNFPRNet builds upon a robust architectural foundation, drawing inspiration from AI-based learning content generation and learning pathway augmentation. The neural network design strategically incorporates the powerful GPT-2 language model, renowned for its proficiency in probabilistic text generation, to impart a new dimension to personalized educational content creation.

As shown in Fig. 1, a distinguishing element within CNFPRNet is the cohesive amalgamation of the GPT-2 language model and a Conceptual Definition Extractor. This innovative addition complements the existing robust architecture, introducing a novel layer that extracts conceptual definitions to enhance the overall educational content generation process. By harnessing the advanced language generation capabilities of GPT-2 and the Conceptual Definition Extractor's discerning abilities, CNFPRNet aspires to shape a learning environment that not only aligns with students' linguistic and cognitive preferences but also ensures precision in conveying conceptual nuances. It is meticulously crafted to usher in a paradigm shift in personalized learning experiences. Unlike traditional methodologies, this network dynamically adapts to individual learners, offering a nuanced and sophisticated educational environment. The network's design prioritizes the personalization of learning content and recommendations, ensuring alignment with the cognitive needs and preferred engagement styles of each student. These phases unveil the innovative approach underlying our model.

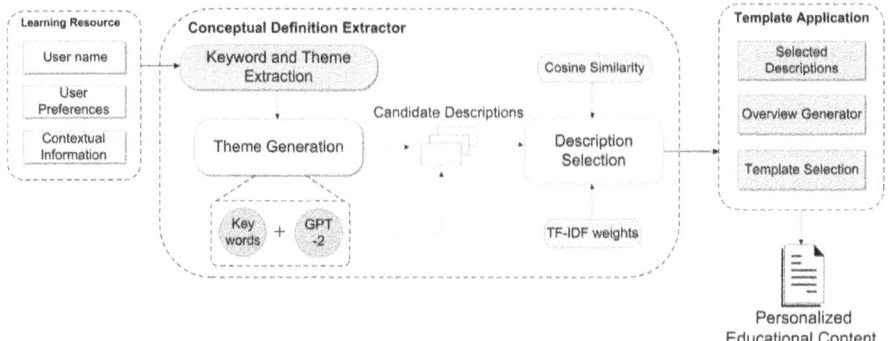

Fig. 1. Schematic Diagram of CNFPRNet

3.2   Conceptual Definition Extractor

In this subsection, we delve into our innovative CDE model, the Conceptual Definition Extractor. This cutting-edge system is designed to craft articulate natural language text, specifically in the format of definitions for any provided keyword or concept. A partial pseudo-code form of Conceptual Definition Extractor is given in Algorithm 1. The definitions produced by this model play a pivotal role in shaping the customized narrative fragments proposed in our study.

Keyword and Theme Extraction
The initial phase of the Conceptual Definition Extractor's workflow involves the meticulous extraction of keywords and thematic anchors from a diverse pool of learning resources. This process is critical for establishing a foundation that accurately captures the fundamental concepts inherent in the learning materials.

In this step, we use TF-IDF [20] (Term Frequency-Inverse Document Frequency) to sift through the vast array of textual data, identifying and isolating terms that encapsulate the core essence of the subject matter. TF-IDF is a common text mining algorithm used to measure the importance of a word to a collection of documents. The algorithm takes into account the frequency of the word in the document as well as in the entire collection of documents to determine the weight of the word. Its formula is given below:

$$TF - IDF\,(t, d, D) = TF\,(t, d) \times IDF\,(t, d) \tag{1}$$

where $TF(t, d)$ denotes the frequency of word t in document d, that is, word frequency. Denotes the inverse document frequency of word t in the document set D, computed using Log. It considers various linguistic and contextual factors, ensuring the extraction of not only common keywords but also thematic anchors that represent the broader, overarching themes of the learning resources.

The goal is to create a comprehensive and representative set of keywords and themes that collectively form a semantic framework for the subsequent stages of the Definition Generator. This meticulous extraction process sets the stage for the model to delve into the intricate nuances of the subject matter, laying the groundwork for the generation of meaningful and contextually relevant descriptions.

Theme Generation

The Theme Generation phase of the Conceptual Definition Extractor is a crucial step in crafting concise and insightful descriptions of overarching themes. This process leverages a state-of-the-art natural language generation model based on GPT-2 (Generative Pre-trained Transformer 2), known for its proficiency in probabilistically generating subsequent words in a sequence.

For each keyword extracted from the learning resources, the GPT-2-based model receives these keywords as initial input. These keywords serve as the core concepts around which the model will generate thematic descriptions. The GPT-2 model initiates the generation process using the provided keywords. It progressively generates text based on the contextual understanding derived from its pre-training on a diverse range of data. GPT-2 excels in capturing language structure and semantics, enabling the coherent construction of complete thematic descriptions. As shown in Table 1, the model produces multiple candidate descriptions for each keyword, ensuring a broad and comprehensive coverage of potential thematic facets (Table 2).

Description Selection

Description Selection is a crucial step in the Conceptual Definition Extractor's workflow, where a judicious process is employed to choose the most fitting description from the multiple candidates generated during the Theme Generation phase. This step ensures that the final definition selected aligns with the overarching theme and provides a clear and insightful representation of the given keyword or concept.

Table 1. Examples of the Theme Generation

Keyword Input	GPT-2 Generation
Climate change	Climate change is a global phenomenon that refers to the long-term alteration of Earth's climate patterns. It encompasses changes in temperature, precipitation, and other atmospheric conditions, primarily driven by human activities such as burning fossil fuels and deforestation.
	Climate change, often referred to as global warming, is a phenomenon characterized by the gradual increase in Earth's average surface temperature.
	The concept of climate change revolves around shifts in Earth's climatic conditions over extended periods. Human-induced activities, notably the release of greenhouse gases, contribute significantly to alterations in temperature, precipitation.
Artificial Intelligence (AI)	Artificial intelligence, commonly known as AI, refers to the development of computer systems capable of performing tasks that typically require human intelligence.
	The field of artificial intelligence revolves around creating intelligent agents that can perceive their environment, learn from experiences, and adapt to changing circumstances.
	From self-driving cars to virtual personal assistants, AI technologies are reshaping the way we interact with machines and process information, with profound implications for the future of technology.

Table 2. Example of a Wikipedia dataset

Topics	Definitional Summaries
Newton's Laws of Motion	Newton's Laws of Motion are three physical laws that form the foundation for classical mechanics.
Chemical Reactions	Reactants, Products, Catalysts, and Chemical Equations
Mitochondria	Mitochondria are double-membraned organelles found in the cells of living organisms, responsible for energy production.
Electric Circuits	Interactive simulations, Video lectures, and Practice Problems for K-12 students studying physics
Cell Biology	Cell Biology is the study of cells, their structure, function, and interactions with their environment.
Renewable Energy Sources	Solar power, Wind turbines, Biofuels, and Sustainable Energy

Each of the candidate descriptions generated in the Theme Generation phase is subjected to a ranking process. Cosine Similarity [21] are applied to assess the relevance of each description to the overarching theme. Cosine Similarity measures the cosine of the angle between two vectors, representing the similarity between two documents or pieces of text. Its formula is given below:

$$\text{Cosine Similarity}(A, B) = \frac{A \cdot B}{\|A\| \cdot \|B\|} \tag{2}$$

where $A \cdot B$ denotes the dot product of vectors A and B, and represent the Euclidean norms of vectors A and B, respectively. For two text documents represented as vectors in a term frequency-inverse document frequency (TF-IDF) matrix, the Cosine Similarity can be calculated based on the TF-IDF weights assigned to each term. In a more specific context, if A and B represent the TF-IDF vectors of two text documents, the formula can be modified to:

$$\text{Cosine Similarity}(A, B) = \frac{\sum_i^n A_i \cdot B_i}{\sqrt{\sum_i^n (A_i)^2} \cdot \sqrt{\sum_i^n (B_i)^2}} \tag{3}$$

where A_i and B_i are the TF-IDF weights of term i in documents A and B, n is the total number of terms in the TF-IDF vectors. This algorithm produces a similarity score between 0 and 1, where 1 indicates perfect similarity, and 0 indicates no similarity. It measures the similarity between the generated descriptions and the target theme, considering factors such as word usage, context, and meaning.

By employing this careful and systematic Description Selection process, the Definition Generator aims to ensure that the final output is not only thematically aligned but also of high quality in terms of language and expression. The chosen description serves as a representative and insightful definition for the given keyword or concept, laying the groundwork for the subsequent Template Application phase.

Algorithm 1

Input: Set of all learning resources (summary) in the segment LR{}
Output: Customized Narrative Fragments
Require: Set of key-phrases K = {K1{}, K2{}, ...} for all learning resources, Dictionary D of all tokens in a learning pathway
    Set each Neighbourhood set N[{}, N2{}, N3{}, ...] to 0;

    foreach keyword k in K do
      Nk ← getNeighbourhood(k);
      intersection-set ← N1 ∩ N2 ∩ N3 ∩ ... ∩ Nn;
      if intersection-set is not null then
        For each term t in intersection-set do
          ranking[] ← getAvgSemanticSimilarity(t, LR{});
        return t with max(ranking[]);
      else
        foreach term1 in N1 ∪ N2 ∪ N3 ∪ ... do
          Lcommon(t) ← number of sets in N having t;
          max-count-keywords ← max(Lcommon);
          if count(max-count-keywords) > 1 then
            foreach term Ik in max-count-keywords do
              Lranking[] ← getAvgSemanticSimilarity(Ik, LR{});
              return Ik with max(Lranking[]);

Function getNeighbourhood(k)
    Input: Dictionary D ← learning pathway tokens
      vectorizeAllTokens(D)
      vectorizeKeyPhrase(k)
      cs = calculateCosineSimilarity(D, k)
      sorted_cs = sortCosineSimilarity(cs)
      selected_tokens = chooseTopTokens(sorted_cs, n)
      N = createNeighbourhood(selected_tokens).
    return N

Function getAvgSemanticSimilarity(c, LR{})
    Input: Candidate token c, Set of learning resources LR{}
      vectorizeCandidateToken(c)
      vectorizeLearningResources(LR{})
      sim = calculateCosineSimilarity(c, Ir)
      simAvg = accumulateSimilarities(sim)
      return simAvg / size(LR{})

Template Application

The Template Application phase is a crucial step where selected descriptions, along with computed metadata, are seamlessly transmitted to the Overview Generator. This collaborative effort results in the discerning choice of suitable templates, intertwining them with the thematic descriptions to create a comprehensive and layered overview.

The descriptions chosen during the Description Selection phase, representing the most relevant and high-quality thematic descriptions for the given keyword or concept, are gathered. Additionally, any computed metadata, which may include additional contextual information or statistical measures related to the descriptions, is also considered. Then, the selected descriptions and computed metadata are transmitted to the Overview Generator, a component of the CNFPRNet designed to handle the aggregation and composition of thematic content into a coherent overview. The Overview Generator engages in a template selection process, choosing appropriate templates based on the nature of the descriptions and the desired structure of the overview. Templates may vary in format, style, and content arrangement to suit the specific requirements of the generated overview. Then, the chosen templates are then seamlessly intertwined with the thematic descriptions. This involves the incorporation of thematic descriptions into predefined sections or placeholders within the selected templates. The goal is to create a cohesive and structured overview that effectively communicates the key concepts and nuances captured in the thematic descriptions.

The final output of the Template Application phase is a comprehensive and layered overview. This overview serves as a succinct yet profound representation of the concepts associated with the given keyword. It maintains clarity, coherence, and information richness, providing a refined output that can be effectively used for knowledge representation and dissemination. By following this Template Application process, the Definition Generator ensures that the generated overview is not only thematically aligned and linguistically refined but also presented in a structured format that enhances understanding and accessibility. The layered overview becomes a valuable resource for conveying precise definitions in a meaningful and organized manner.

4 Experiment Results

4.1 Dataset

In our research, we employed the Wikipedia dataset due to its extensive coverage of various topics and widespread use in education. We specifically opted for the pre-processed Wikipedia dataset tailored for Natural Language Processing (NLP) and Machine Learning (ML) research. This dataset comprises topics along with their summarizations extracted from Wikipedia pages, where the initial sentences function as definitions. The dataset encompasses a total of 5,315,384 data points. To narrow our focus, we selected a subset centered around the Science category, which consists of 200,000 keyword-definition pairs. To facilitate model training and evaluation, the dataset was partitioned into an 85% training set and a 15% test set. It is worth noting that we deliberately refrained from utilizing the entire dataset for training, as expanding the dataset did not yield significant improvements in model performance. The evaluation of both our model and baseline models was conducted using the same set of sampled test data points.

4.2 Implementation

In this study, we leverage the GPT-2 language model, developed by OpenAI, with a specific focus on the medium-sized variant containing 355 million parameters. Referred to as GPT-2 Medium, this model is chosen for its balance between computational efficiency and expressive power. GPT-2 Medium's 355 million parameters enable it to capture intricate linguistic patterns and contextual nuances, making it an ideal candidate for our task of generating personalized educational recommendations. We evaluate our model by comparing it to baseline algorithms such as Attention-Augmented Sequence-to-Sequence Network [22] and Zero-shot evaluation with GPT-2 [23]. For the assessment of our results, we employ ROUGE metrics [24], which serve as the widely accepted standard evaluation measure for tasks akin to ours. ROUGE is a set of metrics used to assess the quality of automatic summarisation and machine translation, mainly to measure the similarity between the generated text and the reference text. The most commonly used of these metrics are ROUGE-N and ROUGE-L, which can help assess the quality and accuracy of the generated text.

$$ROUGE - N = \frac{\sum\limits_{s} \sum\limits_{(n\_gram)} Count_{match}(n\_gram)}{\sum\limits_{s} \sum\limits_{(n\_gram)} Count(n\_gram)} \tag{4}$$

$$ROUGE - L = \frac{\sum\limits_{s} LCS(s, g)}{\sum_{s} |s|} \tag{5}$$

where, s represents the reference summaries, **n-gram** denotes **n** consecutive words, **Count_{match}(n_gram)** denotes the count of matching n-grams between the generated text and the reference summaries, **Count(n_gram)** represents the total count of n-grams in the reference summaries, **LCS(s, g)** denotes the length of the longest common subsequence between the reference summaries and the generated text, and |s| represents the length of the reference summaries. These metrics can help assess the similarity between generated summaries or translations and reference summaries or translations, thus providing a quantitative way to measure the quality and accuracy of automatically generated texts.

4.3 Results

Table 3 unveils the results gleaned from meticulous scrutiny of the test set, offering insights into the performance of both our model and its contextual variant juxtaposed against baseline models. The discerning gaze upon the tabulated data exposes a notable ascendancy in ROUGE scores for both our model and its nuanced counterpart when juxtaposed with their baseline counterparts. Particularly intriguing is the revelation that the context-based input variant manifests a marginal yet discernible augmentation in ROUGE-1 scores, underscoring the nuanced impact of contextual information on the model's linguistic proficiency.

Remarkably, as shown in Table 3, our model maintains parity in ROUGE-2 and ROUGE-L scores, exhibiting consistency to the second decimal place, irrespective of the contextual inclusivity in the input data. This uniformity prompts thoughtful conjecture, leading us to postulate that our model, honed through training in a familiar domain, flexes its linguistic prowess with comparable efficacy on the hitherto uncharted terrain of the test set, irrespective of contextual nuances. However, the strategic incorporation of contextual

Table 3. ROUGE scores averaged across different models on the test set

Model	R-1	R-2	R-L
Sequence to Sequence Network with Attention	0.1947	0.2071	0.1923
Zero-shot evaluation with GPT-2	0.1963	0.0946	0.1762
CNFPRNet	0.2314	0.2328	0.2532
CNFPRNet(with input context)	0.2569	0.2320	0.2508
Model	R-1	R-2	R-L
Sequence to Sequence Network with Attention	0.1947	0.2071	0.1923

information emerges as a prospective catalyst for enhanced inferential acuity, especially in the uncharted expanse of an entirely novel domain. The equipoise in performance underscores the adaptability and robustness of our model, while the subtle divergence in the context-enhanced variant hints at the untapped potential for heightened linguistic acumen in unexplored linguistic landscapes. This nuanced interplay between training domain familiarity and contextual enrichment opens avenues for further exploration, paving the way for more informed and sophisticated natural language processing in diverse linguistic ecosystems.

Moreover, we aimed to gauge the evaluative responses of 40 participants regarding the quality and effectiveness of Customized Narrative Fragments. The 40 participants was divided into two distinct groups, each exposed to different sets of Customized Narrative Fragments. The experimental design involved posing a series of targeted questions to the participants, addressing key facets such as correctness, grammatical accuracy, and overall meaningfulness of the Customized Narrative Fragments. The resulting dataset, comprising responses from the 40 evaluators, was meticulously tabulated and subjected to rigorous statistical analysis.

Q1: Does the Customized Narrative Fragments correctly represent the learning resources?

Q2: Is the Customized Narrative Fragments grammatically correct?

Q3: Is the Customized Narrative Fragments meaningful?

Q4: Does the Customized Narrative Fragments effectively convey the key information?

Q5: Are the Customized Narrative Fragments coherent and logically structured? (Fig. 2)

Upon thorough analysis of the aggregated results, a compelling and consistent trend has surfaced. A substantial majority, surpassing the 70% threshold in every instance, provided affirmative responses, As well as the percentage of almost all responses that are not no's are up and down at 90% signifying a unanimous consensus among participants regarding the favorable attributes of the narrative fragments. Specifically, the commendable evaluations for correctness, grammatical accuracy, and meaningfulness associated with the Customized Narrative Fragments generated by CNFPRNet underscore the model's proficiency in discerning and synthesizing pertinent information tailored to individual preferences and learning profiles. This personalized approach not

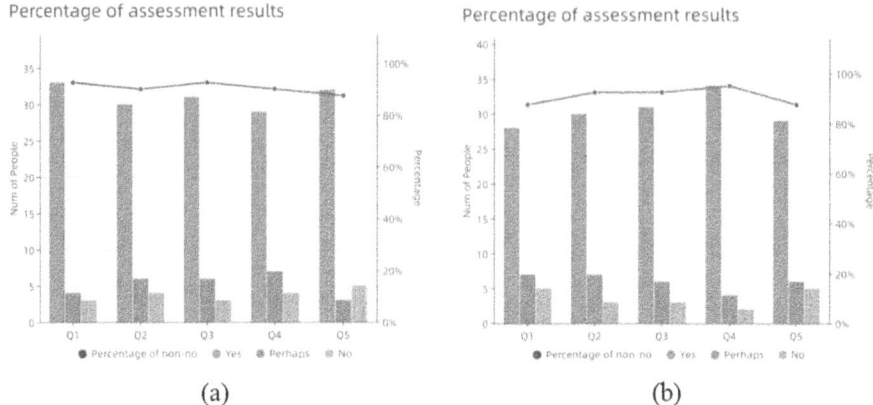

Fig. 2. Experimental results (a) Assessment results for the first 20 participants and (b) Assessment results for the last 20 participants.

only ensures the delivery of precise content but also enhances the overall engagement and efficacy of the learning experience. These experimental findings offer empirical validation for the proposition that CNFPRNet plays a pivotal role in enhancing the quality of personalized education. The model's adaptive nature, as demonstrated by consistent performance across diverse testing conditions, positions it as a robust tool for tailoring educational recommendations in both familiar and novel domains. The results encapsulate the intrinsic significance of CNFPRNet in advancing the frontier of personalized education, providing insight into its potential transformative impact on how educational content is curated and delivered to individual learners.

4.4 Establishing the Threshold for Accepting Definitions

To establish the threshold for accepting the definition, we conducted experiments using both the Multi-Genre Natural Language Inference (MultiNLI) dataset [25] and the Stanford Natural Language Inference (SNLI) dataset [26]. The two datasets, containing sentence pairs from various genres labeled as entailment, neutrality, and contradiction, proved ideal for evaluating the model's ability to assess semantic similarity. In Table 4, we provide instances illustrating each of the three sentence pair categories, drawing examples from the MultiNLI dataset.

To address this, we assess semantic similarity among sentence pairs employing both ELMo and GloVe-based sentence embedding techniques. ELMo, a contextualized word representation model, captures nuanced semantic nuances by considering word context. On the other hand, GloVe offers a global perspective on word meanings through pretrained word vectors derived from large-scale text corpora.

Table 5 unfolds the nuanced tale of semantic similarity scores, revealing the outcome of deploying two distinct sentence embedding methodologies-ELMo and GloVe-on sentence pairs meticulously reviewed by human evaluators. A discerning prowess in distinguishing between diverse sentence types is evident in both embedding techniques.

Table 4. Examples of the MultiNLI dataset

Type	Sentence 1	Sentence 2
Entailment	A black dog is running across the street.	A dog with dark fur is sprinting down the road.
Neutral	The cat is sitting on the windowsill.	A feline is perched by the window.
Contradiction	The sun is setting behind the mountains.	It's dawn and the sun is rising over the hills.
Type	Sentence 1	Sentence 2
Entailment	A black dog is running across the street.	A dog with dark fur is sprinting down the road.
Neutral	The cat is sitting on the windowsill.	A feline is perched by the window.

Table 5. Determining Semantic Similarity Threshold

Type	ELMo		GloVe		Type	ELMo		GloVe	
	MultiNLI	SNLI	MultiNLI	SNLI		MultiNLI	SNLI	MultiNLI	SNLI
Entailment	0.6212	0.5933	0.5717	0.5381	Entailment	0.6212	0.5933	0.5717	0.5381
Neutral	0.5802	0.5501	0.5604	0.5203	Neutral	0.5802	0.5501	0.5604	0.5203
Contradiction	**0.4371**	0.4037	0.3943	0.3619	Contradiction	**0.4371**	0.4037	0.3943	0.3619
Type	ELMo		GloVe		Type	ELMo		GloVe	
	MultiNLI	SNLI	MultiNLI	SNLI		MultiNLI	SNLI	MultiNLI	SNLI

Significantly, ELMo and GloVe showcase this discriminatory acumen, with GloVe offering a more pronounced distinction, especially in its application to the MultiNLI dataset. Consequently, we have chosen to leverage GloVe for our definition selection endeavor.

In the quest to establish a definition acceptance threshold, a thorough examination of semantic similarity scores led us to identify a threshold that not only surpasses the average Contradiction score but also elegantly approaches or exceeds the scores associated with Neutrality. To enhance clarity, we have boldly presented this threshold in Table 5, showcasing its seamless alignment with the Contradiction column in the MultiNLI dataset. By rounding off this threshold value, we now possess a definitive criterion for the selection of definitions. This strategic approach ensures a robust and finely nuanced determination of semantic similarity, highlighting the model's adeptness in distinguishing conflicting statements and those leaning towards neutrality or entailment relationships.

The results of this experiment have provided valuable guidance and optimization for the overall model. By determining the semantic similarity threshold required to accept generated definitions, we can improve the accuracy and efficiency of the model. This helps to filter out irrelevant or low-quality definitions, thereby enhancing the quality of the final generated content. Furthermore, the analysis incorporating the SNLI dataset and the MultiNLI dataset have validated the model's performance in a broader semantic context, enhancing its robustness and reliability. Therefore, the results of this experiment provide important support and guidance for improving and optimizing the performance of our natural language generation model.

5 Conclusion

In this research, we introduced CNFPRNet, a comprehensive framework with semantic models for automatically generating extra learning content and enhancing pathways. Our focus was on creating interactive pathways aligning with traditional narrative expectations. The Conceptual Definition Extractor model, designed for generating definitions based on keywords, showed promising results in evaluations. Comparative assessments demonstrated its effective generalization across diverse domains. Human evaluations of the automatically generated learning content were positive, assessing quality and relevance within pathways. Notably, evaluations were conducted in a controlled setting, with recognition of the need for future assessments in real-time or classroom environments.

Moving forward, our research aims to evaluate the effectiveness of automatically generated learning content in real-world scenarios, such as classrooms. Additionally, we plan to measure increased engagement facilitated by our augmented learning pathways. Despite imperfections in our prototype, our findings emphasize the significant potential of systems like CNFPRNet as content generators for creating engaging learning experiences. These systems lay the foundation for developing learning environments that efficiently use open learning resources. Our exploration marks a substantial step towards shaping the future of education through innovative content generation.

Acknowledgement. The work was supported by the Fundamental Research Funds for Yunnan Provincial Key Laboratory of Wisdom Education Open Fund Key Subjects (YNSE2024B001) and the Construction of Experimental Platform for Artificial Intelligence Specialization for Industry-Teaching Integration(231107612172327).

References

1. Renz, A., Hilbig, R.: Prerequisites for artificial intelligence in further education: Identification of drivers, barriers, and business models of educational technology companies. Int. J. Educ. Technol. High. Educ. **17**(1), 1–21 (2020)
2. Hashim, S., Omar, M.K., Ab Jalil, H., et al.: Trends on technologies and artificial intelligence in education for personalized learning: systematic literature. J. Acad. Res. Progressive Educ. Dev. **12**(1), 884–903 (2022)
3. Korkmaz, C., Correia, A.P.: A review of research on machine learning in educational technology. Educ. Media Int. **56**(3), 250–267 (2019)
4. Bachiri, Y.A., Mouncif, H.: Artificial intelligence system in aid of pedagogical engineering for knowledge assessment on MOOC platforms: open EdX and moodle. Int. J. Emerg. Technol. Learn. (Online) **18**(5), 144 (2023)
5. Fan, A., Gokkaya, B., Harman, M., et al.: Large language models for software engineering: Survey and open problems. arXiv preprint arXiv:2310.03533 (2023)

6. Shemshack, A., Spector, J.M.: A systematic literature review of personalized learning terms. Smart Learn. Environ. **7**(1), 1–20 (2020)
7. Pedro, F., Subosa, M., Rivas, A., et al.: Artificial intelligence in education: challenges and opportunities for sustainable development (2019)
8. Al, D.A.: Acceptance of artificial intelligence in teaching science: science teachers' perspective. Comput. Educ. Artif. Intell. **4**, 100132 (2023)
9. Foffano, F., Scantamburlo, T., Cortés, A.: Investing in AI for social good: an analysis of European national strategies. AI & Soc. **38**(2), 479–500 (2023)
10. Grassini, S.: Shaping the future of education: exploring the potential and consequences of AI and ChatGPT in educational settings. Educ. Sci. **13**(7), 692 (2023)
11. Chen, Z.: Artificial intelligence-virtual trainer: innovative didactics aimed at personalized training needs. J. Knowl. Econ. **14**(2), 2007–2025 (2023)
12. Boughanem, H., Ghazouani, H., Barhoumi, W.: Facial emotion recognition in-the-wild using deep neural networks: a comprehensive review. SN Comput. Sci. **5**(1), 1–28 (2024)
13. Chen, Y., Li, X., Liu, J., et al.: Recommendation system for adaptive learning. Appl. Psychol. Meas. **42**(1), 24–41 (2018)
14. Embarak, O.: Towards an adaptive education through a machine learning recommendation system. In: 2021 International Conference on Artificial Intelligence in Information and Communication (ICAIIC), pp. 187–192. IEEE (2021)
15. Bian, C.L., Wang, D.L., Liu, S.Y., et al.: Adaptive learning path recommendation based on graph theory and an improved immune algorithm. KSII Trans. Internet Inf. Syst. (TIIS) **13**(5), 2277–2298 (2019)
16. Gao, M., Xing, J., Yin, C., et al.: Personalized recommendation method for English teaching resources based on artificial intelligence technology. J. Phys. Conf. Ser. IOP Publishing **1757**(1), 012104 (2021)
17. Wei, X., Sun, S., Wu, D., et al.: Personalized online learning resource recommendation based on artificial intelligence and educational psychology. Front. Psychol. **12**, 767837 (2021)
18. Zheng, F.: Personalized education based on hybrid intelligent recommendation system. J. Math. **2022**, 1–9 (2022)
19. Neethirajan, S.: Artificial intelligence and sensor innovations: enhancing livestock welfare with a human-centric approach. Hum.-Centric Intell. Syst. 1–16 (2023)
20. Aizawa, A.: An information-theoretic perspective of TF–IDF measures. Inf. Process. Manage. **39**(1), 45–65 (2003)
21. Rahutomo, F., Kitasuka, T., Aritsugi, M.: Semantic cosine similarity. In: The 7th International Student Conference on Advanced Science and Technology ICAST, vol. 4, no. 1, p. 1 (2012)
22. Cho, K., Courville, A., Bengio, Y.: Describing multimedia content using attention-based encoder-decoder networks. IEEE Trans. Multimedia **17**(11), 1875–1886 (2015)
23. Radford, A., Wu, J., Child, R., et al.: Language models are unsupervised multitask learners. OpenAI blog **1**(8), 9 (2019)
24. Lin, C.Y.: Rouge: a package for automatic evaluation of summaries. Text Summarization Branches Out, 74–81 (2004)
25. Cheng, I., Harris, W.: Deep Learning for Natural Language Inference
26. Choi, H., Kim, J., Joe, S., et al.: Evaluation of bert and albert sentence embedding performance on downstream NLP tasks. In: 2020 25th International Conference on Pattern Recognition (ICPR), pp. 5482–5487. IEEE (2021)

Research on Intelligent Guide Glasses Based on Multi Algorithm Fusion

Shiyue Zhang, Huijun Zhan, and Yanqing Wang$^{(\boxtimes)}$

Nanjing Xiaozhuang University, Nanjing Jiangsu 211171, China
wyq0325@126.com

Abstract. According to the survey data, most of the blind people encounter accidents when they go out alone, and in order to build a good atmosphere for the construction of a barrier-free environment, the state has issued relevant laws and regulations to help the visually impaired participate in and integrate into social life equally, fully and conveniently. In this context, this project researches and designs smart guide glasses based on CV and 5G and sound coding mapping technology, providing safer and more considerate services for the blind and helping the visually impaired to "see" the wonderful world. Because the blind can not get the environmental information, so the use of cameras to obtain environmental information, we mainly use the low latency, large bandwidth and slicing technology of 5G to provide exclusive network guarantee for the guide glasses, to create an intelligent visual assistance system, the use of CV (computer vision) to detect and identify the basic travel environment such as blind roads and zebra crossings, when the glasses obtain environmental data, special three-dimensional stereoscopic voice coding will be carried out, and different visual information (such as the type of obstacles, Directions and distances, etc.) are mapped one by one with different sounds or different rhythms to convey sound information to the blind.

Keywords: Intelligent guide glasses · balanced development of education · CV+5G · computer vision · binocular parallax · ultrasonic ranging · YOLOv5+conLSTM

1 Introduction

According to data from the China Disabled Persons' Federation, there are approximately 12.63 million visually impaired people in China, making it the largest blind population worldwide. However, in China, visually impaired and assistive device companies have long been dominated by low-tech and low-growth enterprises. The "Guidelines for Basic Assistive Devices for Persons with Disabilities (2020 Edition)" refers to visual aids for the visually impaired, limited to magnifying glasses, low vision eyes, electronic visual aids, etc., presenting low technological added value characteristics. The intelligent products that can be used by the blind population are extremely scarce, and there are few related independent intellectual property rights.

From a foreign perspective, although there are similar intelligent guide devices, the cost is too high, and the possibility of introducing them into China is not very high and

K. Zhang et al. (Eds.): CSEI 2024, CCIS 2448, pp. 266–281, 2025.
https://doi.org/10.1007/978-981-96-3738-6_20

is almost negligible. The market for smart guide devices is still a blank and smart guide glasses have the huge advantage in this market gap. They can quickly occupy the market, and the industry competition pressure is not particularly high.

According to the "Basic Information Survey of Visually Impaired People" released by Time Data, 30% of visually impaired people do not go out; 46% of visually impaired individuals go out every week and need to be accompanied by family and friends; and only 24% of visually impaired individuals go out weekly and do not require accompaniment. With the development of society and progress in medicine, the demand for vision restoration and visually impaired assistive technology is becoming increasingly strong. It is urgent to utilize the latest scientific knowledge and equipment to research new rehabilitation and assistive technologies and devices. How to help visually impaired people achieve a life close to that of ordinary people? How to enable visually impaired individuals to travel with dignity?

The construction of a barrier-free environment is an important symbol of the progress of social civilization. On June 28, 2023, the approval of the Law of the People's Republic of China on the Construction of a Barrier-free Environment aimed to promote the construction of a barrier-free environment with the power of the rule of law. Over the past year, the concept of accessible humanities, civilization awareness, and rule of law construction have gradually deepened and become intertwined with the field of special education, attracting attention from as a whole [1]. In order to promote the joint construction, governance, and sharing of an accessible environment by academic research in the field of accessibility, and assist in the inclusive development of special education, this article studies intelligent guide glasses based on multi-algorithm fusion, which can provide a lot of help for visually impaired people and safeguard them. At the same time, it is very portable, which can free the hands of visually impaired people and is not easy to lose, making it the most convenient and reliable for daily carrying. By designing this intelligent guide glasses based on CV and 5G, it can maximize the improvement of the quality of life for blind people, allowing them to live a more dignified life. It is committed to solving the problems of blind people's lives and helping them see the world. We create an intelligent visual assistance system through 5G low latency and high bandwidth, using 5G slicing technology to provide exclusive network support for guide glasses. Together, we take on the task of analyzing and solving pain points to provide them with more care and help more visually impaired people return to normal life.

2   Research on Intelligent Guide Glasses Based on CV+5G

This article designs intelligent guide glasses based on CV+5G+sound encoding mapping technology, providing more safe and thoughtful services for the special group of blind people, helping them "see" the wonderful world.

Due to the inability of blind people to obtain environmental information, cameras are used to obtain environmental information. We mainly use the low latency, high bandwidth, and slicing technology of 5G to provide exclusive network support for guide glasses, and create an intelligent visual assistance system. Guide glasses use cloud and edge APIs to achieve the use of deep learning to transmit real-time images obtained by smart glasses cameras to the edge for computing travel through the 5G network. By dispersing the complex image processing functions in visual assistance to the edge of the network, leveraging the high-speed and stable 5G network and powerful edge cloud processing capabilities, the computing processing latency is greatly improved and the weight of the terminal is reduced:

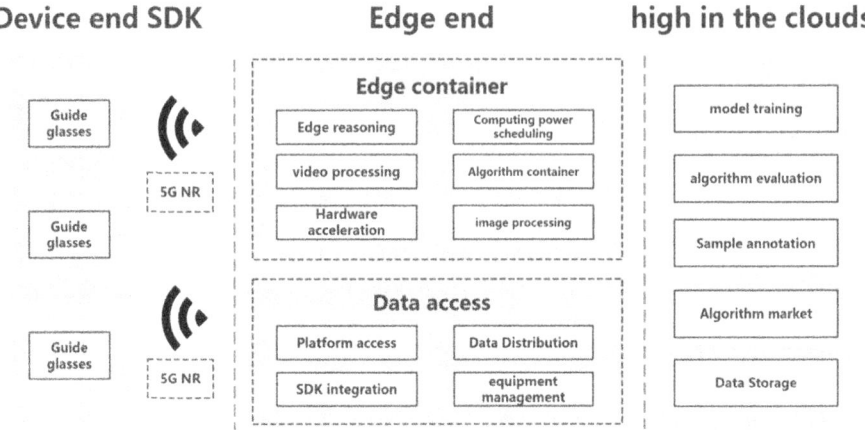

Fig. 1. Architecture diagram of guide glasses

At the same time, CV (computer vision) is used to detect and identify basic travel environments such as tactile paving and zebra crossing. Three cameras are used for glasses, as shown in Fig. 2. One is a regular color camera, which is mainly used to capture environmental information and for image recognition in the later stage. There are also two depth cameras with visible light and infrared night vision functions, which can use the principles of binocular disparity and ultrasound to measure the distance between the object in front and the user. A binocular distance measurement visual system is built to avoid visual obstacles, and voice reminders and fall alarms are implemented through headphones, ensuring the safety of blind people in all aspects.

Based on infrared binocular cameras, large-scale stereo matching is performed with the assistance of natural light and structured light to obtain dense depth maps. Using the mean shift algorithm calculate the distance, direction, and size of the nearest obstacles and map them to stereo sound. Blind people can achieve obstacle avoidance based on the sound they hear.

Based on the reflection and reception of light, the distance is calculated by emitting infrared radiation, receiving infrared radiation, and calculating the time difference. Given that the speed of light is $3 \times 10 \wedge 8$ m per second, the distance is equal to

$$\text{speed of light} \times \text{time difference} /2 \tag{1}$$

The one-stage detection algorithm significantly enhances the detection rate due to its end-to-end characteristics. The key of the algorithm is to directly extract the features of the input image through the backbone network, and then directly obtain the location and relevant information of the target, such as YOLO series, RetinaNet, SSD, etc. Redmon

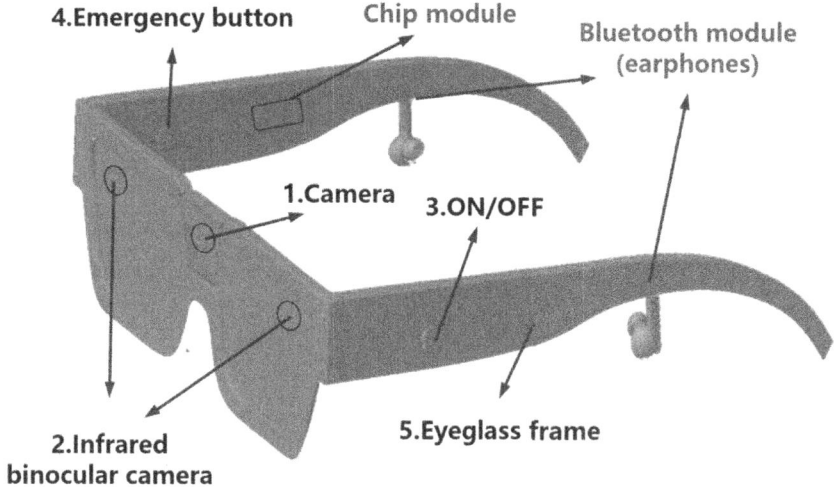

Fig. 2. Diagram of Guide Glasses

et al.[2] have developed the innovative YOLO algorithm, which is the first of the YOLO series. YOLOv1's unique network architecture design, turns the object detection problem into a regression problem, thus achieving an efficient object detection rate.

In 2020, Ultralytics LLC released the open source code for YOLOv5, which has a similar infrastructure to YOLOv4 [3] but provides stronger scalability. In order to meet different memory requirements, YOLOv5 has built five different versions of the model, namely YOLOv5-N/S/M/L/X.

The figure below shows the main structure of Yolov5. Among them, the backbone network extracts features from the input image; the hub component fuses or combines these features to produce more complex and rich feature representations.

Ultimately, the head component uses these features to make predictions, generate detection frames, and predict the kind of target (Fig. 3 and Fig. 4).

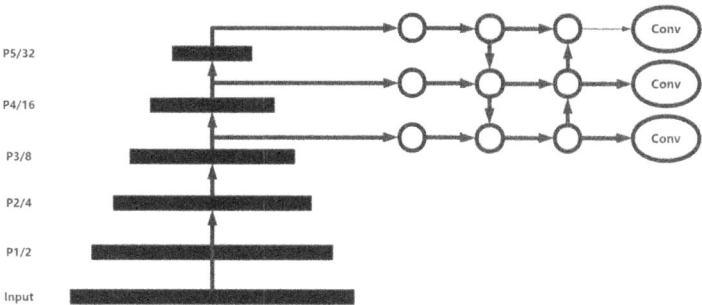

Fig. 3. YOLOv5 Structure Diagram

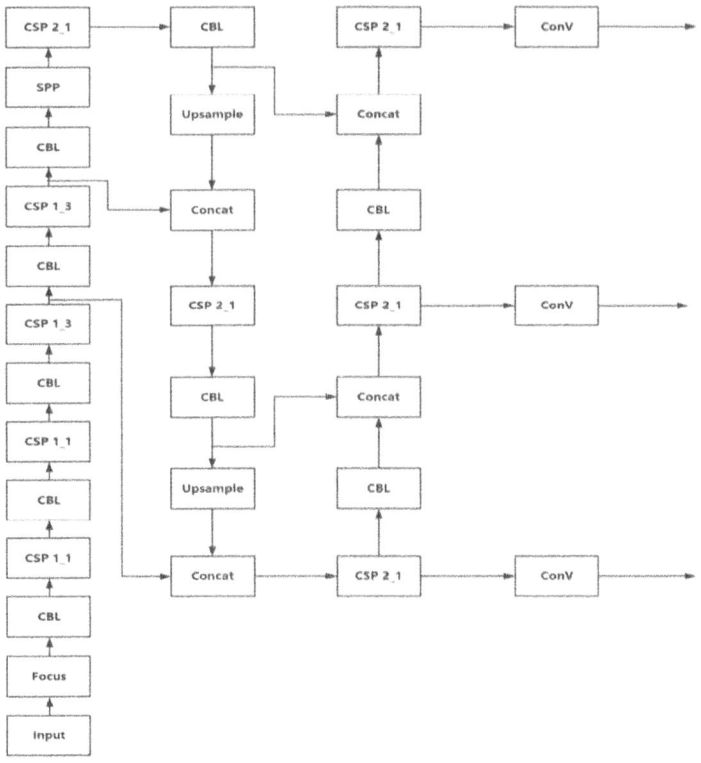

Fig. 4. YOLOv5 Specific Module Diagram

The specific module diagram of YOLOv5 is shown in the figure above. The YOLOv5 network specifically includes modules such as CBL, Focus, CSP1_x, CSP2_x, and SPP. YOLOv5 extracts 5 feature layers through the backbone network, F1, F2, F3, F4, F5. Among them, F3, F4, and F5 extract rich feature information. Pass these three layers to the neck for further feature extraction. The neck of YOLOv5 completes feature fusion, combining different levels of semantic information and using FPN+PAN structure. Its structure was proposed in YOLOv4 [4], which upsamples high-level features and fuses low-level information. In order to better utilize data and avoid overfitting, YOLOv5 uses data augmentation methods so that the network can learn more features from an enhanced image. There are many data augmentation strategies that can be used in this model, including Mosaic augmentation, MixUp image blurring, etc. The loss function defined by YOLOv5 consists of three main components. YOLOv5 has two optimization algorithms to choose from, namely, SGD and Adam, with the Adam optimization algorithm being used by default. SGD has problems such as slow descent speed, frequent fluctuations, and difficulty in stable convergence. However, compared to standard gradient descent, it has the potential to obtain better convergence results and is often used in online learning. Adam is an adaptive learning rate optimization algorithm that performs better in practice, converges faster, and is more effective compared to other adaptive learning algorithms [5].

In 2020, the Google brain team proposed the EfficientDet object detection series model [6]. Its backbone network is EfficientNet [7], a framework series with advantages such as fast and high precision, and excellent performance. The EfficientNet feature extraction network completes preliminary feature extraction and has excellent feature extraction capabilities. As a first stage network, the EfficientDet series network completes information extraction through the backbone network, and innovatively proposes the Enhanced Feature Extraction Module (BiFPN) at the neck to extract enhanced features. Finally, at the head, integrate the features to achieve object detection.

Using EfficientNet as the backbone of the EfficientNet network, 7 feature layers, P1-P7, were extracted through multiple downsampling. Among them, P1 and P2 do not have rich semantic information due to insufficient downsampling. The P3, P4, and P5 layers have undergone more downsampling to complete the preliminary extraction of the feature extraction network. P6 and P7 have high semantic information.

YOLOv5 controls the number of different channels to achieve version networks that occupy different memory sizes. The EfficientNet series adopts the method of Composite Scaling, which unifies controllable parameters into a defined parameter and achieves a series of networks by controlling the size of the parameter. Unify the depth, width, and resolution parameters into the same defined scaling parameter, and achieve dynamic control and adjustment of the three through control. Through composite scaling, the EfficientNet series can be extended to achieve higher accuracy and compressed to effectively save computational resources. The default optimizer for EfficientDet network is SDG. The EfficientDet network proposes using the Fast Normalized Fusion method instead of the Softmax normalization method, which results in faster computation (Fig. 5).

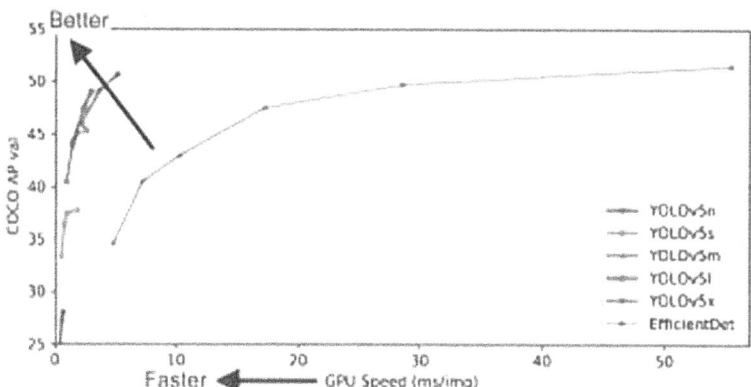

Fig. 5. Different model metrics on the COCO dataset

EfficientDet and YOLOv5, as object detection models, have better performance in small object detection compared to other detection models. The COCO dataset is rich in small targets. The figure above shows the average AP value obtained by training multiple network models with IoU and step size changes. Compared to EfficientDet, YOLOv5 achieves the same AP with faster computation speed. The deeper and wider versions of

YOLOv5 network have higher AP values. In order to balance accuracy and algorithm running speed, we chose YOLOv5 for obstacle detection and recognition.

Among them, we use computer graphics (or deep learning) methods to analyze the image, identify several regions where objects may exist (first look), crop these regions, and put them into an image classifier for classification (second look). Divide the image into a $\times$ a grids, generate bounding boxes based on the grids. The task of the grid is to predict what category the objects in this box will be. The categories are represented by one hot encoding (i.e. each category corresponds to one or more registers, and 0/1 is used to identify whether the target belongs to this category, and each target can only have one category). It can be seen that there are indeed two bounding boxes in each box, some of which have thicker borders and some have thinner borders. This is a manifestation of different confidence levels, with higher confidence levels being thicker and lower confidence levels being thinner. Using a Non Maximum Suppression (NMS) technique based on intersection to union ratio, confidence is used to predict how confident an object is in the box. The object with the highest confidence is selected, and the rest is deleted, i.e., confidence is used for maximum suppression. According to the position of the box, sort and output the number of obstacles and the number of different areas three regions: far, medium, and near.

Meanwhile, we combined the convLSTM model to indicate the obstacle position based on the temporal order. We discovered the working principles of the fully connected layer and the global average pooling layer through research, and found that in the fully connected layer, the convolutional layer was unfolded into a vector, and the classification for each feature map was completed in two steps. However, for the global average pooling layer, these two steps were combined into one. This can provide a more intuitive explanation of the true meaning of the global average pooling layer, which is to perform regularization operations on the entire network structure, with the goal of preventing overfitting. Furthermore, the global average pooling layer eliminates the black box features of the fully connected layer and directly assigns actual meaning to each channel. The experiment also compared the Accuracy value, and in terms of accuracy, the ConvLSTM network based on the global average pooling layer was slightly higher than the ConvLSTM network based on the fully connected layer, with accuracy generally above 90%, so we improved it to the ConvLSTM network based on the global average pooling layer.

To continuously improve the model's performance and stability, we can integrate YOLOv8+convLSTM based on deep learning image classification models to achieve visual obstacle avoidance + voice reminder + fall alarm functions. In obstacle avoidance, we mainly focus on whether an object is moving quickly, so inputting the difference between frames is better, which will also reduce the calculation volume. Therefore, when identifying items, first perform frame difference processing on consecutive two frames of images to obtain the instantaneous motion target picture in the video, then use the DarkNet-53 network to extract features from this picture, and finally input each moment's feature into the improved GAP-based ConvLSTM network to model a video sequence. Finally, through the built-in video detection model, we perform item recognition and classification, as shown in Fig. 6.

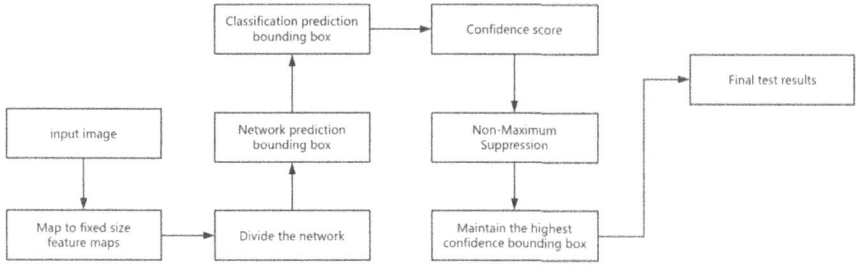

Fig. 6. YOLO+LSTM obstacle recognition

Therefore, we can design a pair of guide glasses with obstacle and object recognition functions based on infrared binocular cameras and target detection algorithms, a zebra crossing detection function based on YOLOv5 and LSTM, a red light detection function based on color extraction, machine learning, and YOLOv5, precise positioning and navigation function, fall warning function, and a yet-to-be-developed face recognition function.

Due to the inability of blind people to see, the three-dimensional information of the environment that can be obtained through cameras must be transmitted to users through methods other than visual perception. The form we adopt is sound. After glasses obtain environmental data, special three-dimensional speech encoding is performed to map different visual information (such as the type, orientation, and distance of obstacles) with different sounds or rhythms, and transmit the sound information to the blind. Through continuous learning and experience, the blind will judge the information of the surrounding environment based on the received sound, and transform the image information into sound information, ultimately achieving the goal of "seeing" the world.

3   Experimental Analysis

3.1   Gesture Processing

The YOLO based pedestrian crossing detection algorithm is used for blind people to find and locate pedestrian crossings at traffic intersections. Train the YOLO model with zebra crossings and preprocess the images, including adjusting brightness, contrast, denoising, etc., to improve the effectiveness of zebra crossing detection. Analyze the output of the target algorithm to obtain the specific location of the zebra crossing. At the same time, determine whether the current zebra crossing is suitable for traffic or whether the current time point is suitable for walking by checking whether there are pedestrians and vehicles around the zebra crossing and the traffic lights next to the road, and convert it into voice prompt information to output to the user. After training on 1000 images, we obtained the data results shown in Figs. 7, 8, and 9:

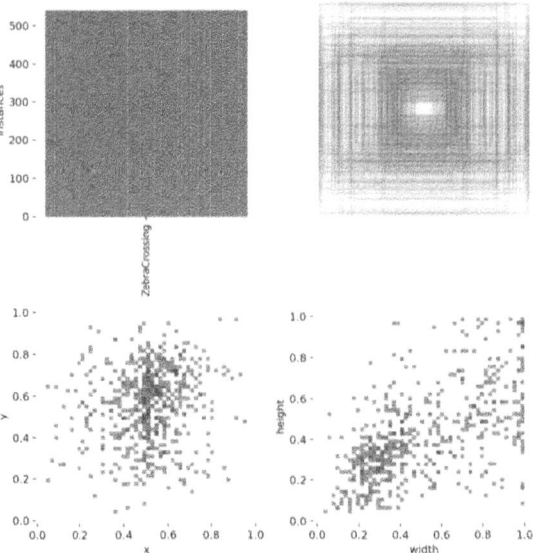

Fig. 7. Training data situation chart

Annotation: Fig. 1: Left one: data volume for each category, right one: bounding'box of labels, left two: center point coordinates of labels, right two: width and height of labels matrix;

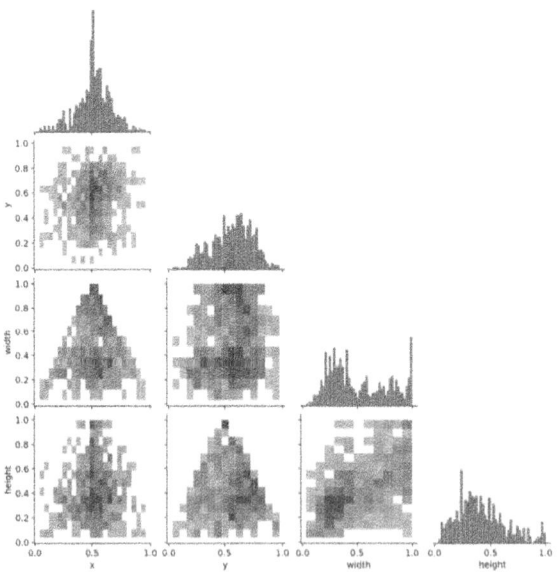

Fig. 8. The situation of annotating data x,y,w,h

Annotation: x, y, w, h are the center of the labels, the width and height of the array. On the top diagonal: their respective distribution histograms. Other positions: their distribution between each other;

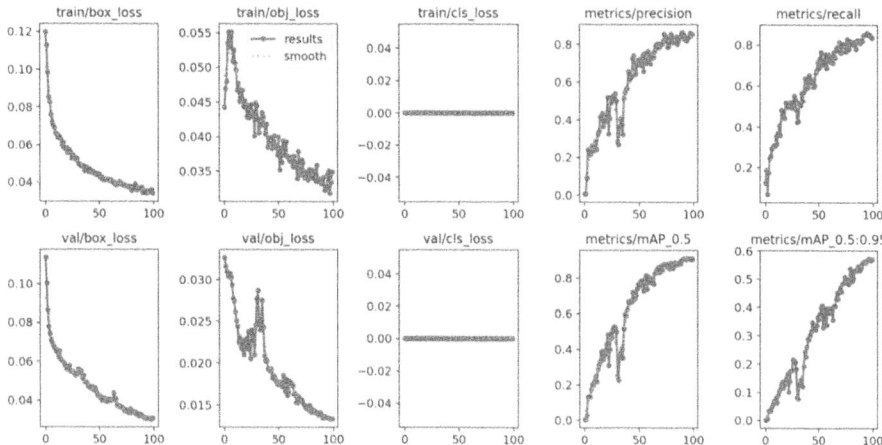

Fig. 9. Process data during training

After the above training analysis, we obtained the results. We used the weight file obtained from the training to recognize two sample images, selecting the front view and top view. The recognition results are shown in Figs. 10, 11.

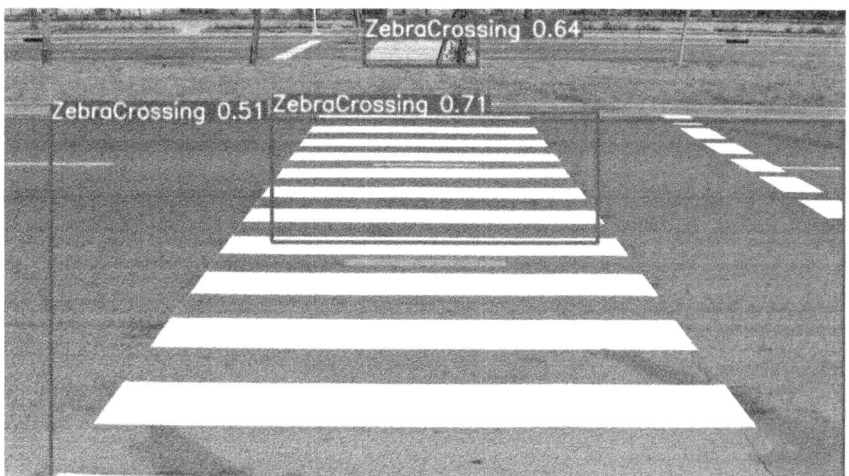

Fig. 10. Test recognition image

Fig. 11. Test recognition image

3.2 Traffic Light Detection

A pedestrian traffic light detection algorithm based on color extraction and machine learning can accurately detect the position of traffic lights in images in real time and provide the status of traffic lights. The corresponding color rectangle of the traffic light is selected as the detection result, and then the recognition result is transmitted to the user in an audible manner.

Realize the recognition of traffic lights through six steps:

Firstly, obtain images or videos of traffic scenes through image acquisition. In actual use, we will use a camera to capture real-time images. Subsequently, image preprocessing is performed to improve the effectiveness of traffic light detection. This may include adjusting the light intensity and contrast of the picture, denoising, and applying color space transformations. Then, using YOLOv5 object detection, traffic signals in the image are detected using YOLOv5 or other object detection algorithms. When training the YOLOv5 model, it is necessary to use an image dataset containing traffic lights for training, so that the model can recognize traffic lights in different states (red, green, yellow). Furthermore, processing the detection results, the output of the object detection algorithm, obtaining the location, category, and possible status information of traffic signals. This may require defining some rules or using a state machine to determine the current state of traffic lights (red, green, yellow). Next, conduct a state continuity assessment. For the determination of traffic light status, it may be necessary to consider the detection results of several consecutive frames of images to reduce the false detection rate. For example, traffic lights are considered green only when green lights are detected on multiple consecutive frames. Finally, output the results. The judged traffic light status, issue corresponding voice prompts to the blind. In order to further boost the performance of the pattern, we adopts two effective methods in data augmentation strategy: Mosaic augmentation [8] and Copy_maste operation [9]. Mosaic enhancement involves slicing four images and randomly concatenating them into a new training image. This strategy not only enriches the background information of the images, but also helps boost the performance of small target. Specifically, it increases the frequency of small targets appearing in the image and promotes the learning of small targets through the contraction of large targets. On the other hand, the Copy_maste operation focuses on enhancing the model's recognition ability by pasting more small targets (such as traffic lights) on the image. Considering the poor detection performance of traffic lights in complex backgrounds such as trees, buildings, and elevated bridges, this strategy helps to distinguish traffic lights from the background more effectively, thereby significantly improving the performance of small object detection models [10].

After training on 1000 images, we obtained the data results shown in Figs. 12, 13, and 14:

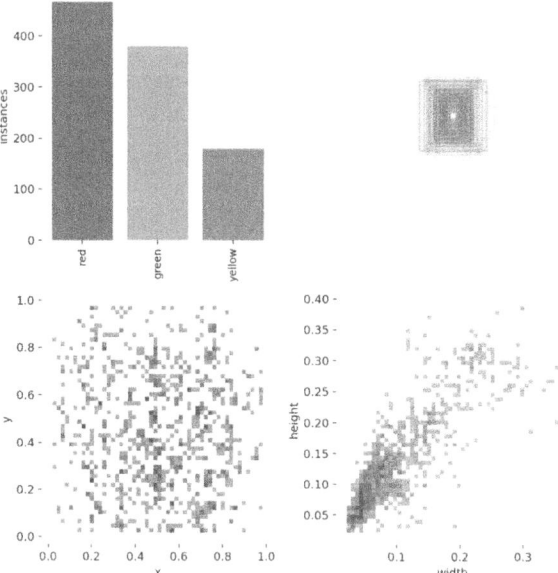

Fig. 12. Training data situation chart

Annotation: Fig. 1: Left one: data volume for each category, right one: bounding'box of labels, left two: center point coordinates of labels, right two: width and height of labels matrix;

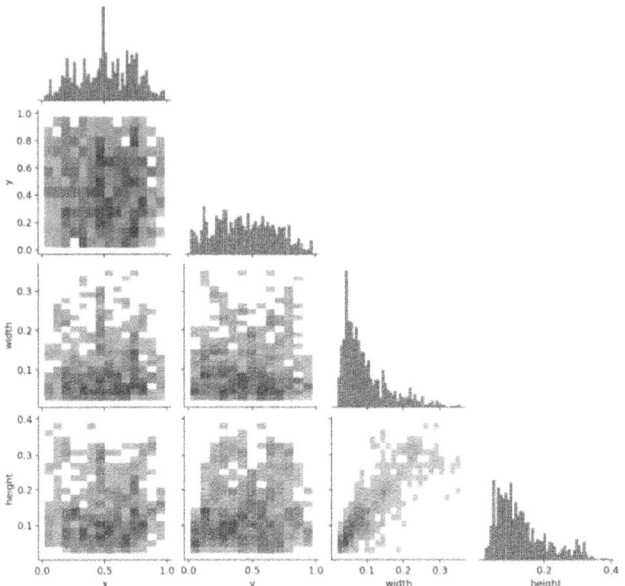

Fig. 13. The situation of annotating data x, y, w, h

Annotation: x, y, w, h are the center of the labels, the width and height of the array. On the top diagonal: their respective distribution histograms. Other positions: their distribution between each other;

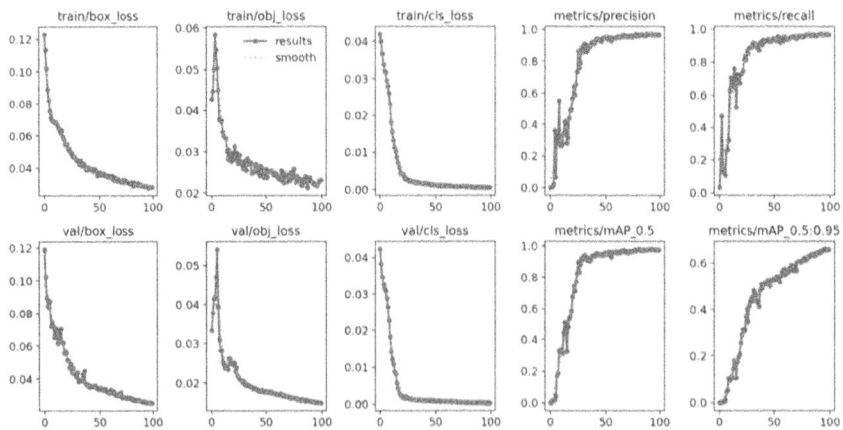

Fig.14. Process data during training

Based on the analysis of the above results, we used the weight files obtained from training to recognize two sample images. The recognition results are shown in Figs. 15 and 16.

Fig. 15. Test recognition image

Fig. 16. Test recognition image

We selected photos from different time periods for testing to determine whether light has a significant impact on the recognition of traffic lights (red, green, yellow). Through on-site sampling, we found that light has little effect on traffic light recognition, greatly improving the safety of blind people crossing the road, as shown in Fig. 17 and 18.

4   Summarize

This article uses CV+5G+sound encoding mapping technology to install an intelligent visual assistance system, combined with binocular disparity and ultrasound to build a binocular distance measurement visual system. YOLOv5 and LSTM time series prediction models are used to achieve visual obstacle avoidance, voice reminder, and fall alarm functions, fully ensuring the safety of blind people. Intelligent guide glasses can be applied in the following scenarios:

City streets and roads: Guide glasses can help visually impaired people walk safely on city streets and roads by providing information about streets, vehicles, pedestrians, and other obstacles.

Public places and buildings: Guide glasses can provide information about public places and buildings, such as entrances, exits, stairs, elevators, etc., helping visually impaired people better understand their surroundings.

Fig. 17. Earlier time

Fig. 18. Late time

Tourist attractions and museums: Guide glasses can help people with limited vision gain a deeper appreciation and understanding of the history and culture of these places.

Social occasions: Guide glasses can help people with limited vision perceive and interpret their surroundings more accurately, so that they can integrate into social activities more effectively.

References

1. Ye, J., Wang, L., Lu, J., et al.: Integration of the perspective of barrier free environment construction and inclusive development of special education (written discussion). Modern Spec. Educ. **16**, 4–17 (2024)

2. Redmon, J., Divvala, S., Girshick, R., et al.: You only look once: unified, real-time object detection. In: 2016 IEEE Conference on Computer Vision and Pattern Recognition (CVPR), pp. 779–788 (2016)
3. Bochkovskiy, A., Wang, C.Y., Liao, H.Y.M.: Yolov4: Optimal Speed and Accuracy of Object Detection. arXiv e-prints (2020). arXiv:2004.10934
4. Wang, C.Y., Bochkovskiy, A., Liao, H.Y.M., et al.: Scaled-Yolov4: scaling cross stage partial network. In: 2021 IEEE/CVF Conference on Computer Vision and Pattern Recognition (CVPR), pp. 13024–13033 (2021)
5. Wanyi, Z.: Research on image based traffic light detection and recognition technology. Univ. Electr. Sci. Technol. China (2024). https://doi.org/10.27005/d.cnki.gdzku.2023.005296
6. Tan, M., Pang, R., Le, Q.V.: Efficientdet: scalable and efficient object detection. In: 2020 IEEE/CVF Conference on Computer Vision and Pattern Recognition (CVPR), pp. 10778–10787 (2020)
7. Tan, M.X., Le, Q.V.: Efficientnet: rethinking model scaling for convolutional neural networks. In: International Conference on Machinge Learning, vol. 97 (2019)
8. Bosquet, B., Mucientes, M., Brea, V.M.: Stdnet-St: spatio-temporal convnet for small object detection. Pattern Recogn. **116**, 107929 (2021)
9. Zhou, S., Wang, H., Nie, C., et al.: Design and experimental evaluation of nighttime trafficsign detection and classification based on low-light enhancement. In: 2022 6th CAA International Conference on Vehicular Control and Intelligence (CVCI), pp. 1–6 (2022)
10. Wang, X., Wang, D., Li, S., et al.: Low-light traffic objects detection for automated vehicles. In: 2022 6th CAA International Conference on Vehicular Control and Intelligence (CVCI), pp. 1–5 (2022

Study on the Teaching Reform of Course Design from the OBE Perspective

Wanting Ji[✉], Tingwei Chen, Han Shi, Yanling Xu, and Xin Zhang

Liaoning University, Shenyang 110036, China
zhangxin@lnu.edu.cn

Abstract. In the context of new engineering, computer education has led to new requirements for cultivating talent with an innovative spirit, practical ability, and comprehensive interdisciplinary ability. Traditional computer science practice course Course Design often focuses on the cultivation of a single skill but neglects improvements in students' comprehensive quality and ability to adapt to future social needs. Therefore, guided by the outcome-based education (OBE) perspective, results orientation, and the principle of continuous improvement, this paper studies the aspects of course objectives, course content, teaching methods, course evaluation, etc., and establishes a multi-dimensional student-centered course teaching system. This reform aims to integrate the concept of new engineering and cultivate students' innovative thinking, practical ability, and comprehensive interdisciplinary ability by optimizing the course content, teaching methods, and evaluation system to meet the needs of future social and technological development. The results of course reform have been applied to other computer science-related majors, which is highly important for improving students' comprehensive quality and employment competitiveness.

Keywords: Course Design · Course Construction · Computer Science Major

1 Introduction

With the robust emergence of a new round of industrial technological revolution and the advancing development of cutting-edge technologies, such as big data, cloud computing, and artificial intelligence, various industries are increasingly expressing precise and urgent expectations for university talent cultivation. In recent years, society's demand for engineering and technical talent has undergone a profound transformation, from traditional professional boundaries to the new field of new engineering, which is highly cross-integrated and innovation driven, and it is urgent to cultivate interdisciplinary talent with comprehensive quality and innovation ability [1–3].

Unfortunately, an escalating imbalance between talent supply from educational institutions and demand from enterprises has become increasingly evident. This is mainly because of the acceleration of technology iteration and the complexity of application requirements. The traditional teaching mode of Course Design has increasingly highlighted its limitations, and it is difficult to fully meet the current and future high-standard

K. Zhang et al. (Eds.): CSEI 2024, CCIS 2448, pp. 282–292, 2025.
https://doi.org/10.1007/978-981-96-3738-6_21

demands of computer professionals [4–6]. Therefore, as a key part of the strategy of new engineering, the implementation of comprehensive and profound innovation in the teaching process of Course Design for computer science-related majors has become a core path to improve the quality of education and cultivate high-quality computer professionals with international competitiveness.

The concept of new engineering advocates the construction of a disciplinary ecology deeply integrated with emerging and traditional engineering, aiming to cultivate diverse and innovative outstanding engineering talent that can lead to future technological and industrial changes [7–9]. It emphasizes interdisciplinary integration, the integration of production and education, and an international vision while focusing on stimulating students' innovative thinking and strengthening their practical operation, teamwork, and lifelong learning abilities. This trend presents greater challenges and expectations for the teaching of computer practice courses.

To enable students to truly master practical skills to solve complex engineering problems, the teaching process must be closely aligned with the background of new engineering, uphold the outcome-oriented educational concept, and constantly deepen the reform and exploration of practical courses [10]. By optimizing course content, strengthening practical teaching, promoting industry-university-research cooperation, and expanding international exchanges, we are committed to cultivating future engineers with interdisciplinary knowledge, an innovative spirit, and an international vision and contributing wisdom and strength to the sustainable development of society.

With the background of new engineering, traditional Course Design faces many challenges. On the one hand, course content often lags behind the development of technology and does not cover most cutting-edge knowledge and technology. On the other hand, existing teaching methods are relatively simple and lack effective training on students' ability to innovate and solve complex engineering problems [11, 12]. Therefore, it is urgent to reform and innovate the practical teaching process of Course Design for computer science-related majors to meet the needs of new engineering education.

Course Design is a comprehensive professional practice course. It aims to help students further consolidate their basic computer theories and professional knowledge by simulating the complete development cycle of software projects from demand analysis and architecture design to system implementation and testing. It improves students' professional skills and practical abilities, cultivates students' independent learning and rigorous scientific style, and enables them to solve complex engineering problems in the computer-related field.

This round of Course Design reform focuses on three core objectives:

(i) The practicability of the course content. The course structure should be optimized, and the teaching content should be updated to ensure that the course content keeps up with the technological frontier and enhances the practical innovation of students.

(ii) The interaction of teaching methods. Flexible teaching methods, such as case teaching and project-driven methods, are adopted to stimulate students' enthusiasm for learning and exploration and improve teaching effects.

(iii) Diversity of the course assessment system. The systematic collection of students' learning process data provides a multi-dimensional evaluation of students' ability training and improves students' comprehensive quality.

In addition, effective practical reform can promote the construction of teachers, promote the overall improvement of teachers' professional quality and teaching ability, and provide a solid foundation for training high-quality computer talent.

In summary, this round of course reform adheres to the core concept of a student-centered approach, closely designs the course content around the goal of ability cultivation, and builds a set of scientific and reasonable course evaluation systems to ensure the objectivity and effectiveness of teaching effects. This round of reform not only has theoretical guiding significance but also shows its unique practical value in practical applications, effectively promotes the improvement of students' ability to solve complex engineering problems, and significantly enhances their employment competitiveness.

Recently, this achievement has been widely used in the teaching practices of computer majors in universities, promoting improvements in professional teaching quality and students' comprehensive quality.

1.1 Existing Problems

The main problems of Course Design of the computer science major include the following:

 (i) Disconnection between theory and practice knowledge. Traditional course teaching tends to reproduce theoretical knowledge but ignores the effect of practical operation. This weakens the ability of students to solve practical problems and limits the exploitation of their practical and innovative potential, making it difficult to effectively transform theoretical knowledge into practical application ability.
 (ii) Course content lags behind market demand. Course content fails to keep up with the development of the industry's rapid pace and the lack of timely entry into the latest technology trends and emerging fields. As a result, graduates are not competitive enough in the job market, and adapting to rapidly changing market demand is difficult, which affects the breadth and depth of their career development.
(iii) Insufficient stimulation of learning interest. Traditional course content involves many programs, which lack innovation and attraction. This makes it difficult to stimulate students' enthusiasm for learning, and some students may lose their motivation for learning, affecting the learning effect and the willingness to continue learning.
(iv) Single evaluation system. The traditional course evaluation system focuses too much on the final results, ignoring the process results. This approach cannot fully and truly reflect the learning state and growth trajectory of students, which limits the accurate evaluation of students' comprehensive ability and learning effect.

1.2 Goal of Reform

To address the above problems, our course team has systematically reformed Course Design with the guidance of engineering education certification standards and the comprehensive use of various means. This round of reform closely follows the core concepts of interdisciplinary integration of new engineering and innovation-driven integration of production and education and involves comprehensive and in-depth exploration in multiple dimensions, such as teaching goal setting, course content updating, teaching process optimization, and assessment system improvement.

Specifically, this round of reform has achieved remarkable results and the following objectives:

(i) Constructing a scientific and reasonable course structure, realizing the deep integration of theoretical knowledge and practical ability, and promoting the effective transformation of students' theoretical knowledge into practical skills.

(ii) Integrating new technologies, new methods, and the actual needs of the industry into course teaching greatly enhances the practicality of the course content so that students can master the latest skills required by the industry.

(iii) Project-driven, case teaching, and other diverse teaching modes are adopted to stimulate students' interest in learning, improve class participation, and thus subtly improve the teaching effect.

(iv) Paying attention to students' mastery of theoretical knowledge and the cultivation and assessment of their practical ability, innovation ability, and teamwork ability to achieve a comprehensive and fair evaluation of students' learning results.

2   Reform Strategy

Course Design aims to enable students to master the whole life cycle of website construction under the browser/server (B/S) architecture through systematic learning and practical operation. The course content covers the key links from demand analysis, architecture design, front-end development, back-end development, database design and management, system testing, and maintenance. Through the study of this course, students can not only independently complete the development tasks of small and medium–sized B/S architecture websites but also cultivate the ability to independently solve complex engineering problems and the spirit of innovation in technological exploration, laying a solid foundation for their future careers. Therefore, the following reform strategies are proposed:

(i) Clear teaching objectives. Through the introduction of practical project cases and the combination of theoretical knowledge with practical operation, students are organized to develop and implement projects so that they can master knowledge and skills in practice and improve their practical ability and innovation ability.

(ii) Rich course content. Cooperation and exchanges with enterprises should be strengthened, teaching content should be updated in a timely manner, the introduction of cutting-edge technologies and emerging fields should be introduced, and the pace of industry development should be maintained.

(iii) Diversified teaching process. A variety of teaching methods and means to stimulate students' learning interest and enthusiasm are adopted. Students are encouraged to participate in extracurricular science and technology activities and competitions to develop their innovative spirit and teamwork skills.

(iv) Multi-dimensional evaluation system. The form of process evaluation should be enriched, a comprehensive and objective evaluation should be conducted, and the teaching results of the course should be continuously improved.

2.1 Clear Teaching Objectives

With the further advancement of engineering education certification, we clarified the teaching objectives of Course Design by closely combining student-centered and output-oriented teaching concepts in engineering education certification.

To accurately locate the teaching objectives of this course, our course team carried out a multi-dimensional survey, which included going deep into the industry frontier enterprises, contacting the graduates of this major, and investigating brother colleges and universities. Through the collection of information from various sources, the course team refined the core teaching objectives of the course:

(1) Knowledge objective: To lay the core foundation and ensure that students understand and master the core theoretical knowledge of computer science, including data structure, algorithm design, programming languages, database technology, etc.
(2) Skill goal: To strengthen practical ability and cultivate students' practical programming ability, complex system design and development ability, problem-solving ability, and team cooperation ability.
(3) Quality objectives: Improving students' comprehensive quality, cultivating their innovative thinking and critical thinking, strengthening professional ethics education, and enhancing their sense of social responsibility and career mission.

Moreover, to ensure the refinement and implementation of the above teaching objectives, our course team has further decomposed the overall objectives of the course into four specific subobjectives after several rounds of demonstration and discussion. As shown in Table 1.

Table 1. Links between course objectives and graduation requirements.

Graduation requirement	Course objective	Weights
Problem analysis	By reading literature, industry norms, and technical standards, students can apply engineering fundamentals and professional knowledge to conduct comprehensive and systematic analyses of complex engineering problems such as website design and data analysis	10%
Solution development	For complex engineering problems that need to be solved, students can use modular or object-oriented design concepts to design software system solutions that are efficient, maintainable, and meet requirements	40%
Professional norm	In the whole cycle of software development, students can consciously abide by the professional ethics and moral norms of software engineers, systematically complete software testing, and ensure the quality and stability of software	25%

(continued)

Table 1. (*continued*)

Graduation requirement	Course objective	Weights
Lifelong learning	Cultivating students' awareness of active learning and self-drive. Students can constantly update the professional knowledge system in the computer field, and improve their professional skills to meet the needs of the rapid development of the industry	25%

2.2 Rich Course Content

After the course objectives are defined, our team has enriched and updated course content to ensure that students not only have a solid theoretical foundation but also keep up with the pace of technological development and can solve practical problems. To this end, the following measures have been taken to enrich the course:

(i) Integration of classics and frontiers. By retaining the core knowledge of classic computer science, such as the data structure, algorithm design, programming language, and database, the course actively integrates cutting-edge technology content, such as big data, artificial intelligence, and the Internet of Things. Through case analysis, project practice, and other means, students can understand and master the application of these new technologies in practical projects.

(ii) Strengthening of practice. We set up various practical units, from simple programming exercises to complex system development, and each unit is closely designed around the course objectives to improve students' programming ability, system design, and development ability. Moreover, students are encouraged to participate in off-campus practical activities such as open-source projects and enterprise internships and apply their knowledge to solve practical problems.

(iii) Interdisciplinary integration. We strengthen cross-integration with other disciplines, such as mathematics, physics, and economics. By introducing cases and problems in related fields, we can broaden students' horizons and cultivate their interdisciplinary thinking and problem-solving abilities.

(iv) Introduction of the industry case. We cooperate with local enterprises to introduce real industry cases as teaching materials. By analyzing the problems, solutions, and implementation effects of these cases, students can gain an in-depth understanding of the current situation and development trend of the industry and cultivate their professional quality and teamwork ability.

(v) Addition of elective modules. According to students' interests and career planning, we set up multiple elective modules, such as mobile application development. Students can choose the appropriate modules for in-depth study according to their own needs to meet the needs of different career directions.

Through the implementation of the above measures, we strive to make the course content richer, more diversified, and cutting-edge and provide students with a comprehensive, in depth, and challenging learning environment to promote their overall development.

2.3 Diversified Teaching Process

To achieve the course objectives, we also designed a structured, interactive, and practice-oriented teaching process as follows.

(i) Stimulation of interest. At the beginning of each class, students' interests and curiosity are stimulated through short and fascinating introductions, such as the latest technology dynamic sharing and industry case analysis, to establish a good psychological foundation for subsequent learning.

(ii) Theory teaching and interactive discussion. Various multimedia teaching methods, such as videos and cartoons, are adopted to clearly explain the theoretical knowledge points. At the same time, interactive discussion sessions are set up to encourage students to ask questions and share insights, promote exchanges and cooperation between teachers and students, and deepen their understanding of theoretical knowledge.

(iii) Practical operation and project guidance. The practical operation runs through the entire teaching process, and through the way of "teaching and practicing", students can consolidate theoretical knowledge in hands-up practice. For complex projects, phased guidance is adopted, from demand analysis, design planning, and coding implementation to test and acceptance, and the whole process is tracked and guided to ensure that students master the complete process of project development.

(iv) Feedback and adjustment. We learn about students' learning situations and existing problems through classroom discussions and after-class questions and answers. According to the feedback results, we can adjust the teaching strategy in a timely manner to ensure that the teaching effect reaches the expected goal.

(v) Summary and development. At the end of each class, a summary is carried out to help students identify knowledge points and skills. In this way, students are guided to think about practical application scenarios and future development trends of course content and stimulate their interest in further learning and exploration.

(vi) Combinations of independent learning and collaborative learning. Students are encouraged to use their spare time for independent learning and expand their knowledge by consulting literature and watching online courses. In addition, group collaborative learning is organized to cultivate students' teamwork ability and problem-solving ability through team discussion and project cooperation.

Through the design of the above teaching process, we create a positive, active, and efficient learning environment for students, promote their comprehensive development, and achieve the established teaching objectives.

2.4 Multi-Dimensional Evaluation System

To achieve a comprehensive, objective, and fair evaluation of students' learning results and promote their all-round development, we adopt a multi-dimensional evaluation system throughout the whole learning process. It comprehensively collects students' learning trajectory data and considers students' knowledge depth, skill progression, innovative thinking, practical application, and other multi-dimensional abilities.

In this round of reform, we combine process evaluation with the final assessment. In particular, the process evaluation accounts for 40% of the total evaluation, focusing on the continuous monitoring of students' daily learning behavior, including class participation and homework submission. The final assessment is carried out in the form of a project presentation, accounting for 60%, focusing on the assessment of students' learning results, the completeness of the experiment report, the completion of the project, and the comprehensive application ability. This not only focuses on the students' practical abilities but also examines the students' learning attitudes, preview situations, and written expression ability to ensure the comprehensiveness, objectivity, and fairness of the evaluation and effectively promotes the overall development of the students.

3   Reform Results

Since 2022, Course Design has been engaged in this reform and has completed three rounds of teaching. During this period, the overall achievement of the course objectives each year clearly improved.

As shown in Fig. 1, the course was taught independently by university teachers in 2022, whereas in 2023 and 2024, university teachers cooperated with enterprise mentors to complete the course teaching. With the continuous deepening of reform, the overall achievement of teaching goals has increased annually, and students' learning performance has become increasingly excellent. This fully proves that the teaching reform has achieved a remarkable teaching effect and has injected a new impetus into the continuous improvement of course teaching.

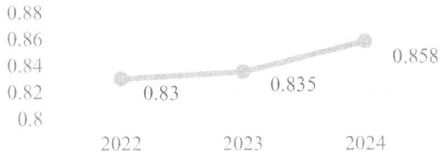

Fig. 1. Overall achievement of course objectives in the past three years.

The results in 2023 are taken as an example. A total of 154 students participated in the course evaluation in 2023, with an average score of 83.5 points, the highest score of 95 points, and the lowest score of 69 points. As shown in Fig. 2, 19 students scored above 90, 82 students scored between 80 and 89, 52 students scored between 70 and 79, 1 student scored between 60 and 69, and no student scored below 60. In terms of the distribution of grades, the overall grades of students tend to have a normal distribution, which fully shows that the setting of course evaluation standards is reasonable.

As shown in Fig. 3, the achievement of each course objective of 2023 is good (i.e., more than 0.8), indicating that the course objectives are well completed. Compared with the previous year, the achievement of course objectives 1--3 improved significantly, whereas the achievement of course objective 4 decreased slightly.

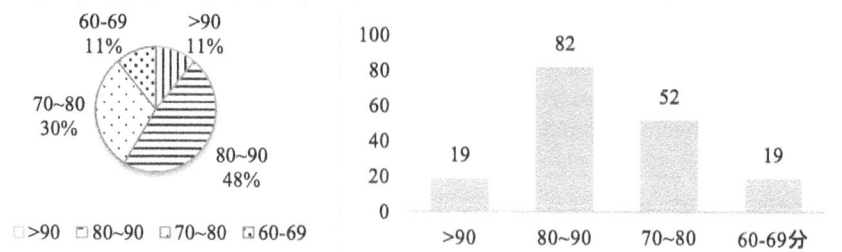

Fig. 2. Distribution of students' total grades in 2023.

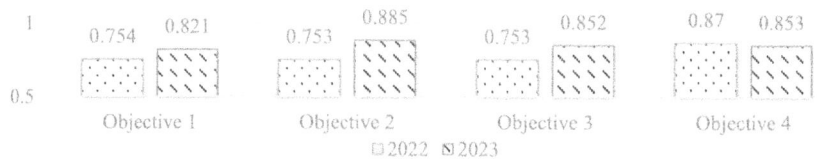

Fig. 3. Overall achievement of the 2023 course goals.

Objective 1 aims to test students' ability to review and understand the literature, perform systematic analysis, and apply professional knowledge. The total score of Objective 1 is 10 points, and the average score of students is 8.21 points (the average degree of achievement is 0.821). Further observation reveals that students' degree of individual achievement is distributed mainly between 0.76 and 0.85, which is relatively concentrated. Compared with other objectives, its achievement is slightly insufficient, and further efforts should be made to improve it.

Objective 2 focuses on developing students' needs analysis ability, software design ability, and innovative thinking. The total score of Objective 2 is 40 points, and the average score of students is 35.4 points (the average degree of achievement is 0.885). Compared with other objectives, its achievement is the best, and compared with its previous year, the achievement has significantly improved, which fully proves that this round of reform has achieved remarkable results.

Objective 3 mainly examines whether students have professional ethics and software testing ability in the process of software development. The total score of Objective 3 is 25 points, and the average score of students is 21.3 points (the average degree of achievement is 0.852). This fully demonstrates that students have a solid grasp of the knowledge points covered by Objective 3.

Objective 4 focuses on cultivating students' self-learning ability, continuous learning ability, and adaptive ability. The total score of Objective 4 is 25 points, and the average score of students is 21.33 points (the average degree of achievement is 0.853). There was a slight decrease from the previous year, mainly due to a very small number of students achieving less than 0.5. Although it affects overall achievement to a certain extent, it can be deeply analyzed as an individual case to further optimize the teaching strategy.

4 Conclusion

Course Design is a comprehensive practical course that integrates theory, practice, and innovation for computer science-related majors and aims to help students understand and master the whole life cycle of B/S architecture website construction through systematic learning and practical operation. Against the background of new engineering, we thoroughly implemented the concept of engineering certification education and actively explored the reform of course teaching.

We aim to cultivate application-oriented talent. Closely combined with the reality of students, we fully studied the characteristics of students' learning, from the teaching content, teaching methods, course evaluation, and other aspects of in-depth reform attempts, and achieved remarkable teaching results. These reforms not only help students better grasp the specific operation of software development but also, more importantly, enhance their ability to apply the computer theory they have learned to solve practical problems.

Recently, the reform of Course Design has achieved a series of results and accumulated valuable experience. In future applications and promotions, we will continue to improve these reform results and enrich teaching experience to achieve greater teaching results.

Acknowledgment. This work was funded by the Ministry of Education industry-university cooperative education project, the Liaoning University graduate quality course construction and teaching mode comprehensive reform research project, and the Liaoning University undergraduate teaching reform project.

References

1. Zhang, X., Zhou, M.: Information and digital technology-assisted interventions to improve intercultural competence: a meta-analytical review. Comput. Educ. (2023)
2. Dai, C.-P., Ke, F., Pan, Y., et al.: Exploring students' learning support use in digital game-based math learning: a mixed-methods approach using machine learning and multi-cases study. Comput. Educ. (2023)
3. Saito, T., Watanobe, Y.: Learning path recommendation system for programming education based on neural networks. Int. J. Distance Educ. Technol. **18**(1), 36–64 (2020)
4. Lin, Y., Pu, Y., Li, C., et al.: Mixed teaching mode of database principle course based on OBE concept. Comput. Educ. **7**, 62–65 (2020)
5. Mendes, B.L.N., SilvaMárcia, T.: Educational data mining applied to a massive course. Int. J. Distance Educ. Technol. (2020)
6. Li, Z.: Analyze the results-oriented concept of professional certification of engineering education. China High. Educ. **17**, 7–10 (2014)

7. Crossley, S.A., Allen, L.K., Snow, E.L., et al.: Incorporating learning characteristics into automatic essay scoring models: what individual differences and linguistic features tell us about writing quality. J. Educ. Data Mining, **8** (2016)

8. Xia, H.: Research on Flipped classroom teaching based on primary teaching principles: a case study of database application technology course. Comput. Educ. **4**, 174–178 (2021)

9. Ugursal, V.I., Cruickshank, C.A.: Student opinions and perceptions of undergraduate thermodynamics courses in engineering. Europ. J. Eng. Educ. (2015)

10. Tan, C., Chen, W., Zhao, L., et al.: Teaching reform guided by the concept of engineering education certification. Comput. Educ. **2**, 123–126 (2019)

11. Lo, C.K., Hew, K.F., Jong, S.Y. :The influence of ChatGPT on student engagement: a systematic review and future research agenda. Comput. Educ. **219** (2024)

12. Chen, H., Lu, W., Du, X.: Exploration and practice of "101 Plan" database course reform. Comput. Educ. **11**, 22–28 (2023)

Teaching Exploration of Artificial Intelligence Courses on the Basis of the OBE Concept

Min Zhang[(✉)] 🆔

Jimei University, Xiamen, Fujian, China
55423261@qq.com

Abstract. This paper explores the application of the outcome-based education (OBE) model in the practice of artificial intelligence (AI) teaching, which focuses on theoretical explanations of traditional teaching methods. Through in-depth analysis of the OBE concept, combined with the characteristics of AI courses, this paper proposes strategies and methods for implementing the OBE concept in AI teaching practice. The results show that the OBE concept can effectively improve the teaching effect of AI courses and improve students' practical ability and innovative thinking.

Keywords: Outcome-based education · Student-centered · Continuous improvement · Artificial intelligence (AI) · Course teaching

1 Introduction

With the rapid development of artificial intelligence (AI) technology, its application in the field of higher education has become particularly urgent, especially in teaching practice. However, how to effectively implement the teaching practices of AI courses to improve students' practical ability and innovative thinking has become an urgent challenge in the current education field. In this context, the output-based education (OBE) model, with its unique educational philosophy and methods, provides a new perspective and strategy for AI teaching practices.

OBE, a concept centered on enhancing the effectiveness of learning, emerged from educational reforms spearheaded by Australian and American academics in the domain of education [1–4]. Sunra et al. conducted a comprehensive exploration of OBE principles and practices, which can offer insights into how OBE reshapes education and its implications for educational policy and practice [5]. It represents a profound change in the traditional education mode [6, 7] and provides a clear direction for the development of AI teaching practices. First, according to the OBE concept, teaching design should start from the actual needs and interests of students, establish clear and definite learning goals, and design teaching activities and evaluation methods to help students achieve these goals. Second, the OBE concept encourages teachers to flexibly use diverse teaching methods and resources to achieve differentiated teaching to meet the personalized needs of students with different learning levels and backgrounds. This can not only stimulate students' interest and enthusiasm in learning but also effectively improve their learning effect and satisfaction. Finally, the OBE concept emphasizes that teachers should pay close attention to students' learning progress through timely feedback and evaluation and constantly adjust and optimize teaching strategies and methods according to the actual situation. This way of continuous improvement helps ensure that students can achieve the expected learning outcomes and helps to improve the quality and effectiveness of teaching.

In summary, the OBE education mode provides important enlightenment and guidance for the teaching practices of AI courses. By practicing the OBE concept, we can better promote the development of AI course teaching practices and cultivate more excellent talent with practical ability and an innovative spirit.

2 Exploration of AI Course Reform Based on the OBE Concept

2.1 Current Situation of AI Teaching in Colleges and Universities

Currently, although most institutions of higher education offer courses related to AI, there are significant disparities in the depth and breadth of the course content. While traditional teaching methods remain dominant, an increasing number of teachers are actively experimenting with more interactive teaching methods, such as case studies and flipped classrooms, with the aim of creating a more engaging and practical learning environment for students [8]. Additionally, the number of practical activities, such as experiments and course projects, is gradually increasing [9]. However, due to insufficient hardware and practice facilities, students' hands-on opportunities remain limited. In the area of teaching materials and resources, although there is ongoing development in the field of AI, we still lag behind top foreign universities. Some institutions continue to face a disconnect between theory and practice in AI education, making it challenging for students to apply their knowledge effectively to real-world problems. High-quality teaching resources tend to be concentrated in a few elite universities, whereas ordinary universities still face shortages in faculty and facilities. Moreover, the evaluation systems for AI education in universities tend to be simplistic, making it difficult to assess students' actual capabilities fully and accurately.

In general, AI teaching in colleges and universities is gradually developing and improving, but many aspects still need to be strengthened and reformed. From the curriculum system to teaching methods, from the construction of teaching staff to the integration of teaching resources, we need to conduct in-depth exploration and improvement to meet the urgent needs of society and industry for the cultivation of AI talent.

In view of the abovementioned teaching status and existing problems, this course will carry out reverse design on the basis of the OBE concept and carry out teaching reform practices from teaching objectives and teaching activities to teaching evaluation. Through this series of exploration and attempts, we will provide students with more high-quality and efficient AI course teaching and cultivate more excellent talents with practical ability and innovative spirit.

2.2 The Necessity of Integrating the OBE Concept into AI Teaching

The OBE concept has profoundly changed traditional education and talent training modes, indicating that the goal of education is not only to impart knowledge but also to cultivate students' ability and quality [10, 11]. This concept coincides with the educational concept of AI course training and has a significant role in promoting the teaching effect of the course. The AI course has been deeply reformed and explored in terms of the three dimensions of the course content system, teaching resources and evaluation mechanism. By overcoming the limitations of knowledge-based teaching, we pay more attention to the problems facing actual production, take output as guidance, and focus on cultivating students' application ability. Such teaching reform aims to cultivate students' ability to solve complex engineering problems so that they can make rapid and accurate judgments and responses in the face of practical problems.

3 Teaching Mode of the AI Course Based on the OBE Concept

3.1 Identifying Learning Outcomes and Defining Clear Objectives

When determining the teaching objectives of a course, we closely combine the talent training objectives and graduation requirements of engineering education professional certification and use Bloom's cognitive theory [12] for reference to achieve the comprehensive development of students' cognition, ability and emotion.

We start by defining what students should know and be able to do by the end of the course.

Objective 1: To cultivate students' political and cultural identity, guide them to understand the industrial background of AI, stimulate patriotism, and firmly establish the idea of "strengthening the country through science and technology". In the process of learning, we pay attention to the ideological and moral education of students to shape their character and feelings while imparting knowledge.

Objective 2: Focus on improving students' scientific and technological literacy so that they can fully grasp the basic concepts, principles and methods of AI. On this basis, we encourage students to carry out in-depth and effective theoretical and applied research on innovative points to cultivate their innovative thinking and practical ability.

Objective 3: attach importance to the cultivation of students' ability for autonomous learning, communication and cooperation and the ability to analyze and solve problems. We expect students to use the theoretical knowledge of AI to solve practical problems and continuously improve their practical ability and comprehensive quality through practical operation and team cooperation.

The OBE concept is highly consistent with the training objectives of the AI course, which helps us better achieve the teaching objectives of the course. By implementing the OBE concept, we can cultivate AI talent with practical application ability and an innovative spirit and contribute to the country's scientific and technological progress and social development.

3.2 Course Design Based on the Teaching Objectives

To ensure that the course is designed to achieve the identified learning outcome, we optimized the teaching content of the course on the basis of the university characteristics and talent training needs of our major, further sorted the knowledge units and points, and formed a unique "3+1" teaching module (Fig. 1). Among them, "3" represents the main line of three teaching modules, which are classic AI, machine learning, including deep learning, and the latest technology. These modules are interconnected and progressive and together constitute a complete knowledge system. "1" represents the ideological and political education of the course, which runs through the entire teaching process and aims to cultivate students' political literacy and feelings toward the country.

Through the implementation of this teaching module, the teaching objectives can be more effectively achieved, and both the acquisition of knowledge and the development of skills necessary for the desired outcomes can be cultivated.

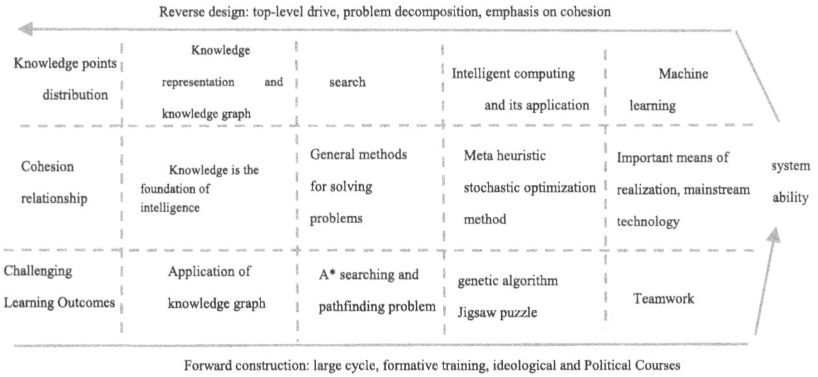

Reverse design: top-level drive, problem decomposition, emphasis on cohesion

Knowledge points distribution	Knowledge representation and knowledge graph	search	Intelligent computing and its application	Machine learning
Cohesion relationship	Knowledge is the foundation of intelligence	General methods for solving problems	Meta heuristic stochastic optimization method	Important means of realization, mainstream technology	system ability
Challenging Learning Outcomes	Application of knowledge graph	A* searching and pathfinding problem	genetic algorithm Jigsaw puzzle	Teamwork

Forward construction: large cycle, formative training, ideological and Political Courses

Fig. 1. Course content framework

3.3 Output-Oriented Diverse Teaching Methods

The OBE concept actively advocates diversified teaching methods; through the introduction of case analysis, the development of practical projects, group discussions and other teaching activities aims to stimulate students' interest and enthusiasm in learning, pay more attention to students' experience in the learning process, and enable students to obtain substantial growth and a sense of gain. This concept not only pays attention to the teaching of knowledge but also emphasizes the cultivation of ability and the improvement of quality. Through practical teaching activities, students can apply their knowledge to the actual situation and improve their ability to solve practical problems.

3.3.1 Case Driven Teaching

Through case-based teaching, students can play their active learning spirit in interactive discussions and gradually form an independent design concept [13]. The flowchart of case-driven teaching is given in Fig. 2.

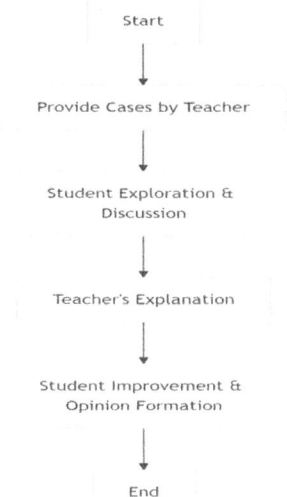

Fig. 2. The flowchart of case-driven teaching

3.3.2 Adopting Project-Based Teaching to Promote Differentiated and Personalized Teaching

Guided by the project and based on the engineering system, students can gain AI knowledge through practical operation and exploration. We propose challenging results to students, allow them to complete the project independently, and cultivate students' professional skills and the professional quality of artificial intelligence.

Teams should be formed reasonably according to students' abilities and interests. Each team should select different difficult project tasks according to their own needs, set appropriate goals, and use the engineering development method (Fig. 3) to clarify the abilities that need to be improved in this course, such as team cooperation, project expression, and innovation.

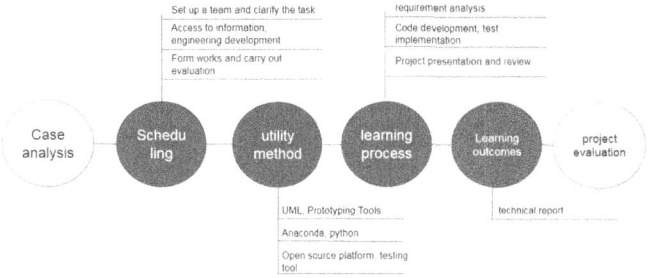

Fig. 3. Engineering development of the AI system

3.3.3 Construction of a Practical Teaching Platform to Support the Achievement of Teaching Objectives

To realize the integrated teaching of "the organic integration of theoretical teaching, experimental and engineering practice ability", new engineering talent should be cultivated as the core goal; knowledge content from the three levels of basic theory, technical methods and practical application should be established; and students' understanding, comprehensive application and innovation ability of knowledge should be improved. As shown in Fig. 4, the practice teaching platform sets AI practice content through three levels, namely, the basic level, the application level and the exploration level, gradually improving students' practical ability and innovative thinking.

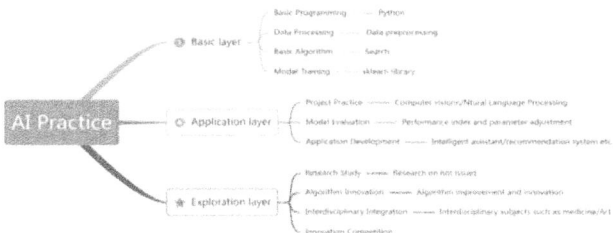

Fig. 4. AI practice platform

Practice teaching is integrated into theory teaching, with a focus on "learning by doing". The appropriate application scenario is selected. Through practical projects and case analysis, students can be guided to apply the theoretical knowledge they have learned to the actual scene and improve their cognition of AI practice ability.

3.3.4 Continuous Improvement and Establishment of a Result-Oriented Teaching Evaluation Mechanism

In the teaching process, this course adopts a combination of various evaluation methods, as shown in Fig. 5, including a comprehensive evaluation of personal assignments, classroom participation, classroom quizzes, experimental reports, team projects and other aspects, to evaluate students' learning achievements and ability improvement to more comprehensively reflect students' learning achievements and comprehensive quality.

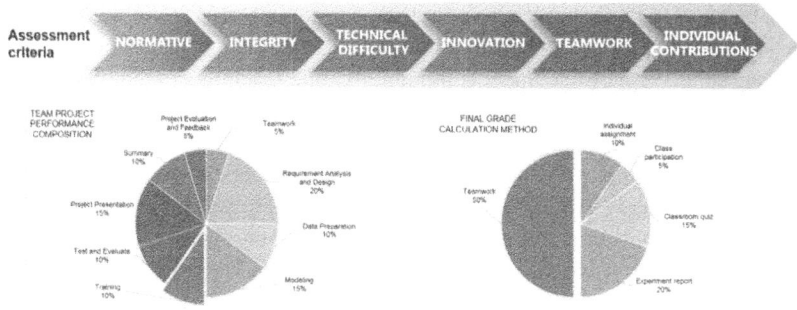

Fig. 5. Assessment criteria

4 Assessment and Feedback of Course Teaching Practice

In the teaching process, we encourage students to provide feedback on the course and teaching methods to continuously improve the teaching quality by continuously adjusting and optimizing the teaching process. The teaching of the course is based on the practice and exploration of classes 1, 2 and 3 of the 2021 network engineering major. At the end of the course, 77 valid questionnaires were collected through a questionnaire survey.

4.1 Statistical Analysis of Course Satisfaction

The survey results of course satisfaction are shown in Fig. 6, which are investigated from three aspects: the overall learning of the course, the theme and content of the course, and the experimental links of the course. The very high satisfaction rates are 77%, 78% and 75%, respectively, and the satisfaction rates are 22%, 21% and 21%, respectively, indicating that approximately 99% of the students are satisfied with the teaching and practice of the course.

Fig. 6. Course satisfaction survey

4.2 Investigation of the Mastery of the Curriculum Knowledge Module

In the course practice, we investigated the difficulty of each teaching module, teaching content and students' mastery. The results are shown in Fig. 7. According to the survey, approximately 46% of the students thought that the teaching content was moderate and could adapt better to their own learning rhythm. Approximately 22% of the students felt that the learning content was more difficult and needed more time and effort to master it. At the same time, 32% of the students thought that the teaching content was relatively simple and could be easily understood and applied.

In terms of learning mastery, we found that only a small number of students (4%) were able to implement complex AI systems, showing high practical ability and innovative thinking. Approximately half (46%) of the students can simply implement the AI system and have certain application and practical ability. However, many students (50%) who only stay at the level of mastering basic concepts and need to further strengthen their training in practice and application ability.

On the basis of the above survey results, in the teaching process of artificial intelligence courses, we need to pay more attention to the learning level and needs of students at different levels and adopt differentiated and personalized teaching strategies to ensure that every student can learn something. We will further optimize the teaching content and methods, provide students with richer and diversified learning resources and practice opportunities, help them better master AI knowledge and skills, and lay a solid foundation for future career development.

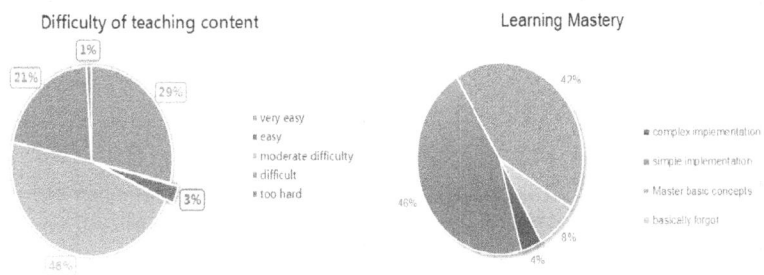

Fig. 7. Investigation of the difficulty of teaching content and the degree of learning mastery

4.3   Survey on the Degree of Interest in Each Module of the Course

The content of interest in each module of the course is investigated, as shown in Fig. 8. The most concerning content of students is machine learning and deep learning, followed by large language models. This survey result fully reflects that students have a strong interest in the current hot topics in the field of AI and shows that our curriculum teaching needs to be closely combined with the needs of development.

In view of this, we plan to increase the proportion of machine learning and deep learning modules in future course teaching and further explore their principles, algorithms and applications. Moreover, the introduction of the latest large language model module and its application will enable students to more comprehensively understand the latest technological developments in this field to improve their comprehensive quality and practical ability.

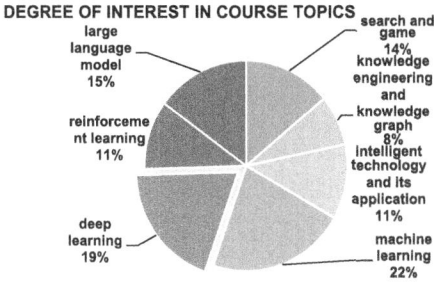

Fig. 8. Survey of interest in course topics

4.4 The Impact of the Curriculum on Graduates' Career Goals

Figure 9 shows the impact of the course on Graduates' career goals. The survey results revealed that the career goals of the vast majority of the students (93%) improved after graduation, but some people believed that the effect of help needed to be improved. In this context, it is necessary to establish a continuous student feedback mechanism, adjust the course content and teaching methods in a timely manner, and provide guidance or supplementary resources for students who need additional help.

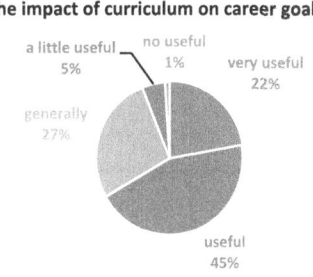

Fig. 9. The impact of the curriculum on career goals

5 Conclusion

The teaching practice results show that AI course teaching based on the OBE concept not only significantly improves students' mastery of AI knowledge but also effectively improves their practical ability and innovative thinking. Compared with traditional teaching methods, the innovation of the teaching mode is that it pays more attention to the harmonious unity of education and talent cultivation and emphasizes the combination of theoretical learning and practical innovation, which not only helps to improve the teaching quality of AI courses but also lays a solid foundation for cultivating AI talent with high professional quality and an innovative spirit.

By continuing to research and refine OBE practices in AI courses, future research could explore how OBE principles can be adapted to different educational settings and cultural contexts within AI classes.

Acknowledgment. This work is supported in part by the Natural Science Foundation of Fujian Province of China (2021J01857) and in part by Education, the Scientific Research Project of Middle-aged and Young Teachers in Fujian Province (JAT210251).

References

1. Lin, X., Wang, Y., Zhang, R., et al.: Ideological and political teaching reform: an introduction to artificial intelligence based on the OBE concept. In: 2022 11th International Conference on Educational and Information Technology (ICEIT 2022), pp. 6–9 (2022)
2. Thirumoorthy, K., Muneeswaran, K.: An application of text mining techniques and outcome based education: student recruitment system. J. Ambient Intell. Humaniz. Comput. (2021)
3. Hussain, W., Spady, W., Khan, S.Z., etc.: Impact evaluations of engineering programs using abet student outcomes. IEEE Access **9**, 46166–46190 (2021)
4. Gang, L., Qin, K., Wan, Y.: CDIO-OBE mode reformation of remote sensing experiment teaching against the background of emerging engineering. Bull. Surv. Mapp. **6**, 140–145+151 (2019)
5. Sunra, L., Aeni, N., Sudding Sally, F.H.: A comprehensive exploration of outcome-based education principles and practices. Asian J. Educ. Soc. Stud. (2024)
6. Hongtao, W., Zhi, L., Yuqian, Y.: Teaching reform of web front end development technology course based on OBE concept. Comput. Educ. **11**, 91–93 (2019)
7. Yushan, Y., Rui, Z.: Reform and practice of teaching mode based on achievement education. Educ. Teach. Forum **12**, 208–210 (2017)
8. Yanhan, L., Zhe, L., Zhiyun, C.: Artificial intelligence course case for new engineering and OBE mode. Comput. Educ. **4**, 94–97 (2022)
9. Min, Z., Yongze, F.: New engineering oriented artificial intelligence teaching practice. J. Jimei Univ. (Educ. Sci. Ed.) **21**, 84–88 (2020)
10. Jiahong, Y.: Results Based Education (OBE): Theory, Practice and Case Study. Education Science Press (2016)
11. Dongxiao, Z., Gaoda, H.: Results based education: ideas, practices and challenges. Educ. Res. **31**, 28–32(2020)
12. Ruixia, W.: The new development of Bloom's goal classification theory and its teaching significance. East China Normal University, Shanghai, pp. 1–56 (2007)
13. Yi, L.: Case guided teaching innovation research of C language programming experiment based on OBE theory. Exper. Sci. Technol. **22**, 1 (2024)

RAC-Based One-Stop Professional Course Teaching Model Exploration and Practice - Taking the Course of "Microcomputer Principles and Interface Technology" as an Example

Xiaorong Wan[1,2(✉)] ⓘ, Yingna Li[1,2], Chuan Luo[1,2], Chuan Li[1,2], and Jinguo You[1,2]

[1] Faculty of Information Engineering and Automation,
Kunming University of Science and Technology, Kunming 650500, China
83020855@qq.com
[2] Yunnan Key Laboratory of Computer Technology Applications, Kunming 650500, China

Abstract. In the context of the country's requirement for academic disciplines to be aligned and mutually reinforcing with industry chains, innovation chains, and talent chains, the integration of education and industry has become an important direction for the reform of higher education. In response to the iterative demand for edge intelligence in the Intelligent Internet of Things (AIOT), the course "Microcomputer Principles and Interface Technology" is deeply integrated with industry and education, establishing a hierarchical model of resource, capability, and commercialization (RAC) layers. It adopts a "one-stop" teaching mainline that starts with microcomputer theory knowledge, relies on hardware development boards, project orientation, competition innovation, and product commercialization training "five points and one line", connects knowledge product channels, integrates ideological and political education in courses, and constructs a multi-dimensional and comprehensive evaluation system to achieve the integration of industry and education from universities to enterprises, classrooms to markets, and from knowledge to products. The innovative teaching mode of this course has achieved significant results in innovative practice. This innovative teaching mode can effectively achieve the knowledge, ability, and quality goals of cultivating new engineering talents, and effectively improve the quality of talent cultivation and teaching. This teaching reform and innovation provide a reference and idea for further exploring the talent cultivation mode of schools and enterprises.

Keywords: Microcomputer Principle and Interface Technology · RAC Hierarchical Model · Course Ideology and Politics · Multi-faceted and all-round evaluation

1 Introduction

In the context of the country's requirement for academic disciplines to be aligned with and mutually promote industry chains, innovation chains, and talent chains, the integration of education and industry has become an important direction for the reform

K. Zhang et al. (Eds.): CSEI 2024, CCIS 2448, pp. 303–315, 2025.
https://doi.org/10.1007/978-981-96-3738-6_23

of higher education [1–4]. In response to the iterative demand for edge intelligence in the Intelligent Internet of Things (AIOT), our college has been building a characteristic course group for electronic design since 2017. We have sorted out 6 courses for first-class course cultivation, among which the basic course "Simulation Electronic Technology Experiment A" was approved for national first-class course construction in 2023, and the basic course "Digital Electronic Technology Experiment" was approved for provincial-level first-class course construction in 2023. As a pivotal course that connects the fundamentals of electronic design and the comprehensive application of the Internet of Things, "Microcomputer Principles and Interface Technology" plays a bridge role in integrating basic theories to achieve application breakthroughs [5–7]. For the electronic design characteristic course group, school enterprise cooperation has been carried out since 2018 to build experimental platforms. In 2019, the UNI-T Enterprise Talent Base was established, and in 2021, a long-term school enterprise cooperation mechanism was established by signing an industry mentor cooperation agreement with UNI-T Enterprise. Industry mentors bring products into the classroom and participate deeply in teaching and practical training, achieving a deep integration of industry and education in this course. The process of school-enterprise cooperation is shown in Fig. 1.

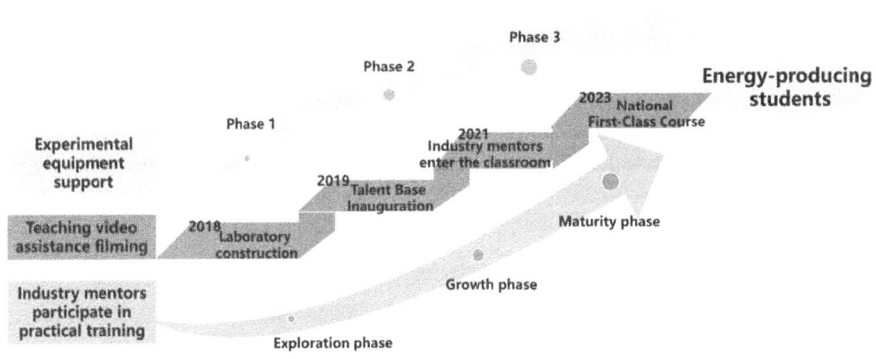

Fig. 1. School-enterprise cooperation process

Common teaching models include traditional lecture-based teaching [8], inquiry-based learning [9], cooperative learning [10], flipped classroom [11], and blended learning [12]. The "Microcomputer Principle and Interface Technology" deeply integrates industry and education and carries out teaching model practices. By establishing a hierarchical model of RAC, it adopts a "one-stop" teaching mainline that starts with microcomputer principles knowledge relies on hardware development boards, project-oriented approach, competition innovation, and product commercialization training along the "five-point-one-line". This approach opens up the knowledge product channel, integrates the teaching process of course ideology and politics, and constructs a multi-faceted and all-round evaluation system. It achieves the integration of industry and education from universities to enterprises, from classrooms to markets, and from knowledge to products. The innovative teaching mode of this course has achieved significant results in practice, effectively realizing the knowledge, ability and quality goals of cultivating new engineering talents, and effectively improving the quality of talent cultivation and teaching. This teaching reform and innovation provide reference and ideas for further exploring the talent cultivation mode of schools and enterprises.

2 Proposal of "Pain Points" in Teaching of the "Microcomputer Principle and Interface Technology" Course

Based on the analysis of the learning situation and feedback from previous student evaluations of the course. The following three teaching issues of "Microcomputer Principle and Interface Technology" course are summarized:

2.1 The Disconnection Between Theory and Market

Theoretical courses are confined to textbooks, and there is a disconnection between teaching and the market, which prevents the matching of theoretical knowledge with product development; practical courses rely on the resources of universities, but the resources of schools are limited. The gap between limited resources and corporate platforms creates a chasm between student learning and the needs of enterprises.

2.2 Insufficient Support for the Achievement of Quality Goalst

In today's context of domestic production of industrial equipment automatic control products, the development of hardware requires systematicity and the need for comprehensive training throughout the product design chain. In addition to having a solid set of professional skills, students must also possess excellent comprehensive qualities, including rigorous engineering standards, a perfectionist craftsmanship spirit, and a sense of national duty. The explanation of course thinking politics cannot fully meet the quality goals of the course, lacking systematic and evaluative aspects.

2.3 The Course Evaluation System is Singular

"Microcomputer Principle and Interface Technology" is a professional course with strong applicability. Traditional tests, experiments, and other components do not sufficiently reflect students' comprehensive design abilities and teamwork skills, and there is a lack of process-oriented assessments, as well as a lack of criteria for evaluating students' higher-order, innovative, and challenging competencies.

3 Measures to Address the "Pain Points" of the Course

The document "Ordinary Higher Education Discipline Professional Setting Adjustment Optimization Reform Plan" points out that disciplines and majors should strengthen collaborative linkages to achieve mutual matching and promotion between disciplines and majors, industry chains, innovation chains, and talent chains. The integration of education and industry has become an important direction for the reform of higher education. Therefore, the direction of curriculum teaching reform follows the development needs of the industry. In 2021, under the guidance of the spirit of documents such as the "Several Opinions on Deepening the Integration of Education and Industry" from the General Office of the State Council, the school, relying on the national first-class professional construction point, carried out innovative practices, applied for the construction of the Artificial Intelligence Industry College, and comprehensively deepened the reform of education and teaching. Taking this opportunity, facing the iterative needs of AIOT edge intelligence, the "Microcomputer Principle and Interface Technology" course has established a hierarchical model of RAC, adopting a "one-stop" teaching mainline that starts with knowledge, relies on development boards, project orientation, competition innovation, and product commercialization practice, forming a "five-point-in-one-line" approach. This method clears the path for knowledge products, integrates the teaching process of course ideology and politics with "comprehensive integration", and constructs a multi-faceted and all-round evaluation system, achieving the path of industry-education integration from classrooms to markets, from knowledge to products, and from universities to enterprises.

(1) Adopting the "one-stop" teaching mainline based on the RAC hierarchical model solves the problem of the disconnection between theory courses and practice. The implementation of the "one-stop" teaching mainline of "Microcomputer Principle and Interface Technology" based on the RAC hierarchical model is shown in Fig. 2.

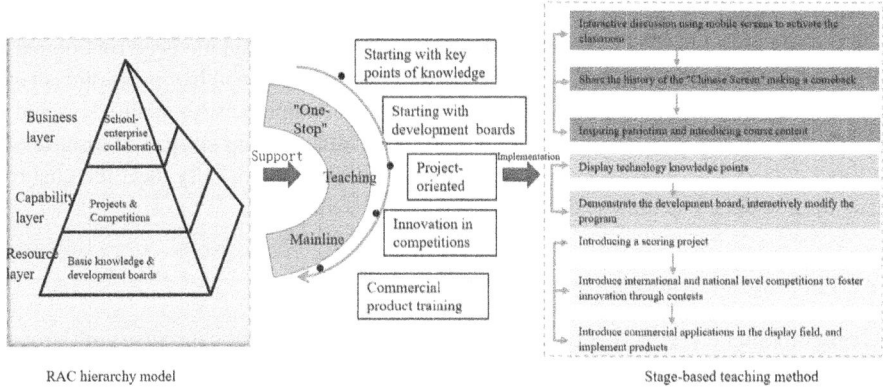

RAC hierarchy model   Stage-based teaching method

Fig. 2. The "one-stop" teaching mainline implementation case of "Microcomputer Principle and Interface Technology".

Combining theoretical teaching, practical operation, and social service, it provides students with a continuous, systematic, and complete phased learning process. Projects connect knowledge points, competitions exercise innovative thinking, and product training allows knowledge to face the market directly, helping students to better grasp the knowledge they have learned, improve learning effectiveness and efficiency, implement knowledge on the ground, and adapt to social needs and employment market demands. The specific implementation process is shown in Figs. 3, 4, 5 and 6.

Fig. 3. Integrating hardware development boards into the classroom

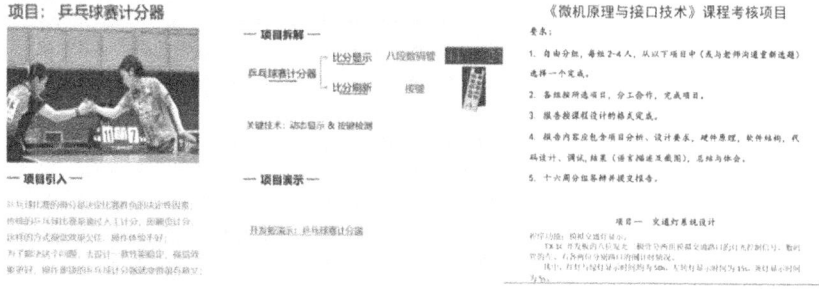

Fig. 4. Project-oriented during the course and final term

Fig. 5. Industry mentors participate in product training

Fig. 6. Students at our school's Blue Bridge Cup competition site actively participate in the contest

(2) Integrating course ideology and politics into teaching content and incorporating course ideology and politics assessment into the evaluation system can address the issue of insufficient support for the achievement of quality goals. Firstly, adhering to the educational philosophy of moral education, deeply explore the elements of thinking politics contained in the "Microcomputer Principle and Interface Technology" course content, integrate ideology and politics elements with professional knowledge, and give full play to the wisdom of the team teachers through various stages such as theory courses, practice courses, and product training to cultivate students' patriotic feelings and the spirit of striving for perfection, and pay attention to engineering standards. By incorporating engineering projects into the teaching content and integrating ideological and political education into the project, classroom teaching can be conducted in a project-based manner to achieve the goal of ideological and political education. The integration of course ideology and politics into teaching content is shown in Table 1.

Secondly, to achieve quality goals, the assessment of course ideology and politics is integrated into the evaluation system. Both the final exam and the process assessment include points for the assessment of course ideology and politics. The final exam supports the graduation requirement indicators: problem analysis, design and development, modern tools, while the process assessment supports indicators: problem analysis, design and development, modern tools, and teamwork, among which problem analysis, design and development, and teamwork all reflect quality goals.

(3) Building a multi-faceted and comprehensive evaluation system to address the issue of singular evaluation. Grading mainly considers two aspects. One is summative evaluation: through exams, the learning effectiveness of students is evaluated, including testing of cognition, understanding, memory, mastery, and application abilities of the prescribed learning content. The other is formative evaluation: through classroom performance, homework, hands-on practice, product training, projects (project defense, and project reports), and other evaluation methods, learning effectiveness is assessed, reflecting students' ideological height, attitude, cognition, understanding, and practical abilities during the learning process. Among these, product training is the application of in-class knowledge points to specific products. The project adopts a team collaboration approach, with 2–4 people in each group and a team leader responsibility system (the team leader assigns tasks and must ensure that each team member is clear about the module they are responsible for, otherwise it will affect the team leader's performance). Product training evaluation and project evaluation aim to reflect high-level, innovative, challenging, and ideological and political evaluation. The grading of this course combines summative and formative assessments, reflecting both learning outcomes and learning processes. Refine and clarify the evaluation requirements, ensure that the evaluation is based on evidence and the assessment is hierarchical, and form a multi-faceted and all-round evaluation system. The implementation of formative assessment can be seen in Figs. 7, 8 and 9.

Table 1. The integration of course ideology and politics into teaching content.

Teaching content	Course Ideological and Political Content and Integration Points	Forms of Teaching Organization	Expected effectiveness of ideological and political education
Chapter 1 Microcontroller Overview Section 3 An overview of the history and current application areas of microcontrollers **Running Light Project**	**Discuss the development history of microcontrollers, the urgent need for breakthroughs by China in the MCU field; the cultivation of learning abilities requires a craftsman's spirit**	Lecture in class **Project introduction**	Starting from the strategic needs of information professionals to shoulder the mission of informatization and intelligentization of traditional industries, gradually infiltrate patriotism, professionalism, national confidence, craftsmanship, team spirit, and engineering standards into the course teaching. Silently promote the core values of socialism, give full play to the educational function of professional courses. Enable students to not only master the basic professional knowledge but also to make good future career development plans. Organize the mission of national rejuvenation, professional identity, and professional knowledge organically, and lay a good foundation for students to enter professional work and society in the future
Chapter 3 C51 Programming Fundamentals Section 4 Programming Standards **Requirements for the end-of-term project report**	**From programming standards to engineering standards, the requirements of standardization are reflected in the project report**	Lecture in class **Project introduction**	

(continued)

Table 1. (*continued*)

Teaching content	Course Ideological and Political Content and Integration Points	Forms of Teaching Organization	Expected effectiveness of ideological and political education
Chapter 5 Control of microcontroller I/O ports Section 1 Output Port Control and Program Design **Smartwatch products**	**Introduce the nation's display field's extraordinary development history and the "comeback story" of Chinese screens from a national perspective, and bring in the introduction of industry leaders to enhance students' patriotic sentiments**	Lecture in class **Project introduction**	
Chapter 5 Control of microcontroller I/O ports Section 2 Input Port Control and Program Design **Humidity and Temperature Controller Products**	**Through the case in 2017 where a Russian rocket launch failed due to an input error, we can draw attention to the importance of focusing on inputs. It illustrates that small details matter and that "a great barrier may be destroyed by an ant hole," meaning even minor things can be of great significance**	Lecture in class **Project introduction**	
Chapter 8 Microcontroller Serial Port and Serial Communication Technology Section 1 Serial Communication Fundamentals **Unmanned Vending Machine Product**	**Discuss multi-computer communication, introduce the Tianhe series of supercomputers, and emphasize the importance of teamwork and communication**	Lecture in class **Project introduction**	

Fig. 7. Homework submission after class

Fig. 8. End-of-term project defense and presentation

4 Innovative Aspects of the Teaching Reform

4.1 The "One-Stop" Teaching Mainline Based on the RAC Hierarchical Model Breaks Through the Knowledge Product Channel

The RAC hierarchical model is divided into three layers: the resource layer, the ability layer, and the commercial layer. The resource layer refers to what is possessed, including the basic knowledge output of the course & hardware development boards; the ability layer refers to what can be done, including course projects and various competitions that students can participate in, allowing learning to begin in the classroom and abilities to be extended outside of class; the commercial layer refers to the value that can be created, including market commercialization products of school-enterprise cooperation practical training, etc. The "one-stop" teaching mainline starts with knowledge, relies

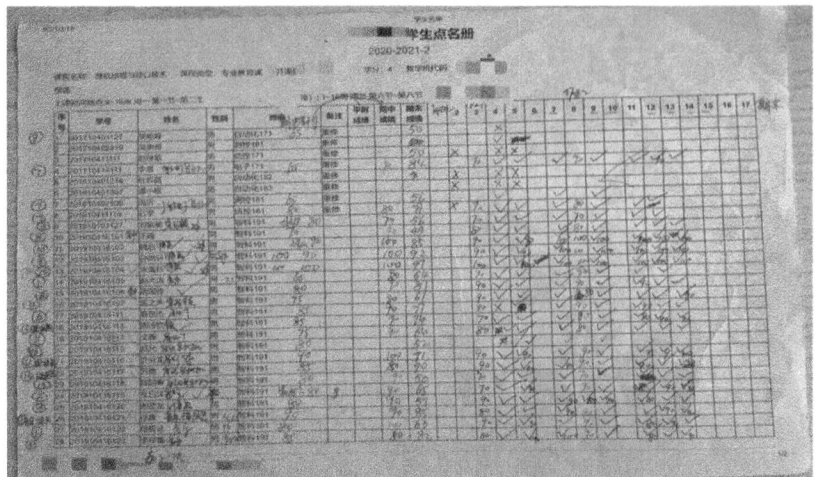

Fig. 9. Project defense grouping and original scoring records

on development boards, project orientation, competition innovation, and product commercialization. It combines theoretical teaching, practical operation, and social service to provide students with a continuous, systematic, and complete phased learning process. Projects connect knowledge points, competitions exercise innovative thinking, and product training allows knowledge to face the market directly, helping them to better grasp the knowledge they have learned, improve learning effectiveness and efficiency, implement knowledge on the ground, and adapt to social needs and employment market demands.

4.2 The "Integration and Application" of Course Ideology and Politics in the Teaching Process Promotes the Achievement of Quality Education Goals

The "integration and application" process of course ideology and politics in teaching includes: integrating course ideology and politics into teaching content and incorporating the assessment of course ideology and politics into the evaluation system. Firstly, adhering to the educational philosophy of moral education, deeply explore the elements of ideology and politics contained in the "Microcomputer Principle and Interface Technology" course content, integrate elements of ideology and politics with professional knowledge, and fully utilize the wisdom of the team teachers through various stages such as theory courses, practical courses, and product training to cultivate students' patriotic feelings and the spirit of striving for perfection, and pay attention to engineering standards. Secondly, to achieve quality goals, the assessment of course ideology and politics is integrated into the evaluation system. Both the final exam and the process assessment include points for the assessment of course ideology and politics. The final exam supports graduation requirement indicators: problem analysis, design and development, modern tools, while the process assessment supports indicators: problem analysis, design and development, modern tools, and teamwork, among which problem analysis, design and development, and teamwork all reflect quality goals.

4.3 Building a Multi-faceted and Comprehensive Evaluation System

The grading criteria for course grades are: 60% for summative evaluation and 40% for formative evaluation. The summative evaluation is conducted through a closed-book written examination; the formative evaluation includes classroom performance, homework, hands-on practice, product training, and projects (project defense and project report). The total score is recorded in a hundred-point system, with a minimum passing score of 60 points. The total grade is calculated as Total Grade = Summative Evaluation Score *60% + Formative Evaluation Score * 40%. The formative evaluation reflects the students' ideological level, attitude, cognition, understanding, and practical skills during the learning process, where product training is the application of in-class knowledge to specific products, and project assessment evaluates teamwork abilities. The aim is to reflect higher-order thinking, innovation, challenge, and ideological and political education.

5 The Promotional Application Effects of the Reform

The teaching effect is good, and students' innovation ability has been significantly improved. From 2020 to 2023, the overall evaluation scores of students in this course have increased for four consecutive years from the 18th to the 21st grade. In 2023, after the integration of industry and education in this course, the total evaluation average scores of students showed a noticeable improvement, as seen in Fig. 10.

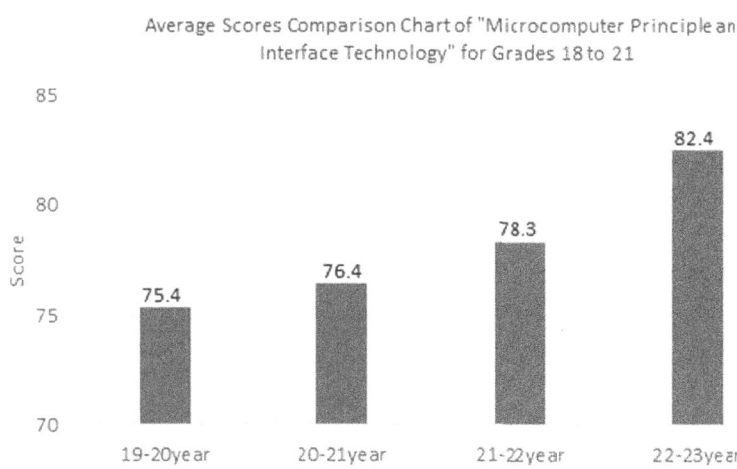

Fig. 10. The comparison chart of comprehensive average scores for the "Microcomputer Principle and Interface Technology" course

Students' autonomous learning ability has greatly improved, and their teamwork and innovation capabilities have significantly strengthened. Students have participated in various academic competitions and have achieved excellent results. In the past three years, the students guided by the main teacher have won 1 national first prize and 1 national second prize in the National College Students' Mathematical Modeling Competition, 3 national awards in the Blue Bridge Cup Group A, and 1 silver award in the ICPC International Collegiate Programming Contest (team competition), and have won 13 provincial-level awards in various academic competitions.

6   Conclusion

Taking the establishment of the Artificial Intelligence Industry College and the cultivation of industry-oriented talents as an opportunity, the "Microcomputer Principle and Interface Technology" course has deeply integrated industry and education. It has innovatively implemented a "one-stop" teaching mainline based on the RAC hierarchical model to address issues such as the disconnection between theory and market, insufficient support for the achievement of quality goals, and a singular course evaluation system. This approach has cleared the path for knowledge products, promoted the achievement of quality goals through the integration of course ideology and politics in the teaching process, and constructed a multi-faceted and comprehensive evaluation system. The innovative teaching model of this course has achieved significant results in practice, effectively achieving the knowledge, capability, and quality goals of new engineering talent training, and effectively improving the quality of talent training and teaching. This teaching reform and innovation quality a reference and idea for further exploring the school-enterprise talent training model.

Acknowledge Fund. Project: Yunnan Province High-Level Science and Technology Talents and Innovative Team Selection Special Project: the Yunnan Province Intelligent Perception and Collaborative Computing Innovation Team (202405AS350001).

References

1. Yan, H.L.: Exploration of professional curriculum teaching reform in the context of integration of industry and education. Automob. Educ. (13), 82–84 (2024)
2. Liu, C.C., Xie, P.: From the perspective of industry-education integration: teaching reform and practice of provincial applied demonstration courses. Comput. Knowl. Technol. **20**(18), 137–139,143 (2024)
3. Yang, J.P., Huang, H., Yuan, Y.Y., Dong, X.H.: From the perspective of industry-education integration: reform and practice of collaborative talent cultivation mechanism between enterprises and universities in applied undergraduate education. J. High. Educ. (11), 147–150, 155 (2024)
4. Cai, Y.M.: Research on the blended teaching model of industry-education integration under the concept of STEM education. Res. Inf. Based Teach. (2), 15–17 (2024)
5. Jia, Y.C., Chen, K., Chang, H.J., Shi, H.Y.: Exploration of teaching reform of "principle and interface technology of single chip microcomputer" course driven by project. Agric. Mech. Synth. Study (12), 188–191, 198 (2024)

6. Hu, F.Z., Guo, H., Xia, X.M., Fan, X.Y.: Exploration of practical teaching reform of microcomputer principle and interface technology under the background of new engineering. Comput. Knowl. Technol. **20**(6), 156–158, 165 (2024)

7. Liao, W.J., Yu, L.J., Fang, J.J.: Exploration of teaching reform for "principles of microcomputer and interface technology". Comput. Knowl. Technol. **19**(3), 131–133 (2023)

8. Pang, L.X., Xu, X.X., Jin, K.K., et al.: The application of flipped classroom based on the "5E" teaching model in physiology teaching. J. Wenzhou Med. Univ. **54**(9), 767–771 (2024)

9. Zhang, J.J., Qiao, S.S.: Reform and practice of research-oriented teaching model oriented to innovative abilities — taking higher mathematics as an example. Stud. Coll. Math. **27**(4), 71–73, 86 (2024)

10. Dai, N.N.: The application of clinical pathology case discussions in pathology education. Contemp. Med. Symp. **3**(10), 164–165 (2015)

11. Zhou, W.L.: Research on the empowerment of college ideological and political education teaching model reform through "micro-courses + flipped classroom". J. Guangxi Coll. Educ. (3), 172–177 (2024)

12. Li, Y., Liu, Z.J.: Under the background of new engineering: exploration and practice of blended course teaching models. J. Arch. Educ. Inst. High. Learn. **33**(5), 70–76 (2024)

Implementation of 'PBL+BL' Teaching Methodology in the "Introduction to Communication Engineering"

Jiao Ding[1], Yuanyuan Pan[2], and Li Yang[2(✉)]

[1] School of Electrical and Electronic Engineering, Anhui Institute of Information Technology, Wuhu, People's Republic of China
[2] School of Medical Information, Wannan Medical College, Wuhu, People's Republic of China
yangli@wnmc.edu.cn

Abstract. From the perspective of an engineer, the knowledge framework is being constructed, and a course textbook is being developed; the course is taught via a combination of thematic lectures and project practices, with teachers from the teaching and research office delivering thematic content on the basis of their expertise and students working in groups to carry out project practices and complete project designs independently; online teaching resources are created to support students' theoretical learning and project practices through the use of smart teaching platforms and tools; an 'N+1' assessment method is used, focusing on process assessment; and the course delves into ideological and political elements, with ideological and political education running through the entire teaching process and all aspects. The effectiveness of course teaching is comprehensively evaluated through course objective achievement, course completion, end-of-term questionnaire surveys, and peer evaluations.

Keywords: Special Topic Lectures · Project Practice · Online Teaching · Ideological and Political Education

1 Introduction

The "Introduction to Communication Engineering" is a significant general course for the communication engineering major at the Anhui Institute of Information Technology. This course offers an overview of the communication engineering major, guiding freshmen to understand the relevant issues accurately. It plays a vital role in training systems for applied talent in communication engineering. The objective of this course is to help students comprehend the nature, characteristics, and role of the profession they are studying. It also aims to establish the correct professional thinking and learning perspective and stimulate students' learning potential.

2   Importance of Reforming Teaching in the "Introduction to Communication Engineering"

The traditional course teaching model comprises 16 h of theoretical instruction, with the course instructor typically being the head of the communication engineering department. Zhang (2015) [1] and Wang (2022) [2] covered topics such as communication applications, communication development, introduction to modern communication theory and technology, communication systems and engineering, an overview of the communication industry, communication engineering majors and disciplines, and the undergraduate teaching system of communication engineering. The final assessment for the course entails submitting a significant assignment on the learning experience in communication engineering. Traditional teaching methods have several drawbacks that hinder effective learning in the field of communication engineering. First, the textbook and content cannot be updated and adjusted promptly to keep up with the fast-changing industry. Second, students do not have sufficient opportunities to ask questions, participate in discussions, and engage in practical activities, which limits their in-depth understanding of the communication profession and skill development. Third, assessment methods are limited to a single form of major assignment, which fails to intuitively reflect students' understanding of professional knowledge. Finally, traditional teaching methods do not effectively cultivate students' abilities for self-directed learning, innovative thinking, and engineering awareness.

Moreover, the objective of this major is to cultivate students with excellent engineering design ability, teamwork skills, self-learning ability, and a strong innovative spirit, in accordance with the latest revised professional training objectives. The major aims to serve the intelligent manufacturing industry and related information technology industries, enabling students to engage in communication system and network design, manufacturing, operation, maintenance, and project management in areas such as mobile communication, computer network communication, and Internet of Things (IoT) applications. To achieve these objectives, it is necessary to reform the course on "Introduction to Communication Engineering".

3   Teaching Practice of "Introduction to Communication Engineering" Using 'PBL (Project-Based Learning)+BL (Blended Learning)'

To address the limitations of conventional teaching methods, a teaching reform is introduced for the "Introduction to Communication Engineering" during the fall semester of the 2023–2024 academic year, specifically for the communication engineering major students in the 2023 grade. This reform integrated PBL and BL to enhance the learning experience.

3.1   Clarifying Course Objectives

The Anhui Institute of Information Technology is an applied undergraduate institution that serves regional economic and social development. The communication engineering major cultivates high-quality applied talent engaged in the design, manufacturing, operation, maintenance, and project management of communication systems and networks. In accordance with the school's position and the requirements for professional talent cultivation, course teaching objectives and ideological and political education objectives are established, as shown in Table 1.

3.2 Self-compiled Textbook for "Introduction to Engineering for New Engineering Electronic Information Majors"

The self-compiled textbook arranges content and teaching from the perspective of engineers, arranges depth and breadth from the standpoint of students, emphasizes the knowledge framework and system, focuses on guidance and thinking, develops students' intrinsic motivation for learning, focuses on methods and practices, overcomes the current situation of too many resources and difficulty in distinguishing between good and bad in the information age, forms a highly condensed overall framework, progressively delves into technical detail, and gradually presents exciting information on electronic engineering technology to future engineers.

The textbook is divided into six chapters, namely, Chapter 1 Overview, Chapter 2 Hardware, Chapter 3 Software, Chapter 4 Information, Chapter 5 Networks, and Chapter 6 Products. Each chapter condenses several core concepts, explained through examples that students need to grasp firmly. These chapters serve as the starting point and foundation for students to think about information and communication issues, as well as the direction and clues for their continuous learning in the future. Zhang (2022) [3] arranged the contents of each chapter in a self-compiled textbook, as shown in Fig. 1.

3.3 Teaching Practices of the PBL+BL Curriculum

The total duration of the course is 32 h, including 14 h of theory, 10 h of project practice, and 8 h of other activities. The other hours involve students watching online videos of project knowledge points before and after class, implementing projects, and writing project design reports. The specific teaching schedule is shown in Table 2.

Group Teaching by the Faculty of the Department of Communication Engineering. The self-compiled textbook "Introduction to Engineering for New Engineering Electronic Information Majors" was used to introduce the seven major topics, emphasizing the knowledge framework and system of the communication major, focusing on guidance and reflection, and developing students' intrinsic motivation for learning. On the basis of the research directions and main courses of the communication engineering department's full-time teachers, corresponding topics are taught, allowing teachers to leverage their strengths to better showcase the characteristics of each topic to students and stimulate students' interest in professional learning.

Blended Learning. The curriculum teachers record microlesson videos on key knowledge points, create online quizzes and discussion topics, and organize project practice reference materials. We use the FIF smart teaching platform (http://www.elearnmooc. com) and Xfaike online platform (https://teaching.xfaike.com) to publish resources, support students' theoretical learning and project practices, provide diverse and personalized

Table 1. Course objectives

Teaching objectives	Ideological and political education objectives
1. Understand the knowledge system framework, application areas, and development overview of communication engineering, establish a strong interest in learning professional knowledge, and enhance professional identity	1. Through learning course-related content, students can develop a strong professional belief, possess excellent professional knowledge and skills, and cultivate good professional behavior habits. They can understand and comply with engineering professional ethics and norms in production and life
2. Having humanistic and social science literacy and a sense of social responsibility, being able to understand and comply with engineering professional norms and ethics in communication engineering practice, and fulfill corresponding responsibilities	2. Continuously learn the latest knowledge in the field of communication, keep pace with the times, be diligent in exploration, and brave in practice. Able to comprehensively apply existing knowledge, information, skills, and methods to practice, continuously integrate, continuously reflect, and propose new methods and new perspectives, with the will, confidence, courage, and wisdom to invent, create, reform, and innovate, forming a spirit of the times centered on reform and innovation
3. Master scientific learning methods for analyzing and designing project cases from hardware, software, and other perspectives, especially how to efficiently learn under information technology conditions. Through project practice, develop certain abilities in self-learning, teamwork, and engineering awareness	3. Understand the impact of the development of communication, major historical events, and other factors on the socialist construction in China, correctly grasp the connotation of the unity of the country and the family, form the concept of the unity of the country and the family, and cultivate deep patriotic feelings. Integrate lofty ideals with personal aspirations, and blend patriotic sentiments with life pursuits
4. Understand the innovative directions and characteristics of the communication engineering profession, learn about relevant entrepreneurial cases, and possess a certain awareness of innovation and entrepreneurship as well as a lifelong learning mindset	4. Reflecting on the historical mission of communicators and the future direction of their own efforts, establishing the correct values, forming a sense of social responsibility, and being able to fulfill the mission, responsibilities, and obligations that should be borne by the country, society, and others in social life

learning experiences, and cultivate students' independent learning abilities and professional learning interests. Screenshots of some online resources for the course are shown in Fig. 2.

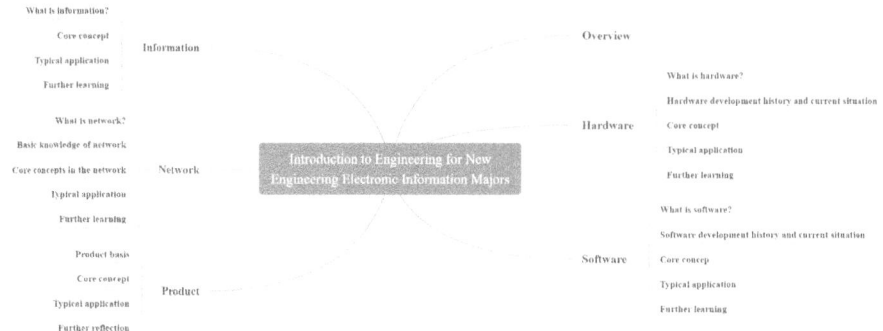

Fig. 1. Chapter content of self-compiled textbooks

Sha (2022) [4], Xu (2024) [5] and Fu (2024) [6] designed teaching methods, teaching activities, and assessments and evaluations of online and offline mixed courses, and the course is divided into three stages of online and offline teaching: preclass preview (online), in-class instruction (offline), and postclass consolidation (online+offline), with specific implementations for each stage, as shown in Table 3.

Project-Based Learning. Deng (2020) [7] and Mao (2024) [8] described the principles for determining project content in project-based courses, and the teachers of the course group combined the content of major communication subjects with common application cases that students are easily exposed to in daily life. On the basis of the teaching objectives of the course, we select projects that are challenging and practical. We compile a project practice guide that can provide objectives, components that may be used, background knowledge and considerations for each project. Shi (2022) [9] introduced in detail the process design of the project in the course of a communication electronic circuit and basic teaching objectives and project content. The specific implementation steps of the course project include the following steps:

(1) Understand the project design requirements. The teacher introduces the project design requirements on the basis of the project practice guide. Students from teams (3–4 people per team) select a project from 5 projects, consult information and understand the project design purpose, task requirements, precautions, etc.;

(2) Self-study background knowledge. Students use resources such as libraries and e-books to collect reference materials related to the project background, understand the project design task and background knowledge, and clarify the focus and scope of self-study;

(3) Design the overall project plan. On the basis of the project design requirements, the team searches and self-studies materials to determine the core components needed for the project, the logical connection relationship between the core components and the Arduino system board, and finalizes the overall design plan for the project;

(4) Breakdown project tasks. The teacher guides the team of students to break down project tasks and make a project execution plan. The team executes project subtasks according to the schedule, with the teacher supervising the process. Figure 3 shows a

Table 2. Course teaching schedule

Theory (14 h)	Project practice (10 h)	Other (8 h)
Topic 1 What is communication? Course content on ideological and political education: China–US trade war Topic 2 Introduction to communication engineering major Topic 3 Fundamentals and applications of hardware circuits Course content on ideological and political education: Self-developed chips, Huawei HarmonyOS Topic 4 Fundamentals and applications of software systems Topic 5 Concepts and applications of information Topic 6 Fundamentals and applications of communication networks Course content on ideological and political education: telecom fraud Topic 7 Product concept and application Course content on ideological and political education: autonomous driving cars, rule of law education	Students conduct project-based practice with Arduino development boards in groups of 3–4 people, with each group completing 5 projects including: design of indoor temperature and humidity detection system, design of digital stopwatch, design of fire alarm system, design of PWM light control system, and design of 1 of the LED dot matrix display system Course content on ideological and political education: Chinese women's volleyball team, Huawei 5G	1. The core components of the learning project include examples of applications of buttons, buzzers, LED, DHT11 sensors, 8×8 dot matrix displays, single-digit displays, and LCD displays. Based on these application examples, complete the corresponding circuit design for the components (4 h) 2. Project software and hardware debugging (2 h) 3. Writing and submitting project design report (2 h)

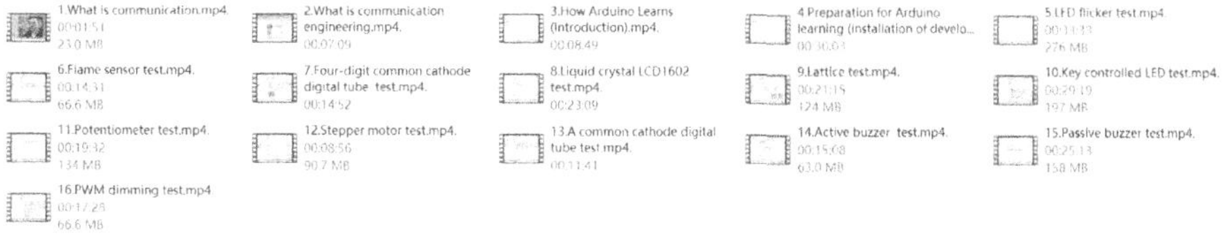

Fig. 2. Course online resources

Table 3. Teaching implementation of blended learning

Teaching stages	Teaching platform	Teacher activities	Student activities
Preclass preview (online)	aike + FIF platform	Post microlesson videos, online practice questions and discussion topics	1. Refer to textbook, practice materials and relevant references, and watch videos on knowledge points; 2. Complete online practice and discussion of corresponding knowledge points in aike
In-class instruction (offline)	Multimedia-classroom + laboratory + aike	Summarize the key points and difficulties in the microlesson videos, provide targeted teaching of knowledge points based on feedback from online practice questions; Use the aike platform to post questions, participate in quizzes, etc., to enhance the classroom learning atmosphere; Use case-based, demonstrative, and inquiry-based teaching methods for knowledge delivery; 4. Project practice guidance	1. Understand the key and difficult points in the teaching content and the knowledge points that have not been conquered by self-study; 2. Actively participate in classroom answering; 3. The group collaborates on project practice, including searching for project materials, self-studying, formulating project design proposals, designing hardware and software, verifying functional, accepting project, etc.

(continued)

Table 3. (*continued*)

Teaching stages	Teaching platform	Teacher activities	Student activities
Postclass consolidation (online+offline)	aike + laboratory + QQ	Answer and guidance	1. Discussing the content of the knowledge points with classmates and teachers; 2. Completing the homework after class; 3. The team works together to complete the project practice; 4. Writing project design report and submitting

    schematic diagram of the decomposition of the design task for the indoor temperature and humidity detection system of Project 1.

(5) Implement project subtasks. Teachers use the FIF platform to provide project-related reference resources and guide students in searching for and evaluating materials. Team members communicate and share their learning outcomes with each other to complete the project subtasks together;

(6) Debug project functionality. On the basis of the overall project design plan, integrate the hardware circuits and software programs of each subtask of the project, debug and optimize the project's software and hardware, and verify system functionality;

(7) Project acceptance and defense. The project team prepares a presentation PPT to showcase the project design process; demonstrates the system physical functionality onsite, presenting the project results and actual operation status; answers 2–3 questions related to the project design;

(8) Submit the project design report. Students should summarize and recap the entire project implementation process, project innovations, insights, etc., write the project design report and submit it.

Ideological and Political Education. Han (2023) [10] and Su (2024) [11] explored how ideological and political elements could be organically integrated with teaching content. The course integrates various teaching methods, such as lectures, case studies, special topics, and subtle inculcation, to seamlessly incorporate ideological and political education elements at appropriate times. It highlights socialist new-era political theories and related ideological and political cases, ensuring that students have more opportunities to participate, think, feel, and experience, thereby further guiding their value orientation and making ideological and political education more effective. Ding (2021) [12] presented the points of ideological and political integration in Table 4.

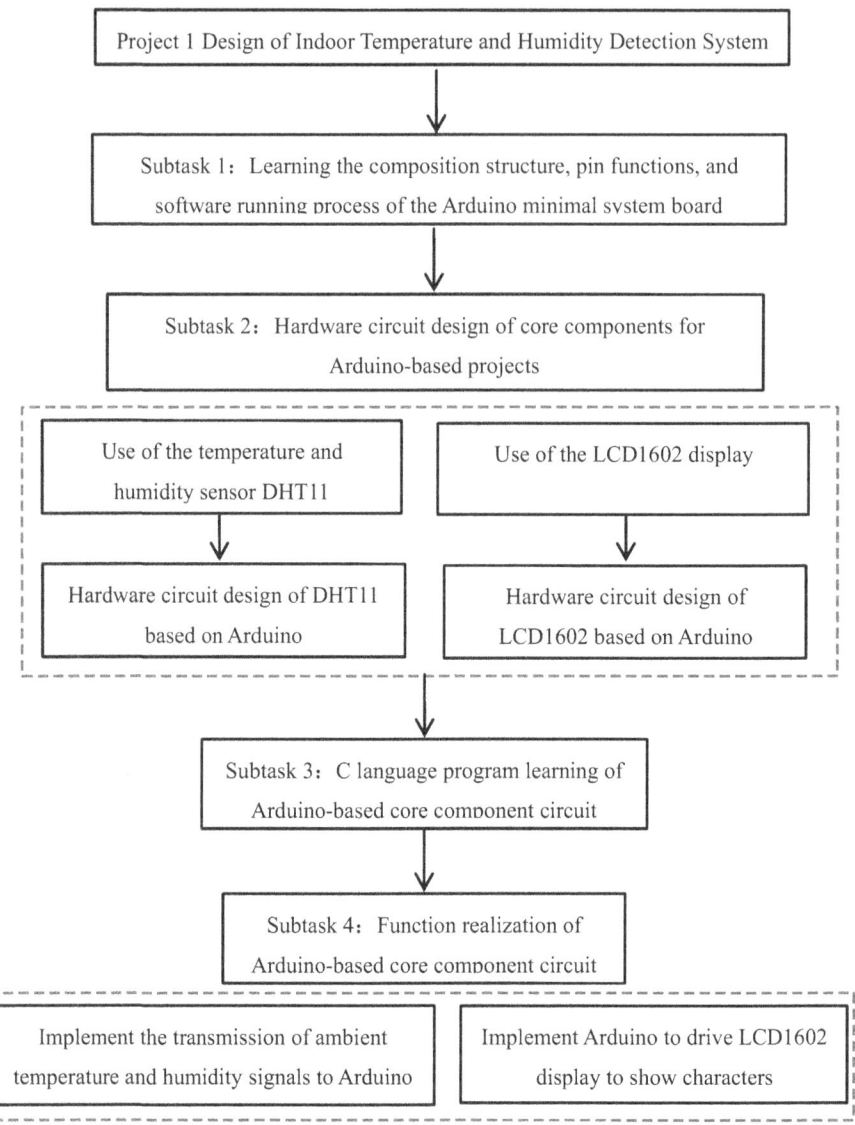

Fig. 3. Task breakdown diagram for Project 1

"N+1" Multidimensional Assessment. Yang (2023) [13] suggested that teaching evaluation is a good way to reflect teaching effectiveness. Ma (2023) [14] and Wang (2022) [15] built a comprehensive evaluation system for the whole process, and the course adopted the "N+1" assessment method, which combines the final examination with the usual performance. The overall score is based on a five-level grading system (excellent: 90–100 points, good: 80–89 points, medium: 70–79 points, pass: 60–69 points, fail: below 60 points). In the "N+1" assessment method, "1" refers to the final examination, which is in the form of a design report with a total score of 100 points, accounting for 50% of the overall score. The "N" represents the usual performance, with a total score of 100 points, accounting for the remaining 50% of the overall score. Usual performance includes online learning, classroom performance, assignments, and project design, each of which is assessed on a percentage basis. The course integrates ideological and political education into the assessment process, incorporating ideological and political education content into classroom performance and project design. The proportion of scores for each assessment component and the detailed assessment rules are shown in Table 5.

In the project design, teachers provide assessment results for each team's division of labor, the rationality and feasibility of program design, and whether physical hardware and software function debugging meets basic functional requirements, project reports, defenses, etc. The specific assessment rules and proportions are shown in Fig. 4.

Table 4. Integration points of ideological and political education in courses

Course content		Ideological and political elements	Teaching approach
1 What is communication?	Current status and future trends of communication technology	Patriotic sentiments and social responsibility	By introducing the impact of the US–China trade war on Huawei, we aim to inspire students to cultivate a sense of patriotism and mission to contribute to the country through technology
2 Introduction to communication engineering	Development history and current situation of hardware	Patriotic sentiments and social responsibility	1. By introducing the suppression of Chinese companies such as ZTE and Huawei by the United States, students are inspired to have a sense of patriotism and mission to serve their country in the field of technology; 2. By introducing Huawei's development of the Kirin chipset and HarmonyOS, students are inspired to have a sense of national pride and confidence in their country

(continued)

Table 4. (*continued*)

Course content		Ideological and political elements	Teaching approach
	Computer network applications	Professionalism and social responsibility	The introduction of telecom fraud warns students of their historical mission as a communicator and their future direction of effort, establish correct values, form a correct sense of social responsibility, and fulfill the mission, duties and obligations that should be undertaken for the country or society and others in social life
	Core concept of the product	Legal education	Through the introduction of product patent applications, students are warned that trademark registration can not harm the social public interests, violate good customs, especially for the registration of "Leishenshan", "Huoshenshan", "Li Wenliang" and other trademarks, is a violation of intellectual property ethics and professional ethics, and students are educated on the rule of law

(*continued*)

Table 4. (*continued*)

Course content		Ideological and political elements	Teaching approach
3 Project practice	Project execution process	Innovative spirit	Taking the Chinese Women's Volleyball Team as an example, students are guided to have firm career beliefs, excellent professional knowledge and skills and good professional behavior habits. Able to understand and abide by engineering ethics and norms in production and life
	Project design	Innovative spirit	Taking Huawei 5G as an example, students are guided to keep pace with the Times, be diligent in exploration, and be brave in practice during the system design process. Able to comprehensively use the existing knowledge, information, skills and methods, apply them to practice, constantly integrate, constantly think, to put forward new methods and new ideas, with the will, confidence, courage and wisdom to invent, reform and innovation

Table 5. Detailed rules for "N+1" assessment

Assessment criteria	Suggested score			Assessment/Evaluation regulations	Corresponding course objectives
Regular performance	50	Online learning	20%	Score according to the completion of uploaded videos on the FIF platform	Course objective 1 Course objective 4
		Classroom performance	20%	Score according to aike attendance, discussion and other participation and completion Elements of ideological and political education assessment: Through the setting of ideological and political related discussion content to assess the cultivation effect of students' patriotism and social responsibility	Course objective 2
		Assignments	20%	(1) Score according to the quality of assignments completion; (2) Each assignment is scored on a percentage basis, and the average score of all assignments is taken as the score for the section	Course objective 1 Course objective 4
		Project design	40%	Score according to the quality of project completion and the defense evaluation Elements of ideological and political education assessment: Assess the cultivation effect of students' innovation spirit and professional ethics through project design	Course objective 2 Course objective 3

(*continued*)

Table 5. (*continued*)

Assessment criteria	Suggested score	Assessment/Evaluation regulations	Corresponding course objectives
Final examination	50	(1) The assessment is based on the project design report, with a total score of 100 points, which will be prorated into the overall score; (2) Comprehensively assessment the students' mastery of knowledge and their ability to analyze and solve problems; (3) If the final assessment score is below 45 points, it will be considered as a fail	Course objective 3 Course objective 4

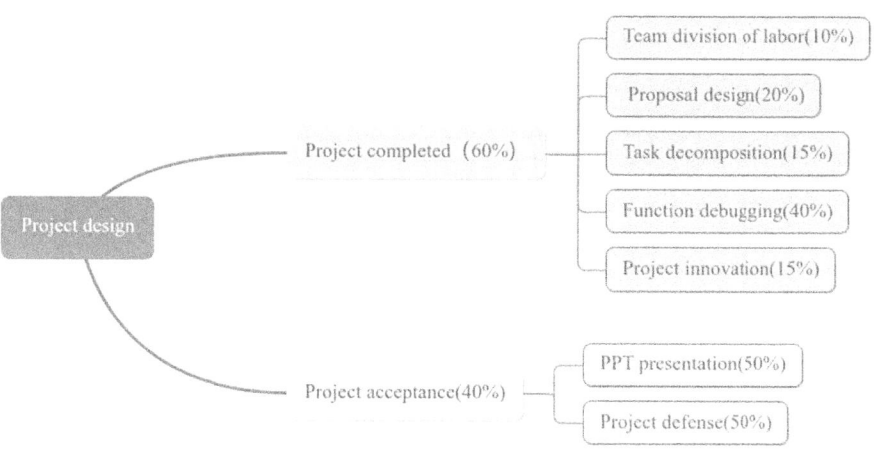

Fig. 4. Assessment regulations of the project design

4 Course Teaching Evaluation

4.1 Student Aspects

Overall Score Analysis. According to the engineering certification requirements and the assessment regulations of the "N+1" course, the analysis of course achievement and the achievement of each course objective are shown in Table 6.

According to the analysis in Table 6, the achievement of course objective 1 is 0.94, indicating that the blended online and offline teaching method enables students to have a better understanding of the knowledge framework, application areas, and development overview of communication engineering. The achievement of course objective 2 is 0.88, indicating that students can understand and adhere well to professional engineering norms and ethics in project practice. The achievement of course objective 3 is 0.85, showing that through project practice, students have a good grasp of the scientific learning methods for analyzing and designing project cases from hardware, software, and other perspectives and possess certain abilities in independent study, teamwork, and engineering awareness. The achievement of course objective 4 is 0.87, indicating that students have been cultivated with a certain level of innovation awareness. The overall course achievement is 0.87, demonstrating that blended online and offline teaching reform based on projects has achieved good results.

Table 6. Course overall performance analysis

Project	Objective								
	Objective 1		Objective 2		Objective 3		Objective 4		
Supporting link	Online learning 50%	Assignments 50%	Project design 50%	Classroom performance	Project design 50%	Final examination 50%	Assignments 50%	Online learning 50%	Final examination 50%
Average score for corresponding support links	5	4.43	8.77	8.79	8.77	21.07	4.43	5	21.07
Target score (corresponding to the score of the supporting link)	5	5	10	10	10	25	5	5	25
Objective achievement	0.94		0.88		0.85		0.87		
Course achievement	0.87								

Analysis of the End-of-Term Questionnaire Survey. After the course, the course team collectively formulated a course survey questionnaire. The questionnaire covers eight dimensions of indicators, including professional understanding, project settings, teaching activity design, teaching methods, teaching evaluation, learning effectiveness, overall evaluation, and teaching suggestions. Multiple evaluation indicators are set for each dimension, and specific evaluation descriptions are provided for each evaluation indicator. A total of 99 students majoring in communication engineering in the 2023 grade participated in the questionnaire survey, and the final course evaluation score was 92.16, indicating a high level of satisfaction with the course teaching among students.

Through the questionnaire survey, students also provided some teaching suggestions, such as conducting the acceptance of two teaching class projects at the same time and place for mutual learning; allowing groups to determine project presenters on their own so that students can play to their strengths and better demonstrate the completed projects;

and in the project defense session, each student in the group answers a question randomly assigned by the teacher, thereby mobilizing students' participation in the projects.

4.2 Peer Review

In the spirit of the document "Notice on Carrying out the Project-based and Hybrid Course Construction during the 14th Five-Year Plan Period", the Anhui Institute of Information Technology initiated 88 project-based and hybrid courses for the 2022–2023 academic year. After all courses for the academic year are completed, an annual inspection and acceptance are conducted. The "Introduction to Communication Engineering" course has been approved as a project-based course. After multiple rounds of review by all members of the school's teaching committee, deans in charge of teaching in various secondary colleges, and heads of teaching and research offices, this course has been rated as excellent in inspection and acceptance, ranking 13th in the evaluation.

According to the inspection and acceptance level and review ranking of project-based courses, the teaching design, implementation process, and implementation effect of this course have been recognized by the school's expert judges. Moreover, it has also played a demonstrative role in the teaching reform of other courses.

5 Conclusion

The "Introduction to Communication Engineering" course is offered in the first semester of the freshman year and plays a very important role in helping students understand the communication engineering profession. On the basis of the shortcomings of the traditional teaching model and in line with the school's educational position and the latest revision of professional talent training objectives, teaching reforms have been carried out for the course. The teaching objectives and ideological and political goals of the course have been further clarified, the professional knowledge framework and system have been reconstructed from the perspective of engineers, a project-based blended teaching model has been adopted, emphasis has been placed on process-oriented assessment of the course, and ideological and political education has been integrated throughout the teaching process. Through the analysis of student data and peer evaluation results, the teaching reform model of the course effectively stimulated students' interest in professional learning; cultivated their self-learning ability, engineering practice awareness, innovative thinking, etc.; achieved the course objectives well; and played a certain role as a demonstration for promotion. The teaching reform of courses is the development trend of future higher education. We should dare to break tradition, create teaching models that meet the needs of talent training in society, improve teaching quality, and enhance students' competitiveness in society.

Acknowledgments. Anhui Institute of Information Technology School-level Master Teacher Cultivation Project (Reform Category) "Ding Jiao" (project No. 22xjmspyjxmsgg02); Anhui Province Higher Education Provincial Quality Engineering Project "Innovative Project for Cultivating Excellent Engineers in Communication Engineering Major" (project No. 2022zybj045); Anhui Province Higher Education Provincial Quality Engineering Project "Exploration on the

Establishment and Implementation Path of Teaching Quality System Model Based on Value-added Evaluation – Taking the Course of 'Database Technology and Application' as an Example" (project No. 2023jyxm0656); Anhui Province Higher Education Provincial Quality Engineering Project "Research on Course Teaching Model for Precision Teaching Based on Big Data" (project No. 2023jyxm0667); Anhui Province Higher Education Provincial Quality Engineering Project "Exploration and Practice of Industry-Education Integration Talent Cultivation Mode in Communication Engineering Major from the Perspective of Collaborative Education" (project No. 2022sx065); Anhui Province Higher Education Provincial Quality Engineering Project "Introduction to Engineering for New Electronic Information Majors" (project No. 2022jcjs058).

References

1. Yanliang, Z.: Introduction to Information and Communication Engineering. China Electric Power Press, Beijing (2015)
2. Guocai, W., Ronghua, S.: Introduction to Communication Engineering. China Railway Press, Beijing (2022)
3. Tianfei, Z., Jinming, P., Minfeng, Z.: Introduction to Engineering of New Engineering Electronic Information Majors. Huazhong University of Science and Technology Press, Wuhan (2022)
4. Sha, N., Guo, M., Gao, Y., et al.: Exploration and practice of online and offline mixed teaching mode – taking "communication principles" course as an example. J. High. Educ. Res. **45**(04), 69–72+93 (2022)
5. Xu, J., Lv, X., Chen, Z., et al.: Exploration and practice of online and offline integrated teaching mode of metallurgical process design and research course. China Metall. Educ. (01), 36–37+43 (2024)
6. Lin, F., Fang, L.: Exploration on online and offline mixed teaching mode of digital electronic technology course. China Educ. Technol. Equip. **01**, 100–104 (2024)
7. Deng, X.: Research on the application of project-based teaching in "introduction to Internet of Things technology" course. Sci. Advice (Sci. Technol. Manag. (05), 104 (2020)
8. Mao, P., Gao, C., Shi, Y.: Project-based teaching practice of communication electronic circuit experiment. Electron. Technol. **53**(04), 416–418 (2024)
9. Shi, X., Chen, J., Jin, W.: Design and implementation of project-based practice teaching of communication electronic circuit course. Lab. Sci. **25**(03), 133–136 (2022)
10. Han, Y., Wu, R., Lu, X.: Ideological and political construction and practice of "introduction to communication engineering" course. J. Electr. Electron. Teach. **45**(04), 105–109 (2023)
11. Su, W.: Exploration and research of integrating curriculum ideology and politics into electronic information engineering major – taking the course "data communication and computer network" as an example. J. Hubei Open Vocat. Coll. **37**(01), 96–97 (2024)
12. Ding, J., Zhang, T.: Research on the ideological and political construction of the course introduction to communication engineering. New Gener. **25**(18), 236–237 (2021)
13. Yang, L., Chen, G., Chang, J., Li, X., Wan, N., Liu, Y.: Exploring the establishment and implementation of a teaching evaluation system based on value-added assessment. In: Gan, J., Pan, Y., Zhou, J., Liu, D., Song, X., Lu, Z. (eds.) CSEI 2023. CCIS, vol. 1899. Springer, Singapore (2024). https://doi.org/10.1007/978-981-99-9499-1_20
14. Ma, C., Chen, H., Jia, Y.L.: Project flipped classroom teaching design and evaluation system construction – teaching reform and practice of "single-chip microcomputer principle and interface technology" course. Educ. Teach. Forum (21), 116–119 (2023)
15. Wang, X., Liu, H.: Research on evaluation method of project teaching based on PBL model – taking object-oriented programming course as an example. Comput. Knowl. Technol. **18**(18), 103–105 (2022)

Substation Operation and Maintenance Training System Based on Virtual Reality and Knowledge Graph

Hao Duan[1], Feng Ye[1(✉)] ⓘ, Nadia Nedjah[2] ⓘ, and Zihao Yang[1] ⓘ

[1] Hohai University, Nanjing, China
yefeng1022@hhu.edu.cn
[2] University of Rio de Janeiro, Rio de Janeiro, Brazil

Abstract. With the increasing complexity and specialization of substation operation and maintenance (Q&M), traditional training methods are insufficient to meet the demands of efficient and comprehensive education. The integration of virtual reality (VR) technology and knowledge graphs (KGs) present new opportunities for innovating O&M training systems. However, existing VR training systems do not fully utilize KGs to provide comprehensive training frameworks, and systems that integrate KGs often lack realism and intuitive scene representation. Moreover, research on applying VR technology and KG to substation O&M training remains relatively scarce. To address these issues, this paper proposes a substation O&M training system based on VR and KGs. The system employs VR technology to construct a highly realistic training environment, offering functions such as equipment operation, fault diagnosis, and emergency response, allowing trainees to engage in hands-on training within an immersive virtual scene. Simultaneously, the system integrates KGs to systematically present the knowledge framework of substations O&M, assisting learners in quickly accessing the required information and enhancing learning efficiency. This system has been applied in three organizations, received positive feedback, and trained numerous O&M personnel, significantly improving training effectiveness and work efficiency, indicating broad application prospects.

Keywords: Knowledge graphs · Substations · Visualization · Operation and maintenance training

1 Introduction

Substations are critical components of power systems, and are essential for the transmission and distribution of electrical energy. Their stable operation directly impacts the safety and reliability of the power supply. However, the complex topology, numerous devices, and intricate structures of substations increase the likelihood of equipment failure and increase maintenance burdens. Therefore, effective training for operation and maintenance (O&M) personnel is crucial [1]. Substation O&M encompasses complex content such as equipment operation, fault diagnosis, and safety regulations. Much of this knowledge exists in regulations, manuals, operating procedures, and training materials, resulting in a steep learning curve and complicating the process of delivering effective training [2, 3].

Traditional training methods rely mainly on document-based teaching, with limited emphasis on hands-on equipment training [4]. Furthermore, using real equipment for training poses risks of damage and is constrained by high costs and maintenance complexities, hindering widespread usage. Additionally, traditional methods lack interactivity and immersion, making it difficult to engage learners and improving training effectiveness.

To address these challenges, increasing attention has been given in recent years to the integration of virtual reality (VR) technology and knowledge graphs (KGs) in education and training. VR technology enables a high degree of interactivity, vividly presenting teaching content and providing users with a synthesized 3D environment that immerses them in a virtual setting [5]. The KG extracts and refines information from large and diverse datasets, constructing a clear and interconnected knowledge structure. This effectively establishes connections among educators, learners, learning resources, and knowledge points, enriching semantic information and facilitating relational features within the data [6]. The combination of these two concepts can leverage their respective advantages, offering a more comprehensive and efficient solution for substation O&M training.

Although existing studies [3–8] have developed training systems based on either VR or KGs, these systems predominantly focus on single-technology applications. For example, the work in [4] creates a realistic training environment using VR technology, allowing trainees to engage in team collaboration and hands-on practice to increase the safety and efficiency of substation maintenance work. However, this system lacks systematic knowledge presentation, making it difficult to support the effective transmission of complex knowledge. In [7], a KG-based educational system was designed for mathematics training for IT professionals, aiming to improve the quality and efficiency of mathematical training. Nevertheless, this system lacks realism and intuitive scene representation, failing to provide an immersive learning experience. Thus, training systems that integrate VR and KGs have yet to be fully explored and validated in the specific context of substation O&M.

In light of this analysis, this paper proposes a substation O&M training system based on VR and KGs, aiming to address the shortcomings of existing systems and improve training outcomes. By constructing a systematic maintenance knowledge ontology and knowledge graphs, combined with realistic and intuitive VR scenes, the system provides O&M personnel with comprehensive, interactive, and efficient training experience. This paper details the design concept, construction methods, and practical application effects of the system, aiming to provide an innovative technical solution for substation maintenance training and promote advancements in related fields.

The structure of this paper is as follows: Sect. 2 provides a review of the relevant literature, emphasizing the application of VR and KGs in training systems, while identifying existing research gaps, particularly in the context of substation-specific scenarios. Section 3 outlines the methodology for developing the proposed substation O&M training system, including the construction of the knowledge ontology, the development of the KG, and the creation of VR environments. Section 4 presents the practical implementation of system and evaluates its effectiveness in enhancing training outcomes. Finally, Sect. 5 summarizes the key contributions of this work and discusses future research directions, such as improving equipment models, expanding the knowledge graph, and integrating multiuser collaboration functionalities to further enhance the system.

2 Related Works

In the field of training, notable research progress has been made in the application of VR technology and KGs. However, most studies focus on the application of either technology individually, and the integration of the two has not been fully realized, especially in substation-specific scenarios where research is particularly limited. This paper reviews related work from three main perspectives and highlight the existing shortcomings in these areas.

2.1 Training Systems Based on Virtual Reality

With the advancement of VR technology, its applications have expanded beyond gaming [9], movies [10] and education [11] to provide substantial technical support for industrial production and training processes. In substation O&M training systems, VR technology has been utilized to construct realistic simulation environments that enhance trainees' practical skills and emergency response capabilities. For example, reference [12] developed an immersive virtual training system for substation electricians, enabling users to interact with the virtual environment via head-mounted displays (HMDs), joysticks, standard keyboards, mice, and monitors. Similarly, reference [13] introduced a VR-based substation O&M simulation system that employs interactive 3D engine technology and gesture interaction techniques to enhance scene realism. This system provides significant personnel support and intellectual resources for power grid operators to meet the demands of modern power system development. However, these systems focus primarily on realistic scene reproduction and operational interactivity, and lack systematic knowledge presentation and structured learning paths. Consequently, they struggle to comprehensively cover the complex knowledge framework required for substation maintenance.

2.2 Training Systems Based on Knowledge Graphs

KG has become a focal point in educational research and applications, facilitating systematic organization, in-depth analysis, and comprehensive utilization of knowledge [14]. A knowledge graph is a structured representation method that forms a vast network by establishing semantic relationships between entities; nodes represent entities, and edges represent the relationships between them. In substation O&M, reference [15] applied a KG to process automation equipment records, transforming redundant equipment information into a knowledge graph. This approach significantly improved the efficiency of querying and identifying equipment information, providing important support for automated substation maintenance. Reference [16] introduced a method for constructing and retrieving KGs for transformer equipment simulation information on basis of physical relationships. The method aims to obtain simulation information for different types of transformer equipment and build a knowledge graph based on physical devices, systems, or their components within the transformer equipment simulation technology domain. These systems categorize and associate substation scene information to construct a comprehensive KG, enabling maintenance personnel to quickly access relevant information. However, they lack integration with intuitive scene presentations and vivid interactive experiences, making it difficult to engage learners' interest and participation during training.

2.3 Integrated VR and KGs in Training Systems

The integration of VR technology and KGs has shown promise in enhancing immersive training experiences through structured knowledge representation. Recent studies have demonstrated this potential across various applications. For example, reference [17] introduces a VR-based approach for interacting with spatiotemporal relationships among entities, offering new ways to visualize and analyze complex historical networks. Additionally, reference [18] combines KGs with steady-state visually evoked potential (SSVEP) brain-computer interfaces, allowing hands-free VR interactions and expanding accessibility in data-rich environments. In specific application domains, the KCUBE project [19] developed a VR-KG framework for curriculum advising, enabling students and educators to explore course relationships within an immersive environment, which facilitates better understanding of academic pathways. Similarly, the Ontodia3D tool [20] extends the Ontodia platform, allowing users to visualize and interact with large-scale knowledge graphs in a 3D VR space. This tool's three-dimensional organization of semantic data improves navigation and comprehension by clustering related information spatially. While these advancements underscore the potential of VR-KG integration, further exploration in specific domains, such as substation training, remains limited, indicating a valuable opportunity for future research.

However, the exploration of integrating VR with KGs in substation scenarios remains insufficient.

In summary, while current research has made progress in O&M training systems based on VR or KGs, significant deficiencies remain in the following areas:

1. Existing VR training systems fail to integrate KGs for systematic knowledge presentation.
2. Training systems that incorporate KGs lack realism and intuitive scenes and equipment displays.
3. Training systems that comprehensively apply both VR and KGs have not yet been fully applied and validated in the specific context of substations O&M.

To address these research gaps, this paper aims to develop a system specifically designed for substation O&M training, combining the advantages of both VR and KGs. By constructing a realistic substation environment and a comprehensive knowledge system, users can practice operations in a virtual space and grasp key knowledge through a dynamic learning process. This innovative approach aims to improve the efficiency and quality of O&M training, providing strong support for future power system management.

Table 1. Example of concept attributes in the knowledge ontology for substation operation and maintenance training.

Concept	Attribute Name	Attribute Description
Equipment	name	Equipment name, e.g., "Circuit Breaker"
	type	Equipment type, e.g., "Protection Device"
	description	Equipment description, detailing the functions of the equipment
Operation	name	Operation name, e.g., "Maintenance"
	description	Operation description, explaining the content and steps of the operation
Fault	name	Fault name, e.g., "Short Circuit"
	description	Fault description, explaining the cause and impact of the fault
Safety Procedure	name	Safety procedure name, e.g., "Emergency Response"
	description	Safety procedure description, explaining the emergency handling process
Personnel	name	Personnel name, e.g., "Engineer Zhang"
	role	Personnel role, e.g., "Technician"
Manufacturer	name	Manufacturer name, e.g., "Siemens"
	country	Country of the manufacturer, e.g., "Germany"
	contact	Manufacturer contact information, such as a website link

3 Methodology for Constructing Substation O&M Training Systems

To build an efficient and comprehensive substation O&M training system, this paper proposes a methodology for system construction on basis of VR and KGs. This methodology encompasses three key steps: the construction of a knowledge ontology for substation O&M training, the development of a knowledge graph, and the creation of VR scenarios.

3.1 Construction of the Knowledge Ontology for Substation O&M Training

Several methodologies exist for ontology construction, including TOVE [18], METHONTOLOGY [21], and the Stanford Seven-Step Approach [22]. The Stanford approach, which use the Protégé ontology tool, is a semiautomated development method that is more mature and widely applied than other methods. Following the guidelines of the Stanford seven-step approach, the steps for constructing an ontology for substation O&M training are summarized as follows:

1. *Define goals and scope*: This step allows us to clarify the objectives of constructing the knowledge graph and define the content scope for substation O&M training. This

may include equipment operation, fault diagnosis and handling, safety procedures, system monitoring, and emergency response.

2. *Organize key terms and define classes*: This step allows us to identify the essential terms for the ontology, define classes—including their hierarchy and attributes—and categorize them, followed by the creation of instances. The knowledge related to substation O&M is sourced from maintenance manuals, operation guides, the technical literature, and expert interviews. After this information is organized, relevant terms are identified, core domain concepts are established, and their relationships are categorized.

3. *Extract and categorize key concepts*: This step allows the extraction of the key knowledge points from the collected information as fundamental units for constructing the knowledge graph, ensuring concept accuracy and completeness. These knowledge points include equipment functions, operating procedures, common faults, and their handling methods.

4. *Classify the concepts*: This step allows one to categorize the extracted knowledge points on basis of logical relationships or O&M processes, such as equipment management, fault handling, maintenance operations, and safety procedures. This classification clarifies relationships among knowledge points, facilitating the subsequent construction of the knowledge framework.

5. *Building the knowledge framework*: This step allows the construction of a structured knowledge framework on the basis of the categorized knowledge points, accurately reflecting the connections and dependencies between concepts. For example, under equipment management, subcategories can include equipment types, operating methods, and maintenance procedures. The framework should ensure a clear hierarchy and logical coherence.

6. *Refine the ontology attributes*: This step allows the establishment of detailed attributes for each concept and relationship, including unique identifiers (IDs), definitions, and feature descriptions, to provide a unified description of each concept and relationship. This step enhances the ontology's scalability and maintainability, ensuring standardization of the knowledge graph.

7. *Evaluating the Quality*: This step allows the constructed ontology to be subjected to expert review to confirm that the concepts and relationships meet practical O&M requirements. On the basis of feedback, unsuitable parts are adjusted or removed to improve the ontology's accuracy and usability.

The adapter pattern is used to demonstrate the tasks related to extracting knowledge points, establishing knowledge relationships, and designing knowledge point attributes, as shown in Table 1. This pattern illustrates the attribute format of the concept.

3.2 Construction of the Knowledge Graph

The construction of the knowledge graph for substation O&M training begins with establishing an ontology framework as the foundation. The main steps include knowledge instantiation, supplementing relationships, and adding attributes.

Knowledge instantiation involves mapping O&M knowledge from the ontologies framework to actual training content, thereby concretizing concepts in training scenarios. Concepts are instantiated sequentially, progressing from higher to lower levels of abstraction.

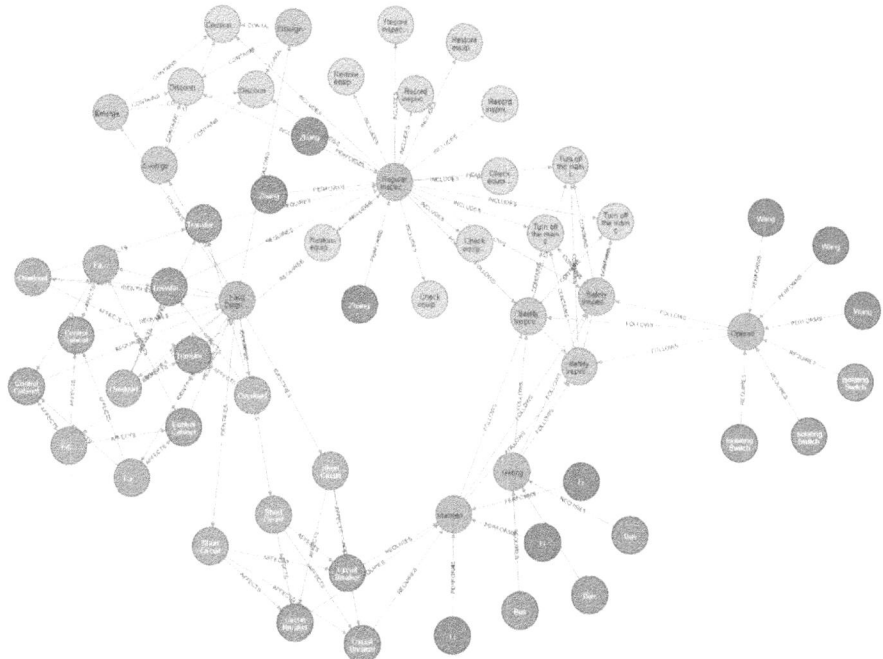

Fig. 1. Knowledge graph for substation operation and maintenance training.

During instantiation, relationships between knowledge nodes are established to align with actual maintenance practices. These relationships typically mirror those in the original ontology framework and adhere to the parameter definitions of the O&M knowledge ontology. This process transitions abstract concepts into concrete ones on the basis of their levels of abstraction.

In the addition of knowledge attributes, each knowledge node is completed with attributes such as identifiers, definitions, and characteristics. The "identifier" ensures uniqueness and is generated by a tool; the "definition" describes the essential features of the knowledge node; and the "characteristics" detail the rules, properties, and unique aspects.

By applying these methods, we construct a substation O&M training knowledge graph comprising 59 entities and 108 relationships, representing 59 knowledge points and 108 direct connections between them, as illustrated in Fig. 1.

3.3 Construction of Virtual Reality Scenarios for Substation Training

The construction of a VR scenario for substation training requires a realistic simulation of the equipment and environment, which is integrated with interactive functionalities for O&M training systems. Figure 2 presents an overview of the VR substation scenario. The following steps are envisioned to achieve this virtual environment.

- *Scene planning and design*: On the basis of the structure and O&M needs of an actual substation, we design the spatial relationships between devices, referencing real layouts. Key equipment such as transformers, circuit breakers, and busbars are arranged to accurately reflect a substation's structure. Attention is given to equipment spacing, safety zones, and main passageways to ensure operational functionality and immersion.
- *3D model construction*: Using tools such as Blender, we create high-precision models of equipment, especially key devices. The models replicate the geometric shapes, sizes, materials, and details of the actual equipment. Polygon counts are controlled to ensure smooth operation.
- *Material and texture processing*: High-quality materials and textures are applied to enhance realism. Materials match equipment surface properties, such as a metallic sheen, and coordinate with lighting effects. Textures include details such as nameplates and wiring to enhance immersion.
- *Scene layout and environment setup*: The 3D models are imported into Unity and arranged according to the plan. Equipment placement reflects actual operational needs, and environmental elements such as ground materials, buildings, and fences are configured. Lighting and shadows are adjusted to simulate the substation's daily environment.
- *Interactive feature implementation*: Equipment supports interactive functions for O&M training. Users can inspect equipment, view status information, or operate circuit breakers via VR devices. Interactive logic is implemented via C# scripts in Unity, enabling responsive device operations.
- *Fault simulation and training tasks*: Fault simulation functionality is integrated to increase training effectiveness. Users can safely handle equipment faults such as transformer overloads or circuit breaker failures, familiarizing themselves with fault characteristics and handling steps.
- *Performance optimization and scene testing*: The virtual environment is optimized by reducing polygon counts, compressing textures, and adjusting rendering settings for smooth operation on VR devices or desktops. Testing was used to verify user interactions, scene stability, and visual realism to meet training objectives.

By following the aforementioned steps, we construct the VR scenario depicted in Fig. 2, which offers a realistic and interactive substation environment. This platform allows O&M personnel to practice equipment operations and fault handling safely, significantly improving training efficiency and effectiveness.

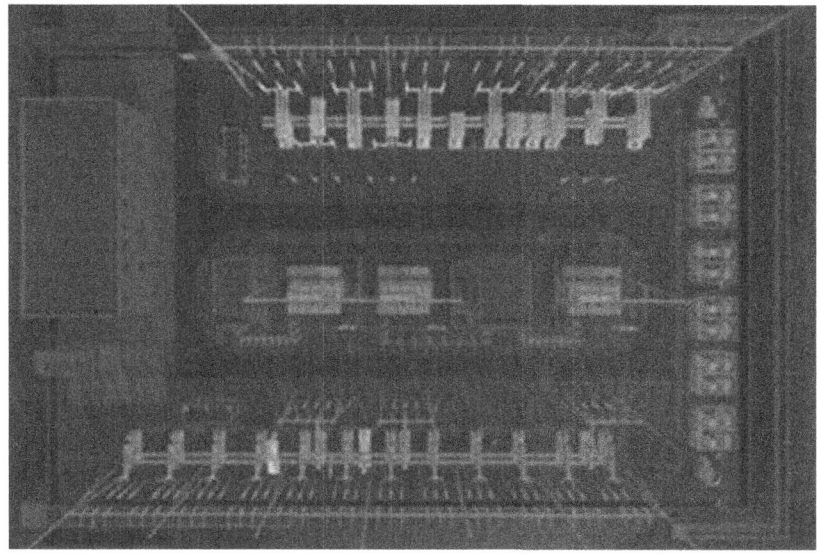

Fig. 2. Construction of virtual reality scenarios.

4 System Demonstration and Application

On the basis of VR and KGs, the Substation O&M training system offers an innovative solution for efficient training in complex substation environments, as illustrated in Fig. 3. The system leverages VR technology to construct realistic substation operation scenarios, providing functionalities such as equipment operation, fault diagnosis, and emergency response. This enables trainees to engage in hands-on training within an immersive virtual environment. Simultaneously, the integrated KG systematically presents the knowledge framework of substation O&M, assisting learners in quickly accessing necessary information and enhancing learning efficiency.

Trainees can interact with the virtual environment via a mouse and keyboard or by wearing VR goggles. By clicking on equipment knowledge nodes within the virtual scene, they can view equipment entities and browse operation manuals, common fault descriptions, and emergency handling procedures. Each node in the knowledge graph represents a specific device or operational process, allowing trainees to flexibly explore the entire graph, thereby enhancing the depth and breadth of learning. In the device operation module, trainees can enter virtual operation scenarios to actually control various equipment, such as starting and shutting down devices or adjusting parameters, familiarizing themselves with operational principles and procedures. In the fault diagnosis module, trainees can access fault simulation scenarios to observe equipment status during faults, understand fault causes, and simulate fault detection and elimination processes. This includes identifying fault signals, analyzing fault data, and implementing appropriate maintenance measures. In the emergency handling module, trainees can simulate emergency response steps and practice procedures for sudden events. For example, when facing equipment anomalies or emergencies, they can follow emergency plans to perform actions such as emergency shutdowns and alarm handling. However, real-world emergency situations in substation operations can have severe and far-reaching conse-quences, such as equipment damage, power outages, and risks to personnel safety. While virtual reality provides a safe and controlled environment for training, there is an inher-ent risk that repeated exposure to simulated scenarios may cause users to underestimate the severity of these events. To address this, the training emphasizes the critical nature of emergency situations through scenario design that reflects the potential consequences and reinforces the importance of swift and appropriate responses. Trainees are regu-larly reminded of the real-world implications of each scenario, ensuring that the training maintains a focus on developing the mindset needed for effective decision-making under genuine high-pressure conditions.

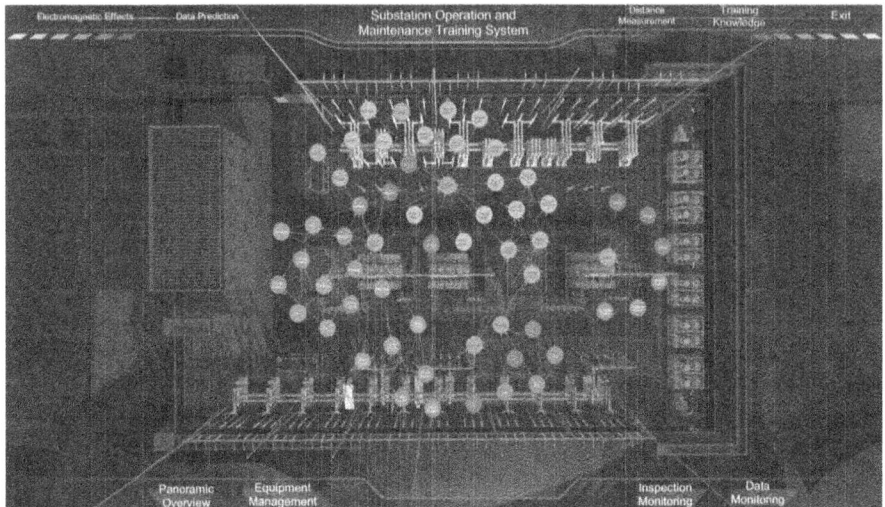

Fig. 3. Substation O&M training system based on VR and KGs.

Building on these interactive capabilities, the system offers significant advantages that enhance the overall training experience. By integrating VR and KG technologies, it provides an immersive environment where trainees can engage in realistic equip-ment operations, fault diagnosis, and emergency response drills within a safe virtual space. This approach not only increases engagement and interactivity but also enables trainees to gain hands on experience that closely resembles real-world scenarios, rein-forcing skill acquisition and knowledge retention. Additionally, the systematic knowl-edge framework provided by the KG allows for efficient access to structured information, enabling trainees to quickly retrieve essential operational details, fault handling proce-dures, and emergency protocols, thereby increasing training efficiency and supporting ongoing knowledge development. The use of VR simulation also reduces the risks and costs associated with traditional training methods that involve real equipment, minimiz-ing potential damage and maintenance expenses while allowing for repeated practice.

Furthermore, the integrated emergency simulation functionality enhances trainees' preparedness for real incidents by providing realistic scenarios for practicing rapid response techniques.

Table 2. Satisfaction scores of the substation operation and maintenance training system.

Dimension	Item	Score
Design and Interface	The system design is aesthetically pleasing and clear	4.80 ± 0.60
	The system is easy to operate and navigate	4.75 ± 0.55
	The interaction design is intuitive and user-friendly	4.70 ± 0.58
Operational Stability	The system runs smoothly without lag	4.85 ± 0.50
	Virtual scenes load seamlessly	4.78 ± 0.65
	Functional performance meets operational requirements	4.82 ± 0.54
Content Richness	The system provides comprehensive operation and training content	4.88 ± 0.62
	Supports simulation and training for various substation equipment	4.83 ± 0.57
	Offers a complete knowledge graph and operational guidance	4.90 ± 0.45
User Experience	The interface is user-friendly and operations are smooth	4.77 ± 0.60
	High user engagement with positive feedback	4.85 ± 0.52
	Convenient review and assessment modules are provided	4.82 ± 0.58
Effectiveness	The system effectively improves users' operational skills and knowledge	4.86 ± 0.55
	Assists users in successfully completing assessments	4.84 ± 0.53
	Enhances work efficiency after system usage	4.88 ± 0.50
Overall Satisfaction	Users are willing to recommend the system to others	4.87 ± 0.56
	The system is highly practical and innovative	4.89 ± 0.58

This system has been successfully implemented in three organizations, training over one hundred O&M personnel, and significantly improving training outcomes and operational efficiency. To evaluate the system's effectiveness, a survey was conducted among 125 trainees, covering four dimensions: design and operation, content configuration, effectiveness, and user intent. The survey included 18 items, rated on a 5 point Likert scale ranging from "very dissatisfied" to "very satisfied," with a total score of 90. The scoring results are shown in Table 2. The average score of each item in the system is 4.60 ± 0.58 (full score of 5 points), and the total score is 81.66 ± 12.18 (full score of 90 points). It performs well in multiple dimensions, and the overall feedback is good. Users highly praised the system's aesthetic design, ease of use, intuitive interaction, and operational stability, particularly in terms of functionality and the smooth loading of virtual scenes, which met operational needs. In terms of content richness, the system provided a variety of simulation scenarios and equipment training, accompanied by a comprehensive knowledge graph and operational guidance, further enhancing user engagement and skill mastery. The system's smooth operation, coupled with positive user feedback, significantly increased work efficiency and helped users successfully complete assessment tasks.

In addition to its successful application in substation O&M training, the system has significant potential for use in other fields that require high-risk operations or complex procedural training, such as aviation maintenance, emergency medical response, and chemical plant operations. Compared with existing training systems, this system stands out through its innovative integration of VR and KG technologies, offering a more immersive environment and a structured approach to knowledge management. While traditional VR-based systems may focus primarily on scene realism and interactivity, they often lack comprehensive knowledge organization, and KG-based systems, though effective for information retrieval, typically fall short in providing immersive, hands-on training experiences. This system bridges these gaps by combining the strengths of both approaches, resulting in improved skill acquisition, emergency response capabilities, and knowledge retrieval efficiency.

However, the system has limitations that are important to acknowledge. Its higher hardware requirements and the complexity of customizing simulation scenarios and knowledge graphs for different fields may restrict its rapid deployment compared with simpler training solutions. In contrast, some existing systems may offer more flexibility with lower equipment demands and easier adaptation, albeit at the cost of reduced training depth and interactivity. Despite these challenges, the system's comprehensive integration of VR and KGs and its demonstrated training effectiveness position it as a powerful tool for advancing high-risk operation training, surpassing the capabilities of many current alternatives.

5   Conclusion

This paper presents an innovative substation O&M training system that integrates VR and KGs to increase training efficiency and effectiveness for O&M personnel. By leveraging VR technology to construct highly realistic operational scenarios, the system provides an immersive learning experience that enhances training intuitiveness and interactivity. The integration of KGs allows for systematic organization and intelligent presentation of operational knowledge, facilitating efficient knowledge retrieval and learning. Deeply integrating VR and KGs, the system offers rich interactive experiences and establishes a comprehensive knowledge management platform, significantly enhancing trainees' practical skills and emergency response capabilities. Successfully implemented in three organizations and training over 100 personnel, the survey results indicate high levels of satisfaction among trainees, particularly with respect to realism and immersion, learning effectiveness, and interactivity. These results highlight the system's substantial benefits in enhancing training outcomes and operational efficiency, underscoring its broad potential for further application.

Importantly, there is still room for further optimization in refining equipment models, expanding the knowledge graph, and developing multiuser collaboration features. Future research will concentrate on enhancing system functionalities, broadening knowledge graph content, and exploring additional interaction methods to comprehensively improve the quality and effectiveness of substation operation and maintenance training.

References

1. Ojeda Misses, M.A., Jiménez, N.J.: Development of a platform with real-time performance for electrical circuits education. IEEE Lat. Am. Trans. **19**(12), 2147–2155 (2021)
2. Peng, Y., Ding, L., Xu, Z., Jiang, Y., Chen, J.: Design and realization of augmented reality based operation training system for operation and maintenance personnel of intelligent transformer substation. In: 2017 IEEE 2nd Information Technology, Networking, Electronic and Automation Control Conference (ITNEC), pp. 1706–1709 (2017)
3. Han, J., Li, Y., Wang, Q., Yang, M., Zhao, J., Zhao, J.: Power skill training knowledge base construction based on knowledge map and improved FP-growth. In: 2021 International Conference on Power System Technology (POWERCON), pp. 1962–1967 (2021)
4. de Oliveira Pereira Neto, J., et al.: An immersive multi-user VR-based system for the training of electrical substation maintenance. In: 2024 IEEE Conference on Virtual Reality and 3D User Interfaces Abstracts and Workshops (VRW), pp. 1216–1217 (2024)
5. Liu, S.: Research on the construction of a dance simulation training system using VR technology. In: 2023 International Conference on Educational Knowledge and Informatization (EKI), pp. 106–109 (2023)
6. Wei, A., Xie, J.: Research on intelligent automatic following collection system for constructing practical training knowledge graph. In: 2024 9th International Symposium on Computer and Information Processing Technology (ISCIPT), pp. 93–96 (2024)
7. Hassan, M., Hossain, M.A.: A VR based children formula feed preparation training simulator with AI-enabled automated assessment features. In: 2022 14th International Conference on Software, Knowledge, Information Management and Applications (SKIMA), pp. 303–308 (2022)
8. Fedonuyk, A., Yunchyk, V., Cheprasova, T., Yatsyuk, S.: The models of data and knowledge representation in educational system of mathematical training of IT-specialists. In: 2020 IEEE 15th International Conference on Computer Sciences and Information Technologies (CSIT), vol. 2, pp. 269–272 (2020)
9. Jung, S., Wu, Y., McKee, R., Lindeman, R.W.: All shook up: the impact of floor vibration in symmetric and asymmetric immersive multi-user VR gaming experiences. In: 2022 IEEE Conference on Virtual Reality and 3D User Interfaces (VR), pp. 737–745 (2022)
10. Yang, X.: Research on improved A* algorithm for camera path planning in VR movie shooting. In: 2023 3rd International Conference on Computer Science, Electronic Information Engineering and Intelligent Control Technology (CEI), pp. 914–918 (2023)
11. Ni, L., Wang, L.: Model study of VR technology in the professional teaching of preschool education. In: 2021 2nd International Conference on Information Science and Education (ICISE-IE), pp. 1490–1493 (2021)

12. Tanaka, E.H., et al.: Immersive virtual training for substation electricians. In: 2017 IEEE Virtual Reality (VR), pp. 451–452 (2017)

13. Wang, M., Gao, F., Zhang, H., Zhao, X., Zhao, C.: Research and development of VR based substation operation and maintenance simulation system. In: 2023 IEEE 3rd International Conference on Power, Electronics and Computer Applications (ICPECA), pp. 445–448 (2023)

14. Wu, P., Zhang, J., Ruan, Y., Chang, G., Wang, Y., Song, Y.: Construction of knowledge graph for substation automation equipment ledger based on Neo4j graph database. In: 2023 3rd Power System and Green Energy Conference (PSGEC), pp. 1080–1086 (2023)

15. Jian, K., Min, D., Xuyang, C., Feng, G., Qianli, Z., Dongqing, W.: Construction and retrieval method of power transformation simulation information knowledge graph based on physical relationship. In: 2024 4th Asia-Pacific Conference on Communications Technology and Computer Science (ACCTCS), pp. 113–117 (2024)

16. Becker, J., et al.: Virtual reality based access to knowledge graphs for history research. In: Knowledge Graphs: Semantics, Machine Learning, and Languages, pp. 144–160. IOS Press (2023)

17. Zhu, S., Yang, J., Ding, P., Wang, F., Gong, A., Fu, Y.: Optimization of SSVEP-BCI virtual reality stereo stimulation parameters based on knowledge graph. Brain Sci. 13(5), 710 (2023)

18. Yun, W., Zhang, X., Li, Z., Liu, H., Han, M.: Knowledge modeling: a survey of processes and techniques. Int. J. Intell. Syst. 36(4), 686–1720 (2021)

19. Li, Q., et al.: KCUBE: a knowledge graph university curriculum framework for student advising and career planning. In: Li, R.C., Cheung, S.K.S., Ng, P.H.F., Wong, L.P., Wang, F.L. (eds.) ICBL 2022. LNCS, vol. 13357, pp. 358–369. Springer, Cham (2022). https://doi.org/10.1007/978-3-031-08939-8_31

20. Daniil, R., Wohlgenannt, G., Pavlov, D., Emelyanov, Y., Mouromtsev, D.: A new tool for linked data visualization and exploration in 3D/VR space. In: Hitzler, P., et al. (eds.) ESWC 2019. LNCS, vol. 11762, pp. 167–171. Springer, Cham (2019). https://doi.org/10.1007/978-3-030-32327-1_33

21. Abdelghany, A.S., Darwish, N.R., Hefni, H.A.: An agile methodology for ontology development. Int. J. Intell. Eng. Syst. 12(2), 170–181 (2019)

22. Jiang, W., Wang, Y., Hu, J., Guan, L., Zhu, Z.: Construction of substation engineering design knowledge graph based on "ontology seven-step method". In: 2021 4th International Conference on Energy, Electrical and Power Engineering (CEEPE), pp. 957–962. IEEE (2021)

Design of the PLC Simulation Experimental Platform Based on Siemens TIA Portal Software

Yongchao Li[1], Jingyu Gao[1], and Shuxin Chen[1,2](✉)

[1] School of Mechanical and Electrical Engineering, Qiqihar University, Heilongjiang, Qiqihar, China
2024936353@qqhru.edu.cn, shuxinfriend@tju.edu.cn
[2] School of Intelligent Computing Engineering, Tianjin Ren'ai College, Tianjin, China

Abstract. In the context of integrated theoretical and practical teaching in higher education, electrical control and PLC technology are fundamental components within the field of industrial control. The promotion and application of these methods are frequently hindered by their high costs, the bulkiness of experimental equipment, and limited application scenarios. To address these challenges in the experimental teaching of this course, this paper employs TIA Portal software to develop a simulation experiment platform based on HMI and the S7-1500 PLC. This platform allows students to intuitively understand and engage with control processes. Teaching experiments confirm that the simulation platform accurately replicates the control processes of real-world scenarios, providing students with an accessible, practice-oriented environment that effectively integrates theory with practice. Furthermore, this study highlights the efficiency, convenience, and cost-effectiveness of PLC technology in electrical control education.

Keywords: TIA Portal software · PLC simulation experiment platform · HMI configuration · Integrated theoretical and practical teaching

1 Introduction

In recent years, the Ministry of Education has been actively driving the transformation of higher education institutions through policy initiatives and collaborative efforts across ministries and provinces, with a focus on enhancing the integration of industry and academia. In particular, in the face of rapid advancements in automation technology, programmable logic controller (PLC) technology has become widely adopted in sectors such as steel, petrochemicals, automotive, and electronics [1, 2]. The growing demand for highly skilled professionals has encouraged universities to further strengthen the link between academic programs and real-world engineering projects. By adopting a "theory-practice integration" approach [3], students not only acquire foundational knowledge but also gain hands-on experience in actual engineering contexts, nurturing their innovative capabilities [4]. This strategy fosters a mutually beneficial relationship between educational institutions and industries, ultimately supporting the development of high-caliber, application-oriented talent.

K. Zhang et al. (Eds.): CSEI 2024, CCIS 2448, pp. 347–355, 2025.
https://doi.org/10.1007/978-981-96-3738-6_26

As a cornerstone of the Mechatronics curriculum, PLC and electrical control technology play crucial roles in developing students' practical skills and technological innovations in the intelligent control of electromechanical systems [5, 6]. The teaching methodology combines theoretical lessons with hands-on experimentation, enabling students to engage in structured lab work that enhances their problem-solving abilities. Through this approach, students are tasked with translating engineering challenges into specific PLC control programs, thereby mastering the intelligent control of electromechanical devices.

2   Challenges of Traditional Teaching Platforms

Traditional PLC experimental methods often lack intuitive clarity, leading to potential human errors that can negatively impact experimental outcomes and fail to meet contemporary educational needs. Students who rely solely on structural diagrams and schematics from textbooks often struggle to fully understand the working principles of electrical components [7]. Additionally, as technology and workflows evolve, the pace of equipment updates tends to lag, rendering experimental projects repetitive and outdated [8]. The primary goal of the course is to equip students with the skills to independently design and debug electrical control systems for specific projects, using PLCs to design and modify general control systems [9].

This paper presents a solution in the form of a simulation experiment platform built on TIA Portal software, incorporating the S7-1500 PLC and HMI, as shown in Fig. 1. By utilizing HMI configurations to simulate and control real-world processes, the platform offers a visual representation of controlled operations, allowing students to quickly verify the accuracy of their programs. This solution overcomes the limitations of offline experimental setups, creating an environment where students can deepen their understanding of professional skills while improving the efficiency and quality of experimental teaching.

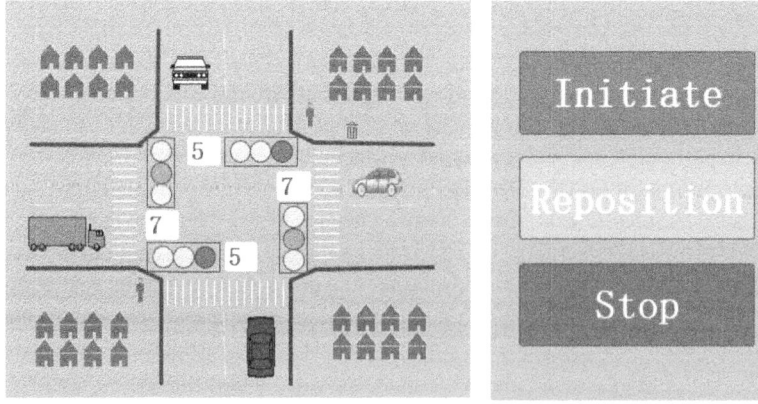

a. Experiment platform interface   b. Experimental platform action buttons

Fig. 1. Simulation Experiment Platform Interface

3   System Design

3.1   Component Hardware Experimental Platform

Currently, commonly used PLC comprehensive experimental platforms typically include Siemens PLCs, physical switches, LED indicators, and control object panels. In these experiments, students write PLC programs on a PC, download them to the PLC, and control the programs via physical switches. These hands-on sessions enable students to apply theoretical knowledge, analyze and solve professional problems, and deepen their understanding of electrical control theory while simultaneously enhancing their programming, design, and application skills.

3.2   Design of the Simulation Experimental Platform Process

The process of using the PLC simulation platform is shown in Fig. 2. As students are beginners, they are often prone to operational mistakes, such as incorrect wiring, overloads, or improper program downloads, which could damage the equipment. The dual verification system between the virtual PLC platform and the hardware platform helps minimize the risk of damage to real hardware and its environment caused by programming errors or logical faults.

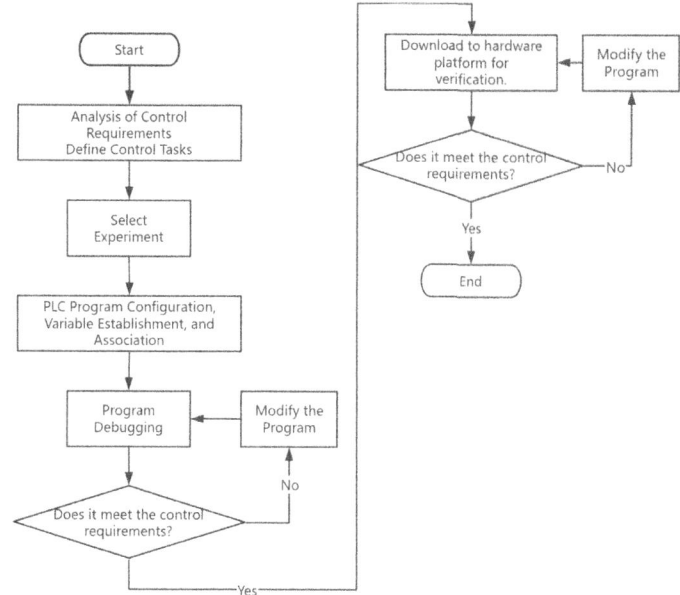

Fig. 2. Simulation Experiment Platform Process Design

3.3 Introduction to the TIA Portal Platform

TIA Portal (Totally Integrated Automation Portal) is an integrated software platform developed by Siemens to streamline the design and execution of industrial automation projects. It combines functionalities such as PLC programming, HMI design, network configuration, and device diagnostics, offering a unified interface and efficient process management. In electrical and PLC control courses, TIA Portal provides a practical platform for students, simulating real industrial environments through modules such as PLC programming and human–machine interface (HMI) design. This enables students to master essential skills such as control logic and equipment debugging. In the era of intelligent manufacturing and automation, proficiency in the TIA portal is essential for enhancing students' ability to apply theoretical knowledge to real-world scenarios.

4 Simulation Experimental Design Example

4.1 Intersection Traffic Light Case

On the basis of the actual wiring conditions at the intersection, the wiring diagram of the traffic lights is illustrated in Fig. 3.

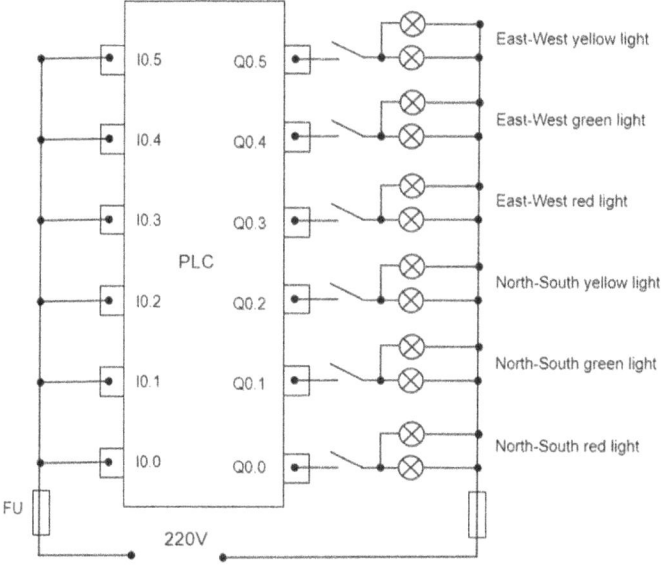

Fig. 3. Wiring Diagram of Intersecting Traffic Lights

4.2 Configuration of the Simulation Experimental Platform System

By utilizing the TIA portal and S7-PLCSIM, the configuration of the simulation experiment platform system is established. A new project is created in TIA Portal, where a new device is added: Controller → 1500 PLC, with the Ethernet interface IP configured to 192.168.0.1. Additionally, a new device is added: HMI → TP900 Comfort Panel, which is linked to the 1500 PLC. As shown in Fig. 4, the left side displays the 1500 PLC, whereas the right side shows the TP900 Comfort Panel.

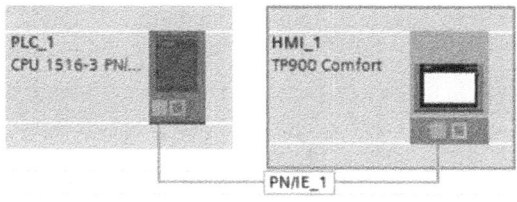

Fig. 4. Configuration Connection Diagram of the Simulation Experimental Plat form

4.3 Design Method for Traffic Light Experiments

In the design of the traffic light control system for the intersection, both the east–west and north–south directions are equipped with red, yellow, and green signal lights, resulting in a total of 12 lights across four sets. After the system is activated, the traffic lights operate sequentially in the following order, as shown in Fig. 5.

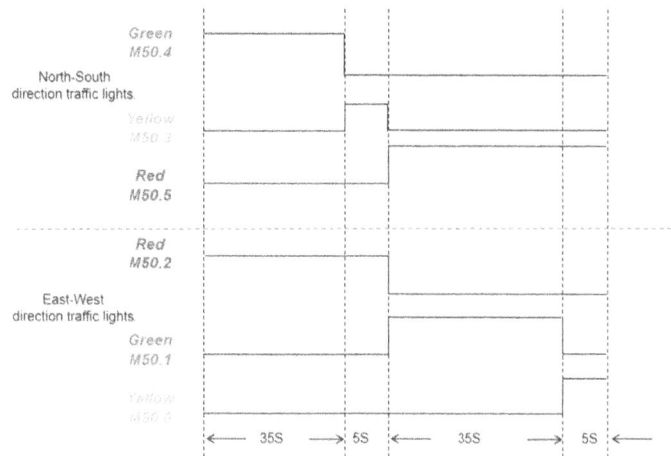

Fig. 5. PLC Control Timing Diagram of the Simulation Experimental Platform

4.4 Building the HMI Screen Configuration

After adding the devices, a user window is created for the project. On the basis of the control requirements of traffic lights, a traffic light experiment window is designed. In the device window, navigate to HMI → Add New Screen, and name it "Traffic Light Experiment Window," with the designed interface illustrated in Fig. 6.

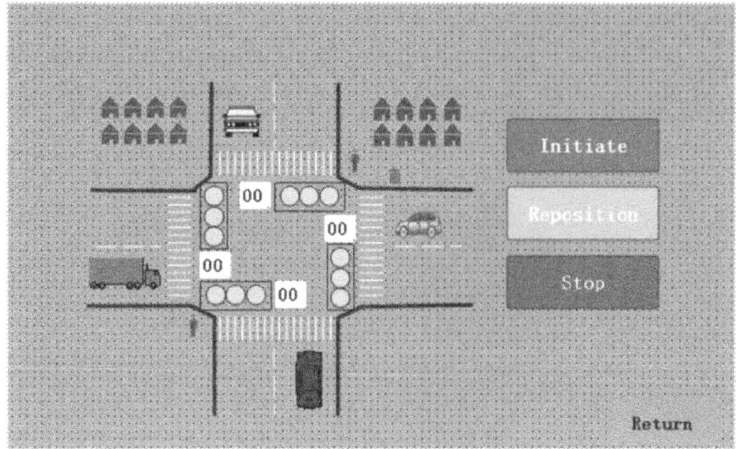

Fig. 6. Configuration Design

4.5 Establishing PLC Variables and HMI Variable Association Channels

To ensure efficient and accurate data exchange between the interface components and the PLC, association channels for variables are established within the HMI [10]. These channels connect the variables in the HMI with their corresponding PLC variables. The establishment of PLC variables and their connections to the association channels is completed in the PLC variable and HMI variable tables, as shown in Tables 1 and 2.

Table 1. PLC Variable Table

Name	Data Type	Address	Accessible by HMI
East–West Yellow Light	Bool	%M50.0	Yes
East–West Green Light	Bool	%M50.1	Yes
East–West Red Light	Bool	%M50.2	Yes
North–South Yellow Light	Bool	%M50.3	Yes
North–South Green Light	Bool	%M50.4	Yes
North–South Red Light	Bool	%M50.5	Yes
Start	Bool	%M52.0	Yes
Stop	Bool	%M52.1	Yes
Run Flag	Bool	%M52.2	Yes
Run Flag (duplicate)	Int	%MW56	Yes
East–West Countdown	Int	%MW58	Yes
North–South Countdown	Bool	%M52.3	Yes

Table 2. HMI Variable Table

Name	Data Type	Connection	PLC Name	PLC Variable
East–West Countdown	Int	HMI_Connection_1	PLC_1	PLC_1
East–West Red Light	Bool	HMI_Connection_1	PLC_1	PLC_1
Eas–West Green Light	Bool	HMI_Connection_1	PLC_1	PLC_1
East–West Yellow Light	Bool	HMI_Connection_1	PLC_1	PLC_1
Stop	Bool	HMI_Connection_1	PLC_1	PLC_1
North–South Countdown	Int	HMI_Connection_1	PLC_1	PLC_1
North–South Red Light	Bool	HMI_Connection_1	PLC_1	PLC_1
North–South Green Light	Bool	HMI_Connection_1	PLC_1	PLC_1
North–South Yellow Light	Bool	HMI_Connection_1	PLC_1	PLC_1
Start	Bool	HMI_Connection_1	PLC_1	PLC_1

5   System Implementation and Testing

5.1   Writing the PLC Control Program

During the allocation of the input and output signals, M auxiliary relays are employed to simulate the signal conditions present in the actual environment. The traffic light control program is shown in Fig. 7.

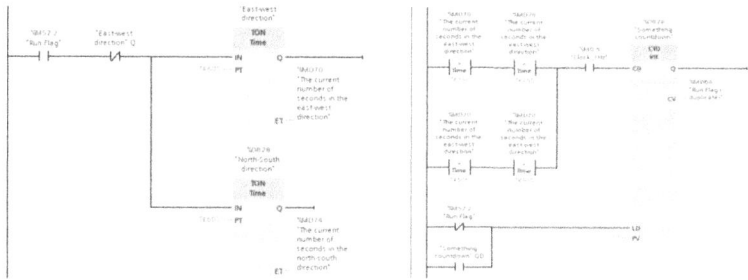

   a.   East–West   Current   **b.**   East–West   Countdown

Fig. 7. PLC Program Design

5.2   System Debugging

After the simulation platform was designed, the PLC program was compiled and down-loaded to PLCSIM. The configuration interface was launched to simulate the operational environment, as shown in Fig. 8. The system initialized the interface using preset initial variable values. Once the HMI start button was pressed, the start flag was activated, triggering the traffic light to enter the predefined cyclic mode. This change was displayed in real time on the touchscreen interface, including the north–south green light status.

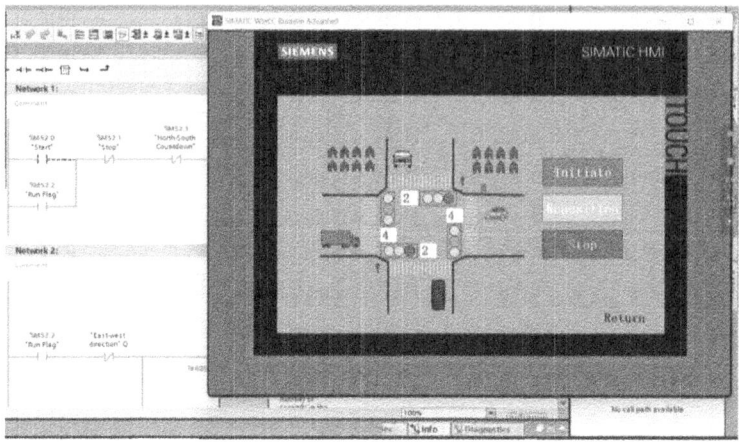

Fig. 8. Traffic Light Simulation Experimental Debugging Interface7 Conclusion

On the basis of the analysis of the test results presented in Table 3 Test Form, all test items have successfully passed, indicating that the simulation platform has performed effectively in terms of start, stop, reset, countdown, and directional light control. All the functions meet the anticipated requirements.

Table 3. Test Form

Test No	Test Item	Expected Result	Actual Result	Pass/Fail
1	Start	Start Successful	Start Successful	Pass
2	Stop	Stop Successful	Stop Successful	Pass
3	Reset	Reset Successful	Reset Successful	Pass
4	Countdown	Display Correct	Display Correct	Pass
5	North–South direction light	Logic Correct	Logic Correct	Pass
6	East–West direction light	Logic Correct	Logic Correct	Pass

6   Conclusion

The experimental results confirm that the simulation platform closely mirrors real-world conditions of the controlled process, significantly boosting student engagement. Its user-friendly and cost-effective nature offers a flexible and efficient learning environment, effectively integrating theory with practice. This solution addresses the challenge of low student participation often seen in traditional experimental teaching.

By increasing flexibility and autonomy in learning, the platform fosters greater student enthusiasm and motivation, aligning with the growing need for practicality and interactivity in modern educational settings. As digital transformation continues to shape teaching methodologies, further optimization and expansion of the platform's functionalities will help cultivate high-quality, adaptable talent that can meet the demands of the intelligent manufacturing industry.

Fund Project. Tianjin Higher Education Undergraduate Teaching Quality and Teaching Reform Research Program (B231403805).

References

1. Wu, J., Xu, X.: Speed control method for marine gas turbines using PLC technology. J. Ship Sci. Technol. **45**(14), 130–133 (2023)
2. Cui, Y.: Research on the application of PLC technology in mechanical and electrical automation control. Nonferrous Metals Eng. **13**(09), 177 (2023)
3. Zhu, J.: Creation and implementation of learning situations in secondary vocational education for 'fundamentals of machinery.' Vocat. Tech. Educ. **39**(05), 44–47 (2018)
4. Liu, D.Z., Zhao, X.Y.: Research and practice on the curriculum system construction of "theory-practice integration" teaching in electromechanical majors. Equip. Manuf. Technol. **03**, 191–193 (2016)
5. Cheng, G., Jiao, S., Liu, H.: Exploration of practical teaching in automation majors based on innovation capability development. Control Eng. **31**(09), 1716–1721 (2024)
6. Deng, C., Chen, Z., Luan, Q., et al.: Construction and discussion of a blended teaching model for electrical control and PLC experimental courses: a case study of motor star-delta starting. J. Educ. Technol. Equip. China (16), 133–138 (2024)
7. Shao, O., Tang, H.: Research on vocational college curriculum reform from the perspective of industry-education integration: a case study of the "motor and electrical control" course. J. Zhenjiang Vocat. Coll. **36**(01), 107–109 (2023)
8. Song, K.: Development of a variable frequency speed control experimental teaching platform based on PLC and MCGS software. Ind. Control Comput. **10**, 47–49 (2019)
9. Zhou, Y., Zhang, W.: Construction of semi-physical simulation experiment device for electrical control and PLC technology. Lab. Res. Explor. **36**(07), 230–234 (2017)
10. Li, G.: Design of S7–1200 PLC simulation experiment system based on MCGS. Electromech. Inf. **11**, 18–21 (2023)

Author Index

K. Zhang et al. (Eds.): CSEI 2024, CCIS 2448, pp. 357–359, 2025.
https://doi.org/10.1007/978-981-96-3738-6

The manufacturer's authorised representative in the EU is Springer
Nature Customer Service Centre GmbH, Europaplatz 3, 69115 Heidelberg,
Germany. If you have any concerns regarding our products, please
contact ProductSafety@springernature.com

Printed and bound by CPI Group (UK) Ltd, Croydon, CR0 4YY

06/05/2026

02103601-0002